AMERICAN CONSERVATISM

NOMOS

LVI

NOMOS

Harvard University Press
I   *Authority* 1958, reissued in 1982 by Greenwood Press

The Liberal Arts Press
II   *Community* 1959
III   *Responsibility* 1960

Atherton Press
IV   *Liberty* 1962
V   *The Public Interest* 1962
VI   *Justice* 1963, reissued in 1974
VII   *Rational Decision* 1964
VIII   *Revolution* 1966
IX   *Equality* 1967
X   *Representation* 1968
XI   *Voluntary Associations* 1969
XII   *Political and Legal Obligation* 1970
XIII   *Privacy* 1971

Aldine-Atherton Press
XIV   *Coercion* 1972

Lieber-Atherton Press
XV   *The Limits of Law* 1974
XVI   *Participation in Politics* 1975

New York University Press
XVII   *Human Nature in Politics* 1977
XVIII   *Due Process* 1977
XIX   *Anarchism* 1978
XX   *Constitutionalism* 1979
XXI   *Compromise in Ethics, Law, and Politics* 1979
XXII   *Property* 1980
XXIII   *Human Rights* 1981

NOMOS LVI

Yearbook of the American Society for Political and Legal Philosophy

AMERICAN CONSERVATISM

Edited by

Sanford V. Levinson, Joel Parker, and Melissa S. Williams

NEW YORK UNIVERSITY PRESS • *New York*

NEW YORK UNIVERSITY PRESS
New York
www.nyupress.org

References to Internet websites (URLs) were accurate at the time of writing.
Neither the author nor New York University Press is responsible for URLs
that may have expired or changed since the manuscript was prepared.

Library of Congress Cataloging-in-Publication Data
Names: Levinson, Sanford, 1941– editor. | Parker, Joel, 1968– editor. |
Williams, Melissa S., 1960– editor.
Title: American conservatism / edited by Sanford V. Levinson, Joel Parker,
and Melissa S. Williams.
Other titles: American conservatism (Levinson, Parker, and Williams) |
Nomos ; 56.
Description: New York ; London : New York University Press, [2016] |
"2016 | Series: Nomos ; LVI | Includes index.
Identifiers: LCCN 2015047791| ISBN 9781479812370 (cl : alk. paper) |
ISBN 1479812374 (cl : alk. paper)
Subjects: LCSH: Conservatism–United States. | LCGFT: Essays.
Classification: LCC JC573.2.U6 A45 2016 | DDC 320.520973–dc23
LC record available at http://lccn.loc.gov/2015047791

New York University Press books are printed on acid-free paper,
and their binding materials are chosen for strength and durability.
We strive to use environmentally responsible suppliers and materials
to the greatest extent possible in publishing our books.

Manufactured in the United States of America

10 9 8 7 6 5 4 3 2 1

Also available as an ebook

CONTENTS

PREFACE

You will find below a series of what we believe to be interesting and stimulating essays on "American Conservatism," taking into account, as will be elaborated below, some inevitably problematic assumptions in defining the topic. This volume has been much delayed; about half of the essays date back to panels of the American Society for Political and Legal Philosophy that were held in January of 2007 (at the annual meeting of the American Association of Law Schools); the remainder were delivered at a conference held at the University of Texas Law School in September 2012. For this reason, papers may reflect perspectives and refer to events that took place a few years apart. The delay is ultimately the responsibility of the editors. Still, it is also relevant, we think, to mention the difficulties inherent in the topic itself. Even in the best of times, preparing a volume on "American Conservatism" would present especially daunting problems.

Before we proceed, however, this NOMOS editorial team has many persons to thank. Not least among these are the membership and officers of the American Society for Political and Legal Philosophy, both for choosing such a provocative topic and for their forbearance in awaiting the completed product. Our gratitude extends as well to the many contributors, commenters, and other participants at the two meetings, which served as launching points for this discussion. Heartfelt thanks are also due the editorial staffers at NYU Press, past and present, for their patient assistance on this and other recent volumes. These include Ilene Kalish, Alexia Traganas, Aiden Amos, Jerilyn Famighetti, Caelyn Cobb, and Karen Verde. Finally, getting to the finish line was aided immeasurably by the assistance of Francesca Eick.

CONTRIBUTORS

CARL T. BOGUS
Professor of Law, Roger Williams University

INGRID CREPPELL
Associate Professor of Political Science and International Affairs, George Washington University

PATRICK J. DENEEN
David A. Potenziani Memorial Associate Professor of Political Science, University of Notre Dame

ELDON EISENACH
Professor Emeritus of Political Science, University of Tulsa

RICHARD W. GARNETT
Professor of Law, Concurrent Professor of Political Science, and Director of the Program on Church, State & Society, University of Notre Dame

GERALD GAUS
James E. Rogers Professor of Philosophy, University of Arizona

ALAN GILBERT
John Evans Professor of International Studies, University of Denver

ARTHUR J. JACOBSON
Max Freund Professor of Litigation & Advocacy, Benjamin N. Cardozo School of Law

KEN I. KERSCH
Professor of Political Science, Boston College

JAMES R. KURTH
Claude Smith Professor Emeritus of Political Science, Swarthmore College

SANFORD V. LEVINSON
W. St. John Garwood and W. St. John Garwood, Jr. Centennial Chair of Law and Professor of Government, University of Texas School of Law

JOHNATHAN O'NEILL
Professor and Chair of History, Georgia Southern University

JOEL PARKER
Former Senior Lecturer, Department of Political Science and Geography, University of Texas at San Antonio

DAVID SIDORSKY
Professor of Philosophy, Columbia University

NATHAN TARCOV
Professor of Social Thought and Political Science and in the College and Director of the Leo Strauss Center, University of Chicago

MELISSA S. WILLIAMS
Professor of Political Science and founding Director of the Centre for Ethics, University of Toronto

INTRODUCTION

SANFORD V. LEVINSON AND JOEL PARKER

Yearly topics are chosen by the general membership of the ASPLP. One can only imagine what was in the minds of the majority who voted for "American Conservatism" as the topic sometime in 2005, when the vote was held. Perhaps some of the voters were interested in what is distinctive about *American* conservatism, as distinguished from "conservatism" across the Atlantic or, ultimately, across the world. Indeed, given that one of the co-editors teaches at the University of Toronto, one can well ask if "American conservatism" includes *Canadian* conservatives, and perhaps even Mexican or Latin American variants. With regard only to the United States and Canada, it is surely the case that one cannot understand the history of the latter without taking into account that it received a substantial influx of immigrants in the late eighteenth century who had rejected in the most dramatic way possible the particular vision thought to be connected to the American Revolution—or, as David Armitage has well argued, the *secession* by thirteen colonies from the constitutional order of the British Empire. To this day, of course, the formal head of the Canadian state remains Her Majesty Queen Elizabeth II, which may (or may not) be important in understanding what continues to separate the two countries and their respective conservatisms. As one moves south, it is of course hard to escape the historical importance of the Roman Catholic Church—and, as in Mexico, the resistance to it—in understanding the conservatism(s) that have been important from Mexico to Argentina.

1

For better or, possibly, for worse, in organizing the panels we interpreted the title to refer—though it is hardly its only semantic "sense"—to conservatism within the political history or culture of the United States. Thus this book begins with an extended conversation that seeks to delineate key aspects of "American conservatism" and its differences from both "American liberalism" and "conservatism" as practiced elsewhere. In the first of these chapters, James Kurth takes a historical approach to the question, teasing out the evolving interaction between economic, socioreligious, and security-oriented aspects of American conservatism. David Sidorsky engages in an equal tour de force, extending the analysis by arguing that each of these three aspects of American conservatism reflects a critical response to the core liberal ideals and attitudes central to that respective arena. They are the two longest essays in the book, deservedly so given the vast expanse of their analyses (and sheer breadth of the topic).

Almost inevitably, one wonders whether a discussion of American conservatism is an implicit invitation to talk about American exceptionalism and the extent to which American conservatism turns out to be just another variety of Louis Hartz's "liberal tradition in America." Sidorsky several times notes, for example, differences between European conservatives, who on occasion praised the virtues of fixed hierarchies, as against American conservatives who instead adopted notions of "equal opportunity" as a mechanism of assuring that success in economic competition would not be based on irrelevant factors (such as having been born into a legally favored group); resultant inequalities would therefore be legitimated on the basis of personal responsibility for one's position in life. Similarly, relatively few European conservatives were critics of government as such, whereas contemporary American libertarians, rightly or wrongly identified as "conservatives" within the American political spectrum, proudly trace their heritage back to Jefferson, Emerson, or Thoreau, among other American figures who were certainly suspicious of government, especially if it took a "consolidated" (and invariably nationalized) form. Along these lines, Patrick Deneen comments that Sidorsky's analysis of conservatism leaves a sense that American conservatism is not conservatism at all, but rather part and parcel of Hartz's American liberalism. Deneen offers "social conservatism" as the only variety of American conservatism that could not be mistaken for liberalism, but for Deneen, that which is fundamentally "American" may be the common ground between conservatives and liberals, not their differences.

In the early twenty-first century, one can scarcely discuss conservatism in America without taking into account controversies about the relationship of church and state. It was certainly not logically entailed that religion during this period would become identified with American conservatism; consider the role that organized religion played, for example, in the Civil Rights Movement of the 1950s and 1960s, as was true of many "progressive" movements, dating to the campaign against slavery. In his recent book on the Civil Rights Act of 1964, for example, Clay Risen emphasizes the vital role played in its ultimate passage by wide-ranging interdenominational and interracial coalitions of religious groups. But in the early twenty-first century, the identification of "religious" and "conservative" sensibilities has become commonplace, especially with regard to the trope of "religious liberty."

Even William F. Buckley, the subject of the penultimate essay in this collection, different from his nineteenth-century European counterparts in having no throne around which to rally, could certainly be viewed as a proponent of recognizing the importance of paying due heed to the altar as instantiated in the Roman Catholic Church. As we revise this introduction in the fall of 2015, it is safe to say that the place of religion, both organized and within the consciousness of individual citizens who "conscientiously object" to performing certain legal duties, has scarcely subsided within politics; one might well regard it as one of the defining realities of contemporary politics in the United States. The most prominent example is surely Kim Davis, the hitherto obscure elected clerk of a Kentucky County who literally went to jail rather than provide to same-sex couples the marriage licenses the U.S. Supreme Court held they were now entitled to, in the bitterly-divided *Obergefell* decision in June 2015. And much notice was taken of the fact that Pope Francis, during what appeared to be a highly successful visit to the United States in September, met her privately and reportedly hugged her (though there was subsequent controversy about who exactly arranged the audience and whether the Pope had been briefed about its importance). Moreover, *Obergefell* as well as an earlier case involving the business corporation *Hobby Lobby* has assured the presence of much future litigation on the ability of at least non-public officials, whether discrete individuals or institutions, to be "accommodated"—which in effect means the ability to avoid compliance with a legal requirement imposed on all other citizens—with regard to their continuing opposition to same-sex marriage, contraception, or abortion. Richard Garnett's essay on the institutional freedom to be accorded religious institutions is especially timely. Ingrid Creppell in her comment on Garnett's chapter argues that the essence of at least one important wing of American conservatism is "anti-governmentism," a striking deviation from the calls for "law and order" that some might identify with conservatism.

It is appropriate, then, that the volume turns next to a more explicit consideration of the relationship among self-described conservatives with the American legal order, including, of course, the U.S. Constitution. Kenneth Kersch reflects on aspects of "legal conservatism" in the twenty-first century, arguing that the Constitution and the common law in America serve as two central examples of the role of constitutive narratives in American conservative thought. In so doing, Kersch argues that too much attention is paid to the putative divisions within the conservative movement and not enough to what these strands have in common: namely, the conservative rejection of all things liberal as having forsaken the truths of the American founding and Constitution. Gerald Gaus carries this claim further, arguing in part that conservatism is better positioned than is liberal philosophy, *contra*-Rawls, to give insights into what a just moral order might look like. Johnathan O'Neill, however, draws a distinction between constitutional conservatism and American conservatism. The balance and restraint crucial to the ability of constitutionalism to deliver the stability it promises are somewhat in tension with the political objectives of the American conservative movement, O'Neill argues. His argument is especially interesting in light of a 2014 book by John Compton, *The Evangelical Origins of the Living Constitution*, noting the emphasis by nineteenth-century Evangelical reformers on the importance of transforming constitutional doctrine in order to overcome such sins as the use of alcohol and slavery, rather than maintain a commitment to the existing constitutional order that tolerated both.

Turning from this focus on conservatism and constitutionalism, our contributors then consider two important figures within the history of post–World War II American conservatism: William F. Buckley and Leo Strauss. Carl Bogus finds in William F. Buckley, Jr., a figure indispensable to American conservatism, for his ability to square the circle contemplated in James Kurth's piece. Bogus credits Buckley with the formation of a coalition among what he describes as the "fundamentalist," "libertarian," and early "neoconservative" elements of the conservative movement. He thus gives as evidence of Buckley's importance the identity crisis that American conservatives have faced "post-Buckley." Just as important, Bogus argues, was his willingness to draw the line against those ostensible mid-century "conservatives" identified with the John Birch Society, who viewed President Dwight Eisenhower as at best a Communist dupe, if not perhaps a more conscious agent of the Soviet Union. In his reply, Eldon Eisenach thinks Bogus has made too much of the internal challenges that conservatism faces looking ahead. For Eisenach, the real story is the lack of anything that might be termed a "coherent liberal political agenda." The success in recent decades of the Republican coalition in American politics is to be attributed more to the ideological "vacuum" on the left than to the role of any one figure or subgroup in the conservative sphere. Eisenach instead finds as threads common to all aspects of American conservatism an emphasis on the family and the importance of the rule of law.

Buckley was of course born in America and educated (or not— his first book *God and Man at Yale,* was bitterly critical) at Yale University; by the time of his death he had become an iconic figure in American culture, not only because of his decades as editor of *National Review,* but also as a result of his long participation on the television program *Firing Line,* carried, paradoxically or not, on the publicly financed Corporation for Public Broadcasting. If anyone can be defined as an unproblematically "American conservative," one might think it was Buckley, the recipient of a Presidential Medal of Freedom from President George H. W. Bush in 1991.

Far more problematic, with regard to identity, is Leo Strauss, the subject of quite distinctive essays by Nathan Tarcov, Arthur J. Jacobson, and Alan Gilbert. Strauss was born in Germany in 1899, served in the German Army in 1917–18, and then enrolled at the University of Hamburg, where he received his doctorate in 1921 under the supervision of Ernst Cassirer. He also apparently sat in on courses at the universities of Freiburg and Marburg, taught by Edmund Husserl and Martin Heidegger. He also intellectually engaged Carl Schmitt. An active member of the German Zionist movement, Strauss left Germany in 1932, first for Paris and then, ultimately, for the United States (and the University of Chicago), where he remained until his death. To put it mildly, he remains a subject of passionate controversy a full four decades after his death in 1973, as revealed by the three essays on his relationship to "American conservatism." And of course, books regularly appear about him, including, in 2014 alone, Michael and Catherine Zuckert's *Leo Strauss and the Problem of Political Philosophy* and Robert Howse's *Leo Strauss: Man of Peace* (2014).

So the question anyone interested in American conservatism must ask is in what sense was Strauss—or another colleague at the University of Chicago between 1950 and 1962, Friedrich Hayek—"American" instead of "European"? (Similar questions, no doubt, could be asked about another influential political theorist of this period, Hannah Arendt, though she has not been claimed as an avatar of American conservatism.) Like Thomas Mann, Strauss emigrated to America, but few people would define Mann as an "American author," or, for that matter, Mann's fellow Californian Arnold Schoenberg as an "American composer." But why, if at all, does the answer matter? We take it that there would be little interest in a volume on "American physics" unless one was particularly interested in the individual biographies of U.S. nationals who happened, say, to end up winning Nobel Prizes in physics. (In which case would Albert Einstein, who spent the last decades of his life in Princeton, New Jersey, qualify? We think not.) There may have been a "Copenhagen school" of physicists who helped to form the basis of quantum theory in the 1920s, but, generally speaking, physics seems to be a cosmopolitan science whose practices and achievements transcend political boundary lines. Political thought, like legal systems, may be more parochial.

Most historians of political thought, we suspect, are quite willing to discuss "German idealism," "British empiricism," and "French social thought," so this *does* imply that even if geography is not destiny, it may nonetheless be important in generating distinctive styles of thought and approaches to considering the great topics of political and legal theory. And all of us are presumably familiar with the standard distinction between analytic philosophy, identified largely with Great Britain and the United States, and what is frankly denominated "continental" philosophy, in which the Continent is obviously Europe and the chief figures include Nietzsche and Heidegger, among others. But one can scarcely understand American conservatism in the post–World War II period without paying due attention to Strauss, as is the case with other émigré theorists. Tarcov argues that it is a fundamental error to denominate Strauss as "conservative" (or, of course, "liberal"). Jacobson, on the other hand, focuses on Strauss's move to America and the impact this had on his thought. He is concerned that Strauss and his followers overlooked, perhaps deliberately, the relationship of fascism to reason, tradition, and the conservative/liberal divide. Whatever label one ultimately places on Strauss the person—is "German-American" a suitable compromise?—it is hard to deny that "Straussianism" and "Straussians" seem to be important in the United States in a way that is not true elsewhere. Just as Buckley is unequivocally American, so too are many of the major figures identified as Straussians. Some have had distinguished academic careers, while some also became more directly involved in the machinery of government. Alan Gilbert's essay focuses on one such fully American Straussian, Robert Goldwin, who became an important conduit for Strauss's ideas—or, at least, certain versions of them—to power-holders within the U.S. government. Gilbert's essay is undoubtedly the sharpest in tone and most likely to provoke at least some readers. This testifies to the fact (or at least possibility) that ideas can have genuine consequences, for good or for ill, as Strauss himself seemed to insist in attacking the baleful consequences of abandoning the wisdom of the ancients for the siren calls of the "moderns" such as Machiavelli, Hobbes, and Max Weber. If one takes politics seriously, as Gilbert most certainly does, it is scarcely possible to write of some of these consequences with dispassion. There are those who love Strauss, and those who deeply dislike (perhaps even "hate") him and at least some of his devotees. Perhaps a newer, younger generation of theorists will write about him from a more detached perspective, but anyone educated before, say, 1980, let alone during the 1960s or '70s, will almost certainly have quite strong views about both Strauss and "Straussianism" (whatever exactly may be thought to be the meaning of the latter).

In any event, it is not only the adjective "American" that makes our topic problematic. Even if one can (or desires to) confidently distinguish between those who are American and those who are not, that still leaves us with the problem of defining "conservatism." We have already adverted to support of the alliance between throne and altar as one definition of at least post–French Revolutionary conservatism. But are there *any* serious descendants of Louis Gabriel Ambroise, Vicomte de Bonald, or Joseph de Maistre in the canon of what we ordinarily think of American conservatism? Neither of these figures, for good reason, is mentioned in Sidorsky's comprehensive overview of strains of American conservatism.

One of the editors of this volume (Levinson) well remembers a graduate course taught by the late Louis Hartz at Harvard on European political thought, which included extraordinarily vivid introductions to Bonald and de Maistre designed to demonstrate their radical differences from anything that might be identified as "conservatism" in America (which Hartz, of course, notably viewed as just another variant of Lockeanism). Consider the fact, for example, that the outstanding list of books republished by the Liberty Fund includes none of their works, even though some of the reprinted works allude to them. This is, not surprisingly, unlike the case with Edmund Burke, whose books are easily available in the United States in many different editions and who continues to be treated as an important intellectual guide by many self-described American conservatives.

But Burke's (or Hume's) conservatism is, of course, very different from nineteenth-century liberalism that, with its vision of a minimal (or night-watchman) state, has been so influential on many contemporary libertarians. Whether or not the U.S. constitutional order instantiates, in the unforgettable jibe of Justice Oliver Wendell Holmes, Jr., "Mr. Herbert Spencer's Social Statics," there can be little doubt that his brand of conservatism, reflected in the work of such undeniable Americans as Yale sociologist William Graham Sumner, is light-years away from the noblesse-oblige conservatism associated with, say, Benjamin Disraeli or, indeed, Otto von Bismarck, who was busy developing the German welfare state at the time that Spencer and Sumner were writing.

Moreover, much of the discussion above involves *domestic* politics and the philosophical issues associated with them. But, of course, there are also divides predicated on what kinds of government and state apparatus are needed to participate effectively in the international order. If Bismarck was in some ways the father of the German welfare state, he is also one of the important figures in the tradition of *realpolitik* or, some would say, *machtpolitik*. Woodrow Wilson, the quintessential "progressive," fought a war both "to end war" and to guarantee the prospects for "democracy," and his successors, in both the Democratic and Republican parties, have certainly been willing to support muscular interventionism on behalf of this goal. One suspects that most self-described conservatives, including, say, Henry Kissinger, with his admiration for such figures as Metternich, would find both of these visions naïve and even dangerous. One might return to the earlier question and ask if Kissinger is an "American conservative," albeit one who, like Strauss, was born in Germany, or simply "a conservative"? But, of course, to identify conservatism, whether American or otherwise, with military interventionism is to ignore one important strain of American conservatism—think in this context of Robert A. Taft—that has been described, especially by its critics, as "isolationism." It was Taft, after all, who vehemently criticized American membership in NATO and Republican senator John Bricker who sponsored a constitutional amendment that would have ultimately reserved to American states the decision about entering into foreign treaties that arguably changed the political order. And Rand Paul, who is currently running for the 2016 Republican presidential nomination, criticizes at least some "foreign entanglements" that are supported by almost all of his opponents among the fifteen candidates still running as of October 2015.

All of the questions raised above could easily have been asked in 2007, the time of the first set of panels from which many of these papers are drawn. What provoked the later, 2012, gathering in Austin, Texas, though, was not only the delay in publication, but also, and more importantly, the obvious changes that seemed to be taking place in the quotidian world of American conservatism. If one defines American conservatism (or, for that matter, American liberalism or American as an adjective in front of any other political category) by reference to the actual behavior of people who identify themselves as American conservatives, one can see significant developments taking place with sometimes dazzling rapidity. In January 2007, for example, there was no collapse of the American economy, no "bailouts," and no Tea Party. John McCain may have been almost literally the last man standing in the competition to represent the Republican Party in the 2008 election, but he had been a "party elder" at least since his near-successful race in 2000 for the Republican nomination. Thus there were many people who predicted his nomination even before the first primary in New Hampshire. But there was, to put it mildly, nothing predictable about his choosing Sarah Palin as his running mate, not to mention the importance that Palin would have in at least some conservative circles in the next several years.

Ron Paul was in 2007 a well-known but almost completely marginal libertarian semi-crank; by 2014 his son, a U.S. senator from Kentucky, was leading some early polls for the Republican nomination (though his support dissipated); and one of his many competitors in 2015 is former Arkansas governor Mike Huckabee, who ran for the presidency in 2008 as a vigorous Christian defending religious values against attack by purportedly rampaging secularists (and who has vigorously defended Kim Davis and suggested that her jailing represented a "war on Christianity"). But Senator Ted Cruz, whose name was known to almost no one in 2007, is competing for much the same constituency as Huckabee and is one of those leading the charge against Jeb Bush, who at least in monetary support appears to have been the early choice of what used to be called "country-club Republicans" (notwithstanding the initial support by financial behemoths the Koch brothers for the unsuccessful campaign of Wisconsin governor Scott Walker).

But the most remarkable feature of the Republican race so far is surely that the three leading candidates, as of October 2015, are Donald Trump, Ben Carson, and Carly Fiorina, none of whom has ever spent even a single day holding public office, even as all three of them profess their deep "conservatism" (as do all of the candidates, for that matter). Trump in particular has emphasized what many would describe as a raw form of nativism predicated on harsh opposition to most immigration. Many mainstream analysts, appalled by Trump's success, are eager to describe him as not "really" conservative at all, but that, of course, only highlights the indeterminacy of the term and contestation over who precisely is authorized to decide who is, and is not, a "true conservative." And analysts of contemporary American conservatism would presumably have to take into account as well the remarkable resignation from the position of Speaker of the House by John Boehner in September 2015 in large part because of his inability to establish any kind of effective control over the "Tea Party" faction of Republicans within the House. The announcement of his resignation, by Senator Marco Rubio, yet another candidate for the presidency, before a conference of conservatives meeting in Washington, was met with remarkably loud and extended cheers.

Perhaps one could write a history of English conservatism in the last forty years without mentioning Margaret Thatcher and her belief, among other things, that "there is no such thing as society. There are individual men and women, and there are families." But surely something would be missing in such a history that so resolutely ignored not only what was going on in the polity at the time, but also the consequences for self-described "conservatives" and those, including members of the academy, who identified with her political projects. For better or worse, American conservatism over the past half-century coincides with the political triumphs of Richard Nixon and then, far more importantly, of Ronald Reagan, of course as well as the two Bush presidencies and other ongoing political developments. But Reagan left the White House more than a quarter-century ago, and, as with disputes within the Democratic Party over the identity of the "true" legatees of Franklin Roosevelt, the Republican Party is faced with similarly contentious debates over the meaning of Reaganism in the twenty-first century.

Part of the practical importance of the fact that Nixon, Reagan, and the two Bushes dominated the White House for almost forty years is that they were enabled to make far more appointments to the Supreme Court than was Bill Clinton. (Jimmy Carter was the only one-term president to be unable to make even a single appointment to the high court, and Clinton, in eight years, was able to make only two appointments.) This basic reality contributes to the near-hegemonic power on the Supreme Court of five conservative Republican justices, though one of the more bizarre features of the 2015 presidential campaign is the charge by Senator Cruz that Chief Justice John Roberts is not at all a true conservative, as evidenced by the fact that he provided all-important fifth votes to uphold the Affordable Care Act ("Obamacare") first against constitutional and then against statutory attack.

It is also the case that these five Republican justices are all Roman Catholic (as is Justice Sotomayor, appointed by President Obama). Is this latter fact relevant? Or perhaps one might ask if it is any more relevant than the fact that this same period also saw the election of the first African American president. All one can say with confidence is that the American social and political orders have developed in ways that almost surely could not have been predicted by anyone writing in 1955 when Hartz wrote his masterpiece (and when, say, electing a Catholic president still seemed highly unlikely and a majority Catholic—and entirely non-Protestant—Supreme Court truly unthinkable). American conservatism, like American liberalism, is a project that necessarily takes place in real historical time, inevitably influenced by what Justice Holmes termed the "felt necessities" of the time. There is, obviously, no necessary agreement on what these necessities may be or, even more certainly, what kinds of measures are required to answer their challenges. Readers of this book will have the advantage of knowing how much of the 2016 primary elections will have turned out and what the results might indicate about "American conservatism." We hope, though, that the following essays offer some illumination as to how one might approach that question.

1

A HISTORY OF INHERENT CONTRADICTIONS: THE ORIGINS AND END OF AMERICAN CONSERVATISM

JAMES R. KURTH

It has long been understood that there is something peculiar, even paradoxical, about conservatism in America. American conservatism is different from conservatism in other countries, even those that were the original source of many other American ideas and ideals, the countries of Europe. Indeed, the very term "American conservatism" is something of an oxymoron. For most Europeans who came to America, the whole purpose of their difficult and disruptive journey to the New World was not to conserve European institutions but to leave them behind and to create something new, often an entirely new life, and even a new identity, for themselves.

In this chapter, I will examine how the paradoxes of American conservatism have unfolded and revealed themselves in the course of American history. In many respects, the history of American conservatism has been the working out of certain inherent contradictions and fatal flaws, beginning with the origins of a distinctive and peculiar kind of conservatism in eighteenth-century America, through its full development during the nineteenth and early twentieth centuries, to the great debacle of this original American conservatism during the Great Depression of the 1930s, to the reinvention and transformation of American conservatism during the Great Stagflation of the 1970s, and finally to the recent debacle of this reinvented conservatism during the Great Recession, which began in 2007 and which continues into the 2010s. I will conclude with a review of the current condition of what now passes for American conservatism.

THE THREE DIMENSIONS OF AMERICAN CONSERVATISM

In recent decades, political analysts have found it useful to interpret American political movements by distinguishing between different policy dimensions or arenas. Thus, conservatives have been divided into: (1) those who are most concerned about economic or fiscal issues, that is, pro-business or "free-enterprise" conservatives; (2) those most concerned with religious or social issues, that is, pro-church or "traditional-values" conservatives; and (3) those most concerned with national-security or defense issues, that is, pro-military or "patriotic" conservatives.

These three arenas are not of equal weight and strength in the conservative movement, however. It is the business elite that, in the long course of American history, has proven to be the most powerful component of the conservative coalition; it has gotten its way on more issues than either the religious or the security conservatives, and it has done so not only within the conservative coalition itself, but also with actual government policies. Calvin Coolidge may have exaggerated somewhat when, in the 1920s, he said that "the business of America is business," but it has been no exaggeration that the business of American conservatism has been business.

It was the achievement of Ronald Reagan that he was able in the late 1970s to unite these three different kinds of conservatism into one grand coalition. This was the culmination of a "fusionist strategy" that had been developing amongst American conservatives since the early 1960s.[1] For a while, especially during the 1980s, it may have seemed that these three kinds of conservatives were natural allies, that they had an "elective affinity" for each other, and that there was no significant contradiction between them. However, as we shall see, pro-business conservatism has always included a tendency toward the disruption and even dissolution of religious ideals and social practices. This is the famous "cultural contradictions of capitalism," identified by social theorists as varied as Karl Marx, Joseph Schumpeter, and Daniel Bell.[2] And in recent decades, pro-business conservatism has also included a tendency toward the dismantling of national boundaries and even dissolution of national identities, and therefore the redefinition of national security. This is the famous "globalization" project of American multinational corporations and financial institutions.[3] It took about two decades for the fusionist strategy to put together the Reagan grand coalition, and then, about two decades after Reagan's departure, that grand coalition began to fall apart.

ECONOMIC CONSERVATISM

In Europe, economic conditions had been shaped by an established landed class and a highly restricted market in land and labor. In America, economic conditions were instead shaped by an open market in land and labor, and this was reinforced and energized by the open Western frontier. The Industrial Revolution of course greatly diminished the relative importance of landed wealth in the economy, but in Europe the traditional idea of an established economic order—supported by the state and by intimate connections between property owners and government officials, between the wealthy and the powerful—was carried over into the new industrial economy (and, to some extent, even into the post-industrial or information-age economy of our own time). Conversely, in America, the idea of an open market was carried over into the new industrial economy (and even into the post-industrial or information-age economy as well). The long-standing American condition of an open market in just about every economic sector meant that there normally was not an established economic order to conserve. If something were going to be conserved, it would normally be the open market or "free-enterprise" system itself. But the idea of free enterprise was a central pillar of the ideology of European, and classical, liberalism, not of European conservatism. This meant that in America conservatism was committed to conserving liberalism, or at least a central pillar of it.[4]

Thus, the Federalists, the Whigs, and the Republicans have successively been considered to be the more conservative political party within the United States, but each of these has also successively been the most pro-business and free-enterprise party. Since business or capitalism is actually one of the most unsettling, even revolutionary, forces the world has ever seen, this means that the conservative party in America has always sought to conserve a revolutionary force. This revolutionary business or capitalist force not only disrupts and destroys existing economic arrangements (Schumpeter's "creative destruction"). It destroys religious, social, and ultimately moral arrangements as well. This means that when religious and social conservatives make an alliance with economic "conservatives" (who are really economic or "classical" liberals, or even libertarians), they are making an alliance with a force that will often choose to betray them. And since the business conservatives are the senior partner within the conservative coalition and the religious and social conservatives are a junior partner, these latter conservatives will be betrayed, and marginalized, again and again.

RELIGIOUS CONSERVATISM

In a pattern similar to that of economic conservatism, in Europe an established state church shaped religious and moral conditions. In America, particularly after the adoption of the U.S. Constitution, religious and moral conditions were instead shaped by the separation of church and state and even by religious pluralism. There was early on a competition between different denominations within the dominant Protestant religion. These competing Protestant denominations were soon joined by the Roman Catholic Church, which itself included a variety of ethnicity-based parishes, and by the Jewish community, which included a variety of congregations with differing views on the relationship between tradition and modernity. Indeed, with all of these competing religious teachings and practices, there soon developed something of an open market in religious ideas and institutions, comparable and parallel to the open market in land and labor—and this too was reinforced and energized by the open Western frontier.

This open market in religious matters, so nicely isomorphic with the open market in economic matters, was a powerful factor generating both a reality and an ideology of free choice in the United States.[5] But another factor lay in the fact that the founding and dominant religion in the United States was Protestantism, rather than some other religion (such as Roman Catholicism or Eastern

Orthodoxy). In its very origins as a distinct religion, Protestantism "protested" the established religion of Catholicism and thereby promoted the idea of some measure of free choice.[6] However, in Europe that choice was mostly the choice of a monarch (especially in the Lutheran or Anglican countries) or of an oligarchy (especially in the Calvinist or Reformed countries). It definitely was not the free choice of ordinary individuals. These European patterns were reproduced in the original European settlements in America, with colonies that were directly ruled by appointed representatives of the British monarch being Anglican (for example, Virginia) and colonies that were ruled by local oligarchies being Reformed (such as Massachusetts).

With the American Revolution and then with the U.S. Constitution, however, the forces supporting established state churches fell away. New denominations, particularly Methodists and Baptists, rose up, especially during the Second Great Awakening (1800s to 1820s), and these denominations very much emphasized the freedom of choice of the individual believer. It is not an accident that the democratic revolution of the Andrew Jackson era of the 1830s was especially robust in those regions of the United States where the Second Great Awakening, Methodists, and Baptists had been especially robust only a decade or two before. Thus, the religious revolution brought by the Second Great Awakening and the democratic revolution brought by the Jackson era greatly reinforced and amplified the religious pluralism, open market, and individual choice that had already begun to characterize the United States. This meant that there was no longer an established religion—and eventually no longer even an established morality and culture—to conserve. If something were going to be conserved, it would be the religious open-market ("free exercise of religion") system. Again, this idea of free exercise of religion was a central pillar of the ideology of European liberalism, not of European conservatism. This meant that in America conservatism was again committed to conserving liberalism, or at least a central pillar of it.

It was thus in the nature of American Protestants that many of them would be inclined to protest this or that religious doctrine or practice and therefore to separate and form new churches or even new denominations. Conservatism in matters of religion was often merely the stance that the older Protestant churches took when they had become the target of all this protesting and separating. Since these churches were continually being left behind, religious conservatism was associated with once-dominant churches that were now dwindling into a minority, and would later dwindle into marginality.

However, there eventually came a time when all Protestants, both old churches and new ones, had something substantial to conserve, and this was Protestantism itself, in the face of the challenges posed by the new religious communities that were coming to America. This began with the arrival of masses of Irish Catholic immigrants in the 1840s, shortly followed by the arrival of far smaller, but still significant, numbers of German Jewish immigrants in the 1850s. Now, all Protestants had something to conserve, at least whatever it was that they held in common that was not Catholic or Jewish.

Various Protestants in various regions and localities did use economic and social institutions to contain the advances of non-Protestants. But Protestants faced serious problems when they tried to use political institutions, including political parties, for the same purpose. By the 1850s, the separation of church and state was very far advanced in the United States, and there was no longer much of a legal basis for excluding non-Protestants from government institutions. Protestant conservatism was contradicted by what had by now become Constitutional conservatism.

The religious—and more broadly, the moral and social—conservatives in America have not been consistently aligned with one political party (such as the Republican Party). In this respect, the religious arena has been somewhat different than the economic one. In particular, the Democratic Party from the 1890s to the 1920s represented many fundamentalist Protestants in the South and in the West, most obviously when William Jennings Bryan was the party's presidential candidate in three elections. Overall, however, the Republican Party has represented the Protestant part of the American population more consistently than has the Democratic Party, with the Democrats being quicker and more effective in reaching out to assist and incorporate new immigrant groups, which were bringing new religions into the United States (as examples, first Catholics and then Jews).

THE SUBORDINATION OF RELIGIOUS CONSERVATISM TO ECONOMIC CONSERVATISM

One of the most powerful contradictions at work within American conservatism has been the different interests and perspectives of the Protestant conservatives versus those of the economic or business conservatives. In their religious identity, most Americans in the nineteenth and early twentieth centuries may have wanted to conserve some sort of Protestant morality and culture. But in their economic identity, many of these same Americans benefited from the admission of new immigrants, even if these were Catholic or Jewish. Businessmen in particular have always wanted cheaper labor, and new immigrants have always facilitated this. From a business perspective, considerations about the immigrants' religion and culture are distinctly secondary (or even lower) in importance. Even ordinary middle-class Protestants benefited from cheaper labor, in the form of domestic servants. And of course it was the businessmen and middle-class Protestants who controlled the political parties, particularly that party which was supposed to be the more conservative one, first the Whigs and later the Republicans. Thus, the party elites—who benefited from free and open immigration—continually overrode the pro-Protestant and anti-immigrant wishes of many working-class voters. Initially, these voters tried to form new political parties (the Know-Nothings in the 1840s and 1850s and the Populists in the 1880s and 1890s), but these parties were soon co-opted and then subordinated by the major political parties dominated by pro-immigration business and middle-class elites. It was not until these elites themselves turned against immigration, that is, when business interests were temporarily overridden by security ones (during the Red Scare of the late 1910s through the early 1920s), that serious restrictions on immigration were enacted (such as the Immigration Act of 1924).

SECURITY CONSERVATISM

The similar dynamics that have been at work in economic conservatism and religious conservatism also have had a parallel dynamic at work in the third dimension of American conservatism, that of security conservatism. This is the conservatism that puts special emphasis on issues of military policy, national security, and at times patriotic or national identity.

In European countries (with the partial exception of Britain), security conditions were shaped by threats from foreign armies existing on all sides and in close proximity. This gave rise to strong centralized states possessing and deploying large standing armies—a state-army complex—or what might be termed an established security system, parallel to the established landed classes and the established state churches that we have already noted. In America, as the Founders recognized, security conditions were instead shaped by the United States being separated from other great powers by oceans and by having neighbors who were relatively weak. George Washington nicely articulated this concept in his famous Farewell Address in 1796:

> The great rule of conduct for us in regard to foreign nations is in extending our commercial relations, to have with them as little political connection as possible. . . . Europe has a set of primary interests which to us have none; or a very remote relation. . . . Our detached and distant situation invites and enables us to pursue a different course. If we remain one people under an efficient government, the period is not far off when we may defy material injury from external annoyance . . . when belligerent nations, under the impossibility of making acquisitions upon us, will not lightly hazard the giving us provocation; when we may choose peace or war, as our interest, guided by justice, shall counsel. Why forego the advantages of so peculiar a situation? Why quit our own to stand upon foreign ground? Why, by interweaving our destiny with that of any part of Europe, entangle our peace and prosperity in the toils of European ambition, rivalship, interest, humor, or caprice? It is our true policy to steer clear of permanent alliances with any portion of the foreign world.[7]

The result of "the advantages of so peculiar a situation" was not exactly parallel to the open markets in the economic and religious arenas (an open market in security is difficult to imagine), but normally there was an absence of military conscription (and therefore a high degree of individual free choice with respect to security issues) and an absence of heavy taxation to support a large military establishment. And even though the Western frontier represented a zone of violence and insecurity for much of the nineteenth century, the very weakness of the Indian tribes or "nations" (as they were called by the federal government at the time) compared with the strength of the European nation-states, meant that the actual conditions of the Western frontier reinforced the general sense within the United States of an unthreatening security environment and of individual free choice in security affairs. This long-standing American condition of security meant that there was not an established security system to conserve. If something were going to be conserved, it would normally be the no-conscription and low-taxation (and free-choice) system. But the ideas of no conscription, low taxation, and free choice combined into yet another central pillar of the ideology of European liberalism, not of European conservatism. This meant that in America conservatism was once again committed to conserving liberalism, or at least a central pillar of it.

THE SUBORDINATION OF SECURITY CONSERVATISM TO ECONOMIC CONSERVATISM

The industrial revolution and more recently the information revolution have been propelled by successive developments in technologies, particularly those that have enabled improvements in transportation and communication—in the ability to move people, goods, and ideas faster and farther. These new technologies obviously provided great profit-making opportunities for new business enterprises that could provide the faster and farther transportation and communication services. But they also provided old business enterprises with new and much larger arenas in which to operate and profit. This meant that each new improvement in transportation and communication technologies expanded the profit-making area beyond the territorial borders of the existing political and governmental units.

Thus, the railroad and the telegraph in the mid-nineteenth century and the automobile, telephone, and radio in the early twentieth century enabled business enterprises to reach (and to push beyond) the borders of any particular American state. Indeed, with these technologies, the most efficient operating and profit-making area had become the territory of the United States, of the

American nation, as a whole. Business firms soon left behind any identification—be it practical, ideological, or sentimental—with the particular state in which they had been founded and incorporated, and they sought to expand to at least the territorial borders of the United States. These enterprises became a relentless and often ruthless force hollowing out the powers of the particular states and transferring these powers to the national government (or, when extinguishing these powers altogether, to no government at all).

For about a century (from the 1850s to the 1950s), the dominant transportation and communication technologies (the railroad, telegraph, automobile, telephone, and radio) reinforced national identity and a nationalist ideology over alternative identities and ideologies, in particular smaller or state ones and larger or international ones. This meant that people who thought of themselves as American patriots or nationalists, and who sought to conserve the American nation and to promote American national interests (as they understood these to be), had a ready and powerful ally in business conservatives. During this era, these two kinds of conservatives came together within the Republican Party. In particular, both nationalist and business conservatives could support protectionism with respect to international trade policy. But once business (especially the bigger businesses) could make more money in the international or even global arena than in the national one, the business conservatives would betray the nationalist conservatives.

For a time this conflict within the Republican Party between a nationalist ideology and an international market was masked by an imperialist ideology—the American nation was simply expressing and fulfilling itself within an expanded, extraterritorial area. But after the debacles of the various European and Japanese imperialisms during and after the Second World War, the imperialist ideology could no longer be legitimate in the United States. Business instead supported an internationalist ideology and eventually a full-blown globalist one. Today, there still remain many American patriots or nationalists, but they are not found among the big businesses and the pillars of great wealth. The nationalist version of American conservatism, like the religious version, has been betrayed and marginalized, and it is now largely found only among small businesses and industrial workers.

The principal reason for this post-national development lies in the same technological process that earlier brought about national development. During the past half-century, new transportation and communication technologies have ushered in new ideas about which political and governmental units provide the best territorial scope for business operations. Thus, the jet airplane and telecommunications, and more recently the computer and the Internet, have enabled businesses to reach and to push beyond the boundaries of particular nation-states—even one as large as the United States—and now the most efficient operating and profit-making area is the globe itself. Business firms soon left behind any identification—be it practical, ideological, or sentimental—with the nation-state in which they were founded and incorporated, and they sought to expand to the very ends of the earth. This was true even with the United States itself, which has provided American multinational corporations and banks with so much support in their negotiations with foreign governments. Although these firms have grown to great strength because of the opportunities and protection provided by the United States, they have ceased to have any real identity with (and loyalty to) America as a distinct nation. These enterprises have been a relentless and often ruthless force hollowing out the powers of the United States (as well as of other nations) and transferring these powers to international financial institutions (such as the International Monetary Fund, the World Bank, and the World Trade Organization) or to "global regimes" or "global governance" (or to no governance at all).[8]

We have examined three dimensions or arenas of American conservatism—economic, religious, and security—and we have seen that, from a European perspective, American conservatism was not conservative at all, but actually was a kind of classical liberalism. Insofar as American conservatism was involved in conserving anything, it was precisely this liberalism.

The three dimensions of American conservatism each had their own distinct logic. However, they also had much in common. First, each conceived of its relevant environment or condition as being relatively open and unconstrained. This meant that units operating within this environment had a good deal of leeway or freedom to do what they pleased (always recognizing, of course, that they would be bumping into other, similar, even equal units,

and this condition would provide its own kind of constraint). Ultimately, the leeway or freedom of the units was so unconstrained
that they could dissolve or disintegrate into their least common
denominator, into their smallest possible element, and this of
course was the individual. Individualism, therefore, was at the
very core and foundation of American identity, and particularly of
American conservatism.[9]

THE GOLDEN AGE AND THE INDIAN SUMMER OF THE ORIGINAL AMERICAN CONSERVATISM

For many decades after the founding of the United States, the
economic, religious, and security conditions that enabled this
pervasive individualism—and the pervasive classical liberalism
and therefore the peculiar and paradoxical American conservatism that was defined by it—largely endured. This was particularly true of the century between the War of 1812 and the First
World War. The American Civil War, which came precisely in
the middle of this century, was an apparent exception, but actually it largely confirmed the distinctive American pattern, and in
any event it only lasted four years. Thus, this particular American century can be seen as a sort of golden age for this peculiar
American conservatism.

Again, one might have expected that the First World War would
bring an end to the distinctive American conditions—it certainly
brought an end to any strong and solid basis for classical liberalism
in Europe itself.[10] However, America's participation in the war was
actually very brief (U.S. forces did not really begin combat operations until March 1918, and these were over in eight months) and
with relatively few casualties (U.S. forces suffered far fewer combat fatalities than any of the other great powers—for example,
only 8 percent of those of France—and even fewer combat fatalities than most of the small participants—such as those of Roma-
nia).[11] Moreover, the wartime experience seemed decisively to
vindicate and even enhance the strengths of both the traditional
American economic system and traditional American moral principles. Consequently, when the war was over, the United States
eagerly and rapidly returned to its traditional ideas and ideals, to
what was seen as "normalcy" in each of the economic, religious,

and security dimensions, and it did so under the leadership of the Republican Party, the political party that was most identified with the great project of American conservatism, that is, of conserving, and restoring, classical liberalism, including its core ideal of individualism.

However, the 1920s were not really a new golden age for American conservatism. Too many changes and challenges had recently occurred within the economic, religious, and security arenas for there to be a full restoration of the American world of the nineteenth century. Rather, the 1920s can accurately be seen as a sort of Indian summer of that world. The decade represents a culmination of the original, and by then traditional, American conservatism, just before that conservatism would be assaulted by the economic challenges posed by the Great Depression, the religious challenges posed by secularization within the American social and cultural elites, and the security challenges posed by the Second World War.

The 1930s: The Great Debacle of the Original American Conservatism

The orderly world and Indian summer of this original American conservatism abruptly came to an end as the 1920s themselves came to an end. It collapsed under the multidimensional assaults posed by the onset of the Great Depression in 1929, the growth of secular ideas (and the growing sense that Prohibition was a failure) in the late 1920s, and the beginning of Japan's imperial expansion in Manchuria and China in 1931–1932.[12] By the election of 1932, it was clear to a majority of Americans that the old conservative order had collapsed.[13] Although it was not so clear that the policies of the Republican Party had been the cause of this collapse, it did seem clear that the party had not done a good job of conserving that order and that it had no convincing plan for how to restore it. The election of Franklin Roosevelt as president and of a large Democratic majority in Congress initiated a whole new era in American history, and in the history of American conservatism more particularly. Indeed, for much of the next half-century, it almost seemed that the history of American conservatism had itself come to an end.

The original American conservatism did not respond well in the 1930s to the multidimensional challenges in the economic, religious, and security arenas. Indeed, it has been widely believed ever since that it failed in each of these three great tests of that time. Consequently, American conservatism was on the defensive and on the decline for several decades. It would not begin to revive—or rather be reinvented—until the fusionist project of the early 1960s, and it would not be truly robust again until the Reagan era of the 1980s. But, as we shall discuss in the concluding sections of this chapter, this reinvented American conservatism is itself now on the defensive and on the decline. Perhaps, in its own way, reinvented American conservatism has failed the great economic, religious, and security tests of our own time.

In the course of the 1930s, conservatives responded to the challenges by essentially splitting into two camps, and this was the case in each of the three arenas. One camp, normally the larger one, essentially abandoned the original conservative (really classical liberal) position. Most economic and social elites made this choice. They adopted instead moderate versions of the political ideology that was coming into being with Roosevelt's New Deal in economic policy, but also with greater secularism in religion and greater internationalism in foreign affairs. Although often called "liberalism," this new ideology envisioned a much larger role for the federal government in many sectors of society; it had much more in common with the Progressivism of Theodore Roosevelt and Woodrow Wilson than it had with classical liberalism. (Indeed, it would be more accurate to call this particular worldview progressivism, rather than the commonly used term of liberalism.) This camp of conservatives, therefore, was hardly conservative at all. Rather, they were merely moderate progressives.

Of course, the original conservatives had not really been conservatives either. They were merely classical liberals. It seems to be the case in America that most so-called conservatives have really been something else. This has confused not only external observers of American conservatism (be they on the European Right or on the American Left), but it has confused American conservatives as well.

However, the second camp, normally the smaller one, largely continued to adhere to the original conservative (classical liberal) position. This was especially the choice of many ordinary persons, particularly small businessmen and Bible-believing Protestants. Although these persons might still form the social elite in small towns, they decidedly did not form the elites in the cities and at the national level. And, step-by-step in the course of the 1930s and 1940s, they ceased to form the elite of the Republican Party. The last Republican presidential candidate to represent some version of original American conservatism was Alf Landon in 1936, and his decisive electoral defeat, even debacle, confirmed the view for most of the Republican leadership that the old conservatism could no longer win elections. For almost three decades thereafter, until the candidacy of Barry Goldwater in 1964, every Republican presidential nominee was some kind of "moderate conservative" or "liberal Republican"—and in favor of some kind of large role for the federal government in many sectors of society (these candidates were: Wendell Wilkie in 1940, Thomas Dewey in 1944 and 1948, Dwight Eisenhower in 1952 and 1956, and Richard Nixon in 1960). The similarity of the policy positions of these Republican candidates to those of their Democratic opponents caused many political commentators to refer to the Republicans as the "me-too" party.

Consequently, if one is interested in American conservatism, one will not find much interesting in the Republican Party during the period that stretched from the late 1930s to the early 1960s, or at least in its leadership and its elite. Insofar as there was a genuine American conservatism during this era, it was found within the minority camp of the Republican Party, whose geographical location was centered in the Midwestern states and whose sociological location was centered in small businessmen, Bible-believing Protestants, and traditional patriots of British or "old-stock" origin. Their principal leader for many years was Senator Robert Taft of Ohio (whom his followers called "Mr. Republican"). After his death in 1954, however, conservatives were largely bereft of any real political leader at the national level, until the emergence of Senator Barry Goldwater of Arizona (who announced his candidacy for this role with the publication of his book *The Conscience of a Conservative* in 1960 and who subsequently ran for president in 1964).

THE MID-TWENTIETH CENTURY: THE GOLDEN AGE OF AMERICAN PROGRESSIVISM

Thus for three decades—from the mid-1930s to the mid-1960s and from the Great Depression to the Vietnam War—American political ideas and public policies were shaped by what was sometimes called "the liberal consensus" (although it was actually a progressive one) and by its counterpart, the conservative marginalization. This era saw such epic American achievements as the recovery from the Great Depression, the winning of the Second World War (with war production largely explaining the economic recovery), the rise of the United States to superpower status, the peace and prosperity of the Eisenhower years, and the apparent taming of the business cycle (with depressions being replaced by mere recessions) by some version of Keynesian policies, be it the "military Keynesianism" of the Eisenhower administration (defense spending accounting for 10 percent of GNP, even in a time of purported peace) or the "economic fine-tuning" of the Kennedy administration. And for these achievements, progressive policies got the credit. It certainly seemed that American conservatism had nothing significant to add, or even to say.

What then explains the conservative revival that eventually occurred by the late 1970s and which took control of the U.S. government with the election of Ronald Reagan as president and of a Republican-controlled Senate in 1980? Conservative thinkers and think tanks (especially neo-conservative ones) ascribe this revival and its success (which they call "the Reagan Revolution") to their own thoughts, that is, to the philosophical and political ideas and policy proposals that they published in their journals (examples include *The Public Interest, The National Review,* and *Commentary*). Standard histories of the conservative movement give a lot of weight to such thinkers (or publicists) as Russell Kirk, William F. Buckley, James Q. Wilson, Irving Kristol, and Norman Podhoretz.[14]

All of this attention by conservative writers to other conservative writers (or to themselves) makes for rather tiresome reading about thinkers regarding whom most American citizens and politicians (including Republican ones) have never thought. In any event, the decisive causes for the revival—or more accurately, the reinvention—of American conservatism lay not in new conservative thinking, but rather in two sets of causes which were more fundamental—and which were less mental and more material. These were, first, the failures of particular progressive policies, which by the 1970s had become apparent to almost everyone, and, second, the shifts that occurred among particular components that formed the social bases of the two political parties and their associated ideological movements.

THE 1970S: THE GREAT DEBACLE OF
AMERICAN PROGRESSIVISM

The progressive policy failures occurred in the same three arenas—the economic, the religious (by now also the moral and social), and the security—that had been the locus of the conservative failures in the 1930s.

The economic arena: Forty years after the beginning of the Great Depression, the United States and the world more generally experienced another great economic crisis, one that eventually came to be called the Great Stagflation. It was similar to the Great Depression, in that the major industrial nations suffered a significant rise in prolonged unemployment. However, the level of unemployment, although prolonged, only reached the level of previous recessions, not of the Great Depression itself. Conversely, this economic crisis was different from the Great Depression in that the major industrial nations suffered a sharp rise in prolonged inflation (with annual rates often at double-digit levels). The conjunction of the stagnation of unemployment and the inflation of currencies gave the prolonged crisis its name, the Great Stagflation.[15]

It was the inflation part that most alarmed middle-class populations and most confounded progressive and "moderate conservative" politicians. By the late 1960s, these politicians had fully embraced Keynesian theories about the proper way to effectively manage the economy. But although Keynesianism certainly could claim to have a solution to the problem of unemployment (which had been the central problem of the Great Depression), it had never focused upon the problem of inflation. With the onset of substantial and sustained inflation after 1968, the United States, as well as many other industrial nations, was confronted with a great economic challenge for which Keynesianism had no solution. Even though the problem of stagflation persisted for years, indeed throughout the 1970s, Keynesian economists were never able to develop a convincing theory of the crisis, and progressive and moderate-conservative (i.e., Democratic and Republican) political leaders were never able to implement an effective policy to tame it. This failure went a long way toward discrediting progressivism in the minds of many Americans, and particularly those in the inflation-impacted middle class.

The religious and social arena: At about the same time as the Great Stagflation and the failure of Keynesian economic policies, there was a somewhat parallel development of dilemmas within the progressive welfare state and a failure of Great Society social policies. By the mid-1970s, it had become clear that something was going wrong with these social policies, particularly with regard to American blacks. Although a minority of blacks seemed to benefit from the policies and entered the middle class (analogous to "the talented tenth" that W. E. B. Dubois had observed as early as the 1900s), the majority of blacks remained caught in a complex of deprived backgrounds, low education, high unemployment, violent surroundings, and extremely high rates of crime. Once again, the middle-class population was alarmed, and the progressive and moderate-conservative politicians were confounded. Progressive sociologists were never able to develop a convincing theory of the problems in the black population, and progressive and moderate-conservative (i.e., Democratic and Republican) political leaders were never able to implement an effective policy to solve them. This failure also went a long way toward discrediting progressivism in the minds of many Americans, and especially those in the crime-impacted middle class.

The evident failure of progressivism to address the economic problems posed by the Great Stagflation and the social problems within the black population, and indeed the direct impact that pro-black policies had upon sectors of the white population, brought about a new set of major changes in the social bases of the two political parties and their associated ideological movements. In particular, two large groups, which had long identified with the Democratic Party, shifted their votes to the conservative wing of the Republican Party. The first was Southern whites, who obviously saw racial issues as a top priority. The second was ethnic Catholics, some even within the working class, who paid the most direct costs for policies of school integration and affirmative action. As a result of these shifts in social bases, the progressive part of the Democratic Party became much more dependent upon and shaped by its remaining components, that is, the media, academia, and municipal-employee and teachers' unions.[16]

The security arena: By the late 1960s, yet another great failure of progressivism and moderate conservatism was becoming manifest. This, of course, was the Vietnam War. The U.S. military intervention in Vietnam, initiated by the Kennedy administration in 1961 and greatly expanded by the Johnson administration in 1965, certainly was an expression of such progressive ideals as internationalism (backed by military interventionism) and nation-building (legitimated by democratic rhetoric). And it was also an expression of moderate-conservative imperatives such as anti-Communism and containment. But by 1968, the U.S. war in Vietnam was clearly going very badly, and for this pressing problem the Johnson administration and the conventional progressives again had no convincing solution. This incapacity of progressives in the face of this great security challenge was a central factor in Lyndon Johnson's decision in March 1968 not to run for reelection that year. It was also a central factor in the election of Richard Nixon as president.

Eventually the progressives were given a second chance at security policy with the election of Jimmy Carter as president in 1976. By now, they had learned from their failure in Vietnam about the costs of military intervention and militant anti-communism, and in its first three years the Carter administration pursued a relatively passive security policy. At the same time, however, the Soviet Union had been emboldened by the U.S. failure in Indochina and by the establishment of Communist regimes in Vietnam, Cambodia, and Laos, and it soon enabled Marxist movements to gain power in a wide range of countries elsewhere. The Soviet Union and more generally Communism seemed to be on a roll, and the progressives seemed to have no convincing ideas or effective policies to meet this challenge.

The resurgent security challenge posed by the Soviet Union and communism was soon joined by a new security challenge

posed by Iran and Islamism. The Carter administration's ineffective responses to the Islamic Revolution in Iran and to the hos-
tage crisis at the U.S. embassy there were widely seen as a humiliat-
ing debacle for the United States. Here was yet another security
challenge for which the progressives seemed to have no convincing ideas or effective policies. This double failure in the security
arena completed the discrediting of progressivism in the minds of
many Americans.

THE LATE TWENTIETH CENTURY: THE REVIVAL AND
REINVENTION OF AMERICAN CONSERVATISM

Given the progressive failures across three policy arenas—adding
up to progressivism's own great debacle—the way was clear for
some kind of conservatism to reappear as a serious force in American history, and this did indeed occur during the 1970s. However,
this kind of conservatism was not really a revival of the original or
traditional American version. Rather, it was something quite different, a reinvention of American conservatism altogether, one that
stretched across all three policy arenas.

The economic arena: As it happened, by the 1970s there was
a body of economic ideas which claimed that it could solve the
problem of inflation (and, in doing so, also the problem of unemployment). This lay in the theories of Milton Friedman and more
generally of what was known as the "monetarist school." Whereas
Keynes and his followers focused upon government spending
and fiscal policy as the balance wheel of the economy, Friedman
and his followers focused upon the money supply and monetary
policy as that balance wheel. And whereas Keynesianism called
upon government (and elected officials) to intervene directly
in the economy through expenditures and taxes, Friedmanism
called upon the central bank—which in the United States is the
Federal Reserve System (and appointed officials who are largely
independent of elected ones but actually quite dependent upon
the executives of major banks)—merely to intervene indirectly in
the economy through interest rates and the overall money supply.
Friedmanism thus advocated a radical shift in the location of the
economy's balance wheel and therefore in the power of those who
would run it.

Although Friedman and his followers were always talking about the virtues of the free market and of conservatism in economic affairs, their approach was not truly a free-market or original-conservative one at all. Instead, they advocated a controlled market in matters of money, credit, and finance, while advocating a free market with respect to almost everything else. And the market in money, credit, and finance was to be controlled by an oligopoly of the major banks, implemented through the Federal Reserve System (whose name made it sound like some kind of government agency, but whose reality made it more a cartel of profit-making banks).

A truly free-market and original-conservative set of ideas about the money supply, and about the general economy, also existed in the late 1970s, and this was found in the theories of Friedrich Hayek, Ludwig von Mises, and what was called the "Austrian school." They argued that the economy, including its interest rates and money supply, should operate without any organized intervention at all, whether by government agencies or by a banker's cartel.[17]

During the era of Keynesian hegemony in economic affairs, both the monetarist school and the Austrian school had been marginalized in academic economics departments and among economic-policy advisors. But the failure and incapacity of Keynesianism meant that these two marginalized alternatives now had an opportunity to supercede it. A main reason why Friedmanism became the alternative that did so, rather than the ideas of Hayek and von Mises, was that the former had a large complex of economic interests (the major banks: "Wall Street") supporting it, while the latter had no such support (the only substantial interests likely to support it were small banks and small businesses: "Main Street").

The monetarist approach was adopted by the Federal Reserve System in 1979 and implemented by its chairman, Paul Volcker, in 1979–1982. Volcker's actions were indeed highly effective (although of course temporarily very painful) in bringing inflation to an end, and in 1983 the U.S. economy began a period of impressive growth that was largely sustained for almost two decades, until 2000. This success in solving the problem of inflation, while also providing for growing employment—for bringing an end to the

Great Stagflation—gave Friedmanism an enormous boost in credibility and prestige. It now became hegemonic in academic economics departments and among economic-policy advisors, and it has held this dominant position for 30 years (1980s to 2010s) after the Great Stagflation, just as Keynesianism had been hegemonic for about 30 years (1940s to 1970s) after the Great Depression. Of course, the Friedman school has been just as insistent and effective in keeping the Austrian school marginalized (and indeed virtually unknown) as the Keynesian school had been before.

Since Friedmanism is not truly a free-market approach (despite its rhetorical claims to be so), what is its relation to American conservatism as this applies to the economic arena? It is most accurately seen as a kind of pseudo-conservatism, not as an example of the original American conservatism. This means that when the "conservative movement" and the Reagan Revolution brought about a "revival" of American conservatism, it was actually bringing about its reinvention on the economic dimension. Consequently, this most central and weighty dimension of American conservatism would not be truly conservative at all, in any real sense of the word (in either its traditional European or its traditional American meaning).

Nevertheless, the pseudo-conservatism of Friedmanism had a very good run at managing the American economy for a very long time (almost 30 years), just like the progressivism or pseudo-liberalism of Keynesianism had had previously (also 30 years). However, as we shall see, the hegemony of the major banks within the hegemony of Friedmanism was a birth defect and fatal flaw that would eventually work its way out and bring about the next great economic crisis, that is, the Great Recession that began in 2007 and that continues until today.

The religious and social arena: During the long era of progressive ascendancy, which included both progressives and moderate conservatives, both Democratic and Republican elites—Bible-believing Protestants had largely remained a component of the original-conservative minority within the Republican Party. However, they did not have any reliable and effective political vehicle, and they were marginalized in electoral policies and in public policy. Then, a number of developments in the 1970s brought about a rise in their potential influence.

First, after several decades of political inactivity, Bible-believing Protestants were awakened and energized by particular progressive advances with regard to moral issues. The most central of these was the issue of abortion, for which a monumental milestone was the Supreme Court decision in *Roe v. Wade* in 1973. Just as Prohibition had been "the Great Crusade" of conservative Protestants for three generations from the 1870s to the 1920s, so Pro-Life became their great crusade for the three decades from the 1970s to the 2000s.

Second, as we have seen, the shifts in the social bases of the two political parties and their associated ideological movements, which were produced by progressive policies and which occurred in the 1970s, brought Southern whites and ethnic Catholics into the Republican Party. As it happened, each of these groups had something important in common with the Bible-believing Protestants who were already in the party. For Southern whites, this was the Protestant part (and, indeed, when Southern whites had been Democrats, many had also been among the most Bible-believing people in America). For ethnic Catholics, this was the Pro-Life part. Thus, the shifts in social bases brought about a new conservative grand alliance with respect to religious and social issues and around commonly shared "traditional moral values."

Of course, traditional conservatives had long been bereft of any credible national political leader (after the death of Robert Taft, Barry Goldwater had briefly been the closest approximation to one, and he was much more a social libertarian than a traditional moral conservative). By itself, religious or traditional moral conservatism was not going to produce a credible national political figure. However, the fusionist project of the conservative movement had laid the intellectual groundwork for uniting social conservatives with economic and security conservatives. And Ronald Reagan, "the Great Communicator," certainly had the gift of being able to speak to the different arenas of traditional conservatism, in words and concepts that they not only understood, but that they loved. It was Reagan who appeared to traditional religious and social conservatives to be, at long last, their authentic political representative and effective political vehicle. And it was he who brought them into the grand alliance of conservatives that provided the electoral base for "the Reagan Revolution."

We have observed, however, that with regard to economic policy, the Reagan era and the following years of Republican political power did not really produce original-conservative policies,
but ones that were merely pseudo-conservative. Much the same
thing can be said for the social policies of the Reagan era and
later Republican rule. Reagan and some other Republican leaders were excellent in their public speeches and pronouncements
with respect to traditional moral values. However, when it came to
implementing these values in actual legislation and practical policies, the results—after a period lasting almost three decades—have
been negligible. The main benefit that traditional social conservatives have received from Republicans in the White House and in
Congress has been four Supreme Court appointments—Antonin
Scalia, Clarence Thomas, John Roberts, and Samuel Alito. And so,
in a sense, the reinvention of American conservatism in the social
arena actually produced another kind of pseudo-conservatism—or
at best quasi-conservatism—one that was parallel and analogous to
the pseudo-conservatism in the economic arena.

Moreover, while the Republicans were in power in the White
House and in Congress, they facilitated a major change in the
demographic composition of the U.S. population—and therefore in the social bases of the two political parties and their ideological movements. This was the great increase in immigration—
including illegal immigration—from Latin America, and especially
from Mexico. Of course, this increase in immigration had originated with the Immigration Act of 1965, which can be seen as one
of the progressive policies of the time, and it had steadily increased
in numbers during the 1970s. However, it was during the era when
reinvented conservatism was in ascendency and the Republicans
were in power that the Hispanic immigration and the ensuing Hispanic births in the United States reached massive proportions. For
example, in the 1980s, Hispanics accounted for 5 percent of the
U.S. population; by the late 2000s, as a group they accounted for
15 percent, surpassing the black population in numbers.

Progressives had their own ideological reasons for facilitating
immigration, based first upon ideals of racial equality and human
rights and then upon the ideology of multiculturalism. But why
did the Republican Party—with its putative social conservatism—
join the Democratic Party in facilitating this massive demographic

and therefore social change? The reason is that the grand alliance of reinvented conservatives were simply ordering their priorities and following the same script as the grand alliance of original conservatives had done in the nineteenth and early twentieth centuries, that other era of open immigration into the United States. That is, the economic interests of business and middle-class conservatives in cheap labor trumped the communal interests of the cultural and social conservatives.

Of course in the long run, since "demography is destiny," this new and massive demographic sector could become a new and massive voting bloc. Given the voting behavior of most previous immigrant groups and racial minorities, it seemed most probable that this Hispanic voting bloc would largely vote for the Democratic Party. However, given the hegemony of business interests in the Republican Party, it is not surprising that the short-term profit-making interests of its business constituency trumped the long-term vote-getting interests of the party itself. And so, once again, re-invented conservatism was revealed to be merely pseudo-conservatism. Indeed, given the massive changes that a new Hispanic bloc could produce in American society and politics in the future, reinvented conservatism was, at least with respect to the social arena, even a kind of anti-conservatism.

The security arena: In the 1970s, a number of policy intellectuals came together to develop a systematic critique not only of the security policies of the progressive Carter administration, but also those of the preceding moderate-conservative Nixon and Ford administrations. They called themselves "neo-conservatives." These thinkers had already developed a systematic critique of progressive and moderate-conservative social policies, but by the late 1970s their principal focus was on the security arena. They were particularly alarmed about the resurgent Soviet and Communist threat and the new Iranian and Islamist threat.[18]

The neo-conservatives proposed a comprehensive program to revitalize U.S. security policy and to strengthen America's leadership in the world. In particular, they advocated: (1) major increases in U.S. military spending and expansion of U.S. military forces; (2) enhanced military assistance to friendly foreign governments that were threatened by Marxist or Islamist movements; (3) enhanced military assistance to insurgent movements that sought to overthrow Marxist regimes (this was the most innovative of the neo-conservative proposals; it would eventually be formulated as the Reagan Doctrine); and (4) renewed willingness to undertake full military interventions, that is, to employ U.S. military forces to overthrow unfriendly governments and to protect friendly ones.

With the exception of (3), these proposals merely called for a revival of previous U.S. policies and practices in the security arena. Indeed, some version of them had earlier been carried out by moderate-conservative administrations (Eisenhower and Nixon) and even by progressive ones (Truman, Kennedy, and Johnson). Even the original-conservative Republican administrations of the 1920s used such methods in dealing with countries in the Caribbean basin and Central America. However, in the era of "the Vietnam syndrome" and the unusually passive security policies of the Ford and Carter administrations, the neo-conservative proposals seemed new, fresh, and vigorous.

The neo-conservative security program was largely adopted by the Reagan administration when it came into office in 1981. As it turned out, that administration and its successor, the George H. W. Bush administration, did achieve a series of extraordinary successes in first reducing and then eliminating the Soviet threat (examples include the Soviet withdrawal from Afghanistan in early 1989, the collapse of East European Communist regimes in late 1989, the reunification of Germany on Western terms in 1990, and finally the dissolution of the Soviet Union itself in 1991). Although the actual causes of the Soviet debacle are complex and disputed, the neo-conservatives naturally claimed the credit for this historic achievement of the Reagan and Bush administrations.

There was still, however, the threat from Iran and from Islamism more generally, and this threat continued to grow at the very time that the Soviet threat was disappearing. And here, the record of the neo-conservatives and the Reagan and Bush administrations is marked by significant failures (examples: the U.S. military intervention in Lebanon in 1964 and the growing threat from Islamist terrorists in the 1980s and early 1990s). Even the apparent successes would later turn into major security problems (as with the U.S. assistance to Islamist insurgents against the Soviets in Afghanistan in the late 1980s and the U.S. victory over Saddam Hussein in Iraq in 1991). And as we shall see in a concluding section of this chapter, the failure of the neo-conservatives would become even more manifest when they became one of the two core groups (the other being the oil industry) shaping the security policy of the George W. Bush administration with respect to the Middle East and Islamism. When the neo-conservatives turned their attention to this region, they largely overlooked the relevant local realities and instead imposed concepts drawn from abstract ideologies that had been developed for other regions, especially for Europe. Thus, they spoke a great deal about "Islamo-fascism" and Saddam Hussein's "Stalinism" and, conversely, about the U.S. success in occupying and democratizing West Germany and Japan after the Second World War.

In what sense, then, can it be said that neo-conservatism is an authentic kind of conservatism with respect to U.S. security policies pertaining to the Middle East and Islamism? It argues for extensive U.S. military involvement, and even U.S. wars, in a region where U.S. national interests are unclear and greatly disputed, and there is little that is conservative about this. It too is more accurately described as a kind of pseudo-conservatism. And it argues for intensive U.S. political involvement to remake Middle Eastern states and Muslim societies, and there is little that is conservative about this. It is more accurately described as a kind of anti-conservatism. Overall, then, neo-conservatism is not really conservatism at all.

THE 2000S: THE GREAT DEBACLE OF REINVENTED AMERICAN CONSERVATISM

And so, in the fullness of time (which in America seems to be after about three decades), reinvented American conservatism brought about its own great debacle, again a debacle great enough to encompass all three policy arenas.

The economic arena: The three decades when Friedmanism and the monetarist school dominated economic theory and the Federal Reserve System dominated economic policy were largely an era of impressive economic growth and prosperity. There were occasional stock market panics or business recessions (1987–1988, 1991–1992, 2000–2002), but overall the U.S. economy seemed to be operating so smoothly that Alan Greenspan and Ben

Bernanke—successive chairmen of the Federal Reserve Board and archetypal exponents of the monetarist worldview—could call the era (and their own management of the economy) "the Great Moderation."

However, near the end of this era and in the aftermath of the recession of 2000–2002, some ominous developments and unhealthy distortions appeared. The economic boom that began in 2003 was based not upon new technologies and investments in productive assets (such as the information-technology boom of 1993–2000), but upon the real estate, especially the housing, sector. And soon, the housing boom became a speculative bubble, which burst in 2007 and then turned into a bust. Since banks had very heavily invested in overvalued real estate and complex securitized mortgages, the housing crisis soon metastasized into a full-blown financial crisis, and since credit and finance is the lifeblood (and in an era of monetarist and Federal Reserve hegemony, the balance wheel) of the economy as a whole, the financial crisis in turn soon metastasized into a full-blown economic crisis. Indeed, this crisis was in many ways—particularly with respect to high and prolonged unemployment—the greatest economic crisis since the Great Depression almost 80 years before, and it was soon given its own name—the Great Recession.[19] It was the major factor causing the Republican Party to decisively lose the presidential and congressional elections of 2008.

It was no accident that the Great Moderation ended with a speculative bubble in housing and complicated securities. For, at the center of this era were the major profit-making banks. Throughout this period, they had relentlessly and successively lobbied government officials to reduce and remove restrictions upon banking activities that had existed ever since the New Deal and Depression-era financial legislation of the 1930s (most importantly, the Glass-Steagall Act of 1933, which limited the risk-taking activities of commercial banks). By 2000, the financial sector had succeeded in abolishing most of the New Deal legislation, and that which remained was very lightly enforced by the anti-regulation appointees of the George W. Bush administration. Then, when virtually no government restrictions remained upon their profit-making activities, the major banks decided that they could make the most profit by investing in familiar and apparently solid ("real" estate) assets, rather than in innovative and apparently risky (but ultimately more productive) enterprises. This kind of decision to invest in the familiar rather than the innovative has long been characteristic behavior for very large and established banks, and it was natural that the major American banks took this path as soon as they could.[20]

And so it was the very ideas, interests, and institutions that brought Friedmanism into power and presided over its long era of success which then, through their excesses, caused an economic crisis that brought their era to an end. And since these ideas, interests, and institutions have caused so much economic disruption and destruction, they can truly be said to be pseudo-conservative, rather than authentically conservative.

Of course, when Friedmanism and pseudo-conservatism was confronted with the challenges of the Great Recession, they were incapable of offering any convincing and effective solutions. In this regard, they were like their predecessors, first the free-market advocates and traditional conservatives when they were confronted with the challenges of the Great Depression and then the Keynesians and progressives when they were confronted with the challenges of the Great Stagflation. But just like these previous great economic crises were eventually addressed and solved with new economic theories and policies, so too we might hope that the current crisis will be also. But just as it took about a decade of crisis before those earlier new theories and policies at last became ascendant, we will probably be waiting for our new solutions to the current crisis for quite some time. In the meantime, despite the disruption and destruction that they have wrought, the major banks and the monetarist school continue to prevail in the making of U.S. economic policy.

The religious and social arena: Since the political representatives of reinvented conservatism produced a good deal of religious and social conservative rhetoric but negligible policy results, there were not any policy failures of reinvented conservatism in the religious and social arena comparable to those in the economic arena and contributing to its contemporary great debacle. However, the choices that reinvented conservatives made with respect to immigration policy from the 1980s to the 2000s finally matured into political consequences in 2008. In that year, Hispanics overwhelmingly (about 70 percent) voted for the Democratic Party, and they provided the margin for victory for many Democratic elected officials. Hispanics repeated this electoral role in 2012. The prospects are that this strong Hispanic identification with the Democratic Party will continue into the future, adding another large voting bloc to the Democratic base, parallel to the one that blacks have long provided to the party. (Together, these two voting blocks of the Democratic Party will greatly outweigh the only comparable voting bloc in the Republic Party, that of white Evangelicals—or, more accurately, white Bible-believing Protestants.) The recent coming into maturity of this great transformation in U.S. electoral politics has contributed a good deal to the great debacle of reinvented conservatism.

The security arena: By the late 2000s, another failure of reinvented conservatism—and particularly of neo-conservatism— was becoming manifest. This was, of course, the Iraq War, joined increasingly by a parallel failure in the Afghan War. The U.S. war in Iraq, which the George W. Bush administration had begun in 2003, was certainly an expression of neo-conservative policies such as a willingness, even eagerness, to employ U.S. military forces to overthrow unfriendly governments and to impose democracy-promotion and nation-building on foreign countries. The same had become true of the way the Bush administration conducted its war in Afghanistan, after its initially successful overthrow of the Taliban regime in late 2001.

By 2006, the Iraq War was clearly going very badly, and for this pressing problem the Bush administration and neo-conservatives deservedly got the blame. This was a major factor in the Republicans' losing control of Congress to the Democrats in 2006. Although the new counter-insurgency strategy of General David Petraeus and the military "surge" authorized by President Bush in 2007 seemed to turn the Iraq debacle around dramatically by 2008, the grueling and growing war in Afghanistan threatened a new debacle. The major cause of the Republican defeat in the 2008 presidential and congressional elections was of course the onset of the Great Recession, but the Afghan War was an additional and substantial contributing factor.

THE 2010S: AMERICAN CONSERVATISM IN THE GREAT RECESSION

The depth, scope, and length of the current global economic crisis—greater than any economic crisis since the Great Depression—has meant that economic and fiscal issues now dominate American politics. Although issues in the religious/social and security arenas are still intensely debated, most of the focus and energy of what now passes for American conservatism is devoted to the economic arena. As we have seen, this has always been the most important arena in American conservatism, and it is now even more central and determinative than before.

The economic arena: The policy response of the George W. Bush administration to the financial crisis of 2008 was completely in keeping with the economic priorities of the reinvented, pseudo-conservatism that had brought about the crisis in the first place, which is to say, massive government bailouts of large financial institutions ("Wall Street"). These bailouts were so massive that they provoked opposition from long-dormant elements within the Republican Party which represented small banks and small businesses ("Main Street"), but when directed at a Republican administration, this opposition was only brief and ineffective (for example, Congress's initial rejection of the administration's TARP plan).

However, the succeeding Obama administration also pursued economic policies which privileged large financial institutions, while not doing much that actually improved the condition of other sectors of the economy (such as unemployed workers). Moreover, the budgets of the Obama administration and the Democratic Congress resulted in a massive expansion of federal deficits and debt (an expansion that had actually begun under the preceding Bush administration and Republican Congresses). Now the small-bank and small-business elements in the Republican Party had Democratic targets to oppose, and their opposition could be more sustained and more effective. The result was the beginning of the Tea Party movement in the summer of 2009, which was able to achieve significant successes in the congressional elections of 2010.[21]

The economic and fiscal thinking of the Tea Party movement had much in common with that of the original American conservatism, and with theorists such as Friedrich Hayek and Ludwig von Mises. It had much less in common with the economic and fiscal thinking of reinvented conservatism, and with theorists such as Friedman and the monetarists. Indeed, the thinking of the Tea Party movement was largely the same as that of the libertarian movement, which had long been a marginal element within the Republican Party.

Consequently, with respect to the economic arena, American conservatism is now split between two tendencies: (1) a partially discredited reinvented conservatism, which nevertheless continues to dominate the leadership or "establishment" of the Republican Party because it corresponds to the economic interests of the party's elites and big donors; and (2) a partially revived original conservatism, which is a significant insurgent force within the Republican Party, because it corresponds to the economic interests of much of the party's base and many of its core voters.

This split was played out in the 2012 primary elections to nominate the Republican candidate for president. From the beginning, indeed as early as 2009, the preferred candidate of the Republican leadership and elite was Mitt Romney. In the early Republican primaries (those with several candidates competing, representing the several different tendencies within the Party), Mitt Romney consistently led with respect to campaign funding and the support of most big donors, but he usually received less than 30 percent of the votes. Conversely, the Tea Party voters often preferred Ron Paul, but they recognized that he could never win the nomination; consequently, their votes were split among several different candidates other than Romney. The party leadership had early determined that their best strategy to achieve a Romney nomination was to split the anti-Romney vote among several different candidates, no one of which could achieve a majority, or perhaps even a plurality, and this strategy proved successful. The insurgent or anti-Romney candidates cancelled out each other. Romney may not have achieved majorities, but he did achieve more pluralities than anyone else, and therefore the nomination. The party leadership calculated that any disaffected Tea Party voters could be corralled into voting for Romney against President Obama in the general election.

The religious and social arena: In contrast to the even greater dominance of economic and fiscal issues within American conservatism since 2008, religious and social issues have been pushed even further to the margins. Both the Republican Party establishment and the Tea Party movement consider religious and social issues to be at best a distraction from the central arena of economic and fiscal issues, and at worst causing an actual subtraction of votes of independents from Republican candidates; consequently, both agreed to marginalize these issues in the 2012 elections. Even such a fundamental and immediate concern of religious conservatives as homosexual marriage was given very little attention in the Republican presidential primaries. The religious conservatives did have a preferred candidate, Rick Santorum (who is a Roman Catholic, not an Evangelical Protestant), and he did score a couple of primary victories, but like the other anti-Romney candidates, he was soon overwhelmed by the Romney strategy and money. And, in the end, the marginalization of Evangelical Protestants even within the Republican Party culminated in the Romney/Ryan nominations, the first major-party president/vice-president ticket in American history that did not include a Protestant.

Meanwhile, the Hispanic percentage of the electorate continued to increase, and their votes continued to go overwhelmingly to the Democratic Party. With all of its focus upon economic and fiscal issues, the Republican Party was not able to develop a coherent and effective strategy to win over Hispanic voters in the 2012 elections. Indeed, many traditional conservatives were opposed to Hispanic immigration, and they found some voice in the Tea Party movement. This drove Hispanic voters even further away from the Republican Party. Some Republican leaders, alarmed by this development, hoped to attract Hispanic voters by having some prominent Hispanic elected official be Romney's running mate (such as Senator Marco Rubio of Florida). But the selection of Paul Ryan brought an end to even these fitful efforts to attract Hispanics.

The security arena: The security arena provides another contrast in the development of American conservatism in the 2010s. In the midst of the continuing global economic crisis, it is not surprising that security and defense issues have been less prominent than before 2008, although they have certainly remained more prominent than religious and social ones. What is perhaps surprising, however, is the continuing articulation of neo-conservative priorities and policies among many Republican leaders. One might have thought that neo-conservatism would have been discredited by its debacle in the Iraq and Afghan wars, but in the election year of 2012, it was just as prominent among Republican candidates for president as it had been in the George W. Bush administration, which put the United States into those wars.

The explanation for the continuing prominence of neo-conservatism in the Republican Party does not lie in the base of Republican voters. Most of these have become critical or skeptical of U.S. military interventions abroad, especially for such remote goals as nation-building and promoting democracy. In particular, the Tea Party movement has largely avoided discussion of security and defense issues, and many of its members take positions similar to those of the anti-interventionist (and anti-defense-spending) libertarian movement. Rather, the explanation lies in the Republican elite, and particularly with some of the Republican Party's big donors. These are found in both older sources of funding, such as the defense industry, and newer sources of funding, such as hedge funds, and they continue to support neo-conservative priorities and policies, particularly with respect to the Middle East.

In the early Republican primaries of 2012, the neo-conservatives' preferred presidential candidate was Newt Gingrich. Indeed, it was funding (in the amount of $15 million) from just one big donor, Sheldon Adelson, a casino magnate, that accounted for there being a Gingrich campaign at all and for its few and brief successes.[22] When it became clear that Romney was going to win the nomination, the neo-conservative donors, including Sheldon Adelson, then threw their support to him. Romney reciprocated by appointing a large panel of advisors, most of whom were prominent neo-conservatives, on security and defense issues and by making a series of well-publicized speeches, which advocated just about every neo-conservative priority and policy. However, there is an obvious contradiction between the fiscal conservatism of a substantial majority of the Republican Party's big donors and the security neo-conservatism of a significant minority of its big donors. This contradiction came to a head during the budget conflicts of 2013, with fiscal conservatism largely prevailing over security neo-conservatism.

What, then, is the contemporary character of American conservatism, half a decade after the debacle of the reinvented version, brought about by the Great Recession and the ongoing global economic crisis? We will sum up the current condition of the conservative coalition in its three component arenas.

In the economic arena, conservatism continues to be dominated and defined by the same kind of big-business, especially big-bank, priorities and policies that have been dominant for many decades. The greatly increased influence in the Republican Party of big donors on its candidates for public office has even strengthened this domination in recent years.[23] But the Party also continues to articulate the rhetoric of the original, free-market conservatism, and this has been enough to retain its small-business and independent-proprietor base among voters. This base has even been strengthened in recent years by the energy and activism of the Tea Party movement, which on economic issues adheres to original-conservative values. In short, with regard to the economic arena, American conservatism is now characterized in its rhetoric by the values of original conservatism—supported by a steady or even strengthened mass base of voters—and in its reality by the priorities and policies of what we have called reinvented conservatism—supported by a steady or even strengthened elite source of donors.

In the religious and social arena, however, the picture is very different. This kind of conservatism is today much weaker and more marginalized than it was only a few years ago. First, there are now very few big donors supporting the electoral campaigns of religious and social conservatives (the only prominent exception in the 2012 elections was a billionaire investor, Foster Friese, who provided the principal financial backing for Rick Santorum). And there has also been a substantial decrease in the number of voters who count religious and social issues as their chief concern when deciding for whom to vote. Moreover, the Republican Party can always be confident that this shrinking—but still essential—part of its electoral base will continue to cast its votes, however unenthusiastically, for Republican candidates and not for Democratic ones. With a very small donor elite and a shrinking and subordinate voter base, it is not surprising that religious and social conservatives are now only a weak and subordinated component within today's American conservatism.

Finally, in the security arena, the picture is again different, a kind of mixture of the contrasting situations in the other two arenas. First, although the number of big donors who prioritize security issues is much smaller than those who prioritize economic ones, their donations have been sufficient to buy the security priorities of Republican candidates, at least until the recent budget crises and resulting constraints on military spending. These priorities have been those of neo-conservatism, not the original ("realist" in current terminology) conservatism; in fact, today, there are virtually no big donors who support realist conservatives as candidates for public office. When we turn from the donor elite to the voter base, however, the situation is reversed. There are very few voters who actually put neo-conservative security priorities and policies (such as U.S. military interventions and democracy promotion abroad) as their chief concern when deciding for whom to vote. Although there are a small number of voters who do make security issues their top concern, the large majority of these actually adhere to realist-conservative security priorities and policies (for example, a strong military to defend America itself).

WHITHER AMERICAN CONSERVATISM?
TOWARD YET ANOTHER REINVENTION

By itself, this review of the various components of the contemporary conservative coalition would suggest that the electoral prospects for the Republican Party in the future are rather poor. There is a well-funded and well-mobilized base for economic and fiscal conservatism, but although this base is strong, it is narrow. Probably no more than 30 percent of the national electorate now votes the way they do because they hold conservative economic and fiscal values, and this is at a time of pronounced economic and fiscal crisis. Of course, within particular congressional districts and particular states, this percentage will be higher, and this will enable economic and fiscal conservatives—when they can make alliances with large numbers of religious/social or security/patriotic conservatives—to win elections to the U.S. House of Representatives (and even to win a majority) or to the U.S. Senate (but where they are unlikely to win a majority). But in general the prospects for conservatives to win presidential elections are doubtful. It is possible, then, that the great debacle of reinvented conservatism in the 2010s will have consequences for American conservatism and the Republican Party similar to those that followed the original great debacle of original conservatism in the 1930s. That is, American conservatism already will have entered into an era where it will mostly be a political minority, while some new version of American progressivism will be in political ascendency.

Of course, most Republican politicians are well aware of these prospects, and they cannot be expected to just passively accept the implications. Rather, we would expect that they will seek to bring about yet another reinvention of American conservatism, a new version, which would provide a broader and stronger base for the Republican Party than the current narrow, incoherent, and withered version. As we have seen, both the original and the reinvented versions of American conservatism were based upon a particular coalition of distinct social components, and so too will be any new reinvention. What might the new social base and new version of conservatism look like, given the electoral realities—based upon the economic and social, but also demographic realities—of the 2010s, and beyond? And here, through a glass darkly, we may glimpse the increasing significance of both race and gender.

The potential role of racial identity: Racial issues, in the form of slavery and the Civil War, were obviously at the origin of the Republican Party and in its ascendency during its first 70 years. However, the Party was never seen as the white party. On the contrary, where blacks were able to vote, they generally voted Republican. It was the Democratic Party in the South (in the once-Confederate states) that was seen, and accurately so, as the white party. More broadly, after the Civil War, the original American conservatism, while neglectful of the interests of black people, did not include white racial identity as an important component, even in its social or cultural dimensions.

However, the coming of the Civil Rights Movement of the 1950s and 1960s—and especially the Civil Rights Act of 1964 and the Voting Rights Act of 1965—brought about a new racial reality in

American partisan politics and a reversal of the racial identities of the Republican and Democratic parties. By the late 1960s, blacks were overwhelmingly voting for the Democratic Party, and whites in the South were largely voting for the Republican Party. Indeed, with their "Southern strategy," Republican leaders made it a major objective to have Southern whites see the Republican Party as the white party. In the South, this new racial and partisan reality has only become more pronounced during the ensuing half-century.

In the rest of America, however, Republican leaders have generally tried to avoid a racial identity being attached to the Party. Rather, as we have seen, they have emphasized economic/fiscal, religious/social, and security/patriotic issues and identities. And what has been true of the Republican Party has been even more true of the reinvented conservative movement. None of the major components of reinvented conservatism have provided any acceptance or even acknowledgment of racial issues and identity as being legitimate. The only exception is in the social arena, where many social and cultural conservatives have criticized affirmative-action policies that have explicitly and directly given preferences to blacks and Hispanics.

These policies seemed to many to be in obvious contradiction to all the language and legislation of the Civil Rights Movement about prohibiting discrimination based on race and about equal rights for all, and it provoked a good deal of resentment—and even delegitimization of the federal government—among many whites. In recent years, therefore, progressives have developed an alternative way of constructing public policies in order to give substantial assistance to blacks and Hispanics. Since a much larger proportion of these two groups is poor, in comparison with whites (and also with Asian Americans), policies that give substantial assistance to poor people will implicitly and indirectly also give such assistance to blacks and Hispanics. There have been at least three major areas where such policies have been implemented in recent years: (1) housing ownership; (2) economic stimulus; and (3) medical care.

There is therefore a growing consciousness among whites, especially among older ones, that Democratic programs not only benefit the poor at the expense of the middle class, but that they benefit blacks and Hispanics at the expense of whites. This consciousness is heightened by current economic realities, because government policies to bring about redistribution of monies from a stagnant or shrinking economic pie impose obvious and painful costs upon the middle class. Changing demographic realities also heighten this consciousness, because the black and Hispanic portion of the American population is steadily increasing, with these two groups already accounting for a majority of births in the United States each year.

Since the conventional identities of Republican voters—be they the identities of either original conservatism or reinvented conservatism—now issue in a voting base that is too narrow and withered to win most presidential and senatorial elections, the Republican Party leadership has to think about how to expand that base, and that probably means adding groups with new identities or ones that are redefined. In particular, the Republican establishment is now trying to somehow persuade many more Hispanics (73 percent of whom voted for Obama in the 2012 presidential election) to vote Republican in the future. However, there are formidable sociological and political obstacles standing in the way of this establishment Hispanic project.

An alternative path for the Republican Party in expanding its electoral base leads from the South to the rest of America, that is, from the Republicans being the white party in the South to the Republicans being the white party in America as a whole. In the 2012 presidential election Romney got 60 percent of the white vote, while Obama received only 38 percent. However, the Republican establishment knows how dangerous and destructive it would be to have an American party system defined and divided along racial lines, even if not explicitly or overtly so, and they are reluctant to take this path.

These considerations lead to a prospective realignment—or rather a sharpening of the current alignment—of the American party system along the following lines: The core voting groups for the progressive coalition and the Democratic Party are (1) blacks; (2) Hispanics; and (3) workers in the public sector. Conversely, the core voting groups for the conservative coalition and the Republican Party are (1) economic and fiscal conservatives; (2) Evangelical or Bible-believing Protestants; and (3) white male workers in the private sector.

The potential role of gender identity: Of course, in this alignment there remains one immense independent or swing group,
and that is white women. A substantial majority of white women
now vote for Democratic candidates, with economic issues being
primary for working-class women and social issues being primary
for middle-class women. If these women continue to vote for the
Democratic Party in the future, the prospects for the Republican Party to win most presidential and senatorial elections will
remain bleak. However, it is also the case that although a substantial majority of single women vote for Democratic candidates,
a significant majority of married women vote for Republican
ones. This suggests that if the Republican Party can find a way
to enhance its appeal to married women, perhaps with policies
that genuinely support families, it might be able to strengthen its
electoral base.

In our long review of the history of American conservatism, we
have seen it appeal over the decades and in successive versions to
a wide array of different groups and interests. But neither original conservatism nor reinvented conservatism ever had much
to appeal to women, if they saw their principal identity to be as
women. The same remains true of the weakened movement that
now passes for American conservatism and of the Republican
Party that is its institutional expression. It will only be if the conservatives and the Republicans can convince large numbers of American women, and particularly married women, that their principal
concern must be to conserve something important to them that
American conservatism will have a future.

NOTES

1. Patrick Allitt, *The Conservatives: Ideas and Personalities Throughout
American History* (New Haven, CT: Yale University Press, 2009), 191–266;
Paul Edward Gottfried, *Conservatism in America: Making Sense of the Ameri-
can Right* (New York: Palgrave, 2007).

2. Daniel Bell, *The Cultural Contradictions of Capitalism* (New York:
Basic, 1976).

3. Bruce Mazlish, Nayan Chanda, and Kenneth Weisbrode, eds., *The
Paradox of a Global USA* (Stanford, CA: Stanford University Press, 2007).

4. This account obviously draws upon the famous argument by Louis Hartz in *The Liberal Tradition in America: An Interpretation of American Political Thought since the Revolution* (New York: Harcourt, Brace, 1955), which in turn draws upon that of Alexis de Tocqueville in *Democracy in America*, trans. Henry Reeve, ed. Francis Bowen (Boston: John Allyn, 1873). Also see Samuel P. Huntington, *American Politics: The Promise of Disharmony* (Cambridge, MA: Belknap, 1981).

5. Lawrence M. Friedman, *The Republic of Choice: Law, Authority, and Culture* (Cambridge, MA: Harvard University Press, 1990).

6. James R. Kurth, "The Protestant Deformation," *American Interest* 1 (Winter 2005): 4–16.

7. George Washington, "Washington's Farewell Address, 1796," The Avalon Project, Lillian Goldman Law Library, Yale Law School, available at http://avalon.law.yale.edu/18th_century/washing.asp.

8. John Fonte, *Sovereignty or Submission: Will Americans Rule Themselves or Be Ruled by Others?* (New York: Encounter, 2011).

9. This is a major theme of Tocqueville, *Democracy in America*.

10. Karl Polanyi, *The Great Transformation*, 1st Beacon paperback ed. (Boston: Beacon, [1944] 1957).

11. Niall Ferguson, *The Pity of War* (New York: Basic, 1999), 295–296 (tables 32 and 33).

12. Charles P. Kindleberger, *The World in Depression, 1929–1939* (Berkeley: University of California Press, 1973); P. M. H. Bell, *The Origins of the Second World War in Europe*, 2nd ed. (New York: Longman, [1986] 1997).

13. Arthur M. Schlesinger, Jr., *The Crisis of the Old Order, 1919–1933*, 1st Mariner Books ed. (Boston: Houghton Mifflin, 2003).

14. George H. Nash, *The Conservative Intellectual Movement in America since 1945*, 30th Anniversary ed. (Wilmington, DE: ISI, 2008).

15. James R. Kurth, "A Tale of Four Crises: The Politics of Great Depressions and Recessions," *Orbis* 55 (Summer 2011): 500–523.

16. Thomas Byrne Edsall and Mary D. Edsall, *Chain Reaction: The Impact of Race, Rights, and Taxes on American Politics* (New York: Norton, 1991).

17. Thomas E. Woods, Jr., *Meltdown: A Free-Market Look at Why the Stock Market Collapsed, the Economy Tanked, and Government Bailouts Will Make Things Worse* (Washington, DC: Regnery, 2009), 63–86.

18. Stefan Halper and Jonathan Clarke, *America Alone: The Neo-Conservatives and the Global Order* (New York: Cambridge University Press, 2004); Murray Friedman, *The Neoconservative Revolution: Jewish Intellectuals and the Shaping of Public Policy* (Cambridge: Cambridge University Press, 2005); James R. Kurth, "The Neoconservatives Are History," *Orbis* 50 (Autumn 2006): 756–769.

19. Kurth, "A Tale of Four Crises."

20. James R. Kurth, "The Foreign Policy of Plutocracies," *American Interest* 7 (November/December 2011): 5–17.

21. Theda Skocpol and Vanessa Williamson, *The Tea Party and the Remaking of Republican Conservatism* (Oxford: Oxford University Press, 2012).

22. Adam Clancy, "What Newt Means," *American Interest* 8 (September/October 2012): 59–63.

23. Thomas E. Mann and Norman J. Ornstein, *It's Even Worse than It Looks: How the American Constitutional System Collided with the New Politics of Extremism* (New York: Basic, 2012), 67–80.

2

AN INTERPRETATION OF AMERICAN CONSERVATIVE THOUGHT: POLITICAL ISSUES, CONCEPTUAL DIFFERENCES, AND ATTITUDINAL DISJUNCTIONS

DAVID SIDORSKY

INTRODUCTION

An interpretation of American Conservative thought has as one of its aims the clarification of the concepts and attitudes that form the background for the political controversies that take place on issues of the Conservative agenda within American political life. In reflecting upon the agenda of political issues, the analysis of American Conservatism has conventionally been divided into three parts: Social Conservatism, Economic Conservatism, and Conservatism in foreign policy with its priority of protection of the national interest.

The assumption of this chapter is that clarification of American Conservative thought can be sought by moving beyond an account of the Conservative positions on issues that are contested in the political arena, which may be termed as the surface or "issues" tier of American Conservative political thought, toward two other tiers in which Conservatism is distinguished from Liberalism. One such tier, which can be termed in this context the second or "conceptual" tier of American Conservative political thought, involves differing interpretations of political concepts. In the analysis of these concepts in this chapter, the selective focus has been placed upon the differing Conservative interpretations of the triad of concepts that became associated with the emergence of Liberal doctrine during the period of the French Revolution, that is, liberty, equality, and fraternity. To a degree, Social Conservatism is related to differing interpretations of the concept of liberty, Economic Conservatism is related to differing interpretations of the concept of equality, and Conservatism in foreign policy with its priority of protection of the national interest is related to differing interpretations or, more correctly, to alternative developments of the concept of fraternity.

Beyond this tier of conceptual analysis, however, there is also an account and analysis of fundamental attitudes, general presuppositions or dispositional tendencies that also distinguish Conservatism from Liberalism in what may be termed, in this context, the third or "attitudinal" tier. This account and analysis accords with the claim advanced in the lines of the Gilbert & Sullivan operetta *Iolanthe*:

> How Nature always does contrive
> That every boy and every gal
> That's born into the world alive
> Is either a little Liberal
> Or else a little Conservative![1]

With reference to the first tier of analysis, that is, the agenda of issues that are contested in the political arena, the claim of *Iolanthe* could be refuted on the ground that subsequent political contests, within a short period of time after the operetta was written, were framed by the opposition between the Conservative Party and the Labor Party rather than the historical duality identified as Conservative or Liberal. In the United States, the division between parties has not been clearly identified as a division between Conservatism and Liberalism. It has often been contended that each of the two main American political parties comprehends a coalition of diverse interest groups.

At the same time, whether by the contrivance of nature or by the perennial emergence of historical patterns, there exist grounds for support of the claim advanced in the poetic line of

W. S. Gilbert that no matter how diverse the political spectrum, extending even to the descriptions of a Chinese Communist Party congress or any particular European fascist party, the polarity of a Conservative wing as opposed to a Liberal wing is characteristically mentioned in the analysis of the contending groups. Accordingly, the examination of the third tier of Conservative political thought involves a selected focus upon a triad of issues that are characterized as representing fundamental attitudes, general presuppositions, or ways of structuring the perception of reality that distinguish Conservatism from Liberalism.

The first disjunction in this third triad is the degree to which any social or historical situation is viewed as a contest between the priority of "the Given" as opposed to the priority of "the Taken" or "the Chosen." The Conservative emphasis upon the recognition of "the Given" and its inherent obligations, as opposed to the Liberal emphasis on "the Taken" or "the Chosen" with its promise of alternative possibilities to realize the new and greater good, marks a significant distinction particularly for Social Conservatism, even though this dichotomy is also present as a generic aspect of Conservative thought.

This disjunction overlaps with the second disjunction of the triad that refers to a fundamental attitude toward the possibility and limits of historical or social change. The Conservative emphasis upon the historical or cultural situation as one in which realized values are to be protected, preserved, and maintained is in opposition to the Liberal emphasis that the historical situation represents a basis for historical discontinuity and revolutionary progress. Conservative thought does recognize and accept the legitimacy or necessity for institutional reform as part of the maintenance of an institution or even its incremental improvement, but it is skeptical regarding any belief in rapid social change as well as any expectation of a transformation of the human condition. This distinction has been particularly evident in Economic Conservatism in its opposition in the recent past to utopian ideologies, such as Marxist socialism, but it is also relevant to more general aspects of Conservatism.

The third disjunction in the tier, which aims to examine fundamental attitudes that are inherent in Conservative thought, involves Max Weber's distinction between an approach to morality that emphasizes "institutional responsibility" versus an approach to morality that emphasizes "ultimate ends" or "ultimate commitments." This distinction may represent a fundamental division of attitudinal approaches toward morality that complement the attitudes that have been represented on the preceding two disjunctions of this triad. It is particularly relevant, however, in Conservatism in foreign policy. As a broad generalization, Conservative thought in foreign affairs has an affinity with Realist positions, while Liberal thought has an affinity with Idealist positions. This may be evident to the degree to which Conservatism envisions foreign policy as protecting a set of limited national interests whereas Liberalism seeks the realization of a set of universal human rights. In this context, Conservative thought would be consonant with a morality of "institutional responsibility" while Liberal thought would hold an affinity with a morality of "ultimate ends" or "ultimate commitments."

Before proceeding to an account and analysis of the dichotomies in concepts or attitudes that distinguish Conservatism from Liberalism in the two underlying tiers of conceptual analysis and fundamental attitudes which constitute the major substance of this chapter, the preliminary question can be raised as to the legitimacy of such a dualistic categorization. The claim in any discipline that its universe of discourse can be separated into two polar opposites, whether Platonism vs. Aristotelianism, introvert vs. extrovert, classical vs. romantic, Liberal vs. Conservative, inevitably invites the rejoinder that all historians of these discourses can be divided into persons who tend to divide the universe into polar opposites versus those who do not. The relevant aspect of this denial of polarity with reference to the contested issues in the political arena can be found in the ways in which lines of disagreement over these contested issues do not always confirm or conform to a coherent division between Liberals and Conservatives. Yet even if polarity avoids the multiplicity and incoherence of particular choices along a spectrum of political issues, it contains a sufficient degree of coherence to permit the effort to identify the views, conceptual interpretations, and attitudes that characterize Conservatism as distinct from the views, conceptual interpretations, and attitudes that characterize Liberalism.

I. The First Tier of Political Issues: The Triad of Social Conservatism, Economic Conservatism, and Conservatism with Its Priority of Protection of the National Interest

A. Social Conservatism

In the case of Social Conservatism, the political issues that have been widely discussed so that they have been referred to as hot-button issues include the separation of church and state, abortion rights, gay marriage, or other emergent controversies that reflect perceived changes in the cultural and religious traditions of the United States. Social Conservative positions on these issues derive from both religious and secular grounds.

The religious groundings can be found in the general theme that a nation whose historical morality as a People has been formed through a covenant with a deity cannot have a political culture that violates significantly the terms of that covenant. The secular groundings do not involve the reference to a covenant with a deity, but appeal to the unanticipated consequences that follow drastic changes in fundamental traditions that are asserted to have governed the human condition over long periods of time. Both of these groundings support a Conservative view on the cultural changes that have marked American cultural history, particularly since the 1960s. From the Conservative perspective, these political issues have been interpreted as negative developments. One Conservative characterization is that these developments in the "cultural wars" since the 1960s have contributed to a breakdown in family values, as evidenced particularly in many black children being raised without fathers, with deleterious consequences for the stability of American society. As previously noted, these issues relate to the different interpretations of the concept of liberty in the second or "conceptual" tier, as well as fundamental attitudes toward what is given and what is to be taken in the constitution of the culture of a society on the third or "attitudinal" tier.

There is special significance, however, to the recognition that American Conservatism includes prominent representatives who do not agree with the majority views of Social Conservatism on several of these contested issues. Thus, it is well known that a significant portion of the Conservative movement and Republican Party leaders and members have strongly supported a woman's right to choose on the issue of abortion. Similarly, a significant portion of the leaders and members of the Conservative movement and the Republican Party have identified equal treatment for gays and lesbians as legitimate aspects of rights of the individual. From this perspective, equality of marriage rights would be a corollary of equality of rights under the rubric of civil rights.

With reference to the polarity generated by Social Conservatism within the political arena, it should also be noted that many Democratic Party leaders whose Liberal credentials are impeccable have supported the sanctity of life movement against complete abortion rights. Similarly, Democratic leaders have supported civil union with the elimination of discrimination on grounds of sexual orientation without supporting a change in the religious tradition concerning the institution of marriage. As previously noted, the demarcation lines on the spectrum of political issues that mark the division of political parties within American politics have never been drawn completely and consistently in terms of Liberalism vs. Conservatism.

Political considerations, that is, the strength of different constituencies within the coalition of groups that enter into the Democratic or Republican Party as well as the perceived sympathies or antipathies of the electorate to various political issues, are a relevant feature in determining the emphasis or lack of emphasis on specific issues in the formulation of the platform documents or in the resonance of political expression throughout any electoral campaign. Thus, it is widely assumed that the issues of Social Conservatism will be de-emphasized relative to the issues of Economic Conservatism during the coming decade.

B. Economic Conservatism

In contrast to this muted emphasis on the issues of Social Conservatism, it is widely assumed that the agenda of economic issues will occupy a central place for the Conservative political movement in the near future. The Conservative proposal is that focus be placed on the issue of heightening economic growth with its implied criticism of the Obama administration policies as responsible for the slow rate of economic recovery since the recession during the entire tenure of the Obama administration. The low rate of growth has resulted in high unemployment, evidenced more by the subnormal rate of participation of the population in the labor force rather than in the rate of unemployment within the labor force as well as by the virtual absence of any increase in wages. The achievement of higher rates of economic growth in past periods of American history with their beneficial consequences for upward social mobility and for the realization of the "American dream" provide the basis for Conservative proposals on a wide range of policy issues that differentiate Conservatives from the Obama administration. These themes, which will be relevant on the level of the "conceptual tier" as well as on the "issues tier," include alternative views on the size and function of government, competing theses on the optimal ratio between the private sector and the public sector, opposing issues of tax policy and deficit reduction, as well as contested issues of entitlement reform including governmental health care policies.

An initial Conservative theme is the need for smaller federal government in the United States. The argument for smaller government has deep roots within American Conservative thought, which has long supported tendencies to prefer action by local or state governments on health, educational, and welfare policies over actions by the federal government.

The connection between the argument for smaller government and lowering the rate of unemployment is carried out through the thesis that economic growth is generated primarily by the private sector. The major economic schools that have influenced American Conservatism since the 1920s have maintained that a strong ratio between the private sector and the public sector must be maintained to realize economic growth and provide the requisite tax base for governmental activities.

Thus, the argument for smaller federal government is connected to the issue of tax policy. The Conservative thesis of lower taxation rates on investment reflects the view of those economists who believe in "supply-side" economic theory. According to this theory, economic growth, and hence job growth, is supported by reducing taxation on the investment sector of the economy. The increase in investment will lead to greater growth of the domestic product, and such growth sustains the upward mobility within American society that has been the distinctively attractive aspect of American egalitarianism for more than a century. This view is clarified by contrasting it with the Liberal economic view that is often supported by proponents of "demand-side" economic theory. According to this theory, economic growth can be realized through reducing taxation on consumption rather than on investment. From this perspective, the argument is that the resulting increase in demand would generate economic growth and job growth. It would also result in greater equality of income distribution since it is argued that reducing taxes on consumption tends to benefit the poor while reducing taxes on investment tends to benefit the rich. Accordingly, there is a focus in the political arena on the contested issue of tax policy. The issue of tax policy also relates to disagreement in the analysis of the concept of equality, which will be the subject of further discussion of the concept of Equality in the second or "conceptual" tier of the division between Liberalism and Conservatism.

The issue of the desirable size of the federal government is connected to the opposing positions within partisan politics on the adequate response to the budgetary deficit of the United States. The Conservative response, which is consistent with the argument for smaller government, is to emphasize the policy view that greater economic growth which would be fostered by less governmental intervention in the economy can result in balanced budgets. To some degree Conservative thought also accepts the reality of the requirement of entitlement reform and cuts in the rate of growth of governmental spending in order to eliminate the deficit.

The Liberal or contrary position is identified with the claim that any cuts in governmental spending will result in excessive harm to those in the lower rungs of American society who have the greatest need for government programs. Accordingly, the Liberal position on deficit reduction has insisted that an increase in taxes must accompany any effort at cuts in spending in any acceptable proposal for reduction of the deficit. According to the liberal view, an increase in taxes on the rich is justified both by the need for greater resources for necessary welfare programs as well as by an effort to lessen economic inequality.

Champions of targeting economic equality like Joseph Stiglitz or Thomas Piketty have emphasized that over the last three decades economic growth has benefited the income of the top decile of American society to a far greater extent than it has benefited the income of the lower deciles. Significantly, another Nobel Laureate at Columbia University has pointed out the increase of $55 trillion in entitlements within the American economy since 1980. Since entitlements tend to benefit the lower deciles, the recognition of this factor represents an alternative perspective in the patterns of American egalitarianism that partially negates the oft-repeated thesis that there has been an extreme increase in inequality in the distribution of income in the United States.

More generally, there is widespread disagreement—usually with the empirical disagreement corresponding with ideological differences—over the interpretation and measurement of economic inequality in the United States. There exist great differences between the comparison of asset ownership and patterns of consumption, as well as with the inclusion or exclusion of governmental programs in the statistics of poverty. Significant differences in the measurement of the quality of life of the population of the poor in the United States can be attributed to different ways of calculating the economic importance of improvements in health care, standards of housing, and changes in the availability and reliability of such diverse objects as telephones, computers, cars, television sets, or air conditioners.

Beyond such specific areas of disagreement, the more general debate between targeting economic growth versus targeting economic inequality as the optimal means for lessening deprivation emerges as a major issue in American electoral politics. As previously noted, this debate is examined below within the rubric of the conceptual analysis of equality.

C. Conservatism in Foreign Policy with Its Priority of Protection of the National Interest

Conservatism in American foreign policy has undergone a dramatic change in the post–World War II period. Historically, the foreign policy of American Conservatism was in alignment with the

vision projected by President John Quincy Adams in a well-known
foreign policy statement of 1821. In that statement, then Secretary of State John Quincy Adams suggested that the United States
could be a "beacon" in support of freedom through its example
and public attitudes. At the same time, it would not intervene in
foreign disputes even for justified causes of freedom and independence. In his statement the United States "goes not abroad in
search of monsters to destroy. She is the well wisher to the freedom and independence of all. She is the champion and vindicator
only of her own."[2]

This approach was represented in Conservative or Republican opposition to liberal Wilsonian idealism particularly at the
end of the First World War. After entering the war on the allied
side, President Wilson had projected a more active role for
American foreign policy in global affairs, particularly in his vision
of the participation of the United States in the League of Nations.
The Republican withdrawal from Wilsonian idealism and from
membership in the League of Nations has received much criticism as contributing to the negative developments in Europe and
Asia that preceded the Second World War. At the same time, it
is recognized that even with President Wilson's policies, the primary responsibility for political arrangements in Europe in the
1920s and 1930s was to be carried out by the United Kingdom
and France.

In contrast to the historical foreign policy of the United States,
which was initially formulated as "no entangling alliances," there
emerged a consensus with overwhelming Conservative support
that the primary goal of protection of the national interest required strong American actions in support of the stabilization of
the international world order in the post–World War II period.
This change in the Conservative approach was signaled by the
decision to maintain American troops in Germany and Japan after
the Second World War. This approach was secured by Conservative
votes in favor of American participation in the defense of Europe
through the North American Treaty Organization (NATO) and
in the defense of Asia through the Peace Treaty with Japan. This
approach was also demonstrated in the American commitment
during the Eisenhower presidency of a residual American military
force in South Korea. Like the American military forces that have

remained stationed in Germany and Japan for seventy years since the end of the war, American forces have held positions in South Korea as a deterrent force for the entire period since the armistice agreement that ended the Korean War.

Accordingly a corollary of this consensus approach that was accepted and promoted by the Conservative movement, and that can emerge as a current political issue, is the failure of the Obama administration to maintain a residual American force after it had declared victory in Iraq. From the Liberal perspective, this withdrawal seemed justified because of their condemnation of the war in Iraq. From the Liberal perspective, particularly in the Liberal media, the war was condemned virtually from its outset as an unwinnable "quagmire" that was excessively costly and unjustifiable with reference to American losses that numbered 4,200 at its conclusion.

From a Conservative perspective, the failure to maintain a small but necessary residual force represented a violation of the need to maintain the victory and stability that had been achieved. The maintenance of such a force was a required American policy even if one were to reject the justification for the initial intervention against the regime of Saddam Hussein. The Conservative argument is that this precipitous withdrawal left the door open for the subsequent penetration of Iraq by Iran as well as for the partial occupation of Iraq by ISIS. The Conservative argument can be grounded historically through the recognition that any American military victory since the Second World War has been accompanied by the accepted necessity of continued American military support as part of the stabilization of the international world order.

At the same time, particularly since the war in Iraq and Afghanistan, there is recognition that American public opinion would not support new and continual acts of American military intervention in the resolution of security threats to the United States originating overseas.

Consequently, for the Conservative perspective on foreign policy issues with its priority of protecting the national interest, there are significant challenges on shaping the role of the United States in the stabilization of the international order. If electoral outcomes are related to issues of policy, then the relevant issues involve the respective adequacy of alternative policy responses to these challenges. Without undertaking a complete tour d'horizon, these challenges have arisen with special force during the second term of the Obama administration in such different spheres as eastern Europe, the Middle East, and Asia.

In eastern Europe, the most recognized challenge is represented as Ukraine's quest for greater independence from Russia concomitant with greater association with the West. A Conservative formulation of the issue involves the assertion that Obama has shown excessive weakness in his relationship with President Putin. The challenge is formulated in the assertion that America must demonstrate that it is a reliable ally for the countries of eastern Europe without unnecessary provocation of Russia and without the threat of military intervention beyond the standard commitments to NATO members. Thus the challenge is identifying an adequate response for the needed support of Ukraine and Georgia to sustain their freedom and independence alongside their ongoing obligations as neighboring countries that border Russia.

In the Middle East, the set of challenges appears to be even more formidable. Again the Conservative criticism of the Obama administration is that it has shown an inability to sufficiently distinguish potential allies from potential adversaries and has vacillated in the implementation of policy. The list of the challenges that require new or heightened responses indicates the policy issues that are being contested. There is the challenge to American policy of maintaining the nuclear proliferation treaty of 1973 such that it denies Iran the capacity to produce nuclear weapons. Separately or conjointly there is the challenge of reversing Iran's path to hegemony in the region that has already seen substantial progress in Lebanon, Syria, Iraq, and Yemen. While sustaining opposition to Iran, there is the simultaneous challenge of reversing the occupation by ISIS of large territorial areas in Syria, Iraq, and Libya.

There is a more general challenge in the long term for the development of an American foreign policy that would foster movement toward the restoration of state authority and stability throughout the entire Middle East, in light of the breakdown of the structures of state authority that had mostly been established at the end of the First World War. These states, including Iraq, Syria, Lebanon, Libya, Yemen, and Sudan, have recently been partitioned among contending power groups whose loyalties are derived from ethnic, tribal, and sectarian divisions. Such a movement would contribute to the American struggle against the export of terrorism.

In Asia, the challenge to the United States of being and being perceived as a reliable ally has emerged as an issue in foreign policy. Apart from its formal defense alliances with Japan, Taiwan, and South Korea, the United States has become a resource in support of the integrity of the boundaries of Vietnam and Indonesia. At the same time it must adjust appropriately to the need of China to be recognized as a major power both in economic influence and as an important member of the international order.

In addition to these challenges, as will be noted below in the discussion of conceptual differences and attitudinal disjunctions, Liberalism in foreign policy has tended to place much greater emphasis on American support for the extension of programs of the United Nations and for the realization of universal human rights through the agencies of the United Nations than has Conservative thought in foreign policy. The Liberal agenda also places greater importance on the role of American foreign policy in confronting what it believes to be the root causes of insecurity, terror, and war, such as poverty, malnutrition, and illness.

While recognizing the legitimacy of these areas of concern for American foreign policy, the Conservative tendency is to support the view that the policies of independent nations represent the major ways for progress in these areas. For these independent nations their policies on the development of the private sector and free competitive markets (including states as diverse as India, China, Poland, Chile, and Estonia) have provided evidence on the progress that can be achieved in comparison with the record of many governmental programs supported by international agencies.

The Conservative thesis with regard to the history of American post–World War II foreign policy is that the policies that have aimed at the priority of protection of the national interest with the recognition of the role of the United States in stabilizing the international order during the past seventy years have contributed strongly to the maintenance of a peaceful international order that has enabled diverse states to realize political freedom, economic development, and significant measures of international trade and cooperation.

The current domestic mood that is represented as disengagement or withdrawal from military intervention admits, relative to future electoral decisions, two contrary future developments. On the one hand, it can mark the early phases of a turning point in postwar American foreign policy that will lead to further American withdrawal and the end of an era in which the United States has been the primary stabilizing force in the international world order. From the Conservative perspective, such a disengagement or withdrawal would signify a global return to the conditions that prevailed in 1913 and in 1938, when European and Asian states were threatened by aggressive neighbors without the overpowering weight of American deterrence. On the other hand, the future development can be marked by continuity with America's established roles in deterrence of aggression and support for the stability of the international order. The realization of this role presupposes adequate responses to the challenges on foreign policy issues that have been previously cited.

The underlying division between Liberals and Conservatives on foreign policy issues remains deep. This division can be demonstrated through an analysis in the second or conceptual tier of this chapter of the Liberal emphasis on the place of human rights in foreign policy with its background concept of shared humanity, which has found expression in the metaphor of universal fraternity or the brotherhood of man. The division can also be demonstrated via analysis of the Conservative emphasis on the place of national interests in foreign policy in which the metaphor of fraternity is replaced by the less familiar metaphor of otherhood with its recognition of the need for protection of the national interest against the unavoidability of adversarial antagonism in a dangerous world.

This distinction between a more "universalist" Liberalism and a more "particularist" or national interest Conservatism in foreign policy can also be analyzed in the third tier of this chapter as representing a disjunction between a morality of ultimate ends as contrasted with a morality of institutional responsibility. These conceptual differences and attitudinal disjunctions will play their part in shaping the issues of political controversy between Liberalism and Conservatism over the role of the United States in world affairs.

II. The Conceptual Tier: Liberty, Equality, Fraternity

The starting point for the analysis of American Conservative thought that has been identified in this chapter has been the conventional distinction between Social Conservatism, Economic Conservatism, and Conservatism in foreign policy. In terms of the analysis of concepts, it was also suggested that Social Conservatism reflects a significant difference in the interpretation of the concept of liberty, Economic Conservatism reflects a significant difference in the interpretation of the concept of equality, and Conservatism in foreign policy reflects a significant difference in the interpretation of or, more correctly, an alternative development of the concept of fraternity.

The triad of liberty, equality, and fraternity does not originate within American Conservatism, however, but indicates an obvious reference to the slogan values of the French Revolution. Yet, the significance of this triad of concepts is not limited to the time and place of the French Revolution. Edmund Burke laid significant foundations for Conservatism as a general movement of thought in his set of arguments against the French Revolution in his *Reflections on the Revolution in France.*[3]

Burke's argument set a pattern for future Conservatism in two ways. He argued that the "idea of a revolution" as a rapid and violent change within a society was not necessary. The positive goals of any movement for change could be realized without revolutionary violence or societal disruption by the more effective means of incremental reform. Burke further argued that the concept of a revolution with its implication of a complete transformation of the human condition, which represented the projection of an ideal of the perfectibility of human nature to be realized in the short span of a revolutionary period, was illusionary, quixotic, and could readily become a means for self-destruction. Thus, the particular arguments of Burke against the French Revolution could be generalized to become part of a permanent intellectual heritage of Conservative thought or providing, in T. S. Eliot's phrase, a "usable past" for America and elsewhere.

Against this background, the analysis of different interpretations of Liberty, Equality, and Fraternity are not limited to a historical inquiry but are crucially indicative of the differences between Liberalism and Conservatism.

A. *Social Conservatism and the Interpretation of Liberty: The Balance between Liberty and Order as Distinct from the Maximization of Liberty*

One point of departure for the distinction between Liberalism and Conservatism on issues that fall along the axis of Social Liberalism and Social Conservatism is provided by an analysis of differing interpretations of the concept of liberty. Both Liberals and Conservatives strenuously maintain the view that they are supporters of the realization of the ideal of liberty or freedom in political society and in the life of the individual. Yet, there is a significant distinction between Liberals and Conservatives over what constitutes the realization of the ideal of liberty.

One way of identifying the difference between Liberals and Conservatives on the issue of liberty is the clarification of the difference in understanding of the terms that constitute the correlative opposite to liberty. This interpretation of the difference between Liberal and Conservative views is derived from the linguistic analysis of ordinary language that characterized the thought of the English philosopher John Austin.

Austin identified a number of terms whose meaning depended upon the identification of their correlative opposites or, in Austin's phrase, the correlative opposite "wore the trousers." Thus, in the area of metaphysics, Austin argues that the meaning of the term "real" could be known in diverse contexts only by identifying the correlative opposite as "appearance," "fiction," "fake," "counterfeit," "paste," "plastic," "phony," "superficial," "dummy," "illusion," or "sense data" as the case may be. Similarly, liberty or freedom was a term whose meaning was known through the identification of its correlative opposite. Thus, a seat could be free as opposed to occupied, while it could also be free as opposed to having a price. A person could be free as opposed to being a slave, while another person could be free since he had been cured of his addiction. Further, a freethinker was not a person who had been liberated from enslavement or addiction, but was a person who had no religious belief, as contrasted with a free spirit who is not identified by the criterion of opposition to religious belief but by opposition to conventional or conformist attitudes. A person could be free as opposed to bound, but could also be free as lacking in appropriate self-restraint.

In some contexts, liberty is appropriately contrasted with terms like "slavery," "tyranny," and "coercion." In those contexts, the characteristic norm for a proponent of liberty is to call for its maximization with the abolition or elimination of its correlative opposite, such as slavery, tyranny, and coercion. It is not considered a justified norm of liberty to seek a balance between the values embodied in the idea of freedom or liberty and the values embodied in slavery, tyranny, and coercion. Accordingly, as a generalization from these contexts, liberty has been identified as a value to be maximized and has even been considered as an absolute value or a "trumping" value. This emphasis on the maximization of liberty is particularly evident in aspects of Liberal political philosophy.

In other contexts, liberty is appropriately contrasted with such correlative opposites as "security," "order," "self-restraint," "authority," and "law." Proponents of liberty do not seek to abolish the correlative opposite of order or to eliminate the correlative opposite of self-restraint in achieving a free society or a free individual. An appropriate norm for the realization of liberty in society or in the life of the individual may be a balance between the value of liberty and such values as security, order, self-restraint, authority, and law, which involve limitations upon choice and upon the initiation of action. As a generalization from these contexts, limits on liberty are justified as part of a quest for balance among plural values. This emphasis on balance and pluralism is particularly evident in aspects of Conservative political philosophy.

This distinction between the Liberal emphasis upon the maximization of liberty and the Conservative emphasis upon the balance between liberty and other values can be investigated through examining the disjunction that occurs between Liberalism and Conservatism in three different formulations of the value of liberty in the history of political philosophy.

The first formulation involves the connection between Liberalism and the doctrine of natural rights, as distinct from the Conservative view that has been critical of doctrines of natural rights since it locates the genesis of rights within the legal framework of an historical society. The second formulation is to be found in the acceptance of John Stuart Mill's *On Liberty* as possessing canonical status for Liberalism, since Mill's theses have been the subject of Conservative criticism particularly on the relationship between the individual and the society. A third formulation is available in John Dewey's emphasis on freedom of inquiry as the necessary condition for Liberal society, while Conservative critics who embrace pluralism recognize that freedom of inquiry can be limited by the weight of other values.

Thus, in that genus of Liberal theory that is characterized by its adoption of a doctrine of natural rights, specified forms of liberty are identified with natural rights so that they become absolute and inalienable. In American Liberalism, there is an embedded tradition that freedom of speech, freedom of the press, and religious freedom are natural rights that cannot be violated. Along this line of argument, in the contemporary idiom such designated rights are analogized to "trumps," such that other values are ordinary suits. On this analogy, any balancing among values is skewed because even the highest value of a non-trumping kind can be overruled as a violation or infringement when set against the trumping value of liberty.

The recognition of the contrary tendencies within Conservatism is marked by the identification of David Hume as the contemporaneous Conservative critic of a theory of natural rights. The drama inherent in this polarity is evident in Thomas Jefferson's several references to Hume's writings as "pernicious." (It provides a piquant detail that Jefferson's term of castigation was repeated and underlined so that it led his heirs to remove Hume's books from the library legacy that was made on Jefferson's behalf to the University of Virginia and the Library of Congress.) Hume's denial of a doctrine of natural rights has been followed throughout the history of Conservative thought by support for values that competed with liberty for priority. Within political philosophy, these have ranged from religious duties, historical traditions, public order, social utility, and other plural forms of public or private virtue that share the denial of a right to individual freedoms as an inalienable absolute right.

This analysis of liberty on the conceptual tier cannot enter into the details of the continuing disputes over specific issues that would serve to confirm or refute the distinction between the claim of the maximization of liberty against other values as the Liberal thesis, in contrast to the balancing of liberty against other values as the Conservative thesis. Yet, this distinction seems to be compatible on its face with approaches to recent and current issues. One illustration is provided by the apparent protection of freedom of speech as including the right of a minister to burn the Koran. The request by the president of the United States and by the chairman of the Joint Chiefs of Staff that he refrain from such a public burning on the ground that it heightens the risk of death to American troops abroad is insufficient to justify a legal limitation upon the absolute liberty which is derived from freedom of speech under the First Amendment as judicially extended to freedom of symbolic speech. The contrast with the constraint that is imposed by law upon the burning of leaves in one's own garden because of potential environmental harm provides support for the thesis that freedom of speech is considered to be an absolute value, so that its maximization avoids the balancing among values that is a feature of the adjudication among norms in a pluralistic society. A similar example is the refusal by a television network and its anchor to withhold publication of images taken at Abu Ghraib prison, denying a request from the chairman of the Joint Chiefs of Staff. In that example also, the primacy of freedom of the press was asserted without a need for balance or limitation by other values, such as the protection of American troops serving in Iraq. Yet despite such examples and widespread support for absolutist interpretation of such freedoms as speech and press, there are numerous illustrations within Liberal public policy and judicial practice of the recognition of the need for balance among plural values.

The Liberalism of John Stuart Mill also explicitly sought to justify the maximization of liberty against competing values without any appeal to doctrines of natural right. Mill recognized the necessity of limitations on liberty in any human society, but sought to minimize these limitations. Thus, Mill recognized that liberty can be limited in cases where a person's exercise of freedom would cause harm to others but rejected the value of limiting freedom in cases where such limits would restrain a person from doing harm to himself.

In contrast to Mill's approach that maximizes liberty, the social practices of most societies have embedded within them various

limitations on liberty that Mill rejected. The norms of many societies aim at some protection for individuals against their own self-
destructive tendencies, including attempted suicide during periods of depression. Again, many societies require the respect for
and protection of the institutions that are accorded highest priority of place, so that freedom of the individual to violate the domain
of such sancta is limited. Further, even those societies that do
not provide special protection for their own sancta do recognize
such competing values as those of traditional morality, historical
cultural norms, and civic order, which may legitimate constraints
upon individual freedom beyond the Millean criterion of doing
harm to another individual. So significant are these conventions
on limitations of liberty that the term *l'ordre publique* has received
widespread and cross-cultural recognition as a term of art whose
value can be invoked to justify limitations upon individual freedom. For Milleans, the response to the recognition of these competing values is an effort to maximize liberty, in contrast to the
more Conservative effort to seek a balance between these values
and the value of liberty.

To a significant degree, the difference between Millean Liberalism and Conservative thought on issues of liberty arises from
the competing models of the relationship between individual and
society. For Millean Liberals, the ideal of liberty is manifest when
the atomic person of individual integrity stands in opposition to
the coercive dominations of government and the power of institutions. This individual person of integrity is, as it were, free to realize his own lifestyle through his experiments in living without the
coercion or authoritative influence of inherited traditions, normative culture, and regulative institutions.

For critics of Millean Liberalism, from Fitzjames Stephen to Justice Patrick Devlin to Judge Robert Bork, the individual is condi-
tioned and influenced and in some ways subject to coercion by
family obligations, a limited set of vocational options, a determi-
nate range of social decisions, and given choices of style and taste
in life. Accordingly, the difference between Millean Liberalism
and Conservatism on the value of liberty reflects the line that can
be drawn between the vision of the free individual as a person who
can, to a significant degree, create his own self-identity and realize
experiments in living that are free of the range of practices and

traditions of the society and the vision of a free individual who is exercising choice among a range of limited options that had been set to a great degree by the traditions, norms, and institutions of the environing society.

Within American Liberalism, John Dewey severely criticizes Millean Liberalism for its excessive individualism and rejects the doctrine of natural rights for its absolutism. For Dewey, value claims, including claims for particular freedoms, are hypotheses that are open to verification by experience. Consequently, for Dewey, albeit without an utilitarian calculus, limitations on freedom can be justified if they provide a verifiable increase in values for the society.

Yet for Dewey, pluralism of substantive values presupposes freedom of inquiry as an absolute methodological value. Since decisions among values must be made on the evidence in accordance with the practice of scientific inquiry, any block upon the road of free inquiry is impermissible. The decision process would be marred and the validity of the decisions would be delegitimized if the process of free inquiry were aborted.

Despite the logical power of the Deweyan emphasis upon the strategic necessity of freedom of inquiry in the decision-making process, the thesis breaks down in practice. Particularly during the horrors of the Second World War, it became evident that scientific research in fields that were associated with weaponry should be limited for moral reasons. Thus, the postwar ban on research in methods and materials for the conduct of biological warfare can be justified even if such a ban sets limits on inquiry in areas and techniques of biology that could hold promise for good. Such examples of limits upon scientific inquiry can be multiplied readily.

One recent surprising block on the process of inquiry was the request by federal authorities in medical research that scientific journals refrain from publishing submitted articles that provided information that could be useful to terrorist groups on techniques for transferring viruses from diseased animals to human beings. During the past decade, there has been an extended argument as to whether embryonic stem cell research and cloning of human beings violates moral values. It would appear that a consensus among practical moralists and biological practitioners has been achieved according to which embryonic stem cell research falls within the line of moral legitimacy while cloning of human beings falls outside that line. The relevant point in this context is that a line can be drawn between cases where freedom of scientific inquiry overrules moral concerns and cases where moral values set limits upon complete freedom of scientific inquiry.

From the perspective of Social Conservatism, the recognition that a line can be drawn which limits freedom of inquiry represents in some measure a vindication of the attitude of Social Conservatism as contrasted with the Liberal tradition from natural rights through Mill to Dewey on the limitation of liberty.

The thesis that has been developed in this analysis has stressed the general presupposition within Conservatism of a balancing between freedom and other values as distinct from the Liberal presupposition that freedom represents a trumping value in confrontation with other values. Yet, this thesis is open to challenge by a straightforward empirical survey of Liberal and Conservative attitudes that would focus upon attitudinal differences toward different areas of concern. Such a survey would suggest that the priority ascribed to freedom within Liberalism or Conservatism is relative to the area of application.

Thus, a distinction can be drawn between the priority of freedom as it relates to areas of national security and areas of morality as contrasted with the area of economic affairs.

In the area of national security, as a thumbnail sketch ranging from the size of defense budgets in the 1950s through legislating the Patriot Act after 2001 to the response to the leaks by Edward Snowden, Liberals have viewed Conservatives as excessively prone to governmental intrusion in areas of individual liberty, while Conservatives have viewed Liberals as unrealistic in refusing to recognize the need for governmental protection against the possibility of hostile activity.

Similarly, as a thumbnail sketch, in the area of personal or traditional morality, Liberals have viewed Conservatives as excessively zealous in involving government in the legislation of morality with consequences that exclude the full range of individual expression of plural values and limit the freedom of the individual's choice of a particular way of life. Conversely, Conservatives have viewed Liberals as oblivious to the need for shared moral foundations in support of the ordered structure of a society and willing to grant individuals an excessive freedom to change fundamental moral institutions, both of which could potentially result in societal self-destruction.

In the area of economic affairs, however, Liberals have been prepared to support governmental intervention that limits freedom of the individual for the sake of such values as social welfare or distributive justice. On the other hand, Conservatives have stressed the priority of limiting governmental intervention in the marketplace so as to allow individual freedom in the operation of free markets to realize long-term greater economic growth.

The point of these examples is that they suggest that the general thesis of the Liberal priority of freedom is relative to the area of practice. Consequently, an inquiry into the differences between Liberalism and Conservatism would focus upon the reasons for greater emphasis on the values of national security and public morality in Conservative thought compared to a weaker emphasis on national security or public morality in Liberal thought. Similarly, an empirical inquiry is required to account for the reasons for a positive attitude that favors governmental intervention in economic affairs in Liberal thought, as compared with a negative attitude that is critical of governmental intervention and economic affairs in Conservative thought.

Irving Kristol, the leading neo-Conservative of his generation, used a commencement address to speculate on what seemed to him to be the apparent inconsistency within Liberalism of outlawing a particular cosmetic for which there was some evidence of potentially harmful effects on health, while supporting legalization of the recreational use of marijuana for which there was much greater evidence of potentially harmful health effects. The resolution of this inconsistency was partially available in that the challenge to the cosmetic took place under the rubric of consumer protection, which represents a governmental intervention in the area of economic affairs that is usually justifiable within liberalism, particularly when directed against corporate culture or corporate profits, while the challenge to marijuana took place under the rubric of legislation of individual morality, which represents governmental intervention in the area of personal morality that is not usually justifiable within liberalism, particularly against dissident culture. There are many other historical roots that can help explain the differences between Liberalism and Conservatism regarding governmental intervention in national security or traditional morality as distinct from intervention in economic affairs. At the same time, it should be recognized that Conservative support for free markets is also not absolute. A free market does not refer to an unregulated market, but to a market that does not have monopolistic or state-administered prices. Accordingly, for Conservatives the concept of free market is consistent with a well-regulated or strongly regulated market.

Despite the need for further inquiry into the ways in which the historical roots of Liberalism and Conservatism have influenced their prioritization of values in different areas, the general thesis that Liberalism aims at a greater priority for the maximization of liberty while Conservatism aims at a greater emphasis on balancing freedom with other values can be sustained.

B. Economic Conservatism and the Interpretation of Equality

In proceeding from the discussion of Social Conservatism to Economic Conservatism with reference to the conceptual tier, the issue of the meaning and importance of the second concept of the triad, equality, occupies a central place.

1. Liberal Positions and Conservative Positions in the Spectrum of Interpretations of Equality

The truistic observation that Liberals and Conservatives disagree on the meaning and importance of the concept of equality provides a convenient starting point for the analysis of American Economic Conservatism. This starting point includes a review of the spectrum of interpretations of the concept of equality that range from a minimalist kind of egalitarianism, through several intermediate positions, to those that seek to maximize substantive economic equality. The minimalist end of the spectrum begins with the recognition of a generalized notion of "equality of concern" for all human beings in recognition of the importance of the distinction between being human and being other-than-human. Such a concept of equality of concern for humanity does not bring with it substantive equality in the distribution of goods or equality of result in socioeconomic positions. This form of equality is not trivial, however, since its significance lies in its recognition of prima facie opposition to any arbitrary killing or starvation of human beings, or to inflicting needless suffering upon them.

The subsequent position on the spectrum is occupied by a notion of formal equality, which can be identified as an "equality of rights" or "equality before the law" for all the members of a particular society. Critics of this notion of formal or legal equality have continually pointed out that this falls far short of substantive equality in the distribution of goods or of equality of result in socioeconomic positions. One of the more familiar illustrations of such criticism was the remark of Anatole France that the law in its majestic formality and impartiality prohibits both the millionaire and the pauper from sleeping on the park bench.

Proponents of formal or legal equality have not only acknowledged but also supported this limitation of formal equality from substantive equality. The idea of equality before the law was considered to be compatible with the criterion of the legitimacy of differentiation among persons for relevant reasons only. In its classic formulation, the principle of legal equality goes back to Aristotle, where it is asserted as a criterion of "formal justice," that is, the principle that similar cases are to be treated similarly, with the implication that differentiation among persons must be for relevant reasons only. From this perspective, "formal equality" or "legal equality" brings with it the principle of hierarchy. Thus, the appropriate correlative opposite of equality is not simply inequality, but a hierarchy derived from discrimination for irrelevant reasons. The principle of equality may be considered to be compatible with this kind of differentiation when inequality is understood as discrimination for irrelevant reasons. Accordingly, equality may require, in the development of social institutions, the necessity of differentiation for relevant reasons. Thus, those who have opposed inequality in American society have often historically instituted laws against discrimination on grounds such as race, religion, or gender, while recognizing legitimate reasons for differentiation among persons. Consequently, a hierarchy that is based upon rational reasons can be interpreted as consistent with egalitarianism in a society.

Even at this early stage of the spectrum, a difference of attitudes that indicates the division between Liberalism and Conservatism can be suggested. The concept of equality as formal or legal with its amplification through differentiation among persons for relevant reasons can be interpreted as necessarily producing inequality that is "inequality of result." Accordingly, another correlative opposite of formal or legal equality emerges as inequality that is identified with differences among persons in the distribution of goods or in the attainment of socioeconomic position. The Liberal tendency, even as it accepts the principle of formal equality, has also been one of seeking ways to minimize inequality of result within a society.

In charting the movement along the spectrum from minimal concepts of equality toward greater egalitarianism, the familiar phrase of "equality of opportunity" appears as a concept that seems to go beyond equality of rights or equality before the law. The concept of equality of opportunity, however, does not possess strict reference, but seems to be vague and metaphorical, often depending upon an analogy between the complex institutions of a society and an athletic contest, particularly a race in a track meet. If a society or an economy were like an athletic contest, particularly a sprint race, then equality of opportunity would be understood as the requirement that each runner in the race has the same starting point. Such a metaphor, however, immediately breaks down as an explication of equality of opportunity. On the one hand, by virtue of the differences in their inherited genetic abilities and the differences in their access to health, treatment, and training, the runners of the race do not have an equal opportunity to arrive at the finish line at the same time even if they all begin with the firing of the gun at the same starting line. On the other hand, it is difficult to interpret any race to the top in a social or economic enterprise as the equivalent of either a sprint or a marathon. The pattern of successful outcomes in a competitive marketplace of a society does not match the criteria for winning trophies at track meets.

To the degree to which the social activity of achievement of position or wealth under a condition of equality of opportunity could be analogized to an athletic competition, a more feasible analogy would be to a steeplechase race. The reason for this analogy is the diversity of challenges that are faced by the runners of the race so that the outcomes reflect diverse talents, including an element of luck, which renders the outcome not completely predictable. Accordingly, in a sense, the difference in genetic background or in training is cancelled out so that the idea that there is an equality of opportunity for winning among all the runners of the race can receive a measure of support and confirmation.

There are obvious ways in which inequalities of opportunity can be limited, proscribed, or eliminated. Accordingly, the concept of equality of opportunity can have its major use as a directive toward the elimination of irrelevant reasons for discrimination with the result that opportunities for persons might tend to greater equalization. Thus, to the degree to which inequalities have been the result of the denial of opportunity to persons on discriminatory grounds, the concept of equality of opportunity can have a meaningful reference. Along these lines, equality of opportunity could be defined as the exclusion of discrimination for irrelevant reasons, such as the familiar trio of race, religion, and gender. In the use of the term "égalité" in the French Revolutionary slogan triad, the opposition was directed to discrimination on the grounds of noble birth. Hence, the move toward equality of opportunity was characterized by the phrase "carrières ouvertes aux talents."

A functional analysis of equality of opportunity as a directive against arbitrary discrimination, however, appears to confirm the idea that an explicit formulation of the constituent elements of a society that provides equality of opportunity is difficult to achieve, and such a formula would be even more difficult to implement. In any human society the fact of great differences among individuals, which seem to be partly genetically caused and manifest themselves virtually from birth, indicates the difficulty of creating a social structure in which opportunities would be equal. Further, in any society the historical inheritance of great differences in the capacity and willingness of families to provide support for the opportunities of the next generation virtually guarantees unequal opportunities. Accordingly, the effort to realize equality of opportunity in some egalitarian societies has involved, at times, extreme measures of coercion directed toward leveling the differences among persons who possess unequal opportunities for success.

The difficulties that have been identified in the interpretation of the concept of equality of opportunity point to a disjunction between Conservative thought and Liberal thought in their approach toward the realization of an appropriate egalitarianism in American society.

Within American Liberal thought, there has been recognition
that equality of opportunity is not achievable without the addition of directed efforts toward its realization. This recognition
has prompted efforts toward the achievement of "fair equality of
opportunity," to use John Rawls's term. Fair equality of opportunity requires champions of the ideal of equality of opportunity to
move beyond policies that outlaw discrimination for irrelevant reasons toward the introduction of programs of "Affirmative Action."

Liberal proposals for Affirmative Action have included different grounds for their introduction. One such ground has been
the thesis that American history has resulted in placing particular
racial, ethnic, or gender groups at a disadvantage in the competition for preferred positions in American society. From this perspective, different policies for affirmative action are needed to rectify
the historical record of discrimination against designated groups.
These policies range from support for educational and training
programs for members of historically deprived groups, through
specified measures for assisting the placement of members of the
designated groups in preferred positions, to actual targets of pro-
portionate numbers or "quotas" for inclusion of members of designated groups in preferred positions in American society.

It is well known that the grounding of affirmative-action policies by reference to particular groups that have suffered historical
deprivation has generated political controversy and judicial argument. One significant counterargument, which has been given
notable recognition by both Liberals and Conservatives, has been
the thesis that some affirmative action policies impose a reverse
form of discrimination upon individual persons who bear no
responsibility for the original acts of discrimination against the
groups designated as having suffered historical deprivation.

There have been other grounds advanced in support of Liberal
policies of affirmative action. The much publicized report of the
Kerner Commission, in response to the urban race riots of the
1960s, suggested that the United States should avoid the perceived
risk of becoming a bifurcated society in which one historically
privileged segment of racial, ethnic, or class groups occupies the
higher strata of the society, while another historically deprived segment of racial, ethnic, or class groups occupies the lower strata of
the society. Affirmative-action policies could be adopted in order to

overcome this risk of bifurcation. Such policies have been directed toward ways to realize upward mobility for members of specified groups that are designated as historically deprived including the criterion of gender and in some cases sexual orientation.

One Conservative rejoinder to programs of Affirmative Action that require a high degree of social engineering through application of quotas or the use of different sets of academic or vocational standards would be the argument that the United States as a society of multiple opportunities has provided many ladders of upward mobility for members of historically deprived groups, including large immigrant populations, during its entire economic history.

Thus, American Conservative political thought has consistently supported the thesis that a high rate of upward mobility has been a constant feature of American society. This record of upward mobility antedates the programs for affirmative action that emerged during and after the 1960s. It is not a Conservative doctrine, however, to exclude all programs of affirmative action that are intended to increase upward mobility in American society. Yet, upward mobility in the United States has had as its political prerequisites only equality before the law, or equality of rights, which involves the exclusion of any caste-like societal bifurcation or the permanent exclusion of groups from the exercise of the opportunities that are available to other members of the society.

One other ground for the justification of programs of affirmative action has been an appeal to the value of diversity. The thesis of champions of diversity seems to be that the adoption of diversity, that is, class, racial, ethnic, or gender diversity, as a criterion for recruitment and admission into institutions such as universities, corporations, or other work places, is an intrinsic good. The defense of diversity often appeals to the claim that an increase in these kinds of diversity in the membership of any institution will inevitably result in a number of values including an increase in intellectual resources, a greater breadth of competing opinions, an improved range of perceptiveness, a heightened ability to exercise empathy in different contexts of human experience, and the greater possibilities for understanding the real world in which the participants of these institutions are operating. The proponents of diversity, however, have not subjected their policies of admission or recruitment to an empirical test as to whether they increase or lessen the assumed values of improved intellectual resources, a broadening of competing opinions, a wider range of perceptiveness, a heightened ability to exercise empathy in different contexts of human experience, and greater possibilities for understanding the real world. The evidence that would compare a set of criteria for admissions or recruitment based on diversity of class, race, ethnicity, or gender with more traditional criteria or with criteria based upon a meritocratic principle has not received empirical confirmation or refutation.

Within Conservative thought, the recognition of the difficulties of realizing the notion of equality of opportunity have not led primarily to a strategy of trying to achieve fair equality of opportunity through affirmative-action policies, but to support the perennial ideal of America as a society which provides the conditions for a high rate of upward mobility, often referred to as "the American Dream." The version of egalitarianism that has emerged in American Conservative thought is not to be realized by efforts to rectify historical or inherent differences among the members of the society, but to preserve the political, economic, and social institutions that permit and enhance the possibilities of upward mobility for any member of the society. Five elements can be identified in the Conservative version of an appropriate American egalitarianism.

The first of these elements is that American society must meet the requisite standards of formal equality, equality of rights, or equality before the law. The explicit exclusion of slavery, serfdom, any form of second-class citizenship, or even a permanent hereditary underclass is required. The equal formal right to participation in American society by all of its legal members cannot be violated. Whatever the empirical patterns of differentiation in American society, the assumption has been, and remains, that every person is potentially capable of economic and social achievement.

The second and more confirmable or refutable element requires the existence of multiple opportunities in American society. Consequently, on the presumption that complete equality of opportunity is not realizable in any society, its important replacement is to be found in the fact that American society can be justifiably identified as an "opportunity society." Such a justification depends for its verification upon the historical record that American society has provided multiple opportunities for members of the diverse groups that have constituted the American people.

The third element is the requirement that, in addition to multiple opportunities, there are also multiple ladders for upward mobility. Consequently, upward mobility in the United States has been relatively free from constraints that require members of the society to proceed through a favored set of educational institutions, to pass through specified choke points, or to move along proscribed rungs in order to achieve wealth, political leadership, or social position.

The fourth element (which can be interpreted as a counter to economic equality in significant context) is economic growth. In one reading of the American economic record, economic growth has been the most important prerequisite for upward mobility. The multiple opportunities for members of the lower strata of the economy to increase their wealth presuppose a positive growth rate for the gross national product. Thus, champions of upward mobility have accepted the historical record as confirming the fact that the United States has shown a growth rate of the gross domestic product in excess of 3 percent since the Civil War. The significance of this figure is sharpened by the identification of a growth rate of this magnitude as involving a periodic doubling of the gross national product in less than 25 years. Conservative thought in economics includes a high degree of confidence in the dynamism that is built into the operation of free markets such that an economic growth rate that would permit upward mobility in the United States will not come to an end.

The fifth element within this pattern of American egalitarianism mandates that the poorest persons in America will not suffer abject misery and extremely severe deprivation. From this perspective the economic growth and the legal rules of the United States will guarantee a "safety net" such that the lowest strata of the population will be free from starvation or lack of food, from inadequate water for drinking and sanitation, from circumstances that are strongly destructive of personal health or involve debilitating social pathology.

From Adam Smith's formulation of "Classical Liberalism" to the present, the Conservative view has emerged as recognizing the necessity for three economic sectors. Alongside the function of free markets as the dynamic instrument of economic growth, the necessity of a governmental sector to secure defense, public education, and other needs of public interest has been recognized. In addition, Adam Smith identified a not-for-profit sector, which historically included the Church, as providing eleemosynary institutions. This sector has been expanded in American society to include a large number of philanthropic foundations with diverse purposes that are intended to serve the public interest. The recognition of the importance of the governmental sector and the not-for-profit sector in Conservative thought does not diminish the primacy that is accorded to the private sector or free-market sector as the dynamic element that is prerequisite for economic growth.

The priority that is placed within American Conservatism upon upward mobility as constituting a major aspect of American egalitarianism contrasts with the Liberal emphasis on realizing a greater degree of substantive equality and its currently sharpened focus against the perceived growth in economic inequality among individuals in American society.

Proceeding further along the spectrum of maximization of equality, Liberal thought has interpreted the concept of equality as going beyond "fair equality of opportunity" toward forms of substantive equality. This is probably best evidenced by the extreme acceptance and popularity of the theory of distributive justice of John Rawls. Its resonance in the 1950s indicated the recognition that the intellectual collapse of Hegelian or historicist Marxism, in its effort to equate equality and justice, could be replaced by a rationalist Kantian theory that would maintain an intrinsic connection between equality and justice. With reference to the spectrum of interpretations of equality, Rawls advanced beyond fair equality of opportunity toward a form of substantive equality formulated by the "difference principle." Rawls's formulation of the difference principle holds that inequalities are arbitrary, except when they are for the benefit of the most disadvantaged. Accordingly, the difference principle would seem to support substantive equality among all members of a society, with the seemingly limited exception of the case where the inequality is to the benefit of the most disadvantaged. Such a direct application of the Rawlsian difference principle, however, does not correctly identify Rawls's intentions. For Rawls, the difference principle is not intended to apply to particular historical or empirical situations, but to represent hypothetical principles for negotiation among rational individuals in the establishment of the rules for distributive justice in a society.

Conservative thought would clearly challenge the application of the difference principle in any real economic context on the ground that a plurality of reasons are to be considered as providing legitimate justification for economic differences among different individuals in the society. In particular, Conservatives would include differentiations of income that emerge from the operation of free markets as justified in unequal distributions. As noted above, however, this apparent issue between Conservatives and Rawlsians cannot be joined, because Rawlsians do not argue that the difference principle is directly applicable in the empirical context of a free-market economy, offering it instead as a guiding hypothesis that could be applied in ways that would allow free markets to operate.

Nonetheless, in clarifying the spectrum of interpretations of equality, with reference to the application of the difference principle to a society as envisioned by Rawls, it is significant to note its potential results. Since, according to the difference principle, inequalities are permitted when they are for the benefit of the most disadvantaged, the following economic illustration could be tested. Consider two societies in which one society exhibits virtually complete equality within its population but has an extremely low or even negative growth rate over a significant period of time, while another society has great disparities in income between the rich and the poor in its population while possessing a very high economic growth rate over a similar period. It is demonstrable that the poorest person in a society with a high growth rate would possess a superior income to the richest person in the former society of equals with a low growth rate. Thus, if the difference principle were applicable, inequalities would be justified in a society with a higher growth rate. The historical example is provided by the difference between an egalitarian Maoist China in which the overwhelming majority of the population were equally poor and the current economic regime in China in which virtually all of the unequal strata of the population enjoy a standard of living that is superior to that enjoyed by virtually all the members of the preceding Maoist regime. The placement of the difference principle within the spectrum of equality is subject to its own patterns of interpretation.

Proceeding further along the spectrum toward the maximization of equality, one arrives at the concept of substantive equality among all members of the society. Substantive equality had been formulated as an ideal for the economic society of the ancient city-state of Sparta, which was a closed, small, and primarily agrarian society. The vision embodied in the constitution of Sparta was augmented and enhanced in a variety of social experiments that have ranged from religious institutions, to Tolstoyan farms, to communal collectives. In the Marxist vision, substantive equality could be realized without the constraints that were identified with "Spartan" life, since Capitalism was to have "solved the problem of production" so that Socialism could distribute goods in abundance with complete equality. Thus, the Conservative rejection of substantive equality was consistent with its long-term criticism of Marxism, just as the Liberal rejection of substantive equality marked its abandonment of Marxist utopianism.

There is one Liberal interpretation of egalitarianism in terms of substantive equality that was formulated in Bernard Williams's "The Idea of Equality." It is especially relevant to the conceptual issues between Liberalism and Conservatism in the contemporary period since it relates to the expansion of health care, an issue that has been central to the controversy between Liberals and Conservatives in the United States in the recent past.

Williams initiates his analysis of the idea of equality with the recognition that both Liberals and Conservatives accept the formal concept of equality, that is, the principle that differentiation is for relevant reasons only. Williams moves beyond this minimal agreement with the thesis that the sole relevant reason for the delivery of health care is the treatment of the illness of the patient. Since the need of the patient is the sole relevant reason for the health care, the introduction of any other reason, including financial or economic considerations, would be an irrelevant reason that would constitute a form of irrationality. Thus, in Williams's theoretical account of "The Idea of Equality," the application of the minimal criterion of formal equality in health care generates the practice of substantive equality usually formulated in the phrase: "To each according to his need."[4]

The Conservative response to Williams's argument does not focus upon its theoretical adequacy but upon its applicability to real world conditions. Thus, a Conservative counter to Williams's thesis involves the recognition that the introduction of need as the sole relevant reason for the delivery of a product or a service, like health care, can be sustained only if the supply were infinite or the supply were perennially much larger than the demand.

Consequently, in establishing a system of health care there are relevant reasons for adopting policies that can increase or maintain supply as well as decrease or lessen the burdens in meeting the needs and demand for health care.

Thus, there are relevant reasons within a health care system for using resources to develop and maintain an adequate cadre of health care practitioners, including surgeons, doctors, nurses, aides, an innovative pharmaceutical industry, and resources devoted to medical research in addition to or even on par with resources for the treatment of patients. In widening the horizon from the treatment of the individual to the development of the health care system, relevant reasons emerge that cannot be correctly attributed as need.

The status of need as the sole relevant reason is also challenged in a review of one significant area of contemporary treatment of illness, namely, organ transplants. In most areas of organ transplantation the demand is much greater than the supply. The criterion of need as the sole relevant reason would require a random lottery for all applicants with the inevitability of death falling upon those in the less lucky portions of the lottery. One rational response has been the introduction of alternative criteria for receipt of the organ other than the equal criterion of "need."

One such criterion or reason is the length and quality of the life of the individual that is expected after a successful transplant. Such a relevant reason would result in an unequal place for patients who are very old or suffer other illnesses that provide lesser expectations for length and quality of life after the transplant. Another much contested reason is the genesis of the illness that required a transplant. In many lists, persons whose irresponsible behavior is considered the cause of the illness, as in alcoholism as the cause of cirrhosis of the liver, are placed below those whose illness cannot be attributed to irresponsible behavior.

A morally interesting challenge to Williams's thesis of need as the sole relevant reason is generated in those cases where close relatives of the patient have volunteered to provide the organ, such as a kidney. The availability of the organ for the specified patient can be considered a relevant reason for his preferential treatment. Substantive egalitarianism could require that the kidney of the volunteer relative should enter into the available pool for all patients, with no discrimination among the individuals other than need. In such an arrangement, the patient who is the relative of the volunteer receives the enhanced benefit of the greater supply but does not realize the direct benefit of the relative's contribution.

Such an egalitarian process, however, clearly carries the price of a disincentive to the relative who does not wish to volunteer his kidney for the general good but for the sake of his close relative. Thus, in the complex human relations that have an impact upon health care, a factor other than need has emerged as a relevant reason in treatment.

As a more general matter, apart from a special field like organ transplantation, other factors including economic factors like the costs of the delivery of health care may become relevant reasons. The maintenance of a health care system requires that the gross national product increase sufficiently at the rate necessary to sustain the costs of the system.

The issue of the relevance of costs for the treatment of illness is bypassed in the analysis of Williams, who considers cost to be distinct from need as the sole relevant reason for treatment. The issue of cost cannot be bypassed, however, in the operation of the institutions that govern the practice of health care. Many advocates of universal health care have themselves commented upon the great expansion of costs of health care during the past three generations. Health care costs represented only 5 percent of the gross domestic product two generations ago and doubled to 10 percent in the next generation. Currently, health care costs in the United States are estimated at approximately one-sixth of the gross domestic product. There is obviously a limit to the rise of this percentage far below the past rate of its doubling in each generation.

This issue has not yet arrived at a climactic point that would necessitate hard choices.

The recognition of cost as a relevant reason generates a variety of possibilities in adequately sustaining health care toward the shared goal of optimal treatment of the illnesses of all members of the population. Alongside Williams's egalitarian thesis of the rationality of need, there is a Conservative emphasis on decision making for optimal economic rationality in providing treatment. The difference between Liberalism and Conservatism on these issues does not focus upon any disagreement over the principle of seeking to meet the need for treatment of illness but upon the measures to be adopted in meeting these needs, particularly upon the Conservative emphasis on priority of individual freedom of choice and the operation of markets in contradistinction to the Liberal emphasis on governmental programs for realizing universality of access to health care.

One of the final stages in a survey of the spectrum of concepts of egalitarianism would be a complete equality of result or of substantive equality along lines that were projected in socialist, Marxist, and anarchist theories. Liberalism, in contrast to socialist, Marxist, and anarchist theories, has generally accepted the inevitability of some forms of hierarchy in every society that involves differentiations of power and of financial position. One recurrent Conservative theme, as previously noted, has been that the socialist ideology has held, at various times, a significant influence on European and American Liberalism. As a result, Liberal programs have often moved beyond the values of equal rights, equality of opportunity, and social welfare policies toward a goal of equality of result or substantive equality. The current emphasis within liberalism on income inequality reflects the interpretation of the egalitarian ideal as a realization of substantive equality with its policy implications for more progressive taxation and measures for income redistribution.

There are extreme forms at either pole of the spectrum of equality that move beyond the relevant contexts of this chapter on the conceptual differences between Liberalism and Conservatism. At one end of the spectrum, the identification of strong concepts of hierarchy within English or Continental Conservatism before the nineteenth century can be noted. Thus, subordination of the common people, or the lower classes, to the ranks of the nobility, or to the upper classes, was legitimized even though such subordination often resulted in oppression of the common people at the hands of the nobility and of the poorer classes by the wealthier.

At the other pole of substantive equality, two extreme examples can be cited. The first of these is found in the well-known myth of Procrustes. Procrustean egalitarianism requires a leveling such that all persons must fit in a bed of the same size with a result that those whose legs are too short will suffer the pain of their being stretched and those whose legs are too long will suffer the catastrophe of having them cut. The applications of this metaphor can be found in some historical periods, like that of the Cultural Revolution in Maoist China.

The second extreme illustration of egalitarianism is available in the phenomenon of malice. A Nordic medieval example is the anecdote in which a person is offered by a deity to receive anything he wants on condition that his neighbor will receive twice as much. The response of the malicious egalitarian is "oh Odin strike me blind in one eye." Cases of economic malice in which persons lessen their own economic benefits in order to achieve harm to those whom they envy or hate can often be found. In the rhetoric that reflects anti-capitalist resentments it is not uncommon to discover and identify economic policies that are directed to harming the rich and that provide no benefit or are counterproductive to the welfare of the poor.

This survey of major positions along a spectrum of definitions of equality ranges beyond the areas of disagreement that divide Liberals from Conservatives. At the same time, competing positions that have been delineated within the spectrum demonstrate conceptual differences that underlie policy disagreements on major issues in which Liberalism and Conservatism have undertaken divergent roads.

2. The Debate between Targeting Economic Growth and
Targeting Income Equality through Redistribution as the
Optimal Way to Lessen Deprivation and Poverty

Beyond disagreement over competing interpretations of the concept of equality, Liberalism and Conservatism have disagreed over

the best means for lessening deprivation and poverty. Such a disagreement can also be understood as representing alternative
interpretations of what would constitute an appropriately egalitarian society.

From the Liberal perspective, an emphasis on aspects of substantive equality, or equality of result, as the fulfillment of an
egalitarian ideal has indicated policies that favor redistribution of
wealth. From the Conservative perspective, an emphasis on aspects
of equality of rights, or of equality before the law, as the fulfillment of an egalitarian ideal has indicated policies that favor economic growth and upward mobility. Consequently, a major line of
policy disagreement between Liberalism and Conservatism can be
identified as a debate between targeting economic redistribution
or targeting economic growth as the optimal way to lessen deprivation and poverty in American society. In such a debate, there is an
element of conflicting attitudes and values as well as competing
empirical hypotheses.

In the attitudinal or value sphere, proponents of redistribution
policy have targeted equality as intrinsically related to justice and,
more particularly, to distributive justice. The realization of equality is considered to be an intrinsic value, and from this perspective
equality is identified as connected to the value of justice, which
is considered a supreme or inviolate value within a society. Thus,
in any economic structure, substantive inequality, that is, the existence of great differences in income and assets between those at
the top and those at the bottom of the society, is in itself judged
to be evidence of injustice. Critics of this connection between
equality and justice have argued that when equality and justice
have been connected so intimately, the moral imperative to do justice has sanctioned an approach toward the realization of equality that has overruled the balancing of competing values and has
justified extreme and excessively coercive means to achieve the
egalitarian goal.

The Conservative view has been that justice is independent
from substantive equality. One obvious example is the existence of
unequal abilities that merit praise rather than leveling, indicating
the absence of a societal sense of injustice. Thus, the inequality
of ability in theoretical physics between Einstein and the majority
of the world's population, like the inequality of talent in musical

composition between Mozart and this majority, provides grounds for celebration rather than for the stigma of injustice. In economic contexts, the connection between inequality and injustice usually presupposes that the inequality is based upon such factors as an unfairness that has been built into the historical economic "system" that reflects domination by the stronger over the majority, the exploitation of the lower class by the ruling class, or the existence of discrimination for irrelevant reasons.

According to the Conservative theory of Justice that originated with Aristotle, as noted previously, justice is not only compatible with substantive inequality, it necessarily results in substantive inequality through generating a hierarchy. The grounds for this are twofold.

One ground is an argument for the ontological necessity of inequality advanced by Professor Ralf Dahrendorf. According to that ontological argument, every social system draws a distinction between those who obey its laws, rules, or regulations and those who violate these laws, rules, or regulations. Since those who commit violations must be punished in some manner, and those who do not commit violations must be rewarded to some degree, inequality is inevitable in any set of social arrangements that are governed by rules. Consequently, the values of justice and equality cannot be equated.

The second ground is the requirement of formal justice that there should be no differentiation among persons for irrelevant reasons. The logical obverse of this requirement is that differentiation among persons is only permitted for relevant reasons. Such differentiation for relevant reasons necessarily brings with it substantive inequality, so that the moral imperative of Justice is not equated with an intrinsic virtue of substantive equality.

As noted above, the debate between targeting economic growth and targeting economic equality involves empirical issues. Proponents of targeting greater equality of income or assets through redistribution have contended that policies and institutions that produce greater inequality of income and assets can be shown to be causally connected to increased deprivation and poverty. The assumption of such an analysis is that the "distribution" of a greater portion of income and assets to the higher strata of the society will result in a smaller portion of income and assets to be available for distribution to the lower strata of the society. Thus an unequal distribution of income and assets results in greater deprivation and poverty than would be the case with a more egalitarian distribution. Generally speaking, the targeting of greater equality of assets and income involves the adoption of policies that support efforts to redistribute wealth from the higher strata to the lower strata of the society. Advocates of redistribution contend that effective redistribution can be carried out by a variety of measures that include improving vocational education for the poor, strengthening labor unions, implementing policies of progressive taxation, and directing transfers of wealth through welfare programs.

Proponents of targeting growth contend that substantive inequality is compatible with lessening deprivation and poverty. The empirical disagreement sharpens with the thesis that targeting economic growth that results in a great disparity of income and assets between those in the higher strata and those in the lower strata of the society can be a more effective way to lessen deprivation and poverty than targeting equality of income and assets through redistributive policies. The assumption of such an analysis is that an increase in growth, even if it results in a disproportionate increment to the higher strata, will provide sufficient benefits for the lower strata so that deprivation and poverty are lessened. Moreover, the benefits of growth can be realized in a wide range of areas. The economic growth of a society ranges over many fields including the improvement of technology, medical practice, and environmental standards. In most modern societies, these kinds of growth cannot take place on a restricted or segregated basis such that an isolated segment of the population could be completely excluded from the benefits that accrue as a result of the general development of the society. Accordingly, it has often been demonstrated that growth can have positive outcomes for persons at the lower strata as well as for persons at the higher strata of the economy. This is evidenced by such data as the virtual elimination of polio, malaria, and diphtheria in the United States as well as the technological availability of telephones, television, air conditioning, and automobiles in virtually all economic strata of the society.

The debate between targeting growth and targeting equality of income and assets has been carried out in a number of contexts.

These include the following: (a) interpretations of twentieth-century political and economic history; (b) contending theses in political philosophy; (c) divergent theories of economics with alternative policies of taxation; and (d) opposing metaphors.

(a) Interpretations of Twentieth-Century Political and Economic History

Contemporary American Conservatism has developed to a significant degree as a reaction to major ideological and political movements in the twentieth century. Thus, one of the historical springs of American Conservative thought is found in its critical reaction to the Communist regimes in the Soviet Union and Maoist China. These origins are particularly evident in American neo-Conservatism, whose dominant figures, from Sydney Hook and James Burnham, through John Dos Passos to Jeanne Kirkpatrick and Irving Kristol, began their political careers on the Left and moved in various stages from anti-Communism in foreign policy to Conservatism that included support for free-market economics.

The belief that Liberal thought in the United States had moved in the direction of greater sympathy for Marxist and Socialist ideologies, particularly in the 1930s, was a significant feature of American Conservatism. From the perspective of Conservative critics of these tendencies in Liberalism, American Liberalism had compromised its own integrity through its support for socialist regimes, including totalitarian socialist governments, tending to overlook grim reality in the sway of rhetorical affirmation of the ideals of economic and social equality. Consequently, the subsequent revelation by the Communist leadership of the institutionalized atrocities that took place within the Soviet bloc and Communist China confirmed and strengthened the Conservative tradition of criticizing Liberalism for bearing within it a strain of pro-Socialist ideology.

Conservatism in the United States had supported free-market economics in the 1920s. During the 1930s it had carried out a continued, albeit ineffective, criticism against the policies of the New Deal. With the failure of Socialist economics within the Soviet Union, Communist China, eastern Europe, and many other Third World countries, as well as the pre-Thatcherite socialist economy of Great Britain, the Conservative tradition in the United States became even more closely connected to free-market economic theory. Thus, the historical interpretation of the rise and fall of socialist ideology reinforced American Conservatism in its critique of Liberalism and in its commitment to free-market economics.

Thus the interpretation of the history of the success and failure of the economic policies of different governments throughout the twentieth century provided support for advocacy by American Conservatism of an economic policy that targeted economic growth through the operation of free markets rather than a redistribution of wealth as the optimal means for lessening deprivation and poverty. In specified governmental policies, President Lyndon Johnson's Liberal "War on Poverty" was followed by President Reagan's Conservative emphasis on economic growth as the better way to lessen deprivation in the United States.

In the recent past the debate between targeting economic growth versus targeting economic redistribution as the optimal means for lessening deprivation has continued with unabated intensity, even though the relevance of the disagreement over the historical interpretation of the political and economic movements of the twentieth century has receded.

(b) Contending Theses in Political Philosophy

In political philosophy, the debate between targeting economic growth versus targeting economic redistribution is reflected in the disagreement over the importance of the private sector as compared to the role of government. Within Conservatism, the thesis of the priority of the private sector has had diverse sources of support. This support, as previously noted, can be traced back to classical liberalism in the writings of Adam Smith, which identify the dynamic or growth factor of the economy as attributable to the private sector. For Smith, in contrast to the "visible hand" of government, an "invisible hand" operates in free markets to achieve optimality of prices whether for labor or for goods, with the result of optimal economic growth. Even with Smith's addition to the private sector of a governmental sector, which provided for national defense and public education, as well as a not-for-profit sector that provided a safety net for the most vulnerable persons in the society, the greatest portion of economic activity was to take place in the private sector as the condition for successful economic development.

A more recent source of support for the priority of the private sector moves beyond the political issue of the size of government to the connection between Conservatism and the economic theory of free markets. An argument against large-scale governmental intervention has been derived from the Austrian School of economics, including the writings of Ludwig von Mises and Friedrich von Hayek. The argument of the Austrian economic theorists seeks to prove that economic growth will not take place if the ratio of public sector economic activity to private sector activity rises above a calculable numerical ratio. From this perspective, reliance on the government to become the major agency for economic growth or the agent for the redistribution of the society's wealth along more egalitarian lines is inevitably counterproductive. This thesis reflects a disagreement in attitudes between Liberals and Conservatives, but it is also subject to confirmation and refutation by future empirical evidence.

The debate in political philosophy has also related to the Conservative thesis that the freedom of the society is intrinsically connected to limits on governmental intervention in the economy. From the Hayekian perspective, excessive governmental involvement in economic affairs leads to the breakdown of the "rule of law," which is a necessary condition for political freedom.

To a degree, American Economic Conservatism has accepted the thesis that an increase in the economic activity of the public sector risks limiting individual freedom. In economic theory, the debate would join between Hayekian advocacy of free markets and the Keynesian approach to greater governmental intervention in contra-cyclical policies in fiscal and monetary affairs. These contending views have been sustained despite significant changes among both Conservative and Liberal economic theories.

The criticism of governmental intervention has been supplemented by the continuing tradition in American political theory that supports local or state government as distinct from federal government. It also has roots in the historical tradition of American political thought that mistrusts "Big Government." This tradition has been traced back to Calvinist religious tendencies in the

American colonies, as well to the constitutionalist preference for Montesquieu's doctrine of the "separation of powers" over the Lockean theory of "legislative supremacy" in the generation of The Founders.

(c) Divergent Theories of Economics with Alternative Policies of Taxation

One more specific area of disagreement is found in arguments for alternative policies of taxation that derive from disagreement between the "supply-side" and "demand-side" economic theorists. Thus, there is a divergence on taxation policy that is connected to the issue of targeting growth versus targeting greater equality through redistribution.

Proponents of supply-side economics have argued in favor of reducing taxes on investment. Such a reduction would involve, in the standard phrase of the opposition, "cutting taxes on the rich." The supply-side argument is that an increase in investment, which can be realized through cutting taxes on capital, will produce a greater benefit for the economy in terms of a higher rate of growth, resulting in a greater reduction in unemployment than would result from an alternative tax policy. Further, the argument is that raising taxes on the private sector would result in a transfer of wealth to the public sector, which is less efficient in increasing the economic growth rate and in the reduction of unemployment.

From the demand side, the alternative proposal has been to cut taxes on the poor with the claim that this would increase demand and result in an increase in consumption that would also benefit economic growth. The issue, then, is often formulated as competing economic hypotheses capable of empirical confirmation or refutation of the supply-side or demand-side approaches. Within American Conservatism, the thesis has prevailed that lower taxes on investment, even as it bears the stigma of "cutting taxes on the rich," is a policy that achieves economic growth and therefore realizes benefits for all strata of society including those on the bottom rungs.

Apart from the general debate over supply-side theory versus demand-side theory, advocacy in the public forum involves prognoses for the application of these policies to current situations. Liberals and demand-side economists have argued that there is an

abundance of unused capital available for investment on the balance sheet of the major corporations at the present time so that
the key to improving the current low economic growth rate is to
increase demand through cutting taxes on consumption, which
can be identified as "cutting taxes for the poor." Conservatives and
supply-side economists have argued that the extremely high rates
of corporate and capital gains taxes in the United States, which are
greater than those in other nations competing for investment, are
a key factor in these current low growth rates of the economy that
would be improved by lowering taxes.

The shaping of attitudes in the spectrum of Conservatism
and Liberalism does not wait upon the verification of empirical
hypotheses on these complex matters. Thus, at the risk of over-
simplification, there is some relevant insight to be gained by a
review of the competing metaphors that have been applied in the
long divergence between Liberalism and Conservatism over economic growth versus greater substantive equality through redistribution as the way to lessen deprivation and poverty.

(d) Opposing Metaphors

One theme of Liberal economic views has been to consider the
overall sum of goods in an economy on the metaphor of a pie. The
visual graphs of economic performance that use illustrations of a
pie being cut into slices or sectors of diverse proportions is familiar in the explication of the distribution of an economic product.
The metaphor supports the idea that targeting greater equality
through redistribution is like "distributing" equal slices of the pie
to each member of the society. The alternative of providing some
members with larger slices and others with smaller slices is then
considered to be a violation of fairness. It is generally recognized
that, for pragmatic reasons, it may be necessary to provide greater
reward in the form of increased slices of pie to some members, but
this inequality is considered to represent a compromise with an
ideal of justice or fairness that would require equal shares for each
member. Champions of equality characteristically illustrate the
patterns of distribution of shares with the goal of demonstrating
the great disparity, particularly in assets, that is the portion held
by the wealthier deciles of the population compared to the more
diminutive slices held by the poorer deciles of the population.

In this connection, the phrase of the 1 percent versus 99 percent emerged as a slogan of the Occupy Wall Street movement. The phrase can be traced back to its use by Franklin D. Roosevelt in his campaign for the senate in New York in 1910.

The competing metaphor to the notion of equal slices of a pie is that of the hierarchical rungs of an extension ladder. Such a ladder can theoretically reach higher and higher on its upper rungs while also achieving greater altitude for the lower rungs of the ladder. From the perspective of those who make use of this metaphorical model, the greater distance between those on the top rungs of the ladder and those on the bottom rungs of the ladder does not represent a deprivation for the lower rungs. The relevant issues for the reduction of deprivation and poverty according to this metaphor are threefold. One of these issues is the rate and degree of upward mobility on the ladder such that persons along the lower rungs of the ladder have a reasonable chance of moving toward a higher rung. The second issue is whether those persons who occupy the lower rungs of the ladder will experience improvements in their economic welfare and quality of life during their lifetime even if they do not rise significantly in their relative position on the ladder. The third issue is transgenerational, that is, whether the succeeding generation will be able to realize a higher position on the rungs of the ladder or an improved status in economic welfare and in the quality of life over the preceding generation.

Liberal critics of the metaphor of the extension ladder who advocate greater redistribution argue that responses that provide positive views on these three issues are excessively optimistic in light of America's economic future and the misdistribution of assets that has prevailed over the past three decades. Conservatives who support this metaphor argue that positive responses on these three issues remain justified because of possibilities of growth of the American economy as an economy of free markets.

The competition between metaphors, such as the fixed pie versus the extension ladder, has also been directed to contending metaphors that use the image of the movements of water. Thus, critics of economic growth used as a method to lessen deprivation or poverty have fixed upon the metaphor of a "trickle-down" of water to depict the view that most economic growth benefits the rich and only a very small proportion reaches the poor. This castigation of economic growth as trickle-down economics has been advanced in support of the need for economic redistribution as a condition for the lessening of deprivation or of poverty.

A direct response to the phrase trickle-down was provided by Congressman Jack Kemp, a supply-side advocate who achieved legislation of lower taxation on capital. Congressman Kemp, whose Buffalo constituency included or abutted Niagara Falls, advocated for the value of economic growth in the reduction of poverty and deprivation through his substitution of the metaphor "Niagara Falls down" for "trickle-down." Along similar lines, President Kennedy, to the surprise of many, strongly advocated tax cuts on higher rates of income upon his entering the presidency. The metaphor he used in favor of this lowering of taxation of capital to support greater economic growth also referred to the movement of water with the phrase: "A rising tide lifts all boats."

There is a contrary metaphor that was formulated by Warren Buffett as applicable in a different context of economic activity. Buffett pointed out that only when the tide recedes is it possible to perceive who is naked in the water. The context of this remark is the identification of economic bubbles. The relevance is that economic recessions recur after periods of economic growth, often with negative consequences for persons at the bottom rungs of the economic hierarchy.

Finally, there is a set of competing metaphors between iconic figures of Conservative and Liberal thought that relates to trees. John Maynard Keynes, in his 1920s essay "The End of Laissez-Faire," developed the thesis that the free marketplace, with its implicit preference for growth of goods rather than their egalitarian distribution, represented a Darwinian struggle.[5] Keynes developed the metaphor that those animals with the longest reach and strongest aggressiveness plucked the best fruits of the tree, thereby relegating those of lesser reach or aggressiveness to poverty and deprivation. Through this metaphor the marketplace of a laissez-faire economy represented a struggle for "survival of the fittest." Despite the similarities between economic competition and Darwinian struggle that Keynes sketches in this essay, Keynesians would themselves agree that the acceptance or rejection of Social Darwinism does not imply the acceptance or rejection of free markets.

One competing metaphor that also refers to trees makes use of the analogy within Burkean Conservatism to society as organic. Social and political change does not take place as if society were a machine with changeable parts or capable of revolutionary transformation but must be incremental like the organic growth of a tree. William Butler Yeats applied this metaphor in the following way:

> And haughtier-headed Burke that proved the State a tree,
> That this unconquerable labyrinth of the birds, century after
> century,
> Cast but dead leaves to mathematical equality.[6]

In the context of Liberalism versus Conservatism, on greater equality through redistribution versus growth, the thesis ascribed to Burke is the rejection of the dead leaves of equality in contrast to the desirable growth of the tree itself with its higher and lower branches.

Disagreement between competing metaphors, like disagreement over opposing attitudes and in contrast to disagreement about alternative empirical hypotheses, is not considered to be decidable on the basis of empirical evidence. Yet, the acceptance of metaphorical statements, like the commitment to attitudes, does depend to some degree upon their support by empirical evidence. This empirical evidence often provides the reasons that are given to justify Liberal or Conservative attitudes. At the same time, empirical evidence can also provide rationalizations for attitudes that are maintained independent of the relative strength of the evidence.

Consequently, despite the value of continued economic knowledge of the beneficial or counterproductive consequences of economic growth or economic redistribution for lessening deprivation and poverty, the ongoing debate does not admit of a consensus resolution. At the same time, within American Conservatism, economic growth is prioritized both as an empirical hypothesis and as a measure of value. The Conservative matter is that, as an empirical hypothesis both in reference to the past as well as to the future, economic poverty and deprivation will be lessened by policies that support economic growth. American Conservatism also includes the belief that the values associated with economic growth, such as freedom of choice for the individual, can contribute to the morality of a society in greater measure than the values associated with redistribution such as equality.

C. Conservatism in Foreign Policy and the Interpretation of Fraternity: The Priority of National Security or National Interest and of Human Rights in American Foreign Policy

In considering Conservatism in foreign policy as a parallel to Social and Economic Conservatism, the idea of fraternity can be introduced as a parallel in the conceptual tier to preceding discussions of liberty and equality. There is a significant difference, however, since Conservatism in foreign policy involves an extension or reinterpretation of the concept of fraternity beyond the scope of its use in the eighteenth century to a far greater degree than the interpretation of liberty or equality. In the eighteenth-century context, the concept of fraternity was applied to the rights of individuals to citizenship within the nation-state, which were no longer to be dependent upon the traditional ties of birth or religion. Traditionalist Conservatives in the eighteenth century had placed a higher value on patriarchy than fraternity, resulting in the restriction of citizenship to those persons who were judged to have a shared relationship with the fatherhood of the nation through birth and religion. Since the eighteenth century, both Liberals and Conservatives have accepted as truistic the view that citizenship in a nation-state ought not to require or support distinctions that are based on birth or religion. One result of the changing context of the concept of fraternity has been its extension to the area of international relationships, as illustrated by such phrases as "the universal brotherhood of man" as an ideal for the international order.

Like liberty and equality, the idea of fraternity can also generate an ambiguity in the determination of its appropriate correlative opposite. The correlative opposite of fraternity, as a democratic ideal of government, could be considered as a statement of opposition to any form of patriarchy or matriarchy, that is, to the legitimacy of government by the elite groups that traditionally exercise authority. In some current contexts, the correlative opposite of fraternity, as well as to patriarchy, is sorority, with its emphasis on the need for women to liberate themselves from the patterns of historical domination by the opposite gender. In an alternative context, including parties that express xenophobic views, the correlative opposite is anti-brotherhood or prejudice against some human beings.

With reference to contexts of international politics, Liberal Cosmopolitanism has asserted the value of fraternity as the belief that all nations can participate equally in the community of nations as an implementation of the ideal of the "brotherhood of man." Nationalist claims would counter such cosmopolitan universality with the recognition that not all people are brothers, since others are cousins, distant relatives, friends, associates, strangers, fellow citizens, aliens, competitors, adversaries, or even enemies. In the international context of non-xenophobic nationalism, the correlative opposite term to fraternity is not anti-brotherhood or pro-prejudice but various kinds of particularist "otherhood." Accordingly, the denial of an ideal of "fraternity" can represent the recognition of the obligations and constraints imposed by the requirement of particular allegiances and the identification of particular social and political boundaries. Supporters of the value or legitimacy of these differentiated patterns of obligation reject the thesis that this support entails any denial of fundamental rights or deprivation of basic goods for "others," that is, for persons who do not share the bonds that bind a particular community, nation, or alliance.

It is difficult to imagine any extension or expansion of cosmopolitan universality that would totally erode and replace the particularist bonds of primary association, like family, that are built into the human condition. The development and existence of differentiated, unequal, and greatly varying forms of obligation among persons and groups that range from bonds of family to relationships of work through voluntary associations and national ties have set the framework for Conservative attitudes in culture and politics. As a loose generalization from the history of Liberal and Conservative thought, Liberalism could be identified with its tendency to challenge the fixity or "closedness" of historical boundaries and to seek the elimination of inequalities and differences across territories, cultures, and classes in support of historical transformation

that would bring societies nearer to an ideal of universal brotherhood. Conservatism has been identified with a tendency to challenge the theme of universal brotherhood through its emphasis
on the values associated with particularist allegiances or traditions
and the legitimacies of historical boundaries.

The recognition of the differences on the nature and ideal of
fraternity points to the differences between Liberalism and Conservatism in American foreign policy in the twentieth century.

From a polar interpretation of Liberalism, there is the position
that American foreign policy ought to be motivated by Idealism,
which involves strong support for international institutions like the
United Nations and the priority of advocacy for universal human
rights in all nation-states. From this perspective, the pursuit of
national interest is not necessarily rejected as a pursuit of selfish
ends but is placed within the context of achieving national security
through establishing the rule of law in international relations by
international forums and agencies. The policies that are preferred
in order to realize the ideal goal of international peace include
development of the specified agencies of the United Nations that
provide for security and the rule of law among nations. Such policies will confront the "root causes" of war through the elimination
of poverty, the reduction of arms, and the increased potentiality of
international projects of cooperation on issues of global concern.
Such a cosmopolitan policy will comprehend within its scope the
protection of the national interests of the United States without
the need to resort to the capacity of the United States to project
power abroad in protection of its security interests.

From a polar view of Conservatism, American foreign policy
ought to be motivated by Realism, which involves the recognition
of the realities of "otherhood," rather than fraternity, such that
there would be strong support for the protection of national interests in a world that contains states with conflicting interests as well
as non-state groups who carry out adversarial and hostile actions.
From this perspective, the protection of national interest is a priority that requires military force, including sufficiency in nuclear
arms, membership in shared military alliances like the North
Atlantic Treaty Organization (NATO), and a robust ability to deter
aggression, including the confrontation and deterrence of acts
of terrorism. At the same time, the priority of national interest is

compatible with a lesser priority of supporting the furtherance of democracy or the protection of human rights in other countries.

The analysis in this chapter, which stresses the differences in the conceptual tier between American Liberalism and American Conservatism in the area of foreign policy, recognizes that there has been a degree of consensus and convergence of views in the conduct of American foreign policy during significant parts of the postwar period.

During the immediate postwar period, a consensus emerged about the continuing projection of American power in Western Europe and Japan. During that same period, there may have been the theoretical opportunity but there was no desire to expand the American capacity to project power abroad toward the realization of an American empire that would resemble the historical European empires of the eighteenth and nineteenth centuries.

Yet major foreign policy issues have been continually contested throughout the postwar period, and a significant line can be drawn between Liberal approaches and Conservative approaches in numerous areas of foreign policy. These included the debate between a Conservative position emphasizing the importance of American nuclear sufficiency including deterrent capacity, as contrasted with Liberal proposals for the internationalization of nuclear weapons at the United Nations or for a unilateral nuclear freeze by the United States. They also included the support for American military buildup through NATO in Europe and for continuing American military presence in Asian allied nations. The contrasting view was critical of American actions in support of a containment policy against the Soviet Union on the ground that such a policy reflected unrealistic, ideologically based assessments of the threat from the Soviet Union and its Communist allies or satellites including Communist China and North Vietnam. To a degree, Liberals also argued that American policies that were designed to strengthen alliances with various pro-Western states in the world, that had ranged from Iran in the Middle East to Taiwan in Asia, were excessive projections of American power abroad, as contrasted with the need for greater American support for the United Nations and its international agencies as well as a greater contribution of economic aid to Third World and developing nations. A dramatic illustration is the difference in meaning between the term "Cold Warrior" as used by Conservatives and Liberals. For most Conservatives, a Cold Warrior referred to a person who advocated strong measures in defense of what was termed the free world in the "long twilight struggle" that needed to be waged against Soviet Communist aggression and subversion.[7] For many Liberals, the term Cold Warrior referred to a fanatical person whose paranoia led him to place himself in the position of fighting the ideological specter of communism and its insidious witchcraft in an unnecessary and imaginary war.

In a sketch of the differences between examples of contrasting positions of Liberalism and Conservatism on these contested issues, their divergence parallels the difference between the Realist tradition and the Idealist tradition in American foreign policy. The Realist tradition has supported the stress on protection of national interest where interests are identified with more material factors, including territorial integrity, security interests, and economic assets. The Idealist tradition supports a greater stress on America's role in supporting democracy and human rights, including social and economic rights, of citizens within all nation-states of the world.

American Conservatism has bridged the dichotomy between "protection of the national interest" and "advancement of universal human rights" in two ways. In one way, selective support for human rights has been utilized as a component of a policy whose goal is to support the national interest. One example was the human rights outreach to dissidents in the Soviet Union or in other Communist states in Eastern Europe, which contributed to the national-interest goal of weakening the Soviet Union as a major military adversary power. A second way is to recognize that the correct interpretation of national interest can include a degree of support for American values. An example is the effort to realize greater international stability through support for the spread of democracy and for economic aid in poor countries. The basic justification for American Realism and Conservatism is that the projection of American power abroad in U.S. foreign policy through nuclear sufficiency, major coalitions with European and Asian states, and regional defense agreements with various states in the Third World have resulted in the absence of major world wars during the past nearly 70 years, in sharp contrast to the catastrophic world wars that took place during the preceding 30 years. This realistic appraisal does not represent triumphalism since it is compatible with a recognition in retrospective analysis of significant errors in policy during the entire postwar period. From the Conservative perspective, the achievement of a degree of stability in the international order in the postwar period through American leadership in the projection of military power outside the territorial boundaries of the United States has contributed to the possibility of roads to freedom and democracy for a large number of states in the aftermath of large colonial empires, brutal totalitarian regimes, and two world wars.

For the portrait of Conservatism in foreign policy, it is also necessary to take note of Conservative criticism of aspects of Liberalism or Idealism in foreign policy. One area of this criticism is its opposition to Idealist or Liberal efforts to strengthen the role of the United Nations, particularly in Security Affairs. Conservatives accept the role of the United Nations as an international forum for discussion of issues, as a mechanism for some appropriate humanitarian intervention, as a keeper of peace in minor conflicts, and as an organization whose special agencies can make important contributions in particular projects in health, education, and economic development. Such a realistic recognition, however, excludes a transfer to the United Nations of control of security issues that can impinge upon American national interest, including an international legal system that could indict or try American military or civilian leaders. One important reason for this opposition to the extension of the power of the United Nations is that this international organization is judged to be politicized, that is, its decision-making procedures have been shown to be subject to political manipulation by a majoritarian coalition of Third World states often allied with Russia or China. The influence of this political majority is evident in the function of the agencies whose burden is the protection of human rights, with the result of selective criticism of a few designated states, such as Rhodesia and South Africa in the past and Israel past and present, and selective avoidance of criticism against violations by states in the political majority, including Zimbabwe and Libya.

One historical example may serve to illustrate the importance of the blurring of the distinction between juridical decision making and political decision making. In the development in the United Nations of the norms for international justice through an International Criminal Court, the assumption has been that the court operates as an apolitical juridical institution. Its function is considered to be analogous to that of a judicial proceeding in issues of domestic crime. The international context, however, would demonstrate an inevitable political dimension that blurs the distinction between a judicial procedure and a political decision.

Significant examples of the inseparability of seemingly juridical decisions on human rights issues from political considerations of strategic interest in consequence of juridical decisions were particularly noteworthy during the Carter administration, with its strong advocacy of human rights as "the soul of American foreign policy." In the late 1970s, there was a judicial determination that both North Korea and South Korea were guilty of violations of human rights with an ensuing recommendation that member states of the UN should reduce the arms supply to both North Korea and South Korea. As a juridical verdict, there was no distinction made on political grounds between the two States. Yet as a matter of political reality, the Soviet Union and China, which were the primary donors of arms to North Korea, would not reduce these shipments while the then president of the United States, in response to obligations to the United Nations, was prepared to cut American arms supplies to South Korea. Thus, the realistic consequence of this apolitical, juridical decision would be that a dictatorial ally of the Soviet Union would be advantaged while a much more democratic ally of the United States would be disadvantaged. The status of the United States as a "reliable ally" in maintaining the peace on the Korean peninsula would be weakened. The political consequences of seemingly impartial juridical decisions are relevant for the desirability or the harmfulness of these decisions.

A much more consequential example is provided by a plausible interpretation of the Iranian Revolution in 1979. President Carter's advocacy of human rights was carried out by the establishment of a new position in the State Department, namely, an assistant secretary for human rights. Accordingly, there was strengthened American policy directed against the Shah of Iran for his violations of free speech and his intelligence agency's suppression of street protests by the Mullahs. The consequence of this limitation on the exercise of authoritarian power by the Shah was the weakening of his regime due to the increase in the protests of the Islamists against his secular government. The outcome that was projected by the State Department's human-rights advocates was to bring about the election of a leading pro-democracy politician, Shapour Bakhtiar, to the office of the prime minister of Iran. In the event, Bakhtiar's government lasted less than 48 hours. With the arrival of the Ayatollah Khomeini from Paris, Bakhtiar fled to Europe where he was subsequently assassinated by a team from the Iranian Revolutionary Guard. Although the practices of the Shah in violation of the human rights of the Mullahs were temporarily restrained, the consequence of the replacement of the Shah by the Ayatollah Khomeini represented a great setback for both strategic interests and human rights. This example strengthens the relevant Conservative thesis that advocacy of human rights cannot be separated from the political consequences of such advocacy in a realistic foreign policy.

The opening theme of this section of the chapter contrasted the concept of fraternity with its correlative opposite of otherhood. The ideal of fraternity in international relations, with reference to the United Nations, was expressed in poetic terms by Alfred Lord Tennyson in a poem that President Harry Truman, who was "present at the creation" of the United Nations, carried in his wallet. The relevant lines of the poem read:

> Till the war-drum throbb'd no longer, and the battle-flags were
>   furl'd
> In the Parliament of man, the Federation of the world.[8]

The contrasting value lacks the visionary scope of Tennyson's poem. Yet, a policy of support for American national interests that was initiated in the postwar period with the Truman doctrine, as applied to Greece and Turkey and subsequently followed by the inauguration of NATO, has provided a basis for international peace more effectively than the idealistic vision of a "federation of the world" that supports pursuit of universal human rights throughout the world.

For the purpose of differentiation between Conservative and Liberal approaches to foreign policy, the distinction between support for the national interest and support for universal human rights has been sketched in polar terms. In historical situations, however, this differentiation functions as differing emphases and priorities. It would be a canard to portray Liberalism as completely ignoring support for national interests in foreign policy, although it would be legitimate to recognize its identification of national interest with foreign aid abroad rather than with military alliance or to note its consideration of American projection of power in support of national interests in the postwar period as having been excessive. Along such lines, within some enclaves of liberal thought, a lessening of American ability to project power abroad or to possess the capacity for intervention would be beneficial to the United States and to the world. Similarly, Conservatives do not completely ignore support for human rights in American foreign policy, although they accord it a lesser priority.

In important periods of twentieth-century history, support of national interests has been accompanied by support of human rights in American foreign policy. Thus, the two greatest victories of American foreign policy in the twentieth century, the destruction of the Nazi regime in Europe and the containment and collapse of the Soviet regime, were motivated in pursuit of American national interests even though they resulted in great improvement in human rights for large populations. Despite the recognition that these theoretically opposing tendencies may be conjoined in particular historical situations, there remains a significant conceptual difference between the Liberal approach, driven by a degree of faith in the possibilities of international human rights or universal brotherhood, and the Conservative approach, which reflects its great concern for protection of national interests in a world in which forces of destructiveness and disorder are never eroded.

III. THE THIRD TIER: A TRIAD OF ATTITUDINAL AND VALUE DISJUNCTIONS

The differences between Conservatism and Liberalism can be examined beyond the concepts of liberty, equality, and fraternity, through an analysis of disjunctive attitudes and values. This third tier will include the analysis of the distinction between the "given" and the "taken" or "chosen," the division between the attitude that emphasizes historical continuity as opposed to belief in the possibilities of historical discontinuity or transformation, and the disjunction between a morality of institutional responsibility and a morality of ultimate ends or ultimate commitment.

A. *Conservatism and Liberalism: The "Given" and the "Taken" or "Chosen"*

1. The Given Versus the Taken or Chosen in Religious, Metaphysical, and Moral Thought

In seeking to identify a third tier of fundamental attitudes or presuppositions that distinguish Conservatism from Liberalism, one significant analytical distinction is that between perceiving or structuring the world as "given" and perceiving or structuring the world as "taken" or "chosen." The polarity between these two approaches can be traced in such diverse domains as religious thought, metaphysics, and morals. The significance of this distinction for Conservatism and Liberalism also is demonstrable in differing interpretations of human nature.

In religious thought, this polarity can be identified in the difference between an emphasis upon the Creator and the values of the Created, in contrast to an emphasis upon the Redeemer and the values of Redemption. An emphasis upon Creation tends to bring with it a sense of obligation toward the preceding and given realities of the world. A virtue that accompanies this sense of obligation has been identified by George Santayana, a philosopher who has also authored works in Conservative political philosophy, in his *Reason in Religion* as "piety," which Santayana defines as "loyalty to the sources of our being."[9] An emphasis upon Redemption tends to bring with it the opportunity for individual choice in changing the existing conditions of the world, often accompanied by messianic faith in an ideal world in which the transformation of humanity is to be realized.

Criticisms have often been formulated, both on secular grounds and on nontraditional religious grounds, of a religious emphasis on the "Given," particularly with its virtue of piety. Thus, Bertrand Russell's Liberalism in his essay "A Free Man's Worship" asserts that a free person must "defy with Promethean constancy the evil of a hostile universe, keep its evil ever before us, ever actively hated."[10] Such a perspective provides a starting point for Russell's account of proposed "roads to freedom" that suggest changes in the ways in which society is ordered.

In metaphysics, the polarity between the "Given" and the "Taken" or "Chosen" can also be delineated. The Classical Metaphysical tradition involves a quest for that immutable Being or beings (whether Forms, Substance, Extension, Monads, Mind, Matter, or atoms) that are "necessarily presupposed" or "Given," in order to explain the everyday appearances and empirical objects of the world. The metaphysical views of Pragmatic analysis, for example, differ in their explicit negation of the identification of Being with an immutable entity as antecedently Given, but involve an interpretation of the ultimate realities of the world to be those entities or beings that are taken to exist as a result of the processes of future and ongoing scientific inquiry.

A parallel division is readily demarcated in the interpretation of morals. One perennial approach requires that moral decisions be grounded in fixed and unchanging prior structures. The nature of these prior structures has taken different forms in different philosophical periods and environments. These have ranged from Sinaitic revelation in Biblical interpretation and the structure of the form of the good in Platonism, to the rational demonstrations of the existence of Natural Law in medieval philosophy and the metaphysical presuppositions of the rational moral principle in the Enlightenment, to innate Intuitions in twentieth-century philosophy. In contrast, John Dewey stressed the interpretation of moral laws or principles as empirical hypotheses that are open to revision and are chosen in light of the analysis of their future consequences for social stability and human growth. In a different representation of the emphasis on the Taken or the Chosen that provided the basis for a political approach toward an extreme political movement to the "Left" of Liberalism, Existentialist ethics has argued that moral decisions have no antecedent basis in any given standard, but are to be understood as choices affirmed or commitments adopted by individuals in a nihilistic and contingent universe.

Moral issues that are debated in contemporary social thought also reflect Liberal and Conservative differences over the priority of the Given versus the Taken or Chosen. An analysis of the ways in which persons are related to their environing circumstances exhibits a spectrum of possibilities that range between those relationships that are perceived to be virtually completely Given, and those relationships perceived to be virtually completely Taken or Chosen. Thus, at one end of the spectrum the past history, genetic inheritance, ethnic identity, native language, and gender of a person are considered to be Given. From this perspective, a person's relationship to his past history is Given such that those who would invent or revise the facts of their past history are often considered to be living a lie or committing a fraud, rather than choosing or taking an alternative interpretation of their own historical past. Again, although many persons choose to transcend their ethnic identity, the ethnic inheritance of a person can be considered to be a Given. A person's relationship to his genetic inheritance also represents a position at the Given end of the spectrum, although the possibility of choice of genes is apparently within the realm of scientific achievement. Similarly, Conservative thought has assigned greater importance to genetic inheritance. Conservative tendencies in education, for example, have assigned greater importance to genetic inheritance than Liberal tendencies, which stress the dimensions of change that are open to environmental influence. The native language of a person appears to be a Given so that a decision to replace the native language by a chosen language does not establish an alternative native language but replaces the Given by a second or chosen language. The relationship between sexuality or gender and the Given or Chosen has been contested. Although there may be a consensus against the use of sexual stereotypes of masculine identity or feminine identity in child development, the idea of raising children in neutral sexuality so that the choice of gender could be decided in later life is not generally practiced. The question of individual choice in taking gender identities emerges only in later life, and attitudes toward the exercise of choice in this area probably do reflect, as a matter of empirical sociology, differences between Conservatives and Liberals.

The contrary view is asserted in Sartrean Existentialism, according to which the individual's situation is never determined by previous facts or the Given. Every human relationship to the environing circumstances is freely chosen by the individual self, including, for Sartre, the creation of his own self-identity. Accordingly, the

Givenness of one's birth is interpreted as an exercise in free choice. The Sartrean claim has been supported by the interesting argument that if the person, upon reaching self-consciousness about the facts of his birth, usually in adolescence, decides not to commit suicide, then he can be said to have freely chosen the option of his being born.

Even if one were to accept the thesis of the virtual impossibility for personal development to take place without the Givens of a historical past, such as genetic inheritance, sexual identity, or, arguably, a native language, it is plausible that persons could be raised in neutral religion or neutral citizenship with the decision as to religious membership or civic obligation postponed until the person's arrival at an age to which responsible choice is ascribed. Nonetheless, contemporary social practice generally involves the decision regarding initial religious affiliation or citizenship to be given at birth rather than chosen at maturity. In this connection, most nation-states mandate citizenship to be obligatory at birth with specified conditions upon the choice of abdication of citizenship, such as prior payment of taxes.

In educational practice, an explicit demarcation has long been drawn between the Conservative approaches identified as "classical" education and the Liberal approaches identified as "progressive" education. The significance of this division as reflecting the distinction between the Given and the Taken can be demonstrated through the emphasis in the classical curriculum upon the study of the canon, or the "Given" great works that the present has inherited from the past. In contrast, progressive education has tended to emphasize curricula that are chosen and electives that are taken by the individual student so that each person can become the source of his own authority in critical inquiry and free expression.

The question as to whether the option of vocation or the option of marriage is Given or Chosen varies with the practices of a culture. Traditional societies, whose practices go far beyond contemporary American Conservatism, have sought to ensure that the preceding generation maintains control over the marital choice or the vocational choice of the next generation through marriages arranged by parents and vocations inherited from parents. The Conservative tendency, through emphasis on given familial obligation and the role of given authority, has been directed toward some limitations of complete freedom of choice in areas of vocation and marriage. The Liberal tendency, through its emphasis on individual freedom and on the legitimacy of skepticism toward given authority, has sought to expand the choices available for the next generation in areas of vocation and marriage. Accordingly, Liberal critics can charge Conservatism with rigidity and the risks of excessive domination by the past in these areas, while Conservative critics of Liberalism can charge it with the risks of greater disorder and societal breakdown.

In the many and complex dimensions of human relationships, neither the possibility of complete coercion by the past nor the possibility of complete freedom from the past in shaping the future appears to be available, so human options in advancing social change require some mixture of the Given and the Taken or the Chosen. In the recent history of the United States, Conservatives have tended to be more concerned with the preservation or conservation of various institutions of American life including religion, traditional marriage, and constitutional practices, while Liberals have been more focused upon the possibilities of reform. Decision making by Conservatives and Liberals cannot be bound by affinities for the Given or the Taken in general, but will and should vary with the specific nature of the Given and the empirical possibilities of the Chosen.

2. The Given Versus the Taken or Chosen in Interpretations of Human Nature in Its Political Context

Political theories in which justifications have been developed for Authority, Sovereignty, or the State have as a rule also provided interpretations of human nature. These interpretations exhibit a great range of differences in their ascription of the Given and the Taken or Chosen, that is, between the thesis of a fixed human nature with unchanging fundamental characteristics and a plastic human nature that is open to possibilities of the transformation of its fundamental character.

In an effort to identify a spectrum of the interpretations of human nature between fixity and plasticity, the Hobbesist view of Man that was developed in his sketch of the original State of Nature can be referred to as representative on the Conservative side of the divide, and the Deweyan view of Human Nature can be referred to as representative on the Liberal side of the divide.[11]

For the Hobbesist, a fixed human nature possesses as its basic desire, drive, or right the protection and preservation of the self and its interests with an accompanying willingness to use virtually all possible means for the realization of its basic desire. In accord with this interpretation of fixed human nature, the Hobbesist recognizes that human beings will always have the need to place locks on the doors of their homes for security and the need to protect any contracts into which they have entered with a reservoir of power. Consequently, for the Hobbesist, war or the readiness for war is a perpetual aspect of human history. From this perspective, the modification of human functioning in the social order is possible, but the complete transformation of the human condition is a wishful, illusory, or delusionary misinterpretation of such a fixed human nature.

The Hobbesist view does not represent the ultimate pole in the spectrum of interpretations of fixed human nature that has had an impact within Conservative thought to the present. For the Hobbesist, human nature is innately aggressive and potentially brutal in its drive to protect or secure its interests, but Hobbes's portrait of the rational pursuit of interests by fixed human nature does not include self-destructive or malicious behavior. Thus, the Hobbesist, like the Machiavellian, recognizes that persons will wreak havoc in the protection of their interests, but unlike the figure of a Machiavel, as envisaged by Shakespeare in the person of Iago, human beings do not act to hurt others maliciously or seek to destroy another for the pleasure of the activity at the price of harm to their own interest or at the cost of their own self-destruction. The Hobbesist's sad record of human nature, which reaches its nadir in the well-known phrase that life can become "solitary, poore, nasty, brutish and short," does not manifest the "motiveless malignity" which Coleridge ascribed to Iago's human nature or exhibit the genocidal realities that have punctuated the twentieth century. Consequently, the interpretation of human nature that is required to explain the political history of the twentieth century involves recognition of other elements, such as malice or self-destructiveness, as part of fixed human nature beyond the Hobbesist conception of man as driven by rational self-interest.

American Conservative thought in the postwar period demonstrated an effort to recognize the significance of the apparent reversal of Progressive Enlightenment in the regressive genocidal actions that preceded and took place during the Second World War. One example of this aspect of American Conservative thought is the importance ascribed to the theological writings of Reinhold Niebuhr. The Niebuhrian perspective, according to which human nature was rendered to be consistent with the Christian doctrine of "Original Sin," influenced the Conservative critique of Liberalism for its failure to appreciate the reality of Evil.[12] Thus, the events that had dominated a significant portion of the political history of the twentieth century could not be explained by a Hobbesist kind of "interest theory" of human nature, but required that an alternative and darker understanding of human nature should be applied to the study of political behavior. The more recent developments that have taken place after the immediate postwar period and the period identified as "The Cold War," such as recurrent genocides, terrorism, and the ubiquitous phenomenon of suicide bombings, have heightened the relevance of the understanding of human nature within American Conservatism.

For the Deweyan, human nature is plastic. Thus human nature, throughout its long history, has adapted to harsh historical environments by developing its potential for survival, often through the use of force. The plasticity of human nature indicates its available opportunities to adapt in different ways to an environment that has been rendered more secure by virtue of the development of scientific knowledge. These opportunities include potentialities for cooperative enterprise, greater understanding of the world and of the self, as well as heightened opportunities for peaceful discourse and communication among all persons who share common human nature. In accord with this interpretation of plastic human nature, Deweyans have advanced social policies particularly on the reform of democracy and on Liberal education. Deweyans sought to transform what they considered to be the authoritarian public school into a cooperative democratic forum for critical inquiry. For Dewey, the exercise of authority for security and order in families and schools should depend upon the rationality and cooperativeness of the members of the institution rather than upon the power of its ruler. From this perspective, the modification of the conduct of human nature in society could be extended to lead to substantial change within the record of human history. Such change was extended to include support for the project of the abolition of war, that is, a convention for "outlawing" war along the lines proposed in the Kellogg-Briand pact of 1928, as a means for resolving disputes among groups and nations.

The Deweyan view does not represent the ultimate pole of interpretations of plastic human nature that has had an impact within Liberal thought. More than a century before Deweyan Liberalism, the Enlightenment vision of Condorcet suggested the progressive perfectibility of human nature. Condorcet's vision included transcendence of imperial colonialism and war toward universal peace. Beyond these achievements, Condorcet's interpretation of the Enlightenment projected the extension of the length of human life and the transformation of human nature. Consonant with Condorcet's Enlightenment vision, twentieth-century Liberalism (even as it rejected the eschatology of Marxism) was influenced by an interpretation of history as demonstrating that different stages in progressive historical development could bring about transformative improvement in human nature.

Along these lines, the interpretation of human nature that developed within Liberalism moved beyond Millean Liberalism and the Deweyan view of the plasticity of human nature to include a measure of Positive Liberty, with its support for the liberation of the human potential toward the realization of the perfectibility of human nature. Accordingly, Liberal thought has included a belief that social progress through scientific inquiry in the natural and social sciences as well as greater international cooperation could lead to the prevention or elimination of poverty, war, and other scourges that have accompanied human history from the beginning.

In contrast to the Liberal emphasis upon the perfectibility of human nature, the Conservative emphasis has been upon the inevitable limitations of human nature as demonstrated by the reality of evil. Consequently, utopian aspirations have not only been abandoned in Conservative thought but have been a major target of the Conservative criticism of Liberalism. The Conservative approach has been more limited with its emphasis upon the preservation of existing values that require protection recurrently against differing enemies of freedom and order. The defense of freedom permits and supports incremental reforms that result in various kinds of human progress. Such an approach by Conservatism can be criticized as failing to motivate human aspiration toward social and political ideals, particularly in view of the importance of the consideration expressed by the phrase: "a man's reach should exceed his grasp."[13] Yet the rejection of utopianism does not exclude sustained efforts at amelioration of the human condition, including dramatic rates of change in the reduction of illness or poverty and significant limitations upon the length and destructiveness of future wars. As discussed in the next section, these indices of improved outcomes do not involve radical or revolutionary historical discontinuities derived from a transformation of human nature.

B. Conservatism and Liberalism: Historical Continuity or the Possibility of Historical Transformation

Polar interpretations of history as demonstrating inevitable continuity, or as exhibiting a possibility of radical and positive discontinuity, were developed independently of the emergence of Conservative or Liberal attitudes in political philosophy. Both interpretations can be understood as deep truths in the sense in which Oscar Wilde defined a deep truth as anything the opposite of which is also a deep truth. Despite the platitudinous nature of the polarity, however, there are strong reasons for the demonstration of the continuity of history just as there are good reasons for the emphasis that has been placed upon the possibility of change and discontinuity within history.

One possible escape route from these contending perennial truths is an effort to distinguish between a Liberal view and a Conservative view of historical change. Within Liberalism, there has developed a belief that a wide range of choices among institutions is available to every historical society as well as a belief that rational and scientific methods provide great scope for the transformation of any society. Within Conservatism, there has developed the view that there are significant limitations on the range of the choices that are available to every particular historical society as well as a belief that there is a significant gap between the ability to apply rational and scientific methods in the natural sciences as distinct from their application in the sphere of historical practice. These conflicting approaches to historical change have been exemplified, on the one hand, in the Liberal political philosophy of John Dewey and in Conservative political philosophies, on the other hand, in the views of Oakeshott. The comparison and contrast between these two contending interpretations of historical change and an analysis of some of the elements that distinguish each interpretation can provide a basis for examination of the adequacy of Conservative and Liberal approaches to historical change that is relevant for the interpretation of contemporary American Conservatism.

The Deweyan perspective within American Liberalism in the twentieth century had placed great stress upon the development of "scientific method." The discovery of a method that can progressively increase reliable knowledge of the natural environment within every human society brings with it the potentiality for the application of this method to the political, social, and economic problems that have existed in every historical society. For Dewey, the challenge for Liberalism was to achieve in the social, economic, and political spheres a degree of reliable knowledge and the ability to apply this knowledge to the resolution of the historical problems in a way that was analogous to the ability of the scientific method to resolve what he identified as the "problematic situations" that arose in confronting the natural world. Accordingly, the key to achieving progressive change in an historical society was the development of the social sciences to the comparable degree of prediction and control that had been realized in the natural sciences.

In the analysis of the Deweyan thesis, it is useful to identify the significance of the term "progressive." For Deweyans, the scientific method guaranteed the progressivity of knowledge. Progress in science was inevitable since the scientific hypotheses that were developed in experimental investigations were to be accepted by the community of scientific inquiry only if they explained all the data that the previous hypothesis had explained as well as predicting new data that could be verified and was confirmed. Progressive improvement of any historical institution, whether the educational system or the economic practices of a society, could be realized by the continuing application of the method of the social sciences to the theory and practice of the institutions. For Deweyan Liberalism, the promise of the social sciences, such as political science, economics, or what Dewey had termed the "science of education," could be realized in the progressive development of a historical society: the United States.

Unlike Marxism, which had interpreted progressive development to be historically inevitable with the coming to power of the proletarian class, Deweyan Liberalism bore within it a recognition of the fragility of progress and the commitment to democracy. For Dewey, the challenge of education for citizenship was to bring into being a democratic public of "concerned citizens" who would be capable of investigating the options available for the improvement of society and of participating in the realization of the successful application of the social sciences to the problematic situations that required resolution in their society.

Deweyans were not unaware of the realistic appraisal that the promise of social scientific knowledge, particularly regarding predictability, had not yet been fully realized. They also recognized the challenge involved in arriving at a democratic decision by free individuals who would carry out the application of social scientific knowledge to long-standing institutions that embodied vested interests and latent human prejudices. At the same time, the Deweyan Liberal vision could look forward to the progressive overcoming of these difficulties so that an America free of poverty and war was a conceivable future outcome along the path of progress.

The expectations generated by the applicability of the scientific method in Deweyan liberalism have been lessened by some disillusionment regarding the link between scientific progress and societal progress that took place during the threat of nuclear war or of chemical or biological warfare. Yet, confidence in the wisdom of transferring the consensus among scientists into economic or social policy has continued to shape liberalism. The use of the study of economics in the operation and control of American economic practices has grown. Despite the progress in the field of economics, confidence in planned economies has weakened since the 1930s.

One of the more dramatic illustrations of the applicability of science involves the debate over climate change. Almost all members of the Liberal community accept what is labeled as the "scientific consensus" for global warming and opt for the introduction of constraints on economic practices. Many Conservatives contend that a scientific consensus falls short of the kind of proof and of convergence among those involved in the scientific inquiry that is required for instituting extreme measures of change in economic policy. The standards for acceptance of a scientific hypothesis as formulated by Charles Peirce, who identified progressivity among scientific hypotheses, was not "consensus," which can be arrived at via extension of a trend or by political agreement, but the stronger criterion of convergence through verification of experimentation by all the members of a community of inquiry. One response by some environmentalists has been to avoid the necessity of further scientific proof by labeling the Conservatives as "deniers" of science for the sake of vested interests who resist necessary rational change. One rejoinder by some Conservatives has been the contention that the advocates of theories of global warming have been motivated by an animus or hostility against capitalism and free markets, which foster economic growth rather than scientific evidence. From this perspective, the environmentalist efforts to save the planet are rooted in preexisting intentions to limit American economic growth. In theory, all aspects of the dispute should be resolved by future scientific inquiry, although aspects of the political debate demonstrate differences in attitudes that may not be resolvable by future scientific inquiry.

The Deweyan Liberal approach emphasized its pragmatic tendency rather than the utopian temptation. Just as absolute truth for Deweyan pragmatists was asymptotic for the process of progressive scientific inquiry, so a vision of utopia was unnecessary in order to undertake Liberal reform. Yet, as previously noted, the issue of the possibility of revolutionary transformation of the human condition in history has generated conflicting responses from Liberals and Conservatives. The differing approaches to the term "revolution" in these usages indicate a difference in attitude toward the general phenomenon of historical change as distinct from a particular evaluation of the consequences of a specified instance of rapid change in a political, social, or cultural domain. This generalized antipathy toward the possibility of positive revolutionary transformation in history is an example of the link between the

English Conservative thought of Edmund Burke and the tradition of American Conservatism.

The Burkean themes within American Conservatism have stressed the limitations that historical institutions place upon radical or revolutionary historical change within any society. From this perspective, different societies represent historical realizations of their respective institutional traditions, or in the phrase of the English philosopher of Conservatism, Michael Oakeshott, "the intimations of a tradition," in plural ways. Accordingly, any particular society is not available for transformation by a universal social scientific methodology.

From this perspective, the belief that scientific method can be applied to provide progressive solutions to societal problems is illusory or exaggerated. In an analogous context, Burke stressed the difficulty of transferring technological knowledge to the understanding of political institutions. Burke wrote:

> An ignorant man who is not fool enough to meddle with his clock, is however sufficiently confident to think he can safely take to pieces, and put together at his pleasure, a moral machine of another guise, importance and complexity, composed of far other wheels, and springs, and balances, and counteracting and co-operating powers. Men little think how immorally they act in rashly meddling with what they do not understand.[14]

Along these lines, Conservative thought accords with aspects of an Oakeshottian criticism of "Rationalism." The assumption that a person can possess a kind of competence in "political science" that can provide a basis for institutional change in the absence of a tradition of practice or experience within the political, social, or human environment of particular historical institutions represents, for Oakeshottians, a path to catastrophe. From that perspective, excessive confidence in the social sciences, and particularly the extension of that confidence to the thesis that persons have mastered "the science of history," is partly responsible for the episodes of moral regression that took place in the totalitarian regimes during the twentieth century.

Conservative skepticism toward the universal applicability of social scientific knowledge as well as Conservative ascription of value to particular historical traditions need not lead to Relativism.

Particular historical traditions admit of objective comparative evaluation. Conservative thought can conclude that scientific predictability of the consequences of particular kinds of political arrangements is not available while also recognizing that some forms of institutional practice are more beneficial or harmful to members of the society than others. Consistent with the recognition of plural traditions, Conservative thought can accept the view that every society will require some structure of political authority and some framework for economic development. The difference in value between a structure of authority that is autocratic, and relies almost exclusively on coercive force to achieve its acceptance, as distinct from a structure of authority that is democratic, and relies on electoral processes to achieve consent of the governed, is not a matter of taste or solely reflective of different historical traditions. An objective difference in value can be affirmed even if the understanding of such a difference is not analogous to the comparison of differing observational outcomes in a crucial experiment in physics.

Similarly, the difference in value between a command economy, in which administered prices are set by the government, and a free-market economy, in which prices are set by market intersection between the supply of goods provided by producers and the demand for goods by consumers, is also not a matter of taste or solely reflective of different historical traditions. An objective difference in value can be affirmed even if the understanding of such a difference is not a verifiable theorem of social science but involves some recognition of the value ascribed to freedom. Thus, Conservative thought includes the recognition of the need and potential for social change and reform, even if it does not share Liberal confidence in the progressivity of reform derived from the applicability of social scientific knowledge.

The Conservative perspective can recognize three different features of historical change, which may avoid the ascription of being platitudinous because they have been subject to denial in modern history. One aspect of Conservatism is the emphasis on the legitimacy of conserving and preserving institutions or practices that exist and presumably have stood the test of time. A second aspect of Conservatism involves the imagination of disaster so that there is a recognition of the need to protect institutions that are characteristically vulnerable to the phenomenon of a changing environment, including risks of decline, regression, or various kinds of disaster. A third aspect of Conservatism involves the potentiality of reform and change in light of a recognition, as noted above, that some institutions and practices are, on objective grounds, more valuable or preferable than others. Yet, the Conservative position toward historical change involves the denial of the kind of perfectibility of human nature that was envisaged by Condorcet or is implicit in the conception of a continuous progressive movement.

The grounds for this denial of perfectibility can be identified, as noted in the preceding section, with the interpretation of human nature as limited. This negative attitude toward perfectibility can also be identified, as previously noted, with the Conservative reaction and response to the tragic consequences of the attempts to institute a transformative historicist vision in twentieth-century Socialist societies in Europe and Asia.

The Pluralist thesis that is a feature of American Conservative thought involves an alternative argument against historical perfectibility. The Pluralist thesis implies the impossibility that a single rationally coherent set of values can be realized to provide an ideal transformation of historical conditions. The Pluralist thesis, as developed in Isaiah Berlin's "On the Pursuit of the Ideal," can be directed against the main social visions of historical transformation, including systematic progressive reform or what has been termed "social engineering."[15]

The Pluralist argument is that the introduction of any value necessarily brings with it a limitation upon an alternative value in social practice. Thus, to use examples that can be traced back to Plato's "Republic," the realization of an important value, namely that each person is to pursue the vocation for which he is best suited, would necessarily bring with it some denial of the freedom of the individual to pursue a vocation which he likes even though he may not be optimally suited for it. Analogously, the adoption of the value that requires appropriate knowledge as a prerequisite for the right of decision making in an enterprise would necessarily exclude or limit the important democratic value that persons who suffer the consequences of decisions ought to have the right to be involved in the making of these decisions. Examples of these kinds of conflicts or dilemmas are available in all areas of social practice. They serve to deny the possibility of an ideal transformation of the human condition, which will eliminate the grounds for future conflict or mark the realizability of any idealized "end of history."

For educational institutions, there is an inevitable dilemma between the value of excellence that leads to the setting of exclusionary high standards for admission and the value of equality that leads to greater inclusiveness and accessibility through policies of open admission. For judicial institutions, there is an inevitable dilemma between the value of procedures that relate to the idea of justice and require appropriate redress, restitution, reparation, or retribution for the past wrongdoing of a person, as distinct from the value of procedures that relate to social utility and pursue rehabilitation or redemption of the person for the sake of his future life.

For the Pluralist, the inevitability of conflict among plural, competing values implies the negation of the identifiably monist, Platonic, and Marxist visions of perfectibility that represent a background for Liberal progressive aspiration. The vision of perfectibility is replaced by the more Conservative perspective, according to which societies achieve compromises among values. These compromises may avoid historical regression and catastrophe, or they may result in degrees of improvement in the social conditions, but they do not aim at or achieve the transformation of the human condition.

To the extent to which American Liberalism has been motivated by or committed to policies that seek permanent progress in the human condition without sufficient regard to the unavoidable costs of progress or the price paid in the diminution of some values in the realization of the designated Liberal values, the pluralist argument within Conservatism bears critical weight.

These competing attitudes toward historical change do not represent competing empirical hypotheses that are subject to experimental verification. Thus, an attitude that emphasizes historical continuity is not refuted by an environment of change in which innovation of new products flourishes. The rate of change for products like computers, televisions, and pharmaceuticals differs from the rate of change of human institutions and human nature. Similarly, Conservatives would concede that an attitude that emphasizes historical discontinuity and the possibilities of reform is not totally refuted even if the practices of a number of major institutions can be traced back continuously for the entire history of the nation, including the practices that are consistent with the Common Law, according to which "the memory of man runneth not to the contrary."

Consequently, an attitude toward historical change within Conservative and Liberal thought is identified as a background factor rather than as an empirical hypothesis or as a determinant of policy. A Conservative attitude toward historical continuity is compatible with specific policy proposals that support a major change. One significant example is Conservative support for the partial privatization of Social Security after 75 years of governmental funding. A Liberal attitude toward historical discontinuity is compatible with specific policy proposals that oppose major change. The parallel example is the Liberal refusal to consider significant changes in the funding of Social Security despite the extreme change in life expectancy that has taken place between the inception of the program and its current operation. The multiplicity of variations on policy issues, compatible with background attitudes, does not negate the relevance of the disjunction between Conservative emphasis on historical continuities and Liberal emphasis on the possibility of progressive discontinuities.

C. Conservatism and Liberalism: The Morality of Institutional Responsibility and the Morality of Ultimate Ends or Ultimate Commitments

The distinction between the morality of institutional responsibility and the morality of ultimate ends or commitments has been recognized since Weber's essay, "Politics as a Vocation," with his use of these particular terms as a distinction that sheds significant light on the differences between Conservative and Liberal political thought.[16] In his sociological studies, Weber recognized the tendency of institutions to ascribe a high moral ranking to those members who expressed loyalty to the institution. The existence and functioning of institutions over a long period of time have tended to generate a sense of responsibility among participating members such that duties are owed to the institution and are to be fulfilled on grounds of obligation or ties that have been developed through these institutions. Although Weber's essay provided a name for this kind of morality, a "morality of institutional responsibility," the recognition of this type of morality as a distinct branch within moral phenomenology can be traced back across the ages. In this context, it is relevant to note that the root Latin verb of "ligare," which refers to binding, is present in terms like "religion" and "obligation."

A generation earlier, F. H. Bradley recognized the pattern of such a morality in his essay, "My Station and Its Duties."[17] This pattern reflects the value placed upon the ties that bind a particular responsible moral individual to a particular institution, as distinct from a commitment that directs every human being toward universal moral ideals.

Weber's sociological studies of contemporaneous anarchist groups documented a tendency of freedom from obligation to conventional institutions, including the State and the Family. A sense of responsibility toward institutions was replaced by the expressions of commitment for the ultimate ends of every society, such as Peace and Justice. Without ascribing to Liberal political philosophy an endorsement of Anarchism, it can be recognized that the Liberal side of the polarity between these two aspects of morality is closer to a morality of ultimate ends or commitments than is Conservative political philosophy with its greater stress on conserving historical institutions and accordingly supporting a morality of institutional responsibility.

The analysis of any actual moral evaluation of political actions or policies shows that a combination of some elements of an ethic of institutional responsibility must be conjoined with elements of a morality of ultimate ends or commitments. This conclusion is evidenced by examples of the functioning of either one of these two moral perspectives in complete independence of the other. Caricatures of moral behavior are illustrated in such examples.

With respect to a morality of institutional responsibility, the caricature depicts the loyal and devoted person who faithfully carries out his duties and responsibilities toward an institution that is extremely immoral. A clarifying documentation of this caricature took place during the senatorial committee questioning of the mafia chauffeur, Joe Valachi, during the Kefauver hearings on criminal gang behavior in the United States. The testimony of Valachi was challenged as providing excuses for criminal behavior since he consistently located himself outside the places where murder and mayhem were being carried out. Valachi, in response to this challenge, exhibited a degree of moral indignation. He explained that as a responsible driver of the getaway car he was always at his station ready to perform his duties, which necessarily placed him outside the immediate site of the action. To have been in any other place would have been a dereliction of duty, which would have been incompatible with his sense of his moral responsibility and with his sense of his obligation to the organization to which he belonged. These responses led Valachi to an expansion of his understanding of his own morality of institutional responsibility. Thus, he went on to explain to the senatorial committee that he was constant in his obligation to his family, bringing home all of his pay for his work, rather than following the practice of other mafia members who irresponsibly used their gains for ventures outside the norms of traditional family behavior. The relevant point for this context was the way in which these assertions of morality were part of an awareness, or of making oneself unaware, that this obligation was being rendered toward a criminal organization whose practices were immorally brutal. More generally, a morality of institutional responsibility that has no connection to the end for which that responsibility is being exercised can be viewed as grotesque.

A similar caricature can be drawn in the opposite direction. With respect to a morality of ultimate ends or ultimate commitments, the portrait of the idealistic person who labors with enthusiasm in order to solve such great problems as those of war, poverty, or environmental sustainability, while neglecting minimal obligations in relationships with persons with whom he is associated, demonstrates the inadequacy of this kind of morality in the absence of a morality of institutional responsibility. A dramatic interpretation of this theme was carried out by the literary critic Edmund Wilson in his play, *The Little Blue Light*. Wilson's drama is set within the United States of an imaginary 1950s in which a small group of dedicated Liberals are fighting to preserve the rule of law against a combination of religious bigots and fascist bosses. Unfortunately, the Liberal stalwarts of political reform are being assassinated by a diabolical invention identified as "the little blue light." The little blue light is placed in the home of the targeted person by a close associate, friend, or lover and has the property of exploding with devastating effect whenever the distance between the expressions of public morality and the actions of private immorality are wide enough to release the triggering mechanism. The saving remnant of American Liberalism has taken refuge in a Long Island mansion to undertake its political plan for restoration of American democracy. This plan crucially depends upon a political exposé that is being prepared for their institutional publication. The subsequent acts of vanity, lying, and adultery within this elite Liberal group mark the betrayal of their own institution and bring about the setting up and explosion of the little blue light in the last bastion of American Liberalism. Wilson's political theater exhibits a contradictory aspect of American political life in which political idealism with its working commitment toward ultimate moral ends is combined with immorality in personal relations that involves the neglect of responsibilities toward one's own institutions. More generally, the relevant point for this context is the thesis that a morality of ultimate ends or ultimate commitments cannot be successfully carried out in the absence of a culture of moral responsibility, including responsibility for personal relationships and obligations to necessary social institutions.

Apart from the broader philosophical issues raised by the preceding two examples, their relevance for the characterization of American Conservatism and Liberalism is the shared conclusion that both Liberalism and Conservatism must provide some combination of the important features of a morality of institutional responsibility with the important features of a morality of ultimate ends or commitment in their approaches to policy.

At the same time, the ways of combining these two moralities provide a measure of understanding of the differences between Conservatism and Liberalism. This is demonstrable in Social Conservatism with its expression of greater support for traditional institutions in their understanding of commitment to the moral ends of the society. It can also be identified in Economic Conservatism with its greater support for existing commercial and financial institutions in their commitment to the economic welfare of the society. The significance of this differentiation of contending moralities is even more evident in the area of foreign policy.

In the area of Social Conservatism, a review of contested policy options would confirm the support expressed among Conservatives for designated established institutions such as the family, the traditional institution of marriage, and military institutions. One feature of Social Conservatism is found in the field of education. Historically, Conservatives have tended to support educational curricula that focus upon Western culture and upon a "traditional," characteristically patriotic, presentation of American history, as distinct from Liberal advocacy of multiculturalism and support for cosmopolitan and more critical interpretations of American history.

In the case of Economic Conservatism, the morality of institutional responsibility has tended to oppose radical movements toward rapid social change of dominant institutions like free markets and corporate practices. Both Liberals and Conservatives would agree that reform of economic institutions should be governed by decisions regarding the long-term consequences of these reforms in benefits and in costs. Yet, the contending moralities provide background attitudes in support or in opposition of reform, which is partially independent of the calculus of benefits and losses. This is partially occasioned by the general Conservative view that "unanticipated consequences" with negative implications occur more frequently after economic reform policies have been developed than is projected by Liberal optimism.

One significant debate between Liberalism and Conservatism, which is often cast in moral terms, relates to the legitimacy of monetary contributions to political parties and elections. This debate reflects the difference between a morality of institutional responsibility and a morality of ultimate ends, although it can also be structured as a debate over models for democracy. In the model of democracy that can be identified as a "plural interest group" model developed by Joseph Schumpeter, the ideal of the democratic process includes an appropriate "negotiation of consent" among competing interest groups. Economic regulations would be written with recognition of the need for the democratic process to recognize and incorporate "negotiation of consent" among interest groups carried out through their elected political representatives. Accordingly, as part of this process, interest groups would contribute monetarily within the democratic process.

In contrast, most Liberal theory identifies the public interest as excluding any "pollution or contamination" from special interest groups. In the Rousseauvian model of democracy, for example, the public interest was identified with the interests of "the People," with total exclusion from the influence of private persons or private institutions. Economic regulations are to be written to prevent the influence of special interest groups in economic affairs as necessarily contrary to the public interest. The degree of willingness to replace historical particularist institutions or to recognize the special interests that have developed in the economic arena demonstrates, to a degree, the difference between a morality of institutional responsibility and a morality of ultimate ends.

In the case of Conservatism in foreign policy, a morality of institutional responsibility legitimates support for the historical particularist national interests as a realistic goal of American foreign policy. The exercise of institutional responsibility requires the careful and prudent interpretation of what constitutes the permanent national interest as distinct from apparent, unexamined, or transient interests. The rigorous concept of "the national interest" does not extend, for example, to cases where a particular cause has been the subject of extensive media hype through visually provocative imagery. One illustration is the way in which the portrayal of the suffering of the people of Sarajevo on television led the Clinton administration to initiate a bombing campaign against Serbia that lasted eight months. There was no demonstration that the defeat of Serbia, primarily for the sake of independence of Kosovo, was a legitimate national interest of the United States. The exercise of a morality of institutional responsibility also requires critical evaluation of the means to be used to realize the national interests, including the recognition of the possibility that the risks and the costs of the use of some means may outweigh the desired ends that are achievable. Further, the exercise of a morality of institutional responsibility requires the recognition that other sovereign states have their own national interests, so that the realization of one's own national interests includes the need to balance and even harmonize the interests of one's own nation-state with the interests of other states.

Despite these cautionary and irenical aspects of Conservatism in foreign policy, the distance between a morality of institutional responsibility and a morality of ultimate ends in foreign policy remains wide. Pursuit of a morality of ultimate ends has sought to transcend particularist national interests. These transcendent ends have included actions that are ostensibly aimed at universal peace, such as a call for unilateral nuclear disarmament, and are often considered to be trumping actions against narrower national interest policies. These also include programs for the establishment of an international court for criminal justice whose commitment to a neutral juridical process would trump the political compromises that are compatible with national interests. They also include strong support for the jurisdiction of the United Nations over human-rights violations in all member states that is to be carried out without reference to national interest concerns among sovereign nations.

The distinction between the particularism of the morality of institutional responsibility and the cosmopolitanism or universalism of the morality of ultimate ends overlaps significantly with the distinction between Conservatism and Liberalism. The adoption of a morality of institutional responsibility within Conservatism indicates Conservative skepticism to national commitment to ideal ends in foreign policy, such as universal human rights that transcend the national interest.

For Conservatism in foreign policy, there is another important consequence that is implicit in the distinction between a morality of institutional responsibility and a morality of ultimate ends. That distinction signifies the response of Conservatism to one particular strand of Liberal criticism. This strand of Liberal criticism argues that a foreign policy that supports national interests represents an amoral policy of national selfishness or self-interest, for which the appropriate remedy is a moral policy that adopts a cosmopolitan or internationalist perspective. Such a liberal perspective would require that the United States replace the pursuit of its own national interests with the pursuit of a democratic international world order that could realize shared ideals of peace, social progress, and global sustainability among all the nations of the world. Accordingly, with reference to moral terminology, from this Liberal perspective, the contest is not between two kinds of morality but between a Conservative national interest approach that does not rise to the level of morality and a Liberal internationalism that involves commitment to moral ideals. Thus, the assertion of a duality between a morality of institutional responsibility and a morality of ultimate ends changes the framework in which the debate is cast. A debate, which was structured between a disinterested and hence moral point of view and an amoral or interested point of view, has been converted into a debate between two kinds or aspects of morality.

The challenge that emerges subsequent to the recognition of this contrasting duality of moral perspectives or attitudes is in locating the place or priority within the spectrum of these two moralities that is to be ascribed to support for realistic national interest or to support for idealist human-rights advocacy in foreign policy. In developing these priorities, those who assert a morality of institutional responsibility in the formation of American foreign policy recognize that the major social and political institutions of the United States have been developed in accordance with commitments to values that include democracy and liberty. Consequently, a morality of institutional responsibility in foreign affairs would not exclude some measures for the potential expansion of liberty and democracy abroad even as it recognizes its priority for support of national security interests. For Conservatism in foreign policy, the recognition of a morality of institutional responsibility suggests that the priority of protection of national interests will have pride of place to a greater degree over a Liberal morality of ultimate ends with its heightened concern for the values expressed by the "international community" in the forums of the United Nations. The range of disagreement between Conservatives and Liberals in public debates on foreign policy in the national media, which has been identified in this chapter as the surface tier of American political thought, has received repeated and widespread recognition. The distinction between a morality of institutional responsibility and a morality of ultimate ends or ultimate commitments is connected as an underlying tier of disjunction of attitudes between Conservative and Liberal political thought.

CONCLUDING NOTE

Shortly after the election of Bill Clinton as president of the United States in 1992, the American historian Arthur Schlesinger, Jr.

welcomed this outcome as a Liberal victory. In placing it in historical context, Schlesinger reviewed the presidential outcomes of the
entire twentieth century. He concluded that there had been a pattern of oscillation between Liberal and Conservative presidencies.

Thus Professor Schlesinger identified President William Howard Taft as followed by President Woodrow Wilson as the successive Conservative and Liberal presidents within the opening two
decades of the century. Again, Presidents Harding and Coolidge
were the Conservative presidents whose policies in office in the
1920s contrasted with the Liberal policies of the New Deal throughout the ensuing presidency of Franklin D. Roosevelt of the 1930s.
The presidency of Dwight Eisenhower marked the Conservative
decade of the 1950s, which was followed by the Liberalism of the
1960s during the presidencies of John F. Kennedy and Lyndon B.
Johnson. The presidency of Ronald Reagan and of George W. Bush
had marked the revival of Conservatism in the 1980s. Schlesinger
concluded his review with the optimistic claim that the election of
Bill Clinton would lead to a Liberal decade in American politics.
Arthur Schlesinger, Jr.'s review did not anticipate the reversal of
fortune that was the election of a Republican Congress under the
leadership of the Conservative Newt Gingrich in 1994. Nor did he
anticipate that Clinton's response to the challenge of an opposition Congress would be a form of "triangulation" which located his
pattern of successful compromises between the Liberal wing of the
Democratic Party and the Conservative opposition in Congress. In
relevance to this thesis of the century-long oscillation between Liberal and Conservative presidencies, however, the twenty-first century has noted the relatively Conservative presidency of George W.
Bush, which was succeeded by the Liberal policies of President
Barack Obama.

As of the date of this writing, the beginnings of the campaign
for the 2016 presidency also reflect an ongoing division between
Conservative candidates for the Republican nomination and other
Liberal potential candidates for the Democratic nomination. The
thesis of this chapter has been that underlying this surface tier of
disagreement there are two other tiers that relate to the surface
tier. One of them is a conceptual tier with different interpretations
of such concepts as Liberty, Equality, and Fraternity. The other
is an attitudinal tier with disjunction over attitudes toward the

Given versus the Taken or the Chosen; the necessary continuity of human history versus the possibility of historical transformation and the morality of institutional responsibility versus the morality of ultimate ends or ultimate commitments.

NOTES

1. W. S. Gilbert and Arthur Sullivan, *Iolanthe or The Peer and the Peri*, dir. Edward E. Rice, prod. Collier's Standard Opera Company, Bijou Theatre, Boston, December 11, 1882. Accessed August 30, 2014, at: https://archive.org/stream/iolantheorpeera00gilbgoog/iolantheorpeera00gilbgoog_djvu.txt.

2. John Quincy Adams, "She Goes Not Abroad in Search of Monsters to Destroy," July 4, 1821, *The American Conservative* (July 4, 2013). Accessed April 23, 2015, at: http://www.theamericanconservative.com/repository/she-goes-not-abroad-in-search-of-monsters-to-destroy/.

3. Edmund Burke, *Reflections on the Revolution in France* (Philadelphia: Young, Dobson, Carey, and Rice, 1792).

4. Bernard Williams, "The Idea of Equality," in *Philosophy, Politics, and Society: Second Series*, ed. Peter Laslett and W. G. Runciman (Oxford: Basil Blackwell, 1962), 110–131.

5. John Maynard Keynes, *The End of Laissez-Faire*, 3rd impression (London: L. & Virginia Woolf, 1927).

6. William Butler Yeats, *Blood and the Moon*. Accessed October 5, 2014, at: http://cla.calpoly.edu/~pmarchba/TEXTS/POETRY/W_B_Yeats/1933_BloodandtheMoon.pdf.

7. A phrase used in reference to the works of John Lewis Gaddis. See Patrick J. Garrity, "The Long Twilight Struggle," *Claremont Review of Books* 6 (Summer 2006). Accessed December 27, 2014, at: http://www.claremont.org/article/the-long-twilight-struggle/#.VJ9SskCVAA.

8. Alfred Lord Tennyson, *Locksley Hall.* Accessed October 5, 2014, at: http://www.poetryfoundation.org/poem/174629.

9. George Santayana, "Reason in Religion," in *The Life of Reason: The Phases of Human Progress, Vol. 3* (New York: C. Scribner's Sons, 1905). Accessed May 5, 2015, at: http://www.gutenberg.org/files/15000/15000-h/vol3.html#CHAPTER_X.

10. Bertrand Russell, "A Free Man's Worship." Accessed October 5, 2014, at: http://www.academia.edu/1278006/Bertrand_Russell_A_Free_Mans_Worship.

11. See Thomas Hobbes, *Leviathan*, Reissued edition, ed. J. C. A. Gaskin (Oxford: Oxford University Press, [1996] 2008); and John Dewey,

Human Nature and Conduct, New edition (New York: Barnes & Noble, 2008).

12. Reinhold Niebuhr, *The Children of Light and the Children of Darkness* (New York: Charles Scribner's Sons, 1943).

13. Robert Browning, "Andrea del Sarto," line 98, in *Men and Women*, ed. F. B. Pinion (New York: St. Martin's, [1855] 1963).

14. Edmund Burke, *The Works of the Right Hon. Edmund Burke* (London: Holdsworth and Ball, 1834).

15. Berlin's speech delivered on February 15, 1988 at the Turin Opera House, in his acceptance of the inaugural Senator Giovanni Agnelli International Prize and printed in *The New York Review of Books* 35 (March 17, 1988). Accessed December 27, 2014, at: http://www.nybooks.com/articles/archives/1988/mar/17/on-the-pursuit-of-the-ideal/.

16. Max Weber, "Politics as a Vocation," in *The Vocation Lectures*, ed. David Owen and Tracy B. Strong, trans. Rodney Livingstone (Indianapolis, IN: Hackett, 2004), 32–94.

17. F. H. Bradley, "My Station and Its Duties," in *Ethical Studies* (London: Oxford University Press, 1876), 145–192.

3

CONSERVATISM IN AMERICA?
A RESPONSE TO SIDORSKY

PATRICK J. DENEEN

I. The Conservative Tradition, or Tradition as Conservation

Attempting to describe "conservatism" is a daunting task, since the very word points to a contradiction in terms. Conservatism, as David Sidorsky ably suggests, historically occurred as a response to the French Revolution, the first of the modern monistic political ideologies. Articulated by such thinkers as Edmund Burke against the ideology of the French Revolution that gave rise to the Terror, and further developed during the twentieth century in response to the ideologies of Communism and Fascism, conservatism was not so much a philosophy as a *reaction* to the efforts to realize a utopian brand of political philosophy. As such, conservatism is not really an "-ism" at all, but rather a set of dispositions—one that may even constitute a "framework," as Sidorsky writes—that are arrayed against ideology. The effort to describe "conservat*ism*" is perhaps akin to the effort to describe what makes a *New Yorker* cartoon funny. According to the fictional editor of the *New Yorker* in an episode of *Seinfeld*, *New Yorker* cartoons are—perhaps like conservatism—"like gossamer, and one doesn't dissect gossamer."

Conservatism by definition is anti-ideological, and thereby inherently resists reduction to a set of political dogmas. Sidorsky rightly points out, however, that this resistance does imply several positive beliefs, albeit ones possessing a degree of flexibility that allows the conservative simultaneously to defend a set of loosely related positions without himself falling into ideological rigidity. As Sidorsky suggests, the various strands of conservatism overlap in their opposition to "progressivism," which might be positively construed as a positive insistence upon "imperfectability" or even "realism." For conservatives, "realism" means a firm belief in *givenness* (as Sidorsky argues), that is, a reality that is given and not subject to transformation by humans, at least not without grave consequences. Thus, in the first instance, conservatives embrace a realism about the frailty and flaws of human nature, which they hold to be a permanent condition and not one subject to fundamental transformation. Conservatives manifest a realism about the prospects of political amelioration and thus oppose the modern vision of political perfection or redemption.[1] Because something can be imagined and wished for is not tantamount to its realizability. For this reason, conservatives are mistrustful of ideology in all of its forms, since ideology takes the form of a set of political beliefs to which reality is forced to conform. "Rationalism" is one such form of ideology, since political life, and human beings, are not subject to full rationalization. Conservatives can thus come across as obstructionist, "stick in the mud" traditionalists. The danger of conservatism is one of complacency in the face of ameliorable injustice; the danger it seeks to call attention to is the danger accompanying the belief that a kind of "heaven on earth" can be achieved through politics—a belief that has resulted in the death of millions of people since the French Revolution through the ideologies of the bloody twentieth century.

Because reality is "given"—including the family, city, culture, language, and the tradition into which one is born—conservative realism is reflected in an embrace of political and cultural pluralism, as Sidorsky rightly points out. In this sense, conservatives are the original "multiculturalists," in part because they believe culture is an inescapable and necessary formative force in human life.[2] Human nature requires cultivation, and such cultivation fittingly is the proper function of culture. While human nature is more or less inalterable, culture can take many forms, and, if decent, can support the flourishing of human nature.[3] Nature and culture are not opposed, but rather work properly to support and draw from one another. Culture is properly conceived to bring nature to its fruition (much as cultivation leads to flourishing crops), while nature frames the possibilities and limits in which culture functions (no matter how much cultivation, you can't harvest tomatoes from oak trees). Cultures thus tend to be formed around the experiences of human nature *in* nature: in human terms, birth, coming of age, procreation, sickness, and death; in wider natural terms, seasons, weather, food and eating, natural disaster, gratitude and propitiation.[4]

Conservatism *qua* realism is thus firmly opposed to perhaps the core belief of all modern ideology—the belief in progress. Amelioration, or improvement, is considered possible and desirable, but all such improvements take place within the context of recognized limits of human nature and the natural world as well as the recognition of the need to preserve the overarching fabric of cultures and communities. Conservatism in the West has been alignment with traditional religious belief, in particular a stress upon an Augustinian theology in which the City of Man cannot be transformed into the City of God. Conservatives reject the proposition that the "problems" of human imperfection and original sin can be "solved" through politics or reason. Rule by philosopher-kings, the withering away of the State, or the perfect application of deliberative rationality all represent inappropriate goals that seek to reach a "solution" to the problem of politics.[5] "Improvement," when it occurs, takes place always within a larger backdrop of inescapable imperfection and human frailty. Politics—that is, the condition of imperfect humans attempting to forge a common life in spite of inevitable assertions of self-interest—remains the permanent condition of humankind. Accordingly, conservatives typically commend the political and intellectual virtue of *phronesis*, or "practical wisdom" or "judgment," as a necessary faculty that supports judicious choices between various imperfect options. Phronesis is grounded *not* on abstract rationality or ideology, but rather on the culmination of collective wisdom based upon a thorough grounding in one's own culture, history, and hence a chastened but still hopeful sense of political possibility.[6]

Conservatism *avant la lettre* might be said to describe the default position of much of the lived human life, at least until modern

times. Conservatism, prior to its explicit articulation in response
to modern ideology, might better be described as "traditionalism,"
and, as such, was largely unarticulated as a philosophical phenomenon. As "tradition," it was instantiated through a set of practices,
customs, and most especially, religious traditions. The pre-modern
world was replete with traditions, but largely lacked something
called traditionalism. This is not to suggest that human political experience was absent theoretical considerations, but that those considerations were framed within the context of particular cultures
and histories and with an overarching sense that human perfection or thorough emancipation or human redemption was not and
could not be the proper aim of political life.[7] Conservatism as an
"-ism" was forced to articulate itself (and hence, to become somewhat "unconservative") in response to the first modern ideology—
liberalism and "the Rights of Man." In response to the assertion
that there is a set of criteria, based upon the doctrine of rights, that
determine political legitimacy in all times and in all places, and
hence can and did serve as a perpetual justification for adjudging
and even overturning political authorities that did not embody and
instantiate those rights, conservatism found its voice in alignment
against a form of universalism and anti-culture fundamentally
inimical to the previously unarticulated conservative mind-set.

In explicit reaction to the universalizing doctrines that arose
out of the Enlightenment, and the attempt to put them into practice in the French Revolution, conservatives (or, not inaccurately,
reactionaries, as "in reaction to something") such as Edmund
Burke and Joseph de Maistre appealed to the dignity of existing
custom, the practicality of prejudice, and the steadiness of tradition. Burke scoffed:

> Whilst they [the Revolutionaries] are possessed by these notions, it
> is vain to talk to them of the practice of their ancestors, the funda-
> mental laws of their country, the fixed form of a constitution, whose
> merits are confirmed by the solid test of long experience. . . . They
> have "the rights of men." Against these there can be no prescrip-
> tion; against these no agreement is binding: these admit no tem-
> perament and no compromise: anything withheld from their full
> demand is so much fraud and injustice. Against these rights of men
> let no government look for security in the length of its continuance,
> or in the justice and lenity of its administration.[8]

This condemnation of the universalizing, uncompromising, and monistic philosophy of the Enlightenment was trenchantly echoed by Maistre, who similarly attacked the Declaration of the Rights of Man:

> [T]here is no such thing as a *man* in the world. I have seen, during my life, Frenchmen, Italians, Russians, etc. . . . . But as far as *man* is concerned, I declare that I have never in my life met him; if he exists, he is unknown to me.[9]

Beyond the empirical *falsehood* of wholly rationalist claims to universal humanity are the *dangers* that accrue when applying such rational theories to the unruly reality of particularist politics, attempting to fit particular customs and circumstances into the Procrustean straightjacket of Reason.[10] Against the monism of science and rationalism, a hostility to nature and culture, and the ideology of progress and political redemption, conservatism *qua* "ism" was articulated as a defense of history, culture, tradition, authority, limits, and realism in politics.

Sidorsky rightly understands conservatism to be a set of responses to the French revolutionary assertions of particularly modern forms—that is, universalized, ideological, and monistic—of "liberty, equality, and fraternity." Further, he rightly understands conservatism not implicitly to be a defense of the *opposites* of "liberty, equality, and fraternity" (that is, tyranny, inequality, and parochialism), but rather as criticisms of their ideological and monistic *excesses* (that is, disorder and instability, a hostility to justifiable discrimination in the form of merit, and the neglect of particular obligations and duties). In these respects, his paper is an informative and helpful corrective to the tendency of contemporary academics to dismiss "conservatism" as the cramped and ignorant defense of prejudice and backwardness by "the stupid party."[11]

However, what is true largely in theory, and perhaps more specifically as a definition of conservatism as it arose largely within the European context, fits only tenuously, if at all, in the instance of America and American conservatism.[12] The specifics of Sidorsky's own analysis unwittingly reveal that what is regarded as American conservatism, based on these basic features of conservatism, might be regarded as largely *unconservative*. Indeed, reading Sidorsky's description of certain features of American conservatism, one is inclined to conclude that—by this reckoning of conservatism—what are described as conservative positions are simply versions of liberalism, at best "conservative liberalism." Thus, the question presents itself: is there such a thing as *American* conservatism?

II. Conserving Liberalism?

According to the well-known analysis of America by Louis Hartz, there has only been one philosophical tradition in America—liberalism.[13] Assuming for the moment that Hartz's analysis is largely correct, it is reasonable to ask whether there has in fact ever been a conservative tradition in America. In an era that widely recognizes the importance of conservative politics in America, this question will perhaps surprise many. However, based upon the historical and theoretical understanding of conservatism as described above, and as laid out by Sidorsky, it can be argued plausibly that what passes for conservatism in America is simply one version of the predominant political philosophy of liberalism. If so, then it can be argued that there is no appreciable or significant conservative tradition in America.

Baldly stated, liberalism as a political philosophy is definitionally anti-conservative. Liberalism begins with an assumption that human societies are formed by individuals wholly upon the basis of rational calculation. Governments and societies arise as a result of rational consent, not a combination of nature, culture, and history. Liberalism views society as voluntarist, and hence regards with suspicion any claims to political legitimacy based upon tradition, religion, hierarchy, or custom. Liberalism's earliest articulation—Locke's *Second Treatise of Government*—is a tract that justifies revolution against illegitimate political authority, views marriage as another contract and hence endorses divorce, and challenges traditional authority of parents over children, since parental authority is as capricious as an unchosen political authority. Liberalism, it could be argued, at base seeks to eliminate "givenness," or what it regards as *arbitrariness*, as a constitutive feature of human life, both politically and personally. Its stance toward "givenness" is often one of opposition, a keen sensitivity to injustice and even outrage, and seeks at nearly every turn to remake reality into one that is constructed out of the materials of consent—hence, at base, an artifice. Conservatism, by contrast, understands that certain fundamental aspects of life are *given*, and counsels a degree of acceptance, gratitude, duty, and obligation.

Furthermore, liberalism has been historically aligned with the development of free-market economics, and as such, places a premium upon individual liberty, "creative destruction," economic freedom, "private vice" or self-interest, consumption (as opposed to conservation), and values dynamism and change as opposed to the antique and increasingly antiquated virtues of temperance, austerity, and frugality.[14] While conservative decrials of the ravages of the free market can be found, perhaps the most powerful description of the devastation that free markets wreak on traditional settings was articulated by the anti-conservatives Marx and Engels in the opening paragraphs of *The Communist Manifesto*:

> The bourgeoisie cannot exist without constantly revolutionizing the instruments of production, and thereby the relations of production, and with them the whole relations of society. Conservation of the old modes of production in unaltered form, was, on the contrary, the first condition of existence for all earlier industrial classes. Constant revolutionizing of production, uninterrupted disturbance of all social conditions, everlasting uncertainty and agitation distinguish the bourgeois epoch from all earlier ones. All fixed, fast frozen relations, with their train of ancient and venerable prejudices and opinions, are swept away, all new-formed ones become antiquated before they can ossify. All that is solid melts into air, all that is holy is profaned, and man is at last compelled to face with sober senses his real condition of life and his relations with his kind.[15]

Free markets have been praised for their liberative and creative qualities. Following Sidorsky's example of providing "correlative opposites," however, a conservative assessment would identify the consequences of unfettered free markets as destabilizing to communities, as undermining the necessary virtues for living well, as unleashing avarice and envy, as encouraging a form of life that is exploitative and destructive toward nature, as engendering massive quantities of waste and frivolous innovation, as orienting human life toward crass materialism, as destructive of authority and authoritative claims, and so on. All of these consequences are anathema to a conservative worldview.

Lastly, conservatism has been mistrustful of centralized State power at the expense of local and plural forms of self-governance. Conservatism is sympathetic with the approach of "subsidiarity," in which localities are assumed to be best able to address political issues and challenges unless it is concluded that they are ill-equipped, and hence that a next higher level of authority must be consulted. Certainly in this regard, conservatism is closest in alignment with traditional liberalism—or so it would seem. However, while liberalism is rightly viewed as a political philosophy that seeks to eliminate *illegitimate* state power, it is a political philosophy that has the practical effect of massively expanding what it regards as *legitimate* centralized state power.[16] This aspect of liberalism was present already in the work of John Locke, who, when writing of "executive prerogative," argued that expansive and extensive intrusions of executive power were justified if the consequences were deemed good.[17]

While many arguments might be had over what constitutes "good" consequences, certainly the extension of individual rights, the defeat of arbitrary or traditional forms of authority, and the expansion of free-market economics are several goals that liberalism has embraced and advanced. As such, liberalism has often proven hostile to local forms of governance that minimize or obstruct these various goals, and extensive centralized State power has been brought to bear to defend and expand those non-liberal, "traditionalist" ways of life. Akin to other modern ideologies, liberalism has at points demonstrated impatience with "givenness" and intervened forcefully to remake the world in its own image. This has been true not only domestically—where, over the course of the national history of the United States, the central government has accumulated more regulatory and administrative authority over regions and localities in every era—but can arguably be said to apply with some frequency in international relations as well. Domestically, the defense of civil rights is an exemplary instance; integration in the form of forced busing, more problematically so; the universalization of abortion rights and gay marriage continues to agitate the land and show the liberal devotion to rights to be a homogenizing force. Internationally, liberalism has at times proven to be paternalistic through intervention in backward civilizations with the benign intent of bringing them up to date.[18] Liberalism has often proven to be supportive of diplomatic, economic, and even military efforts to expand the purview of liberal goals, often under the rubric of liberating unfree people or encouraging greater economic development through the spread of free markets abroad.[19] The war in Iraq, aimed at bringing "democracy" and "freedom" to the native population, is only the latest in a series of American efforts to pursue its "manifest destiny" or "make the world safe for democracy."[20] The effort to disentangle international "realism" from this underlying liberal idealism in fact proves exceedingly difficult. Thus, throughout American history, seemingly "conservative" realism in international relations has often been as deeply liberal as its more idealist counterpart, differing only in means but not ends.[21]

Through this all-too-brief encapsulation of the anti-conservative features of liberalism, one can perhaps readily discern that the "correlative opposites" discussed in Sidorsky's exposition of conservatism's critique of modern concepts of liberty, equality, and fraternity are, at least problematically, and perhaps finally not at all, conservative. This should not prove surprising, since the United States is the world's consummately liberal nation. Its founding documents—particularly the Declaration of Independence—are based upon the Lockean thesis justifying revolution against an illegitimate government. It has been boasted as the most dynamic free-market economy in the history of the world, and has been the uncontested engine of globalization and internationalism in the history of the world. One can hardly think of a less "conservative" nation that the United States of America, and must wonder whether there is any appreciable conservative presence in such a nation. Sidorsky's analysis suggests that there may not be.

The three elements comprising modern American conservatism suggests that one is hard pressed to find "conservatism" within the broader context of American liberalism, and, in particular, that American "conservatism" only gains political traction inasmuch as it conforms with dominant liberal norms and assumptions. The three constituting elements of the modern conservative movement, to which Sidorsky rightly points—echoing precisely the "fusion" that was consciously formed at the outset of the modern conservative movement in America by such early founders as William F. Buckley and Frank Meyer—are: (1) Economic libertarians; (2) "National Security" conservatives; and (3) Social conservatives. The first often invoked the ideas of Milton Friedman, Friedrich Hayek, and Ayn Rand for inspiration and overlapped with the other two in their criticisms of an enlarged and activist federal government and their opposition to Communism. The second group, in many cases, were anti-communist liberals (such as Irving Kristol), whose antipathy to Communism led them to embrace the conservative cause. In their more recent iteration, they are known as "neoconservatives," counting among their number William Kristol. The last group is mainly composed of traditionalist Christians and orthodox Jews—a broad coalition of Evangelical Protestants, traditional Roman Catholics, and a smaller number of conservative mainline Protestants, Mormons, orthodox Jews, and Christian Orthodox. For a time they were gathered under the banner "Moral Majority" and gained an intellectual home at the ecumenical journal *First Things* under the leadership of Catholic convert, Father Richard John Neuhaus.

What should be noticed is that the first two "legs" of this tripod in fact conform to the dominant philosophy of liberalism. While social conservatives are at least philosophically and more often theologically in tension with liberalism, they—in spite of their seeming influence—have been largely unsuccessful in advancing their agenda even during periods of conservative Republican ascendance, and today are increasingly regarded as irrelevant and even embarrassing by the mainstream conservative movement. The first two elements of the coalition have had greater success securing their political aims during times of conservative ascendancy, respectively with libertarian-minded economists securing international free-trade agreements and rolling back a number of regulatory regimes, while neoconservatives have successfully defended growing military budgets, an activist military posture (particularly in regard to the Middle East, culminating in the War in Iraq), and a strong partnership with Israel. Meanwhile, social conservatives have seen little success advancing some of their main areas of concern, whether defending prayer in school, reversing *Roe v. Wade*, or more recently, staunching the spread of legalized gay marriage.[22] That is, one might justifiably conclude that the closer a "conservative" worldview aligns with liberalism in America, the more likely it is to achieve political success.

Libertarians often explicitly reject the label "conservative," rightly understanding themselves as opposed to the "conserving" aspects of society, culture, and family, and instead recommending the "creative destruction" of free-market economics. Milton Friedman, for instance, was a self-described "liberal," broadly falling under the rubric of "classical liberal," which emphasizes especially the centrality of individual freedom, expanding markets, and rapid economic change associated with growth and experimentation. He might also have been speaking for Ayn Rand and Friedrich Hayek in statements in which he repudiated the label "conservative" and spoke in favor of the market's role in generating profound and sweeping social and political change: "The nineteenth century liberal was a radical, both in the etymological sense of going to the root of the matter, and in the political sense of favoring major changes in social institutions. So must be his modern heir."[23]

Neoconservatives, like libertarians, are essentially "realist" liberals. They reject "progressive" internationalism for many of the same reasons that libertarians reject "economic progressivism." Both share an historic animus against communism. However, neoconservative international realism in fact manifests itself in a support for expansive nationalism and soft imperialism, particularly use of force and "soft power" to advance liberal democracy. Neoconservative Francis Fukuyama articulated the neoconservative view that liberalism constituted the "end of history"; that with the fall of the Berlin Wall in 1989, there remained no ideological competitor to modern liberalism. Neoconservatism informed, too, the call by President George W. Bush in his second inaugural address to make the "expansion of freedom" the singular goal of American foreign policy: "America's vital interests and our deepest beliefs are now one." This more aggressive, expansionist, imperialistic, and interventionist stance contradicts a traditionally conservative aversion to expansionism, imperialism, and homogenization of the world's governments and cultures.

Social conservatism has often embraced core aspects of both economic libertarianism and neoconservatism, but neither is defining, and, arguably, both actually stand in considerable contradiction to core aspects of social conservatism. The main foci of social conservatives have tended to be "social" issues, often ones related to consequences of the sexual revolution, and particularly center on abortion and, more recently, gay marriage and religious liberty. Social conservatives have received a heightened amount of press coverage, and their influence during Republican primaries has often been noted, but in comparison to the libertarian and neoconservative "legs" of the triad, it is also arguable that they have had the least success securing their main commitments during times of Republican Party ascendance. While true that they have tended to have a significant influence on judicial appointments, given the importance of the Supreme Court on an array of social issues, even the appointment of a number of conservative judges and Justices has not handed social conservatives victories in various causes, as major decisions supported by Reagan appointee Justice Kennedy (such as *Casey v. Texas* and *U.S. v. Windsor*) as well as George H. W. Bush appointee Justice Souter have resulted in defeats for social conservatives. In the meantime, successes of economic libertarians in advancing economic globalization and decreasing regulation on financial centers has contributed to deep insecurity and social dislocation of many who support a social conservative agenda, while neoconservative support of the war in Iraq has disproportionately affected military families who are typically drawn from this segment of society. It is arguable that the very success of the "conservative" movement has only been achieved when its "liberal" elements command, at heavy costs to social conservatism and its supporters.

III. Two Waves of Liberalism in America

These particular political arrangements, while to some extent contingent upon the historical threat of Communism that drew these three "legs" together, more deeply still reflect a profoundly liberal American constitution (in the broadest sense—that is to say, a fundamentally liberal set of assumptions that are pervasively held, regardless of partisan allegiance) that has made America infertile soil for the development of a robust conservative tradition. However, in failing to acknowledge this deeper liberal loam,

Sidorsky does not adequately note the fundamental "liberalism" of American conservatism.

In the first instance, in response to the call for liberty, Sidorsky maintains that American conservatives seek to achieve a balance between liberty and order. Far from being constitutively "conservative," this call for balance lies at the heart of liberalism's effort to balance individual freedom with state power. The Declaration of Independence not only advances a theory of natural rights and a defense of revolution, but also asserts that "to secure these rights, governments are instituted among Men." A defense of governments powerful enough to "secure" rights is a doctrine that lies at the heart of liberal theory: its conundrum, as stated succinctly by James Madison, has always been that "you must first enable the government to control the governed; and in the next place oblige it to control itself."[24] As such, the debate is not between modern liberty and classical conservatism, but an internal debate between varieties of liberalism, and particularly a more "libertarian" liberalism versus a more "statist" liberalism. Historically, a strong national government has been an essential feature of liberalization, the extension of free markets, and individual liberties. Far from representing a "conservative" position, an endorsement of strong centralized government may reflect a deep antipathy to established patterns of local or regional life. Order is the necessary partner of liberty, and may in fact be arrayed together against "conservation."

In the second instance, in response to the call for equality, Sidorsky maintains that conservatives seek to preserve "relevant" forms of differentiation. He categorically rejects that conservatives would seek to "restore" hierarchy based on "birth and religion." Rather, he emphasizes the single relevant form of discrimination currently defended by American conservatives to be differentiation based upon "merit," particularly inasmuch as such forms of merit are seen to support "the functioning of free markets in the economy." That American conservatives, according to Sidorsky, do not acknowledge or seek "restoration" of formerly relevant aristocratic forms of differentiation (such as those based upon birth or religion), and rather seek to defend "talent" as the only "relevant reason for developing hierarchies," reveals how extensively such conservatism is actually at base fundamentally liberal. "Meritocracy" fully comports with the expectations and dynamics of a liberal political and free-market economic order. Merit-based forms of discrimination have been the "heavy artillery" by which older aristocratic orders have been routed, and have been a fundamental contributor to modern mobility and dynamism and the undermining of traditional forms of life.[25] American conservatism, writes Sidorsky, has taken the form of "economic conservatism," by which he means "that the primacy ought to be accorded to the operation of free markets." That a largely unregulated free market has come to be regarded as a constitutive form of American conservatism brings to the fore the doubt that there is an actual conservative tradition in America.

Lastly, in response to the call for fraternity, Sidorsky maintains that conservatives seek to defend the legitimacy of "otherness" in the form of national sovereignty and interests in opposition to calls for "universal brotherhood." As a species of conservative "pluralism," he is certainly correct. However, as briefly addressed above, conservative nationalism in America has always been informed by the identical "liberal idealism" that undergirds supranational theories of cosmopolitanism. While Sidorsky rightly avers that the defense of the inescapability of the nation-state—or particular entities that depend upon an understanding of "otherness"— draws on a conservative worldview, in the case of American internationalism, even "realist" positions are invoked in the name of human rights, democratic self-governance, and free markets. No reputable American leader has defended a "realistic" international policy in the name of expanding imperial power, dominating a market, or resource exploitation. And, in our times, arguments on behalf of relative isolationism from "foreign entanglements" in order to "conserve" republican virtues are not typically heard on the national agenda.

If the positions that Sidorsky highlights are not fundamentally conservative, in what respect do they differ from the position they stand arrayed against? For, certainly, American conservatism understands itself to differ from some kind of non-conservative counterpart. It is not inaccurate to suggest that what is being described is a difference between liberalisms, and in particular, "classical" liberalism as drawn from the philosophy of John Locke and Adam Smith, on the one hand, and "progressive" liberalism as it was further developed in the thought of, among others,

J. S. Mill, Rousseau, Kant, and later, Rawls and Habermas. The
debate is between species of liberalism, or even, as framed by
Leo Strauss, the first two "waves" of modernity.[26] The "first wave"
of modernity, or liberal theory as developed by Thomas Hobbes
and John Locke, if not conservative, nevertheless shares certain
features in common with a conservative worldview. Human beings
possess an unalterable nature that is motivated primarily by self-
interest. Governments are instituted under the assumption that
"men are not angels" nor can be rendered perfect. In contrast to
the second wave of modern liberalism, first-wave liberalism rejects
moral improvement as a justifiable aim of politics. It is suspicious
of government efforts to effect such moral progress. As such, first-
wave liberalism is not a *conservative* political philosophy—it still
rests upon a theory of rights, a justification of revolution, and an
embrace of free-market economics—but it retains some kinship
with an overarching conservative disposition and worldview in its
view of human partiality, frailty, and even wickedness.

By contrast, the "second wave" of liberalism draws inspiration
from the thought of, among others, Rousseau, Kant, and Hegel. It
embraces an "historicist" worldview, viewing humans as "plastic,"
subject not only to material amelioration, but moral improvement.
Broadly, second-wave thinkers hold that human consciousness
itself is subject to alteration, and that, in particular, as human societies evolve and become more global, cosmopolitan, liberal, and
tolerant, people will develop forms of heightened social consciousness, allowing for political forms and economic developments that
are increasingly global and humanitarian. In its most visionary
manifestations, it envisions the end of nations and borders, even
of individuated human consciousness—a "progressive" apotheosis
in which we will achieve a new, doubtless very different form of
"species being," or what the nineteenth-century utopian Richard
Bucke dubbed "cosmic consciousness."

Understandably, first-wave liberalism stands arrayed against
this progressive version of liberalism. Within the American context we call this first-wave liberalism "conservatism," and it does
indeed retain certain key aspects of conservative suspicion toward
progress and moral transformation. Thus, when juxtaposed with
"progressive" liberalism, "classical liberalism" is indeed more conservative. But when juxtaposed to a worldview based in tradition,

authority, social stability, and priority of communal ways of life, first-wave liberalism becomes ferociously critical.[27]

First-wave liberalism is a distant cousin of conservatism—related, if not too closely—and within the context of the liberal American polity, passes for conservatism. However, it is a sibling of second-wave liberalism—critical of some of its main features, but similarly and more fundamentally critical of "the ancestral" and traditional. It may be the only conservatism possible in a liberal regime, but if so, can only be problematically conservative. Whether there is a conservative tradition in America, therefore, remains an open and debatable question, and exploring the ways in which American conservatism remains fundamentally liberal may once again reveal that the fiercest battles are those fought between brothers.

NOTES

1. This conservative disposition was perhaps best captured in Christopher Lasch's phrase, "hope without optimism" in *The True and Only Heaven* (New York: W. W. Norton, 1991).

2. Conservatives differ from contemporary "multiculturalists" inasmuch as they reject the supposition that culture is subject to casual embrace or rejection. Because culture is deeply constitutive, culture is one fundamental source from which judgments are rendered—including judgments about other cultures. See Marc J. Swartz, "Negative Ethnocentrism," *Journal of Conflict Resolution* 5 (March 1961): 75–81. Contrast this position to contemporary assumptions that multiculturalism assures the ready movement between cultures and, hence, non-judgmentalism, such as the argument presented by Kwame Anthony Appiah, "The Case for Contamination," *New York Times Magazine* (January 1, 2006).

3. An early critique of the universalist implications of Cartesian and Hobbesian critiques of tradition and culture, that stresses the close connection between nature and culture, can be found in Giambattista Vico, *The New Science* (Ithaca, NY: Cornell University Press, 1984).

4. Aristotle, *The Politics*, Book 1.

5. See Bertrand de Jouvenel's critique of "the myth of the solution" in *A Pure Theory of Politics* (Indianapolis: Liberty Fund Press, 2001), Addendum, 203–212.

6. Aristotle, *Nicomachean Ethics*, Book 6.

7. See Leo Strauss, *Persecution and the Art of Writing* (Chicago: University of Chicago Press, 1988). One point of contrast between the ancients

and moderns was the effort by ancient theorists to respect the prevailing opinions and beliefs of ordinary citizens. Even were persecution not to be feared, responsible political philosophers respected the traditions and opinions of their city. Beginning with the philosophy of Hobbes, "opinion" was rejected in the name of reason and science.

8. Edmund Burke, *Reflections on the Revolution in France*, ed. J. G. A. Pocock (Indianapolis: Hackett, 1964), 55–56.

9. Cited in Stephen Holmes, *The Anatomy of Anti-liberalism* (Cambridge, MA: Harvard University Press, 1993), 14.

10. Among the most eloquent and classic critiques of the deforming role of ideology and rationalism in politics remains Michael Oakeshott, "Rationalism in Politics," in *Rationalism in Politics and Other Essays* (Indianapolis, IN: Liberty Fund Press, 1991), 1–36.

11. Perhaps atypical for its brazenness if not for its widespread belief throughout the academy, see the interview with Duke University Professor of Philosophy Robert Brandon, in which he stated: "We try to hire the best, smartest people available. If, as John Stuart Mill said, stupid people are generally conservative, then there are lots of conservatives we will never hire. Mill's analysis may go some way towards explaining the power of the Republican Party in our society and the relative scarcity of Republicans in academia. Players in the NBA tend to be taller than average. There is a good reason for this. Members of academia tend to be a bit smarter than average. There is a good reason for this, too." "DCU Sparks Varied Reactions," *Duke Chronicle* (February 9, 2004), at: http://www.dukechronicle.com/articles/2004/02/10/dcu-sparks-varied-reactions.

12. It is perhaps revealing that, in describing "American conservatism," Sidorsky cites Edmund Burke and Michael Oakeshott, an English statesman and a British philosopher.

13. Louis Hartz, *The Liberal Tradition in America* (New York: Harcourt, Brace & Company, 1955).

14. On the anti-conservatism and anti-conservation of free-market economics, see Roger Scruton, *A Political Philosophy: Arguments for Conservatism* (London: Bloomsbury Academic, 2007); most any collection of essays by Wendell Berry, especially *Home Economics: Fourteen Essays* (San Francisco: North Point Press, 1987); *Sex, Economy, Freedom and Community* (New York: Pantheon, 1994); and *The Way of Ignorance* (Berkeley, CA: Counterpoint Press, 2006). Alternatively, one can consult Adam Smith, *The Wealth of Nations*, or Friedrich Hayek, *The Road to Serfdom*, for a defense of free-market economics in the name of liberalism and liberalization.

15. Karl Marx and Friedrich Engels, *The Communist Manifesto* (1848), Part I.

16. Bertrand de Jouvenel, *On Power* (Indianapolis, IN: Liberty Fund Press, 2003); Grant McConnell, *Private Power and American Democracy* (New York: Knopf Books, 1966).

17. John Locke, *Second Treatise of Government*, ch. xiv, "Of Prerogative": "Many things there are, which the law can by no means provide for; and those must necessarily be left to the discretion of him that has the executive power in his hands, to be ordered by him as the public good and advantage shall require: nay, it is fit that the laws themselves should in some cases give way to the executive power, or rather to this fundamental law of nature and government," paragraph 159.

18. See John Stuart Mill's admonition that advanced societies must force the people of backward civilizations to adopt modern liberal forms of life, even if they must be enslaved to do so:

Thus (to repeat a former example), a people in a state of savage independence, in which every one lives for himself, exempt, unless by fits, from any external control, is practically incapable of making any progress in civilisation until it has learnt to obey. The indispensable virtue, therefore, in a government which establishes itself over a people of this sort is, that it make itself obeyed. To enable it to do this, the constitution of the government must be nearly, or quite, despotic. A constitution in any degree popular, dependent on the voluntary surrender by the different members of the community of their individual freedom of action, would fail to enforce the first lesson which the pupils, in this stage of their progress, require. Accordingly, the civilisation of such tribes, when not the result of juxtaposition with others already civilised, is almost always the work of an absolute ruler, deriving his power either from religion or military prowess; very often from foreign arms.

Again, uncivilised races, and the bravest and most energetic still more than the rest, are averse to continuous labour of an unexciting kind. Yet all real civilisation is at this price; without such labour, neither can the mind be disciplined into the habits required by civilised society, nor the material world prepared to receive it. There needs a rare concurrence of circumstances, and for that reason often a vast length of time, to reconcile such a people to industry, unless they are for a while compelled to it. Hence even personal slavery, by giving a commencement to industrial life, and enforcing it as the exclusive occupation of the most numerous portion of the community, may accelerate the transition to a better freedom than that of fighting and rapine. It is almost needless to say that this excuse for slavery is only available in a very early state of society.

A civilised people have far other means of imparting civilisation to those under their influence; and slavery is, in all its details, so repugnant to that government of law, which is the foundation of all modern life, and so corrupting to the master-class when they have once come under civilised influences, that its adoption under any circumstances whatever in modern society is a relapse into worse than barbarism. (John Stuart Mill, *Considerations on Representative Government*, chap. 2)

19. As such, classical liberalism has been closely aligned with imperialism. See Uday Singh Mehta, *Liberalism and Empire: A Study in Nineteenth-Century British Liberal Thought* (Chicago: University of Chicago Press, 1999); and Jennifer Pitts, *A Turn to Empire: The Rise of Imperial Liberalism in Britain and France* (Princeton, NJ: Princeton University Press, 2006). Historically, opponents of liberal imperialism have been conservatives. See, for instance, the opposition of G. K. Chesterton to the enthusiastic imperialism of George Bernard Shaw and H. G. Wells, or, in the American context, William Jennings Bryan's opposition to America's imperialistic ventures under President William McKinley, ably described by Michael Kazin in *A Godly Hero: The Life of William Jennings Bryan* (New York: Knopf, 2006).

20. Of course, this is a complex story, and one well told by Walter A. McDougall, *Promised Land, Crusader State: The American Encounter with the World since 1776* (New York: Houghton Mifflin, 1997).

21. See David Fromkin, *In the Time of the Americans: FDR, Truman, Eisenhower, Marshall, MacArthur: The Generation That Changed America's Role in the World* (New York: Knopf, 1995).

22. It should be noted that social conservatives have had some significant success in securing legislation that either limits or puts up obstacles to the procuring of abortion, particularly at the state level. The Supreme Court has shown some willingness to allow such legislation to stand, as long as it does not prevent outright legalized abortion, particularly during the first trimester.

23. Milton Friedman, *Capitalism and Freedom*, Introduction (1962).

24. James Madison, *Federalist* No. 51.

25. See, generally, Alexis de Tocqueville, *Democracy in America*; David Brooks, *Bobos in Paradise* (New York: Simon & Schuster, 2001), and especially chapter 1, a study in the transformation of marriage announcements in the *New York Times* from the old aristocracy to the new class of "bourgeois bohemian"; and Nicholas Lehmann, *The Big Test: A Secret History of the American Meritocracy* (New York: Farrar, Straus and Giroux, 2000), a study of how the SAT test was introduced by liberal elite university presidents who sought to break the control of old family hierarchies whose sons and daughters attended such schools (accumulating "gentleman's

C's") in order to advance greater dynamism and progress throughout American society.

26. Leo Strauss, "The Three Waves of Modernity," in *An Introduction to Political Philosophy: Ten Essays by Leo Strauss,* ed. Hilail Gildin (Detroit, MI: Wayne State University Press, 1989), 81–98.

27. Consider, for example, an American "conservative" *locus classicus,* Allan Bloom's *Closing of the American Mind,* in which one finds not only lengthy critiques of progressivism, but also of "traditionalism" and even "conservatism." *The Closing of the American Mind* (New York: Simon & Schuster, 1987). See my review on the occasion of the 25th anniversary of the publication of Bloom's book. Patrick J. Deneen, "Who Closed the American Mind," *The American Conservative* (October 1, 2012), at: http://www.the americanconservative.com/articles/who-closed-the-american-mind/.

4

THE WORMS AND THE OCTOPUS: RELIGIOUS FREEDOM, PLURALISM, AND CONSERVATISM

RICHARD W. GARNETT

> We have made [the state] intolerant of associations within itself—associations that to Hobbes will appear comparable only to "worms within the entrails of a natural man."
>
> —Harold Laski[1]

> The State may never become an octopus, which stifles the whole of life.
>
> —Abraham Kuyper[2]

I.

An academic lawyer writing in the early years of the twenty-first century and hoping to productively engage and intelligently assess "American Conservative Thought and Politics" should be forgiven for struggling with the unanticipated difficulty of the question, "what, exactly, are we talking about?"[3] In my own case, this difficulty can be chalked up at least in part to a lack of formal training or advanced study in American history and political thought, but that is not the whole of it. The question *is* difficult, the subject *is* elusive. The former will probably not be definitively and comprehensively answered, nor the latter pinned down, by a law professor.

Lionel Trilling's famous but pat diagnosis and dismissal, it seems safe to say and as Russell Kirk surely showed,[4] was not and—

notwithstanding the burlesque world of right-leaning cable-news programs and talk-radio shows, the sensationalizing and dumbing down of "conservative" books, and the fever-swamp character of so much of the blogosphere[5]—is not the right answer. A half-century or so ago, Trilling surveyed American culture, politics, and intellectual life and concluded, to his regret, that "it is the plain fact that nowadays there are no conservative or reactionary ideas in general circulation. . . . [T]he conservative impulse and the reactionary impulse do not, with some isolated and some ecclesiastical exceptions, express themselves in ideas but only in action or in irritable mental gestures which seek to resemble ideas."[6] Of course, the opposite claim—that is, that *all* of the new and engaging ideas are "conservative" ones—was for a while something of a staple of both triumphalist self-congratulation on the right and anxious self-examination on the left.[7] But then came the 2008 presidential election and, it was reported, the "death of conservatism";[8] soon after that came the Tea Party and forecasts of its "rebirth."[9]

It seems that American conservatism has always been protean, liquid, and variegated—more a loosely connected or casually congregating group of conservatisms than a cohesive and coherent worldview or program. The fact that even our Revolution was, relatively speaking, a conservative one[10]—one that was fueled and animated more by indignation over novel interferences with deeply rooted rights and long-standing institutions than by abstract speculations, Jacobin ambitions, or romantic enthusiasms—could be part of the reason why our conservatism is hard to pin down. After all, even if the British *had* played "The World Turned Upside Down" at Yorktown, it would still have been true that many of our Revolution's leaders and instigators had a very Burkean wariness of such turnings.

In any event, and for whatever reasons, there has always been a variety of conservatives and conservatisms—a great many shifting combinations of nationalism and localism, piety and rationalism, energetic entrepreneurism and romanticization of the rural, skepticism and crusading idealism, elitism, and populism—in American culture, politics, and law. Conceding as much, however, does not make it any easier to identify, describe, or evaluate them.

Even a quick glance at the new-releases table at a Barnes & Noble bookstore, or a few minutes of cursory web surfing or

Twitter-feeding, confirms the daunting definitional and taxonomical challenge of sifting through the colorful, if confusing, array of conservative hues and flavors: Over here, Reformocons, Paleocons, Neocons, Leocons, Theocons,[11] and CrunchyCons.[12] Over there, National Greatness and Compassionate Conservatives, Randians and Fusionists, libertarians and values voters, anarcho-capitalists and distributists, Sam's Club[13] and South Park Republicans.[14] Should the student of American conservatism study up on Randolph and Tocqueville, Voegelin and Kirk, Buckley and Meyer? Or can she stick simply with Mark Levin and Michelle Malkin? Should she subscribe to *Reason* or *First Things?* To *National Review* or *The American Conservative*—or, for that matter, *The New Republic?* Should she follow *Front Porch Republic* or *RedState?* Should she look back to Burke or Paine?[15] Should she make a pilgrimage to Wendell Berry's farm or Ronald Reagan's ranch, or can she safely settle for *The Kelly File* on Fox News at the local sports bar? Who better understands and speaks for the "conservative soul," Andrew Sullivan or Rick Santorum?[16] What do we do and what should we make of a label that has been attached to both Justices Blackmun and Scalia, to *Citizens United* and *NFIB v. Sebelius*, to Judges Posner and Pryor, and to Larry Summers and Lino Graglia? Is it the aim of conservatism, well understood, to "stand[] athwart history, yelling 'stop',"[17] or to push history toward the recognition and protection of that "freedom [that] is the desire of every human heart"?[18] And so on.

II.

It would, again, be dangerous for an academic lawyer to attempt or purport to set down with confidence the boundaries of "American conservative thought and politics." A paper that reduced this subject to, say, a description of the decisions authored by "conservative" or Republican-appointed justices of the Supreme Court, or that conflated it with an account of the post–Civil War or post-1968 evolution of the Democratic and Republican parties, would not do it justice or be of much interest. So, in this chapter, I will play it safe, and start on what feels like very firm ground.

No one would doubt the impeccably conservative bona fides of grumbling about the French Revolution and about 1789, "the

birth year of modern life."[19] Most of us have probably heard the
story that, when asked sometime during the middle years of the
last century about the significance of that Revolution, the Chinese
Premier Zhou En-lai is said to have replied, "it's too soon to tell."[20]
It does not seem premature or hasty, though, to say that, whatever
else it may prove to have achieved or undone, the French Revolution and the reactions to it are responsible for many of the features of our political landscape and debate and for many of the
lines we draw, categories we employ, and labels we attach. More
specifically, what Kirk called "[c]onscious conservatism, in the
modern sense"[21] first arrived on the scene with Burke's *Reflections
on the Revolution in France*, and at least its Anglo-American varieties
have long been pervasively shaped by his reaction.

So, what was he reacting to? Certainly, the Revolution provided Burke with plenty of things to regret and about which to
warn. Important among these were its claims that—in Mary Ann
Glendon's words—"there should be no 'particular associations'
competing for the loyalty of citizens; religion should not be left
independent of political control; and those who refuse to conform to the general will would have to be 'forced to be free.'"[22]
As John Courtney Murray put it, Burke's targets included those
"French enthusiasts" who tolerated "no autonomous social forms
intermediate between the individual and the state," and who
aimed to "destroy . . . all self-governing intermediate social forms
with particular ends."[23] I suggest, then, that to be conservative is
at least and among other things to join Burke in rejecting Rousseau's assertions that "a democratic society should be one in which
absolutely nothing stands between man and the state"[24] and that
non-state authorities and associations should be proscribed.[25] In
other words, to be conservative—borrowing now from the evocative quotations at the beginning of this chapter—is to take up the
cause of Hobbes's "worms in the entrails" and to resist the reach of
Kuyper's "octopus."

Now, the non-state authority that was the most obvious enemy
and victim of the Revolution was, of course, the Catholic Church.
This is not the place for a detailed description of the Assemblies'
aggressive and bloody campaigns against the Church, clergy, and
Christianity generally.[26] It is enough for this chapter's purposes
simply to observe that the 1790 Civil Constitution of the Clergy and

what followed—that is, a campaign to confine Christianity closely to the realm of private belief and to eliminate the Church as an institution or social body with authority and influence—should be seen as essential aspects of the Revolution, to which conservatism was and meaningfully remains a response.

My proposal here, then, is that near the heart of anything called conservatism—of any temperament, worldview, or set of ideas that stands opposite or reacts against the French Revolution—should be an appreciation for the place and role of non-state authorities in promoting the common good and the flourishing of persons and a commitment to religious freedom for individuals and institutions alike, secured in part through constitutional limits on the powers of political authorities. Accordingly, one appropriate way for an academic lawyer to engage "American Conservative Thought and Politics" is to investigate and discuss the extent to which these apparently necessary features or elements of conservatism are present in American public law. Pluralism and religion, in other words, are topics that should provide extensive access to this volume's subject.

III.

To approach American conservatism in this way is not merely to echo the well worn observations that the more religious and church-going among us are more likely to vote for Republicans, that the energetic "base" of the Republican Party includes many motivated-by-faith "values voters," and that many of the social concerns and policy commitments that reliably attach to self-identified conservatives also seem consonant with traditional religious teachings. It is also not to suggest that religious believers, themes, imagery, and arguments are active or deployed only on or to advance the aims of the political right.[27] It is to propose, though, that a central question, or problem, for conservatism is the place of religious belief, religious expression, religious institutions, and religiously motivated action in the political arena and public square.[28]

This has been true for a very long time. In the American context, it is probably not overly anachronistic, just by way of illustration, to distinguish the "liberal" Jefferson from the more "conservative"

Adams by pointing to their contrasting understandings of public religion and its role in securing freedom under law.[29] Shifting to the present, we might consider the perennial and ubiquitous squabbling over religiously themed displays and declarations in public spaces and by public officials. It seems fair to say that "conservatives" can be identified with confidence by their eye-rolling skepticism toward efforts to prevent or marginalize such displays in the name of protecting objectors' consciences and sensibilities (and also, in some cases, by a tendency to overheated and exaggerated claims about "wars" against Christmas).[30] A whole litany of similarly hot-button and exhaustingly familiar issues is available to help us hone in on conservatives and conservatism: vouchers for children attending religious schools, public funds for religious organizations involved in services and outreach to the poor, faith-based rehabilitation programs for prisoners, science education and tolerance-training in public schools, conscience-based exemptions from contraception coverage mandates, morals legislation of all sorts, and on and on.

Perhaps the most efficient sorting device, though, is the idea, or simply the term, "separation of church and state." For many who self-identify as "liberals," it is, ironically enough, an article of faith that this idea is at the heart and perhaps is the entirety of any plausible understanding of religious freedom. On the other hand, for many who call themselves "conservatives," it serves as a call to arms against the forces of Jacobin atheism or as an occasion for an Orwellian two-minute hate. In some quarters, it appears to have become something of a litmus-test requirement that conservatives dismiss talk of "separation" as little more than strategic sloganeering for anti-religious activists. In August 2006, for example, U.S. Rep. Katherine Harris, a candidate for the U.S. Senate known primarily for her role in Florida's 2000 presidential election, caused a stir when she announced that the separation of church and state is a "lie we have been told" to keep religious believers out of politics and public life.[31] On the other hand, no less a religious believer—and, some would say, no less a "conservative"—than the Pope Emeritus, Benedict XVI, made clear his strong commitment to the view that "separation," properly understood, far from being a "lie," is instead "ultimately a primordial Christian legacy and also a decisive factor for freedom."[32]

In 1988, out on the campaign trail, President George H. W. Bush caused a few chuckles—and, more than likely, a few groans—when he recalled being shot down over the South Pacific in World War II:

> Was I scared floating in a little yellow raft off the coast of an enemy-held island, setting a world record for paddling? Of course I was. What sustains you in times like that? Well, you go back to fundamental values. I thought about Mother and Dad and the strength I got from them, and God and faith—and the separation of church and state.

The former president's idea juxtaposition and word association probably strike us as a bit absurd. And yet, in a way, they are entirely American. That "God" and "faith" could not be invoked by the president as "fundamental values," without the addition of "the separation of church and state," speaks volumes about how Americans think about the content and implications of religious freedom. Indeed, as Professor Dreisbach observed, "[n]o metaphor in American letters has had a greater influence on law and policy than Thomas Jefferson's 'wall of separation between church and state.'"[33] For many Americans, this metaphor supplies the "authoritative interpretation" of the First Amendment's Religion Clauses; in Professor Hamburger's words, "vast numbers of [us] have come to understand [our] religious freedom in terms of Jefferson's phrase. As a result, Jefferson's words often seem more familiar than the words of the First Amendment itself."[34]

The idea of "separation" and the image of a "wall" are near the heart of many American citizens' and commentators' thinking about law and religion, about faith and public life, about church and state.[35] Unfortunately, the latter, inapt image can cause great confusion about the former, important idea. As then-Justice William Rehnquist once observed, the image has "proved all but useless as a guide to sound constitutional adjudication."[36] This is, as will be discussed in more detail below, certainly not to question the importance to religious and political freedom of distinguishing the institutions and authorities of religion from those of government. Nor is it to deny that such a distinction was important to many of those who drafted and ratified the First Amendment and should be recognized and maintained in our constitutional doctrine.[37] It is, however, to regret that what should be regarded as an important feature of religious freedom under constitutionally limited government is too often employed as a rallying cry, not for the distinctiveness and independence of religious institutions, but for the marginalization and privatization of religious faith.[38]

How, then, should we understand "the separation of church and state"? It seems to me that separation, correctly conceived, is an essential component of religious freedom. It is neither an obstacle to nor an attack upon that freedom but is instead a necessary structural feature of our constitutional order, through which that freedom is affirmed and protected. It is a principle of pluralism, of multiple and overlapping authorities, of competing loyalties and demands. It is a rule that limits the state and thereby clears out and protects a social space, within which persons are formed and educated and without which religious liberty is vulnerable.[39] As John Courtney Murray once wrote, separation is not—or should not be—secularism but rather a "means, a technique, [and] a policy to implement the principle of religious freedom."[40]

So, why is church-state separation often and widely regarded, both by some of its opponents and by some of its self-styled defenders, as an anti-religious ideology or a policy that mandates a public square scrubbed clean of religious symbols, expression, and activism? Why do some imagine or insist that the separation of church and state requires religious believers to keep their faith strictly private, or to wall off their religious commitments from their public lives and arguments about how we ought to order society? Why are some of us under the impression that respect for church-state separation requires us, as Professor Carter memorably put it, to regard religion as a "hobby," nothing more?[41] To answer these and related questions, it might be helpful to look more closely at the "wall" that is said to separate "church" and "state."

As Professor Witte has noted, this "wall" has, in public law and in public discourse, proved far more "serpentine"—both in the sense of winding and twisting, and in the Edenic sense of "seductively simple"—than is often appreciated.[42] Where did it come from? Certainly, and as is discussed in more detail below, the idea of a distinction between the Church and the political authority, between what Calvin called the "spiritual kingdom" and the "political kingdom," between believers and the world, between the City of God and the City of Man, is much older than the American Constitution and long predates those Enlightenment thinkers widely thought to have influenced it.[43] In Professor Witte's words, although "[s]eparation of Church and state is often regarded as a distinctly American and relatively modern invention," it is, in fact, "an ancient Western teaching rooted in the Bible."[44] Christ's followers were taught to "repay to Caesar what belongs to Caesar and to God what belongs to God"[45]; Pope Gelasius instructed the Emperor Anastasius that "[t]here are indeed . . . two powers by which this world is chiefly ruled"[46]; Pope Boniface VIII identified "two swords, a spiritual . . . and a temporal" (and claimed them both)[47]; and Roger Williams contrasted the "Garden of the Church and the Wilderness of the world."[48]

In the United States, though, the story begins in October 1801, when the Baptist Association of Danbury, Connecticut wrote to President-elect Thomas Jefferson, congratulating him on his election.[49] In their letter, no doubt hoping to ingratiate themselves and their cause to the new president, the Danbury Baptists trumpeted their disagreement with Jefferson's Congregationalist and Federalist opponents, who had energetically scorned him during the 1800 campaign as "an enemy of religion[,] Law & good order," and noted also that their own "[s]entiments are uniformly on the side of Religious Liberty."[50] For the Baptists, the letter explained to the president, as for many other dissenters from Founding-era religious establishments, "religion [is] an essentially private matter between an individual and his God. No citizen, they reasoned, ought to suffer civil disability on account of his religious opinions. The legitimate powers of civil government reach actions, but not opinions."[51]

Jefferson, of course, was "keenly aware of the political implications of his pronouncement on a delicate church-state issue," and he replied a few months later in a well-considered and carefully crafted letter of his own, one that reflected not just his views about the First Amendment and his frustration with the attacks of his political enemies, but also his own anti-clericalism.[52] He wrote, in the letter's key and famous passage:

> Believing with you that religion is a matter which lies solely between Man and his God, that he owes account to none other for his faith or his worship, that the legitimate powers of government reach actions only, and not opinions, I contemplate with sovereign reverence that act of the whole American people which declared that their legislature should "make no law respecting an establishment of religion, or prohibiting the free exercise thereof," thus building a wall of separation between Church & State.[53]

Jefferson's letter was published in Massachusetts shortly after it was received, but it seems to have been forgotten for a half-century thereafter.[54] (Indeed, the Danbury Baptists themselves were reluctant to publicize the letter or its contents.[55]) It does not appear that Jefferson ever employed the "wall of separation" image again.[56]

As Professor Hamburger has explained, the idea of separation between church and state served, during most of the nineteenth century, less as a Jefferson-inspired constitutional doctrine than as an anti-Catholic ideology and rhetorical weapon.[57] However, in the 1879 case of *Reynolds v. United States,* a case involving the bigamy prosecution of a Mormon and one of the Supreme Court's first major decisions interpreting the First Amendment's Religion Clauses, the Justices quoted Jefferson's letter to the Danbury Baptists, invoked the "wall" metaphor, and reported that Jefferson's response "may be accepted as an almost authoritative declaration of the [Clauses'] scope and effect."[58]

The Court did not have occasion to return to the metaphor for almost 70 years. Then, in the landmark 1947 case, *Everson v. Board of Education,* Justice Black went even further than had the *Reynolds* Court, and announced that the First Amendment's Establishment Clause constrains not only the actions of Congress, but also those of state and local officials.[59] Although a narrow majority of the Court declined to strike down a New Jersey law allowing reimbursements to parents for money spent on bus transportation to parochial schools, Justice Black followed *Reynolds* in giving Jefferson's letter, and the "wall," controlling, canonical weight. After a lengthy, if incomplete,[60] account of the Establishment Clause's history, context, and meaning, Justice Black summed up in this way: "In the words of Jefferson, the clause against establishment of religion by law was intended to erect 'a wall of separation between

Church and State.' . . . That wall must be kept high and impreg-
nable. We could not approve the slightest breach."[61] (Some of Justice Black's critics, though—fellow separationists—protested that
he had done just that.[62])

A lot has changed in constitutional law—and, in particular, in
the understanding and application of the Religion Clauses—since
1947. Still, and even though many of these changes have been
departures from strict separationism,[63] what Chief Justice William
Rehnquist once called Jefferson's "misleading metaphor"[64] remains
deeply and—it appears—indelibly ingrained in Americans' thinking about church-state relations and religious freedom.[65] As the
Court has moved in recent years from a no-aid-to-religion understanding of the First Amendment to a more accommodating,
equality-emphasizing view, it has been impossible to avoid warnings that the "wall of separation" is being lowered, knocked down,
dismantled, weakened, or breached.[66] Even as First Amendment
doctrine moves in the direction of "neutral" treatment by government of religious expression and activity,[67] it is charged by some
that religiously motivated or inspired arguments, claims, expression, and activism are—if brought to bear in public discussions or
upon political questions—inordinately "divisive" and inconsistent
with our traditional commitment to church-state separation.[68]

Of course, that some invocations of religious faith in the civic
arena might be unwise, unfaithful, or unseemly does not make
them inconsistent with separation, correctly conceived. To join
Pope Benedict XVI in recognizing—indeed, in insisting on—the
"distinction between Church and State" is not to demand disengagement by religious believers, communities, or institutions.[69] As
Justice William Douglas wrote, in the *Zorach* case, that the "separation" of church and state "must be complete and unequivocal"
does not mean that "the state and religion [must] be aliens to each
other"[70] or that civil society and public life should be evacuated of
religiosity.[71] In the context of the modern, activist, welfare state,
"separation" or "segregation" of church from state—let alone of
religion from public life—seems neither possible nor desirable. We
would do better, in this context, not to invoke or rely on the image
of a "wall of separation," but to think instead in terms of what my
colleague, Professor Rodes, called the "church-state nexus,"[72] with
"nexus" being understood as a "means of connection; a link or

tie."[73] This term suggests not so much a "wall" as a relationship, even a symbiosis, between two distinct things—neither a collapse of the one into the other nor a rigid segregation of the one from the other. In this nexus, churches are not, and must not be, arms or auxiliaries of the state. But the point of this arrangement is not to privatize religion or secularize civil society. It is, instead, to protect religious freedom, which includes the freedom to construct and live a faithful, integrated, public life.

IV.

The claim so far, then, is that there are strong reasons, rooted in themes and commitments that should uncontroversially be regarded as central to the conservative tradition, for endorsing church-state separation, correctly understood, and for neither embracing nor warring against a mistaken version of the idea. And, there are not good reasons for either supporters or opponents of this complex and contested term to reduce it to a mere slogan calling for the retreat and confinement of religion to the private sphere or the censoring or translation of one's political arguments. What the "separation of church and state" describes or demands is not a civic conversation, social landscape, or public order from which religion is excluded or in which religion is closely policed. Instead, it denotes a structural arrangement, and a constitutional order, in which the church—not "faith," "religion," or "spirituality," but "church" —is distinct from, other than, and independent of the state. In this arrangement, the church—that is, religious associations, communities, and institutions—is not above and controlling, or beneath and subordinate to, the state. It is separate, and so it is free.

And yet, consider the nature of so many of the hot-button "church-state" issues and disputes that are the stuff of front-page stories and high-profile court decisions: May governments allow privately owned menorahs and nativity scenes in public parks, or display the Ten Commandments on the grounds or in the halls of public buildings, or include the words "under God" in the Pledge of Allegiance, or open legislative sessions with prayer? May the state ban ritual animal sacrifice, or the religiously motivated use of hallucinogenic tea or peyote? May a child in a public school read a

Bible story from his favorite book, or hand out pencils with a religious message, or start a Christian club? And so on.

Cases presenting questions like these are touted as church-state disputes. And, there is no doubt that they involve important questions about the freedom of conscience, the powers of governments, and the meaning of citizenship. The image of the lone religious dissenter, heroically confronting overbearing officials or extravagant assertions of state power, is evocative and timeless. No account of religious freedom would be complete if it neglected such clashes or failed to celebrate such courage. And yet, while the "state" is (usually) easy to spot in these cases, where is the "church"?

It is not new to observe that American judicial decisions and public conversations about religious freedom tend to focus on matters of individuals' rights, beliefs, consciences, and practices. The distinctive place, role, and freedoms of groups, associations, and institutions were—until fairly recently[74]—often overlooked or underappreciated.[75] This pattern is consistent with the widespread assumption that, because the individual religious conscience is and should be free and protected through law, religion itself is private and religious freedom is possessed and enjoyed only or primarily by individuals. However, an understanding of religious faith, and religious freedom, that stops with the liberty of the individual's conscience and neglects institutions, communities, and authorities will be incomplete. And, so will the legal arrangements that such an understanding produces.

To understand well and appreciate appropriately the separation of church and state, a broader focus is necessary. One needs to consider not only the clashes—both dramatic and mundane—between religious believers and government officials, but also those involving institutions, groups, communities, associations, clubs, and families. That is, our attention needs to be directed, as two leading law-and-religion scholars have put it, at the "distinctive place of religious entities in our constitutional order."[76] Consistent with this line of inquiry, the separation of church and state should be seen, again, as involving legal arrangements and constitutional constraints whose point is not so much to artificially exclude religious faith from our civil and political lives and spaces as it is to respect and protect religious institutions' appropriate independence, jurisdiction, and autonomy. Religious liberty, in other words, involves not only the immunities of believers but also the "freedom of the church."

But what, in the context of contemporary American law and politics, could, or may, one mean by the "freedom of the church"?[77] In my view, this question should be at the heart of our conversations about and understanding of the separation of church and state, and this idea, or something like it, remains, with appropriate translation and evolution, an important component of any plausible and attractive account of religious freedom under and through constitutionally limited government.

V.

Chief Justice Roberts observed recently, in his opinion for a unanimous Court in the *Hosanna-Tabor* case, that the first constraint to which King John agreed (but did not always respect) in 1215 in the meadows of Runnymede was "that the English Church shall be free, and shall have its rights undiminished, and its liberties unimpaired."[78] And, more than a century earlier, during the Investiture Crisis, the idea of *libertas ecclesiae*—the freedom of the church—served, in Professor Berman's judgment, as the catalyst for "the first major turning point in European history"[79] and as the foundation for nearly a millennium of political theory. Armed with this idea, an eleventh-century monk named Hildebrand—who eventually reigned as Pope Gregory VII—orchestrated a campaign in support of his struggle with secular powers for papal control over the church.[80] He also led a "papal revolution" that, as Berman reports, worked nothing less than a "total transformation" of law, state, and society.[81]

For Hildebrand and his allies, the "freedom of the church" was the "assertion of papal primacy over the entire Western church and"—no less importantly—"of the independence of the Church from secular control."[82] What was at stake in Pope Gregory's confrontation with Emperor Henry IV at Canossa—as at the Cathedral in Canterbury a century later, when the "meddlesome priest" St. Thomas Becket was killed by the agents of another ambitious King Henry[83]—was the "principle that royal jurisdiction was not unlimited . . . and that it was not for the secular authority alone to decide where its boundaries should be fixed."[84] As one writer has put it:

Thanks to the Freedom of the Church, and to the resolution of the investiture controversy in favor of the Church, the state . . . would not be all in all. The state would not occupy every inch of social space. Indeed, the state had to acknowledge that there were some things it couldn't do because it was simply incompetent to do them—and that acknowledgment of limited competence created the social and cultural conditions for the possibility of what a later generation of constitutions and democrats called the limited state. The Western ideal—a limited state in a free society—was made possible in no small part by the investiture crisis.[85]

No Justice of the United States Supreme Court has ever mentioned—at least, not according to Westlaw—Hildebrand, Gregory VII, or Canossa in any published opinion. Nevertheless, engagement with the eleventh-century Investiture Crisis, the "Papal Revolution," and the idea of the "freedom of the church" is, I submit, important for understanding constitutionalism generally and, more specifically, religious freedom under law. As John Courtney Murray once observed, persons are not really free if their "basic human things are not sacredly immune from profanation by the power of the state."[86] The challenge, then, for those concerned with preserving this immunity has long been to find the limiting principle that would "check the encroachments of civil power and preserve these immunities" and, according to Murray, "[w]estern civilization first found this norm in the pregnant principle, the freedom of the Church."[87]

Now, it is tempting to assume that such a "great idea" or "revolutionary" principle of limited government in the service of human freedom must be deeply rooted and comfortably well established in our Constitution's text, history, structure, and doctrine. It is not entirely clear, though, that or how it is.[88] This is not to ignore the fact that there are a number of constitutional doctrines and lines of cases that guard churches' ability and right to control their internal structures and operations, to select their own ministers, to propose their own messages, to administer their own sacraments, to conduct their own liturgies, and so on.[89] Still, appearances can be deceiving and it is not obvious or settled that these doctrines in fact reflect a robust underlying commitment in our law to the freedom of the church as a structural principle of constitutional

government. The Court's recent *Hosanna-Tabor* decision notwithstanding, it could be that we are living off the capital of this idea—
that is, we enjoy, embrace, and depend upon its freedom-enabling
effects—without a real appreciation for or even a memory of what
it is, implies, and presumes.[90]

For us today, the principle or idea that does the work of affirming and ensuring that the state is not "all in all" is not the freedom of the church, but the freedom of the individual conscience.
In our religious-freedom doctrines and conversations, it is more
likely that the independence and autonomy of churches, or of religious institutions and associations generally, are framed as deriving from, or existing in the service of, the free-exercise or conscience rights of individual persons than as providing the basis
or foundation for those rights.[91] In this sense, if I am right about
conservatism, these doctrines and conversations are less consonant with Burke's *Reflections* than with the rationalism and roman-
ticism against which he reacted. In any event, an understanding of
religious freedom that purports to respect the rights of belief and
conscience while authorizing or tolerating intrusive government
supervision of churches' expression, rituals, and doctrine is probably a hollow and unstable one. A better understanding—and, as
it happens, a more "conservative" one—appreciates that authentic freedom of religion does not exist when its manifestation in
and expression through the life of non-state institutions and communities is prohibited and that independence and space for such
institutions and communities is both a feature of and a necessary
condition for political freedom.[92] It is one that treats the freedom
of the church, or something like it, as a structural feature of social
and political life—one that promotes and enhances freedom by
limiting government—and also as a moral right of religious communities, not simply as an effect or implication of private, individual claims to freedom of conscience and immunity from government coercion in matters of religious belief.

VI.

In my view, there is and there ought to be a place in American
thought, politics, and law for a "revolutionary" structural principle

like the "freedom of the church." Certainly, at the very least, one hears echoes of this principle in the arguments and opinions in *Hosanna-Tabor*. And, again, there are a variety of constitutional cases, tests, and rules that evoke or resemble it. Most notably, there is the doctrine of "church autonomy" which, in Professor Bradley's words, is "the issue that arises when legal principles displace religious communities' internal rules of interpersonal relations (as opposed to prescriptions for personal spirituality)."[93] So understood, Bradley insists, "church autonomy" is the "flagship issue of church and state," the "litmus test of a regime's commitment to geniune spiritual freedom."[94]

It should be conceded, though, that the "church autonomy" doctrine seems as much a collection of themes, or a grab-bag of discrete holdings in particular cases—a mood, even[95]—as a clear rule, prohibition, or principle: The Court told us, in its battered-but-still-standing *Lemon* decision, that the First Amendment does not permit state action that creates or requires "excessive entanglement" between the government and religious institutions, practices, teachings, and decisions.[96] It commands that the "secular and religious authorities . . . not interfere with each other's respective spheres of choice and influence."[97] In an intriguing line of cases,[98] the Justices have refused to "undertake to resolve [religious] controversies" because "the hazards are ever present of inhibiting the free development of religious doctrine and of implicating secular interests in matters of purely ecclesiastical concern."[99] The Court has affirmed, time and again, the "fundamental right of churches to 'decide for themselves, free from state interference, matters of church government as well as those of faith and doctrine,'"[100] and deferred to church authorities and processes "on matters purely ecclesiastical."[101] The Supreme Court in *Hosanna-Tabor* recently joined the many other courts that have recognized a constitutionally required "ministerial exception" in employment-discrimination cases.[102] And, the Court has approved some exemptions from anti-discrimination or other general laws on the ground that they promote and protect the independence and free-exercise rights of religious institutions.[103]

Still, and *Hosanna-Tabor* notwithstanding, it remains unsettled what exactly are the content and textual home in the Constitution for the church-autonomy principle, and it does not seem unfair to suggest that the doctrine has something of an imprecise emanations-and-penumbras air about it.[104] Many scholars and courts locate the church-autonomy rule in the Free Exercise Clause.[105] Others have looked instead to the Establishment Clause's proscription on "excessive entanglement."[106] The Supreme Court grounded the ministerial exception in both Clauses.[107] Some experts appear to regard the rule as an implication from general, foundational religious-freedom principles underlying the Religion Clauses, such as church-state "separation"[108] or the "voluntary principle."[109] Professor Esbeck has explained that the autonomy of churches follows from the fact that the Establishment Clause is a "structural restraint" on government (while the Free Exercise Clause protects individuals' rights of belief and practice).[110] Something like the church-autonomy rule, if not the rule itself, might be found within the privacy protected by the Fourteenth Amendment,[111] or adjacent to the freedom of expressive association.[112] Perhaps it is reinforced by a correct understanding of the long-neglected freedom of assembly.[113]

It is not only the lack of a clear doctrinal and textual home that might stir up doubts about whether the church-autonomy cluster captures, reflects, or protects the freedom of the church. It is noteworthy that one of the justifying premises sometimes invoked in the relevant cases is the asserted incompetence of secular courts to resolve internal church disputes or to interpret and apply religious rules.[114] Indeed, in some discussions, the immunity of churches' internal decisions is framed as a function of their irrationality, as a result of the asserted fact that "religious truth by its nature [is] not subject to a test of validity determined by rational thought and empiric knowledge."[115] But the fact that answering religious questions or making religious decisions can involve recourse to and reliance on materials with which secular judges are unfamiliar, or even on revelation, is not, in itself, a particularly strong reason for a rule protecting churches' autonomy in matters of governance and structure. Judges confront new substantive areas all the time and the issue in church-autonomy cases rarely has to do with the truth or content of revelation.[116] Indeed, a church-autonomy doctrine grounded ultimately, or even largely, on abstention-like notions

seems to miss the point. Distinguishing "substantive nonentanglement" from "decisional nonentanglement," Professor Berg put the
matter well:

> More important than whether courts avoid theological questions is
> whether religious organizations are substantively free to organize
> themselves and define their mission free from unwarranted govern-
> mental interference. . . . We keep courts out of such questions not
> just for the sake of doing so, but ultimately for the sake of substan-
> tive religious autonomy: when judges make theological determina-
> tions, they may distort and unjustifiably override a church's organi-
> zation and self-understanding.[117]

Pope Gregory VII's objection to Henry's claims of power over the
naming of bishops was not and could hardly have been merely that
the job required the use of technical expertise for which the former, but not the latter, had been well prepared by virtue of his
clerical training.

The laws and canons of a particular church or religious community need not be more inscrutable or inaccessible to a judge
than those of any other entity or voluntary association. But, it
would seem crucial to the success of any proposed translation or
incorporation of the *libertas ecclesiae* principle into our law that
churches not be assimilated and reduced to such associations.[118]
And the Supreme Court explicitly refused, in the *Hosanna-
Tabor* case, to do so, calling "untenable" the suggestion that an
"implicit" right to "freedom of association" renders unnecessary
a ministerial exception grounded in "the Religious Clauses themselves."[119] It is true, as I have discussed elsewhere,[120] that churches,
like many other voluntary associations, play a structural, mediating role in limiting government and preserving space in civil society for the development of, and competition among, values and
loyalties. This does not mean, though, that constitutional doctrines friendly to the formation and expression of such associations capture fully the still-relevant content of the older freedom
of the church idea.

So, a meaningful, appropriately translated principle of the
freedom of the church is not reducible simply to an implication
of civil judges' lack of technical competence and familiarity with
"religious" sources. It should also not be understood merely in

terms of government "neutrality" or as following from the "private" nature of religion and religious belief.[121] That is, the explanation for the freedom of the church has never been merely that religion and religious institutions are and do "private" things that governments do not or should not care about. As Professor Hittinger has pointed out, it is one thing to say that the government lacks authority over religious matters; it is "quite another to assert that, on principled grounds, the government must remain neutral on religion as such."[122] The goal of the *libertas ecclesiae* principle is not government neutrality for its own sake and it is not the domestication or privatization of religion. It is religious freedom, which "cannot be reduced either to [private] individual liberty or to governmental incompetence."[123] Religious freedom, which includes the freedom of the church, is a good to be promoted and not merely the result of, or what is left over after, government neutrality or incompetence.

In my view, the First Amendment can and should be understood to endorse and vindicate what Mark DeWolfe Howe called the "pluralistic thesis . . . that government must recognize that it is not the sole possessor of sovereignty"[124] and therefore as constitutionalizing some version—again, a translated, adjusted, and perhaps "chastened" version[125]—of institutional religious freedom, or the freedom of the church. To some, this view is controversial; clearly, it is both contested and contestable. That it is contested and contestable should be a cause for concern, especially for those situated in or sympathetic to the conservative tradition, because the freedom of the church, as a structural principle and as a reality, matters.

It matters, for starters, because—as was suggested earlier—there is at the very least a plausible argument that it has played and does play an important, even if unnoticed today, role in protecting the freedom of conscience in religious (and other) matters.[126] If Murray was right, and the modern experiment has been to substitute autonomous individuals' individual consciences—whose designated protector would be the liberal state, through the vehicle of individual rights—for the freedom of the church as the guarantor of the social space necessary for meaningful pluralism, then it would appear modern freedom of religion is attacking its own foundations—that, in a way, the immunity of conscience is eating itself. In addition, and again, the case can be made that the freedom of the church has mattered and does matter for the development and sustaining of constitutionally limited government.[127] Constitutionalism as an enterprise would seem to depend for its success, at least in part, on the existence and activities of non-state authorities, and so this enterprise is one to which religious freedom and church autonomy contribute. And, as Professor Brady has explained, freedom for churches and religious institutions makes it possible for them to continue proposing, "prophetically," "national values" and "preserving new visions of social life for us all."[128]

Indeed, the freedom of the church matters more than many of the matters at issue in most contemporary church-state disputes and debates. If religious freedom, grounded on human dignity and directed toward human flourishing, is the good for which we are aiming, preserving a plausible but meaningful church-autonomy principle is more important than insisting on snippets of civil religion on the walls of secular courthouses or inserting them in professions of national loyalty. Even if it is true that the First Amendment is best understood to permit official acknowledgments of religion and public displays of religious symbols, it is also true that such acknowledgments do little to protect religious institutions, groups, authorities, and communities and their important structural and other roles and contributions. The attention directed by many contemporary activists and advocates who identify as "conservative" to such acknowledgments and displays is, if not misplaced, at least underinclusive.

The freedom of the church matters, but it is vulnerable. In part, this vulnerability is connected to the limited, and perhaps dwindling, appeal in public discourse of "church autonomy." We tend to be, generally speaking, enthusiastic about autonomy, but many of us are uneasy about connecting "church" with *nomos*— or with jurisdiction, authority, sovereignty, and so on. Matters are not helped by the fact that the idea is sometimes understood as entailing the unattractive and implausible assertion that clergy and church employees are entirely "above the law" and unaccountable for wrongs they do or harms they cause.[129] And, the freedom of religious associations, communities, and institutions is made more vulnerable by the link that many perceive between church-autonomy principles, on the one hand, and—on the other—sexual abuse by clergy, venality and mismanagement by bishops, and dioceses' declarations of bankruptcy.[130] To the extent the church-autonomy principle is thought to privilege institutions over individuals, or structures over believers, its appeal will suffer, given that people today think about faith—and, by extension, about religious freedom—more in terms of personal spirituality than of institutional affiliation, public worship, and tradition.[131] We are—many of us, anyway—like the woman, Sheila Larson, described by Robert Bellah and his colleagues in *The Habits of the Heart*, who described her faith as "Sheilaism."[132] If we approach religious faith as a form of self-expression, performance art, or therapy, we are likely to regard religious institutions as, at best, potentially useful vehicles or tools but more likely as stifling constraints or bothersome obstacles to self-discovery. If a commitment to the freedom of the church is thought to privilege religious institutions, that commitment's appeal will suffer as special or distinctive treatment for "religion" becomes more controversial.[133]

At perhaps a deeper level, though, it could be that the freedom of the church is vulnerable because of the increasingly widespread acceptance of the idea that liberal values and nondiscrimination norms ought not only to constrain state action, but also to inform state action constraining non-state actors and associations.[134] The tension between the desire and efforts of governments to combat invidious and irrational discrimination and the constitutional and other limits on these governments' power and ability to do so is at the heart of many current debates and recent Court decisions, including *Hosanna-Tabor* and *Christian Legal Society v. Martinez*.[135] This tension reflects and results from the fact that liberal political communities, precisely because they are liberal, are generally thought to be committed to tolerating, and even protecting, illiberal groups, ideas, and expression, and so they "risk being undermined by groups that do not support liberal institutions," values, and aims.[136] And so, as Larry Alexander has observed, liberalism—at least, in its more restrained and less comprehensive forms—in fact "rests on a bedrock of illiberalism. That is, one cannot be a liberal 'all the way down.' If that is so, then it raises the question, at what level does liberalism demand that one be 'liberal,' and why?"[137]

Part of a conservative response to this question has included and should include an invocation and defense of pluralism and of the freedom of the church. Stanley Hauerwas once observed that the "rights of the individual have become the secular equivalent of the church as the means to keep government in its proper sphere."[138] However, he continued, the "very means used to ensure that the democratic state be a limited state . . . turn out to be no less destructive for intermediate institutions than the monistic state of Marxism."[139] Similarly, it is more likely today that churches and their autonomy are regarded as dangerous centers of potentially oppressive power, as in need of supervision and regulation by the state in its capacity as protector of individual liberty and conscience.[140] But if, as Berman proposed, the freedom of the church is not easily separated from both the history and the health of political freedom under constitutionally limited government, it would appear that, in Professor Hamburger's words, the illiberal expansion of "liberal ideals and, more broadly, liberalism could . . . become a threat to freedom."[141] Such a warning would seem very much at home in the tradition of "American Conservative Thought and Politics."

NOTES

1. Harold Laski, "The Personality of Associations," *Harvard Law Review* 29 (February 1916): 425.

2. Abraham Kuyper, *Lectures on Calvinism* (Princeton, NJ: L. P. Stone Foundation Lectures, 1898, photo. reprint 2007), 96.

3. An earlier version of this chapter was presented on January 6, 2007, at the Annual Meeting of the American Society for Political and Legal Philosophy. The theme for the meeting was "American Conservative Thought and Politics." I was and remain grateful for thoughtful and challenging responses to my presentation by Elizabeth Harman, Ingrid Creppell, and Sandy Levinson and for helpful questions from Andrew Sabl, Eric Claeys, Bill Galston, Jacob Levy, Nathan Tarcov, my former teacher Martin Golding, and others. I am also in debt to Professor Levinson and Joel Parker for their generous patience during this chapter's, and this volume's, long gestation. Versions and portions of the paper that was presented at the January 2007 meeting have been published elsewhere, and I have continued to

explore, develop, and—I hope—deepen my understanding of its claims, proposals, and themes. See, as examples, Richard W. Garnett, "The Freedom of the Church," *Journal of Catholic Social Thought* 4 (Winter 2007): 59–81; "Do Churches Matter? Towards an Institutional Understanding of the Religion Clauses," *Villanova Law Review* 53 (Issue 2, 2008): 273–296; "Religious Liberty, Church Autonomy, and the Structure of Freedom," in John Witte, Jr. and Frank S. Alexander, eds., *Christianity and Human Rights: An Introduction* (Cambridge: Cambridge University Press, 2010), 267–282; "'The Freedom of the Church': (Towards) an Exposition, Translation, and Defense," *Journal of Contemporary Legal Issues* 21 (Issue 1, 2013): 33–58. If I were, in late 2013, starting fresh, or writing on the proverbial "blank slate," or putting forward my current and now-more-considered thinking on the paper's subject, I would say some different things and some things differently than I did in 2007. That said, for the sake of historical accuracy and also in order to avoid imposing additional burdens on my colleagues who wrote responses, this chapter is not substantially different from the paper that I presented at the meeting. The title and the opening quotations, though, are new.

4. See Russell Kirk, *The Conservative Mind, from Burke to Eliot*, 3rd rev. ed. (Chicago: H. Regnery, 1960). First published as *The Conservative Mind, from Burke to Santayana* (Chicago: H. Regnery, 1953).

5. See, for example, Andrew Ferguson, "Older & Wiser? A Weekly Standard 10th Anniversary Symposium," *Weekly Standard* 11 (September 19, 2005). "From *The Conservative Mind* to *Savage Nation*; from Clifton White to Dick Morris; from Willmoore Kendall and Harry Jaffa to Sean Hannity and Mark Fuhrman—all in little more than a generation's time. Whatever this is, it isn't progress."

6. Lionel Trilling, *The Liberal Imagination: Essays on Literature and Society* (New York: Viking Press, 1950).

7. See, for example, Jason DeParle, "Goals Reached, Donor on Right Closes Up Shop," *New York Times* (May 29, 2005). "Feeling outmatched in the war of ideas, liberal groups have spent years studying conservative foundations the way Pepsi studies Coke, searching for trade secrets."

8. Sam Tanenhaus, *The Death of Conservatism* (New York: Random House, 2009).

9. Carolyn May, "Cruz: Conservatism Is on the 'Verge of a Rebirth,'" *Daily Caller* (January 26, 2013).

10. See Russell Kirk, *The Conservative Mind: From Burke to Eliot*, 7th rev. ed. (Washington, DC: Regnery, [1986] 2001), 6. "[T]he American Revolution, substantially, had been a conservative reaction, in the English political tradition, against royal innovation." But see Gordon S. Wood, *The Radicalism of the American Revolution* (New York: Knopf, 1992).

11. See Damon Linker, *The Theocons: Secular America Under Siege* (New York: Doubleday, 2006).

12. See Rod Dreher, *Crunchy Cons: How Birkenstocked Burkeans, Gun-Loving Organic Gardeners, Evangelical Free-Range Farmers, Hip Homeschooling Mamas, Right-Wing Nature Lovers, and Their Diverse Tribe of Counter-Cultural Conservatives Plan to Save America (Or At Least the Republican Party)* (New York: Crown Forum, 2006).

13. Reihan Salam and Ross Douthat, "The Party of Sam's Club," *Weekly Standard* 11 (November 14, 2005).

14. Brian C. Anderson, "South Park Republicans," *Dallas Morning News* (April 17, 2005).

15. See Yuval Levin, *The Great Debate: Edmund Burke, Thomas Paine, and the Birth of Right and Left* (New York: Basic Books, 2014).

16. See Andrew Sullivan, *The Conservative Soul: How We Lost It, How To Get It Back* (New York: HarperCollins, 2006), and Rick Santorum, *It Takes a Family: Conservatism and the Common Good* (Wilmington, DE: ISI Books, 2005).

17. William F. Buckley, "Publisher's Statement," *National Review* (November 19, 1955).

18. President George W. Bush, "Speech to UN General Assembly" (September 21, 2004). Available online at: http://www.cbsnews.com/news/text-of-bushs-speech-to-un/.

19. Abraham Kuyper, "Uniformity: The Curse of Modern Life," in *Abraham Kuyper: A Centennial Reader,* ed. James D. Bratt (Grand Rapids, MI: W. B. Eerdmans, 1998), 24.

20. Sanford Levinson, "Bush v. Gore and the French Revolution: A Tentative List of Some Early Lessons," *Law and Contemporary Problems* 65 (Summer 2002): 7, citing Simon Schama, *Citizens: A Chronicle of the French Revolution* (New York: Knopf, 1989), xiii. It is not clear who asked the question; candidates range from Richard Nixon to Archduke Otto van Hapsburg.

21. Kirk, *The Conservative Mind* (2001), 6.

22. Mary Ann Glendon, "Rousseau and the Revolt Against Reason," in *Traditions in Turmoil* (Ann Arbor, MI: Sapientia Press of Ave Maria University, 2006), 39.

23. John Courtney Murray, *We Hold These Truths: Catholic Reflections on the American Proposition,* New ed. (Lanham, MD: Rowan & Littlefield, 2005), 277, 278.

24. George H. Sabine, "The Two Democratic Traditions," *Philosophical Review* 61 (October 1952): 464.

25. Robert A. Nisbet, "Rousseau and Totalitarianism," *Journal of Politics* 5 (May 1943): 103.

26. An engaging and accessible account is provided in Michael Burleigh, *Earthly Powers: The Clash of Religion and Politics in Europe from the French Revolution to the Great War* (New York: HarperCollins, 2005).

27. By way of comparison, consider Steven H. Shiffrin, *The Religious Left and Church-State Relations* (Princeton, NJ: Princeton University Press, [2009] 2012).

28. Compare, for example, Russell Kirk, *The Conservative Mind* (1960), 539, who suggests that the first problem for conservatives is "[t]he problem of spiritual and moral regeneration; the restoration of the ethical system and the religious sanction upon which any life worth living is founded."

29. See generally John Witte, Jr., "Publick Religion: Adams v. Jefferson," *First Things* (March 2004): 20–35.

30. See, for example, John Gibson, *The War on Christmas: How the Liberal Plot to Ban the Sacred Christian Holiday Is Worse than You Thought* (New York: Sentinel [2005] 2006).

31. Jim Stratton, "Rep. Harris Condemns Separation of Church, State," *Orlando Sentinel* (August 26, 2006): A9. See also David Barton, *Myth of Separation: What Is the Correct Relationship Between Church and State? A Revealing Look at What the Founders and Early Courts Really Said* (Aledo, TX: Wallbuilder Press, 1992). More recently, another Republican political candidate, Christine O'Donnell, complicated her run for one of Delaware's seats in the U.S. Senate by asking, during a debate, "[w]here in the Constitution is the separation of church and state?" Of course, there was and is considerably more to her question than was appreciated by those who mocked it. See, for example, Vikram David Amar and Alan Brownstein, "Does It Matter that the Constitution Never Uses the Phrase 'The Separation of Church and State'? The Coons/O'Donnell Debate and the Importance of Constitutional Metaphor," *FindLaw's Writ* (October 22, 2010). Available online at: http://writ.news.findlaw.com/amar/20101022.html.

32. Joseph Cardinal Ratzinger, *The Salt of the Earth: Christianity and the Catholic Church at the End of the Millennium* (San Francisco: Ignatius Press, 1997), 240. See also, for example, Pope Benedict XVI, *Deus Caritas Est*, encyclical letter given at Saint Peter's in Rome (December 25, 2005): "Fundamental to Christianity is the distinction between what belongs to Caesar and what belongs to God . . . in other words, the distinction between Church and State," paragraph 28(a). See also, generally, Richard W. Garnett, "Church, State, and the Practice of Love," *Villanova Law Review* 52 (Issue 2, 2007): 281–302.

33. Daniel L. Dreisbach, "Origins and Dangers of the 'Wall of Separation' Between Church and State," *Imprimis* 35 (October 2006).

34. Philip Hamburger, "Separation and Interpretation," *Journal of Law & Politics* 18 (Winter 2002): 7. See also Philip Hamburger, *Separation of*

Church and State (Cambridge, MA: Harvard University Press, 2002). "Jefferson's words seem to have shaped the nation."

35. See, as examples: Dreisbach, in "Origins and Dangers": "For many Americans, this metaphor has supplanted the actual text of the First Amendment to the U.S. Constitution, and it has become the *locus classicus* of the notion that the First Amendment separated religion and the civil state, thereby mandating a strictly secular polity"; and Hamburger, *Separation of Church and State*, 1: "Jefferson's phrase . . . provides the label with which vast numbers of Americans refer to their religious freedom."

36. *Wallace v. Jaffree*, 472 U.S. 38, 107 (1985), Rehnquist, J., dissenting.

37. See, for example, John Witte, Jr., *Religion and the American Constitutional Experiment: Essential Rights and Liberties* (Boulder, CO: Westview Press, 2000), 48–50. Witte notes that "separation of church and state guarantees 'ecclesiastical purity and liberty'—the independence and integrity of the internal processes of religious bodies."

38. Consider in comparison: John Witte, Jr., *God's Joust, God's Justice: Law and Religion in the Western Tradition* (Grand Rapids, MI: William B. Eerdman's, 2006): 160–162, discussing the "separation and cooperation" of church and state in American Puritan thought and practice; and Hamburger, *Separation of Church and State*, 2, contrasting "a differentiation or distinction between church and state" with "something more dramatic—a distance, segregation, or absence of contact between church and state."

39. See generally Garnett, "Religious Liberty, Church Autonomy, and the Structure of Freedom."

40. John Courtney Murray, "Law or Prepossessions?" *Journal of Law and Contemporary Problems* 14 (Winter 1949): 23–42.

41. See Stephen L. Carter, *The Culture of Disbelief: How American Law and Politics Trivialize Religious Devotion* (New York: Basic Books [1993] 1994).

42. Witte, *Religion and the American Constitutional Experiment*, 209.

43. For example, see generally Carl H. Esbeck, "Dissent and Disestablishment: The Church-State Settlement in the Early American Republic," *Brigham Young University Law Review* 2004 (Issue 4, 2004): 1395–1447.

44. Witte, *Religion and the American Constitutional Experiment*, 210.

45. *Matthew* 22: 21 (New American Bible). The next verse records that when the Pharisees heard this, "they were amazed, and leaving him they went away."

46. The text of this letter from Pope Gelasius I, *Duo sunt* (A.D. 494), is available online through the Internet Medieval Source Book, at: http://www.fordham.edu/halsall/source/gelasius1.html. For more on the letter's context and aims, see generally, as examples, Robert Louis Wilken, *The First Thousand Years: A Global History of Christianity* (New Haven, CT:

Yale University Press, 2012), 170–171; Nicholas Wolterstorff, *The Mighty and the Almighty: An Essay in Political Theology* (Cambridge: Cambridge University Press, 2012), 124–140; Brian Tierney, *The Crisis of Church and State, 1050–1300: With Selected Documents* (Toronto: University of Toronto Press with the Medieval Academy of America, [1964] 1988), 8–15; and Heinrich A. Rommen, *The State in Catholic Thought: A Treatise in Political Philosophy* (St. Louis, MO: Herder, 1945), 523–524.

 47. Pope Boniface VIII, *Unam Sanctam* (November 18, 1302).

 48. Roger Williams, *Mr. Cotton's Letter Lately Printed, Examined and Answered* (London: 1644), 313–396.

 49. "Letter from the Danbury Baptist Association to Thomas Jefferson" (October 7, 1801), on file with the Thomas Jefferson Papers Manuscript Division, Library of Congress, Washington, DC. See generally, for example, Daniel L. Dreisbach, "Sowing Useful Truths and Principles: The Danbury Baptists, Thomas Jefferson, and the Wall of Separation," *Journal of Church and State* 39 (Summer 1997): 455–502.

 50. "Letter from the Danbury Baptist Association."

 51. Daniel L. Dreisbach and John D. Whaley, "What the Wall Separates: A Debate on Thomas Jefferson's 'Wall of Separation' Metaphor," *Constitutional Commentary* 16 (Winter 1999): 631.

 52. Ibid. "The surviving manuscripts reveal that Jefferson's reply was written with meticulous care and planned effect." The letter's political context and the motives and concerns that probably shaped it are described in James H. Hutson, "Thomas Jefferson's Letter to the Danbury Baptists: A Controversy Rejoined," *William and Mary Quarterly* 56 (October 1999): 775–790. See also Hamburger, *Separation of Church and State*, 144–161, noting that Jefferson "elevated anticlerical rhetoric to constitutional law."

 53. "Letter from Thomas Jefferson to the Danbury Baptist Association" (January 1, 1802), on file with the Thomas Jefferson Papers Manuscript Division, Library of Congress, Washington, DC.

 54. James Hutson, "A 'Wall of Separation': FBI Helps Restore Jefferson's Obliterated Draft," *Library of Congress Information Bulletin* 57 (Number 6, June 1998). Hamburger, *Separation of Church and State*, 162: "[H]is epistle was not widely published or even noticed." Professor Dreisbach has noted that Jefferson's Letter to the Danbury Baptists first received wide circulation in 1853, when it was included in an edition of his works. See Dreisbach, "Sowing Useful Truths and Principles."

 55. Hamburger, *Separation of Church and State*, 163–180, contrasting the Baptists' views relating to religious freedom with Jefferson's version of separationism.

 56. Dreisbach and Whaley, "What the Wall Separates," 635.

57. See generally Hamburger, *Separation of Church and State*. See also Witte, *Religion and the American Constitutional Experiment*, 231: "[T]he principle of separation of church and state became one of the strong new weapons in the anti-Catholic arsenal." Compare to Douglas Laycock, "The Many Meanings of Separation," *University of Chicago Law Review* 70 (Fall 2003): 1678, agreeing that, in the early- to mid-nineteenth century, "separation took on a new meaning, roughly but fairly summarized as restricting Catholic influence," but insisting also that "separation" has and has long had many meanings.

58. 98 U.S. 145, 164 (1879).

59. *Everson*, 330 U.S. 1 (1947).

60. See Murray, "Law or Prepossessions?", 40. "The absolutism of [*Everson*] . . . is unsupported, and unsupportable, by valid evidence and reasoning—historical, political, or legal—or on any sound theory of values, religious or social." See generally, as examples, Hamburger, *Separation of Church and State*, 454–478; and Donald L. Drakeman, *Church, State, and Original Intent* (Cambridge: Cambridge University Press, 2010).

61. *Everson*, 16, 18.

62. See Hamburger, *Separation of Church and State*, 463–472; John T. McGreevy, *Catholicism and American Freedom: A History* (New York: W. W. Norton, 2003), 183–186.

63. See, for example, Ira C. Lupu, "Lingering Death of Separationism," *George Washington Law Review* 62 (January 1994): 230–279.

64. *Wallace v. Jaffree*, 472 U.S. 38, 91 (1985), Rehnquist, J., dissenting: "It is impossible to build sound constitutional doctrine upon a mistaken understanding of Constitutional history, but unfortunately the Establishment Clause has been expressly freighted with Jefferson's misleading metaphor for nearly 40 years."

65. See, for example, Dreisbach and Whaley, "What the Wall Separates," 627. "No word or phrase is associated more closely by Americans with the topic of church-state relations than the 'wall of separation.'"

66. See, for example, *Zelman v. Simmons-Harris*, 536 U.S. 639, 686 (2002), Stevens, J., dissenting: "Whenever we remove a brick from the wall that was designed to separate religion and government, we increase the risk of religious strife and weaken the foundation of our democracy." A chapter in Dean Erwin Chemerinsky's recent critique of the Court's "conservative" turn, entitled "Dismantling the Wall Separating Church and State," concludes with the claim that "little is left of the wall that separates church and state." Erwin Chemerinsky, *The Conservative Assault on the Constitution* (New York: Simon & Schuster, 2010), 134.

67. See, as examples: *Good News Club v. Milford Central School*, 533 U.S.

98 (2001); and *Rosenberger v. Rector and Visitors of the University of Virginia*, 515 U.S. 819 (1995). Compare to *Locke v. Davey*, 540 U.S. 712 (2004).

68. See, for example, *Van Orden v. Perry*, 545 U.S. 677, 698–705 (2005), Breyer, J., concurring. Consider by comparison Richard W. Garnett, "Religion, Division, and the First Amendment," *Georgetown Law Journal* 94 (August 2006): 1667–1724, criticizing the argument that judicial predictions or observations regarding political divisiveness along religious lines should determine outcomes in Establishment Clause cases.

69. Pope Benedict XVI, *Deus Caritas Est*, paragraph 28(a). "The Church . . . cannot and must not replace the State. Yet at the same time she cannot and must not remain on the sidelines in the fight for justice."

70. *Zorach v. Clauson*, 343 U.S. 306, 312 (1952). See also, as examples: *Lemon v. Kurtzman*, 403 U.S. 602, 614 (1971), observing that the "line of separation" is not so much a "wall" as a "blurred, indistinct, and variable barrier"; and *Lynch v. Donnelly*, 465 U.S. 668, 673 (1984), "No significant segment of our society and no institution within it can exist in a vacuum or in total or absolute isolation from all the other parts, much less from government."

71. Pope Benedict XVI, *Deus Caritas Est*, paragraph 28(a), writing that church and state are "distinct, yet always interrelated."

72. Robert E. Rodes, Jr., "The Last Days of Erastianism: Forms in the American Church-States Nexus," *Harvard Theological Review* 62 (July 1969): 301–348.

73. *The American Heritage Dictionary of the English Language*, 3rd ed. (Boston: Houghton Mifflin, 1992), 1120.

74. In the years since this chapter was originally presented in 2007, interest in, scholarship about, and litigation involving religious institutions, groups, communities, and associations has increased dramatically. See, as examples: Paul Horwitz, *First Amendment Institutions* (Cambridge, MA: Harvard University Press, 2013); John D. Inazu, *Liberty's Refuge: The Forgotten Freedom of Assembly* (New Haven, CT: Yale University Press, 2012); Garnett, " 'The Freedom of the Church': (Towards) an Exposition"; Steven D. Smith, "Prologue to the Symposium," *Journal of Contemporary Legal Issues* 21 (Issue 1, 2013): 1–14; Andrew Koppelman, " 'Freedom of the Church' and the Authority of the State," same issue, 145–164; and Richard Schragger and Micah Schwartzman, "Against Religious Institutionalism," *Virginia Law Review* 99 (September 2013): 917–986. The minor revisions that I have made to this chapter do not attempt to take fully into account or to engage closely these important and interesting developments.

75. See, for example, Gerard V. Bradley, "Church Autonomy in the Constitutional Order: The End of Church and State," *Louisiana Law*

Review 49 (May 1989): 1064, noting that the idea of "church autonomy" sits uneasily in our law and discourse about religious freedom, because of our "longstanding blind spot . . . concerning groups of all kinds. Liberalism," he continues, "adeptly reasons about the individual and the state, but cannot fathom groups."

76. Ira C. Lupu and Robert Tuttle, "The Distinctive Place of Religious Entities in our Constitutional Order," *Villanova Law Review* 47 (Issue 1, 2002): 37–92.

77. Compare, for example, Garnett, " 'The Freedom of the Church': (Towards) an Exposition" and Smith, "Prologue to the Symposium," with Paul Horwitz, "Freedom of the Church Without Romance," *Journal of Contemporary Legal Issues* 21 (Issue 1, 2013): 59–132.

78. *Hosanna-Tabor Evangelical Lutheran Church and School v. E.E.O.C.*, 132 S. Ct. 694, 702 (2012), noting that the Church's "freedom in many cases may have been more theoretical than real." See also Sir Frederick Pollock and Frederic William Maitland, *The History of English Law Before the Time of Edward I, Vol. 1*, 2nd ed. (Washington, DC: Lawyers' Literary Club, [1898] 1959), 172. "The vague large promise that the church of England shall be free is destined to arouse hopes that have been dormant and cannot be fulfilled."

79. Harold J. Berman, *Law and Revolution: The Formation of the Western Legal Tradition* (Cambridge, MA: Harvard University Press, 1983), 87.

80. Ibid., 94, quoting from the "Introduction" in Gerd Tellenbach, *Church, State, and Christian Society at the Time of the Investiture Contest*, trans. R. F. Bennett (Oxford: Blackwell, 1940), xiv–xv.

81. Berman, *Law and Revolution*, 23. See also Witte, *Religion and the American Constitutional Experiment*, 1–14, discussing the "papal revolution." See generally, as examples, Tierney, *The Crisis of Church and State*; and Robert Louis Wilken, "Gregory VII and the Politics of the Spirit," in *The Second One Thousand Years: Ten People Who Defined a Millennium*, ed. Richard John Neuhaus (Grand Rapids, MI: W. B. Eerdmans, 2001), 1–14.

82. Berman, *Law and Revolution*, 50. See also Witte, *Religion and the American Constitutional Experiment*, 11–12, noting Pope Gregory VII's claim that "[o]nly the pope . . . had authority to ordain, discipline, depose, and reinstate bishops, to convoke and control church councils, and to establish and administer abbeys and bishoprics."

83. In the Academy Award–winning 1964 film, *Becket*, England's King Henry II—played by Peter O'Toole—says of Thomas Becket, the Archbishop of Canterbury—played by Richard Burton—"will no one rid me of this meddlesome priest?"

84. Berman, *Law and Revolution*, 269.

85. George Weigel, *The Cube and the Cathedral: Europe, America, and Politics without God* (New York: Basic Books, 2005), 101. See also Wilken, "Gregory VII," 10: "By desacralizing the authority of the king, Gregory disengaged the spiritual world from political control (at least in theory) and set in motion forces that would alter not only the self-understanding of the Church but also of the state . . . . Deprived of its spiritual authority, the state was forced to conceive of itself anew as a corporate body independent of the Church."

86. Murray, *We Hold These Truths*, 204.

87. Ibid. Also, at 205, arguing that it was the freedom of the Church that furnished a "social armature to the sacred order," within which the human person would be "secure in all the freedoms that his sacredness demands."

88. In *Hosanna-Tabor*, of course, a unanimous Court affirmed that the First Amendment "bar[s] the government from interfering with the decision of a religious group to fire one of its ministers," 702; that the Free Exercise Clause "protects a religious group's right to shape its own faith and mission through its appointments," 706; and that "[a]ccording the state the power to determine which individuals will minister to the faithful violates the Establishment Clause." I regard this as one of the Court's most important religion-related decisions in decades. At the same time, the decision left many questions unanswered and its implications remain to be seen. See generally, as examples: Christopher C. Lund, "Free Exercise Reconceived: The Logic and Limits of *Hosanna-Tabor*," *Northwestern University Law Review* 108 (Summer 2014): 1183–1234; Michael A. Helfand, "Religion's Footnote Four: Church Autonomy as Arbitration," *Minnesota Law Review* 97 (June 2013): 1891–1962; Michael W. McConnell, "Reflections on *Hosanna-Tabor*," *Harvard Journal of Law & Public Policy* 35 (Summer 2012): 821–838; and Richard W. Garnett and John M. Robinson, "*Hosanna-Tabor*, Religious Freedom, and the Constitutional Structure," *Cato Supreme Court Review* 2011–2012 (2012): 307–332.

89. See generally Richard W. Garnett, "Assimilation, Toleration, and the State's Interest in the Development of Religious Doctrine," *UCLA Law Review* 51 (August 2004): 1652–1659.

90. Compare to Murray, *We Hold These Truths*, 215: "On the one hand, modernity has denied (or ignored, or forgotten, or neglected) the Christian revelation that man is a sacredness, and that his primatial *res sacra*, his freedom, is sought and found ultimately within the freedom of the Church. On the other hand, modernity has pretended to lay claim to the effects of this doctrine."

91. See generally, for example, Schragger and Schwartzman, "Against Religious Institutionalism."

92. See Garnett, "Religious Liberty," 279. "[C]onstitutionalism . . . should protect, but it also requires, self-governing religious communities that operate and evolve outside and independent of governments."

93. Bradley, "Church Autonomy," 1061. See also, as examples: Douglas Laycock, "Towards a General Theory of the Religion Clauses: The Case of Church Labor Relations and the Right to Church Autonomy," *Columbia Law Review* 81 (November 1981): 1373–1417; Lupu and Tuttle, "The Distinctive Place of Religious Entities"; and Carl H. Esbeck, "Dissent and Disestablishment."

94. Bradley, "Church Autonomy," 1061.

95. Garnett, " 'The Freedom of the Church': (Towards) an Exposition," suggesting that "the 'freedom of the church' might end up functioning less as a rule, standard, or doctrine (though it will function this way sometimes . . .), and might—somewhat maddeningly—work more like an animating value, even a mood."

96. See *Lemon v. Kurtzman*, 403 U.S. 602, 613–614 (1971).

97. Laurence H. Tribe, *American Constitutional Law*, 2nd ed. (Mineola, NY: Foundation Press, 1988), 1266, section 14-12; see also Eugene Volokh, *The First Amendment: Problems, Cases, and Policy Arguments* (New York: Foundation Press, 2001), 916–921, discussing the rule that "[t]he government may not delegate certain kinds of government power to religious institutions."

98. See *Kedroff v. St. Nicholas Cathedral*, 344 U.S. 94 (1952); *Presbyterian Church in the United States v. Mary Elizabeth Blue Hull Mem'l Presbyterian Church*, 393 U.S. 440 (1969); and *Serbian E. Orthodox Diocese v. Milivojevich*, 426 U.S. 696 (1976). See generally Garnett, "Assimilation," 1652–1659.

99. *Hull Church*, 449.

100. *EEOC v. Catholic Univ. of America*, 83 F.3d 455, 462 (D.C. Cir. 1996), quoting *Kedroff*, 116.

101. *Gonzales v. Roman Catholic Archbishop*, 280 U.S. 1, 16 (1929).

102. *Hosanna-Tabor.* See also, for example, *Bryce*, 289 F.3d at 656, quoting *Rayburn v. General Conference of Seventh Day Adventists*, 772 F.2d 1168 (4th Cir. 1985): "The right to choose ministers is an important part of internal church governance and can be essential to the well-being of a church, 'for perpetuation of a church's existence may depend upon those whom it selects to preach its values, teach its message, and interpret its doctrines both to its own membership and to the world at large.'"

103. See *Corp. of the Presiding Bishop v. Amos*, 483 U.S. 327, 334 (1987): "This Court has long recognized that the government may . . . accommodate religious practices and that it may do so without violating the Establishment Clause," quoting *Hobbie v. Unemployment Appeals Comm'n*, 480 U.S. 136, 144–45 (1987); also at 336, noting that, even if the exemption

at issue were not required by the Free Exercise Clause, an accommodation may take into account the concerns of a religious organization that "a judge would not understand its religious tenets and sense of mission."

104. See *Griswold v. Connecticut,* 381 U.S. 479, 484 (1965): "[S]pecific guarantees in the Bill of Rights have penumbras, formed by emanations from those guarantees that help give them life and substance."

105. See Laycock, "Towards a General Theory of the Religion Clauses"; John H. Garvey, *What Are Freedoms For?* (Cambridge, MA: Harvard University Press, 1996), 139.

106. See, as examples, *Bollard v. Cal. Province of the Soc'y of Jesus,* 211 F.3d 1331, 1332 (9th Cir. 2000), order denying rehearing *en banc,* Wardlaw, J., dissenting: "Though the concept originated through application of the Free Exercise Clause, the Supreme Court has held that the Establishment Clause also protects church autonomy in internal religious matters"; also Lupu and Tuttle, "The Distinctive Place of Religious Entities," 62: "If anything in the positive law of the Constitution confirms the distinctive character of religious institutions, the doctrine of non-entanglement is it."

107. *Hosanna-Tabor.*

108. See, for example, Mark E. Chopko, "Shaping the Church: Overcoming the Twin Challenges of Secularization and Scandal," *Catholic University Law Review* 53 (Fall 2003): 131. "Church autonomy forms one critical aspect of the constitutionally mandated separation between governmental and religious entities that has been expressly noted in the case law."

109. Thomas C. Berg, "The Voluntary Principle and Church Autonomy: Then and Now," *Brigham Young University Law Review* 2004 (Issue 4, 2004): 1606.

110. See Esbeck, "Dissent and Disestablishment" and Carl H. Esbeck, "The Establishment Clause as a Structural Restraint on Governmental Power," *Iowa Law Review* 84 (October 1998): 51.

111. Compare to *Roberts v. United States Jaycees,* 468 U.S. 609, 617–620 (1984); and *Wisconsin v. Yoder,* 406 U.S. 205 (1972).

112. Compare to *Roberts,* 622–624; and *Boy Scouts of America v. Dale,* 530 U.S. 640 (2000).

113. See Inazu, *Liberty's Refuge.*

114. See, for examples: *Thomas,* 450 U.S. at 715, "Intrafaith differences . . . are not uncommon among followers of a particular creed, and the judicial process is singularly ill equipped to resolve such differences"; *Milivojevich,* 714 note 8, "Civil judges obviously do not have the competence of ecclesiastical tribunals in applying the 'law' that governs ecclesiastical disputes"; and *Watson v. Jones,* 80 U.S. 679, 729 (1872), "It is not to be supposed that the judges of the civil courts can be as competent in the

ecclesiastical law and religious faith of [church] bodies as the ablest men in each are in reference to their own."

115. Tribe, *American Constitutional Law*, section 14-11, 1232 note 46. See also Garnett, "Assimilation," 1658–1659.

116. Compare, for example, Lupu and Tuttle, "The Distinctive Place of Religious Entities," 58–59, noting that a "weaker" argument for limiting courts' review of religious matters is their "lack of judicial expertise on matters of religion."

117. Berg, "The Voluntary Principle and Church Autonomy," 1612–1613.

118. See Richard W. Garnett, "A Quiet Faith? Taxes, Politics, and the Privatization of Religion," *Boston College Law Review* 42 (July 2001): 801 note 147, noting that it would be a "mistake to reduce the Church to a mediating institution with a message, or a 'voluntary association with a cause'"; Russell Hittinger, "Dignitatis Humanae, Religious Liberty, and Ecclesiastical Self-Government," *George Washington Law Review* 68 (July/September 2000): 1052, note 111, quoting Pope Leo XIII's complaint that the Church's title to freedom had been reduced to that of other associations and that the "Catholic religion is allowed a standing in civil society equal only, or inferior, to societies alien from it; no regard is paid to the laws of the Church"; and from the same article, at 1053: "What was most important [for the Church in the modern world] was that the Church could be differentiated without reducing itself to the status of other private associations." Compare Lupu and Tuttle, "The Distinctive Place of Religious Entities," 51, noting that "[t]he task of any overarching theory of the constitutional status of religious entities is to identify and elaborate the reasons, if any, that justify treatment of religious enterprises different from secular organizations and from religious believers."

119. 132 S. Ct. at 706.

120. See Richard W. Garnett, "The Story of Henry Adams's Soul: Education and the Expression of Associations," *Minnesota Law Review* 85 (June 2001): 1841–1884.

121. See Murray, *We Hold These Truths*, 210. "[Modern man] does not object to religion, provided that religion be regarded as a private matter which concerns only the conscience and feelings of the individual."

122. Hittinger, "Dignitatis Humanae," 1041. This latter view, Hittinger continues, "implies a radical privatization of religion," a "reduction of the moral and juridical status of the church to that of other private associations," and a "denial that civil authority has any participation in the veridical order of truth."

123. Ibid., 1046, arguing that the government's neutrality with respect to religion is a result of a lack of jurisdiction over religious matters

and is consistent with its "obligation to promote the free exercise of religion."

124. Mark DeWolfe Howe, "The Supreme Court, 1952 Term—Foreword: Political Theory and the Nature of Liberty," *Harvard Law Review* 67 (November 1953): 91. Prof. Howe contended that the Court's decision in *Kedroff v. St. Nicholas Cathedral,* 344 U.S. 94 (1952), reflected its acceptance—at least to some extent—of this "thesis." See generally Richard W. Garnett, "'Things That Are Not Caesar's': The Story of *Kedroff v. St. Nicholas Cathedral,*" in Richard W. Garnett and Andrew Koppelman, eds., *First Amendment Stories* (New York: Foundation Press, 2012), 171–191.

125. See Paul Horwitz, "Defending (Religious) Institutionalism," *Virginia Law Review* 99 (September 2013): 1051 note 11. "[A] modern version of the freedom of the church is a viable concept in contemporary American law and society precisely because it has become so chastened."

126. See, for example, Angela C. Carmella, "Mary Ann Glendon on Religious Liberty: The Social Nature of the Person and the Public Nature of Religion," *Notre Dame Law Review* 73 (July 1998): 1211–1212, noting that the "prohibition on religious establishments ensures that religious associations are free from governmental control so that religious choice is 'both possible and meaningful.'"

127. See, for example, Lupu and Tuttle, "The Distinctive Place of Religious Entities," 84, 87, noting that institutional "separationism" between the state and "some aspects of institutional behavior" serves as a check on totalitarianism and contending that "[f]aith makes comprehensive, ultimate claims, and our anti-totalitarian political commitments preclude the state from supporting means that involve claims upon the whole of lives in that way."

128. Kathleen A. Brady, "Religious Organizations and Mandatory Collective Bargaining Under Federal and State Labor Laws: Freedom From and Freedom For," *Villanova Law Review* 49 (Issue 1, 2004): 81, 167. Also from that article at 157, "For the Church, freedom from state interference is essential so that religious groups can exert a transformative power on the larger world."

129. See, for example, Marci A. Hamilton, *God vs. the Gavel: Religion and the Rule of Law* (Cambridge: Cambridge University Press, 2005), 8, contending that "[i]n recent decades, religious entities have worked hard to immunize their actions from the law" and "lobbying for the right to hurt others without consequences."

130. See, for example, Marci Hamilton, "The Catholic Church and the Clergy-Abuse Scandal," *Findlaw's Writ* (April 10, 2003), available online at: http://writ.news.findlaw.com/hamilton/20030410.html, arguing that "the so-called church autonomy doctrine is not really a legal doctrine at

all, at least as far as the U.S. Constitution and Supreme Court are concerned. Rather, it is an insidious theory that invites religious licentious-
ness rather than civic responsibility."

131. See generally Garnett, "Assimilation," 1662–1665.

132. See Robert N. Bellah, et al., *Habits of the Heart: Individualism and
Commitment in American Life,* Updated ed. (Berkeley: University of California Press, 1996), 221, 235.

133. Consider for comparison Lupu and Tuttle, "The Distinctive Place
of Religious Entities," 39, noting the "shift to a subject-oriented religiosity"
which "leads many to question why religious experiences, commitments,
and communities are different than other intense sensations, beliefs, and
associations." In recent years, the problem of justifying "special" treatment
for religion has attracted renewed and close scholarly attention. See, as
examples, Brian Leiter, *Why Tolerate Religion?* (Princeton, NJ: Princeton
University Press, 2013); Micah Schwartzman, "What If Religion Is Not Special?" *University of Chicago Law Review* 79 (Fall 2012): 1351–1428; Andrew
Koppelman, "Is It Fair to Give Religion Special Treatment?" *University of
Illinois Law Review* 2006 (Issue 3, 2006): 571–604; and Michael W. McConnell, "The Problem of Singling Out Religion," *DePaul Law Review* 50 (Fall
2000): 1–48.

134. See, for example, Bradley, "Church Autonomy," 1063, noting the
problem created by "the forced introduction into the religious community of civil 'nondiscrimination' principles that are at odds with internally
generated norms."

135. 130 S. Ct. 2971 (2010).

136. Michael W. McConnell, "The New Establishmentarianism," *Chi-
cago-Kent Law Review* 75 (Issue 2, 2000): 453–476.

137. Larry Alexander, "Illiberalism All the Way Down: Illiberal Groups
and Two Conceptions of Liberalism," *Journal of Contemporary Legal Issues* 12
(Issue 2, 2002): 625.

138. Stanley Hauerwas, "Christianity and Democracy: A Response,"
Center Journal 1 (Issue 3, 1982): 44–5.

139. Ibid. "Ironically, that strategy results in the undermining of intermediate associations because they are now understood only as those arbitrary institutions sustained by the private desires of institutions."

140. See generally, for example, Hamilton, *God vs. the Gavel.* Compare to Murray, *We Hold These Truths,* 207, observing that the "prophets of
modernity" regard the freedom of the Church "as a trespass upon, and a
danger to, their one supreme value–the 'integrity of the political order.'"

141. Philip Hamburger, "Illiberal Liberalism: Liberal Theology, Anti-
Catholicism, and Church Property," *Journal of Contemporary Legal Issues* 12
(Issue 2, 2002): 694.

5

ANTI-GOVERNMENTISM IN CONSERVATIVE THOUGHT: A NOTE ON GARNETT'S CONCEPTION OF RELIGIOUS FREEDOM

INGRID CREPPELL

Strands in modern conservatism appear strikingly divergent and at times incompatible. Yet, I would hold that the unifying core of conservative thinking in the United States today is anti-governmentism. While not the essence of conservatism, anti-governmentism stands as the most powerful simplification of conservative ideology. When Ronald Reagan quipped in his First Inaugural Address that "government is the problem" not the solution, he captured a persistent strain, and gave it added impetus, in American political culture. Recently, a strong anti-government orientation has proven itself through the Republican-driven government shutdown of October 2013, the Tea Party's continued viability in elections, Paul Ryan's vice-presidential bid with many references to Ayn Rand, and Hayek versus Keynes debates among economists, to name the most salient. But, as Lenin might have put it: there is anti-governmentism and there is anti-governmentism!

Some long-term features of the American political tradition contribute this basic mind-set. Obvious candidates include the founding ideal of limited government, a culture of self-help and localism, the idea of states' rights, individualism, and religious, economic, and political freedom. Government at the federal level—as the set of institutions imbued with the task of insuring citizens' public welfare through national laws and leadership for an unruly and deeply diverse citizen body—has never been viewed in the United States as the apotheosis of the people's soul in the nation-state. But the intensity of the reaction against governmental programs and against the very notion of government as a valued sphere of human effort indicates an extreme swing in the pendulum of public opinion.[1] Many liberals may be disgusted by "government" of the crisis-driven paralyzed sort, yet core beliefs of liberalism favor a positive conception of the potential of political institutions and action. Conservatism of all types, however, seems to demand not just healthy skepticism but downright hostility toward government. This has crystallized a rigid conservatism. Tea Party signs trumpet: "I LOVE OUR COUNTRY: It's Government I'm AFRAID of."

How deep and revolutionary is the animus? How did it come to be this way? For some, the answer focuses on the embedded interests of the economically powerful: politicians are co-opted to institute policies for them. The wealthy, business class, and right-wing politicians propagate the message of deregulation, of getting government out of the way, enabling "individuals" and business to bring back a resurgent powerful American way of life. Many among the losing middle- and working classes respond to this familiar theory, hence anti-government sentiment infuses conservative patriotism. That sentiment cannot be understood mainly as a matter of elite manipulation—why would it work if not for predilections within the American political and cultural psyche and narratives of American history? Conservative commentators and opinion leaders may have initially stoked some of the intensity of anger by tapping into complex forms of reaction in the face of the symbolic power posed by a black Democrat with foreign parentage. Much has to do with a need to identify the cause of economic fragility. Still another major source of hostility derives from the impossible bind in which national governments are put through contemporary global dynamics, where governments must serve their people but simultaneously balance forces beyond their control that contradict many domestic needs. Finally, governmental action to solve national problems, like health care, raises phantoms of "socialism." Strong anti-government conservatives see government as, on the one hand, too intrusive and powerful, and, on the other, as corrupt, biased, weak/inept, and alien.[2] Government then is fixated upon as the fulcrum point of contention.

The phenomenon of anti-governmentism as a trope or principle of modern American conservatism remains a fascinating and complex one that has not received the study it deserves. In this chapter, I comment on a recent version of a conservative critique of government found in Richard Garnett's strong defense of religious freedom. Integral to his argument for religious freedom is the diminution of the power of government, as if an argument *for* robust non-governmental institutions requires the shrinking of government itself and pointedly an attitude of wariness toward government (note the epigram "The State may never become an octopus, which stifles the whole of life"), on the assumption that this is necessarily a zero-sum relationship. I believe this to be fundamentally misguided. Indeed, as will become clear, Garnett's conservative instincts seem to be grounded in different roots than anti-governmentism. Yet the idea that religious freedom and political freedom are only secured when government is restrained serves as bedrock. He writes:

> [N]ear the heart of anything called "conservatism" . . . should be an appreciation and respect for the place and role of non-state author-ities in promoting both the common good and the flourishing of persons and a commitment to religious freedom for individuals and institutions alike, secured in part through constitutional limits on the powers of political authorities.[3]

As Garnett must grasp, an appreciation for the role of non-state "authorities" and a commitment to religious freedom is as much a "liberal" idea as a conservative one; hence, he needs to accentu-ate the conservative imprimatur through strong limitations on the power of political authorities. Before turning to Garnett's argu-ments, I sketch in cursory terms basic considerations for thinking about the government-religion nexus.

THE INTRICATE DANCE OF RELIGION AND GOVERNMENT

How do ideas of religious freedom fit with anti-government con-servatism? Fundamental ideas of American freedom rest upon religion's independence from the state. The predominant conception holds that an emphasis on religious freedom goes hand-in-hand with restriction of governmental power. If we consider classical liberalism as libertarian conservatism, limited government originated in demands for religious freedom against an interfering state. The separation of church and state was protected by a so-called wall to keep government out of religious life, enabling groups and individuals to believe and worship as they chose. Thus, religious freedom is not only compatible with "limited" government, but indeed dependent on it. Those arguing normatively for the restriction of state in order to allow the most expansive "freedom" of religious life might gain traction from the observations of some sociologists. The religiosity of American society, and the proliferation of churches and religious groups, are explained as resulting from the non-imposition of an established national church. Because the state abstains from control over religion, religion flourishes through a vibrant marketplace.[4] This sociological observation would seem to support the normative claim that a government kept out of religion enables a society with more religious freedom.

Government action must be restricted not only when directly aimed at repressing religion, but also when its neutral objectives lead to consequences viewed as harmful by religious believers. For instance, mandating that all employers provide contraceptive coverage under the 2010 health care law, even Catholic hospitals, universities, and social services organizations, was taken as a serious infringement on religious liberty by many Catholics, as forcefully articulated by the U.S. Conference of Catholic Bishops. Mitt Romney highlighted this apparent "war on religion" being waged by the Obama government. Romney posed the question in his presidential campaign, "When religious freedom is threatened, who do you want to stand with?" Thus, government is seen as posing a natural threat, directly and indirectly through its secular aims, to religious individuals and religious groups/institutions. There are softer and harder versions of the anti-government point of view derived from a religious perspective.

A second interpretation of the fit between religious freedom and anti-governmentism accentuates the *incompatibility* of the two. This line of argument contends that religious freedom in a diverse society in fact requires strong and responsive government. If one upholds religious freedom as a freedom *to* and not a freedom *from*—that is, a positive freedom to be a certain kind of person or organization and to act on specific commitments—then one depends on government to enable the fullest practice and expression of one's religious life. Why would that be? While government remains limited and non-intrusive vis-à-vis one's particular individual religious choices, in order to be able to practice those choices among diverse others, citizens depend on active government support both financially and juridically. Think of school voucher programs, or accommodations in the military or other secular institutions for religious observance and practice, or faith-based groups providing social services (anti-addiction or housing programs), which ask for tax breaks or exemptions regarding employees. Indeed, the demand for exemptions and accommodations by religious institutions requires extra resources and a responsive government. It takes more resources and more legitimacy, we might say, to make exceptions than to apply rules uniformly across the board. The contention here then holds that a capacity to achieve one's religion—to be religiously free—essentially requires positive government involvement to make space available—to carve it out in an extraordinarily complex mosaic of religious freedoms. Thus, religious freedom and anti-governmentism are fundamentally incompatible demands: the flourishing of religious freedom cannot rely on weak government. The question to be asked is not how much government (a little or a lot), but how responsive, to whom, and with what consequences.

WHAT GUARANTEES "SOCIAL SPACE" FOR PLURALISM? GARNETT'S ARGUMENT FOR "FREEDOM OF THE CHURCH"

I turn now to Richard Garnett's interpretation of the church-state relationship, as set out in a paper originally entitled, " 'Two There Are': Church-State Separation and Religious Freedom," and that has now been slightly revised for this volume as "The Worms and the Octopus: Religious Freedom, Pluralism, and Conservatism." Garnett juxtaposes his position against a liberal approach to religious freedom, which he contends makes religion primarily an individual private matter. This atomization of religion is flawed in at least two ways: first by not recognizing the essential community-based nature of religious life, and second, by making religion and individual freedom vulnerable to a top-down statist management through ignoring the principled role of the church. Liberalism individualizes and privatizes freedom and thereby hands over constraint to forces of the state, without sufficient respect for intermediary moral institutions. The social space for pluralism is squeezed when the state intrudes to enforce individualized religious freedom. We need, he argues, a much richer conception of the role of religious associations, communities, and institutions. Garnett's theoretical contribution develops a notion of "church freedom" as a necessary condition of religious freedom. His theory supports the trend of anti-government conservatism.

Garnett argues that if we fail to grasp that the separation of church-state is based fundamentally on what he calls the *freedom of the church*, this separation remains vulnerable and incorrectly worked out—"that separation, *correctly conceived*, is an essential component of religious freedom."[5] While he recognizes the Court's affirmation time and again of the importance of church autonomy (see section V of Garnett's chapter in particular for a discussion of the constitutional cases, tests, and rules protecting the autonomy of religious institutions), this cannot suffice. The reasons typically advanced for "protecting" the church from interference have been either pragmatic (government is incompetent to judge on spiritual matters) or have rested on ideas of privacy or neutrality ("religion and religious institutions are and do 'private' things that governments do or should not care about"). These approaches to the status of religion and the present reasoning about church autonomy cannot guarantee real freedom. So what is "the distinctive place of religious entities in our constitutional order"? Garnett proposes a justifying principle of *libertas ecclesiae*. I'll pose two lines of questioning here: why do we need this alternative notion of church freedom? And what exactly does this more definitive role of the church look like vis-à-vis government?

Regarding why we need an alternative church freedom, there seem to be two answers in Garnett's chapter: one social-psychological and the other normative.

First, the conception of church freedom more adequately supports the way in which people come to know and realize religious selves in a human world: we cannot understand the nature and conditions of religious faith and freedom *for individuals* devoid of religious institutions and communities. *Independent and free churches* provide conditions for free *individual* beliefs, not as purely private experiences but as public realization. This argument emphasizes the sociologically and institutionally constituted nature of religious belief, as opposed to vague spiritual sentiments and notions. Individuals live in sociologically rich environments and hence the individual needs this institutional context and discipline—as a matter of shaping and for purposes of expression. Garnett writes:

> If . . . the modern experiment has been to substitute autonomous individuals' individual conscience—whose designated protector would be the liberal state, through the vehicle of individual rights—for the freedom of the church as the guarantor of the social space necessary for meaningful pluralism, then it would appear modern freedom of religion is attacking its own foundations—that, in a way, the immunity of conscience is eating itself.

In his original version of the paper, the last lines recapped one aim of freedom of the church to uphold the First Amendment's protection of freedom of individual conscience. Thus, individual freedom is nurtured in contexts of fellow believers organized and active as groups in public social space. Protecting churches as organized public embodiments of individuals' commitments remains essential to robust religious existence.

But, clearly, this social-psychological and indeed cultural claim rests upon a normative point of view, perhaps about better or worse forms of religiosity. Garnett's normative commitments display his more genuinely conservative side (and not simply in the anti-governmentist fashion), and point to a deeper attitude about the nature of the value of human life. He argues that churches help us avoid reducing religion to "a form of self-expression, performance art, or therapy." Perhaps his critique of the Sheilaism[6] of liberal spirituality comes from a commitment to a view of human life as attaining value through the kind of cultivation and discipline that derive from membership in a moral and spiritual institution, which is the purpose of the church. Individual freedom is not sufficient. That is, the marketplace of religion which renders churches equivalent to other voluntary associations among which people pick and choose makes a person's commitment to religion too fluid and shallow, and renders persons in this type of society certain types of persons. Garnett cares that we think about faith in deeper terms than personal spirituality: "institutional affiliation, public worship, and tradition" matter a great deal. Religion should not be based on loose, transitory, and merely spiritual enthusiasms.

Given these assumptions about the nature of religiosity, what would a principle of *libertas ecclesiae* actually look like? Garnett insists that the church is "distinct from, other than, and independent of, the state." Separation of church and state is correctly understood to mean church freedom which "denotes a structural arrangement, and a constitutional order, in which the church— not 'faith,' 'religion,' or 'spirituality,' but 'church'—is distinct from, other than, and independent of, the state. In this arrangement, the church—that is, religious associations, communities, and institutions—is not above and controlling, or beneath and subordinate to, the state. It is separate, and so it is free." Such a "revolutionary structural principle" certainly diverges from Locke's description of the church as a "voluntary" society on par with a country club or sports team. But what does *separate, independent, and free* signify? One possibility seems too tepid—that the church is simply a separate space within a basically secular society within which one also lives and feels at home. We've already noted that Garnett appears to support the conception of the church as the necessary institution for the sustenance of higher human virtues, which perhaps also improves the world beyond the boundaries of the church. But the language of separate and independent implies more. Garnett suggests that the church acts in some sense to *constrain* secular power; quoting George Weigel, he stresses, "the state will not occupy every inch of social space."

As an explanation of a necessary causal component in the historical genesis of constitutionalism and limited government, Garnett's emphasis on the importance of the church's freedom in relation to the state seems absolutely right. But, after overcoming the continual power struggle between church and state through many centuries in the west, the constitutional state has been established in its modern form. What does it mean, then, for the church to be *separate, independent, and free* in our modern context of secular legitimacy? What would a church that is "free" of the state look like? The fact that some condition or factor (in this case—church freedom) caused or brought about a positive consequence (in this case constitutionalism) does not serve as a *reason* to justify the continued necessity of that factor in that precise form at the present time. Garnett claims that there is no clear constitutional commitment to the freedom of the church ("revolutionarily understood") in American constitutional law and that this is a problem, that there is no evidence of a "robust, underlying commitment in our law to the freedom of the church as a structural principle of constitutional government." The distinctiveness of Garnett's argument must come in his point that a free church is essentially different from the church's standing as a voluntary association in a pluralist society.

At one level, this might imply that as a ballast against a potentially intrusive state we should not be satisfied with individual rights but rather justify and shore up the churches in order to emphasize the state's limitations. I find this proposition perplexing! Do we need other institutions as countervailing forces to the state? In a sociological sense, we certainly do. We require a robust civil society in which individuals are able to live meaningful and communal lives without a totalitarian subsumption into a monolithic state— the specter of the octopus he raised earlier. But, the juridical status of freedom of the institution of the church cannot mean literally an alternative sovereign body. When we search for an answer, however, Garnett goes back to describe the Investiture Crisis in which the church comes to be established as separate, autonomous, and independent of royal imposition, and he engages in a critique of liberal individualism. Yet, he neglects to spell out what *a structural principle of autonomy of the church* entails. If the church is independent and free, how would the following be answered?

- In a debate between church and state, does the church win? Who shall be judge—as Locke posed the vexed question—in these confrontations of authoritative collective moral claims?
- Should people feel a clash of loyalty between their religious commitments and those to their government—nay, are the thicker and more existential ties to churches ultimately more important than to secular society?

- Should the state be prohibited from intervening in cases where discrimination seeping out of a church affects society, or even in cases where offensive practices remain within religious institutions (polygamy)?

What is the practical import if one is striving to enhance church freedom, and would we really want it? Noah Feldman, in an article on redrawing the line between church and state, argues that we ought to "offer greater latitude for religious speech and symbols in public debate, but also impose a stricter ban on state financing of religious institutions."[7] Does Garnett's argument commit him to supporting federal funds for faith-based organizations, or for religious schools that teach that the ultimate source of values is rabbinic law, cannon law, or Sharia? What about the mega-churches that have come to dominate the suburban and urban landscapes of the United States? Could these embody the type of church freedom that Garnett envisions?

I do not believe Garnett has worked out the implications of support for a free church and what it would actually demand as a legal or cultural commitment in the modern American context. In theory, a literal application of a "revolutionary structural principle of freedom of the church" could lead liberal societies back to an early modern clash between the authorities of church and state. Thus, while he may see it as enhancing religious freedom, instantiating the church as separate, autonomous, and independent confuses legal and political grounds and undermines the allegiance to government upon which church freedom itself depends. We could, on the other hand, interpret Garnett's conception of religious freedom as more of a recommendation about political normative touchstones. A more fully reasoned defense of a *separate, independent, and free* church matters because it might serve as a grounds for conservatism emphasizing human value forged through institutional disciplining commitments.

These questions about Garnett's theory of *libertas ecclesiae* point in two directions for their resolution. From one angle, his view of religious freedom as a positive active life depends on a positive view of government—not at all on a repressive conception of government or of secular society as a hostile environment. Thus, Garnett may inadvertently be making a case for the incompatibility between religious freedom and anti-governmentism that I outlined above. Nevertheless, if Garnett insists on the essentially repressive nature of government jurisdiction, his theory of church freedom lends itself to a corrosive and unhelpful anti-governmentism. He would then be challenging the very "basic values upon which the legitimacy of the social system rests," as Lewis Coser phrased it in his famous treatment of social conflict. Conservative thought, driven primarily by a commitment to religious life and religious freedom, must recognize what is at stake: the issue is not one of limited versus expansive government interference, but the recognition of the need and legitimacy of government power to balance divergent pressures within a pluralistic and religiously free society. If we take him seriously, the divergence of allegiance propagated by one's church membership could lead to undermining the very liberal conditions upon which contemporary churches have practiced and their members lived free lives in a pluralist political environment. I do not think Garnett would agree to being part of that alienating trend.

CONCLUSION

In this short comment on Garnett's case for a revived principle of *libertas ecclesiae* as the right interpretation of religious freedom, I have pointed out what I take to be its implicit foundations in a conception of disciplined civic virtue through church association as well as the highly questionable implications for a coherent conception of political legitimacy. His theory seeks to shore up the ballast of religious vitality as a necessary condition of political freedom at the cost of the ballast of governmental legitimacy as a condition of political freedom. While Garnett does not display vituperativeness toward governing institutions, he does leave himself open to the charge of a willingness to fragment the American project. Such arguments as this enhance anti-governmentism even when they do not explicitly seek to do so.

The American project remains an experiment in sustaining a unified and just polity in the face of deep differences of belief (among many other differences). We cannot wish these differences away; to pretend we can, or to force a false unity, is to betray the foundations of American history. The chasms among various

groups in the American political body must be spanned and overcome in some way, at some level. Such a project is possible only
through a commitment to our governing institutions normatively
conceived. Unfortunately today, references to the Constitution
are as much instigations to acrimony as commonality. Thus, we
should see constitutional faith as always intrinsically tied to governing institutions in the American case, and the legitimacy of
those institutions must remain one source of glue keeping disparate communities and interests together. Anti-governmentism acts
as a corrosive of a common American identity. When government
is projected to be the prime source of the problem—an understandable point of view lately but one that seems also to be a self-
fulfilling prophecy—we are led to ask if the very basis for potential
re-grouping and response is undermined, particularly given the
history of American political culture.

It might be helpful to invoke conclusions Lewis Coser reached
in his book, *The Functions of Social Conflict* (1956):

> Internal social conflicts which concern goals, values or interests
> that do not contradict the basic assumptions upon which the rela-
> tionship is founded tend to be positively functional for the social
> structure. Such conflicts tend to make possible the readjustment of
> norms and power relations within groups in accordance with the
> felt needs of its individual members or subgroups. Internal conflicts
> in which the contending parties no longer share the basic values
> upon which the legitimacy of the social system rests threaten to dis-
> rupt the structure.[8]

The distinction between social conflict as a matter of adjustment
and reinvigoration, versus conflict that displays and brings about
a tearing apart, seems useful. Is rigid anti-government conservatism a sign of and a means to wind down the energy of a common American experiment? It certainly stands for a definitive and
uncompromising interpretation of the nature of that experiment,
and shows a kind of blindness to the potentially destructive nature
of denouncing government tout court. Critique of government
must be an incentive to think deeply about what we need to do
together to re-legitimize government, not to paralyze it, but to
make it work for the diverse, cacophonous citizen body of this new
political, economic, cultural, and technological age.

The complex and fertile set of beliefs I listed in the introduction that have made Americans skeptical of state intrusion—ideals of limited government, self-help and localism, individualism, and religious, economic, and political freedom—help American constitutionalism and political ideology to be flexible and facilitate alignments and adjustment to new historical problems and circumstances. How to reconstruct a sense of shared legitimacy? Conservatives should not feel compelled to align themselves with a hardened and extreme form of anti-governmentism—or with its subtler but equally destructive fellow-travelers—but should clarify other strands of their myriad and rich traditions in which the necessity and virtues of government were clearly affirmed.[9]

NOTES

1. See for instance the poll conducted by Pew in October 2013—admittedly just after the reopening of government following the shutdown, available online at: http://www.people-press.org/2013/10/18/trust-in-government-interactive/.

2. Political perceptions hostile to government action may derive from many logics. For instance: (1) government appears essentially corrupt as it operates to fulfill organized and therefore typically special, powerful interests; (2) government appears biased and not to be trusted: given the fragmenting, splintering sense of national identity and unity, people hunker down into factionalized group identities (local, regional, class, racial, lifestyle, professional, and so on); because government cannot be for "all" when there no longer appears to be an "all" or a "we" that citizens can identify with, government action necessarily looks unfair and favoring some over others; (3) government appears weak and impotent to solve major problems, of which the levers of control lie outside any single state's reach; and (4) government appears alien or cosmopolitan—not "national"—due to economic globalization, to which government must attend for state survival. This distant and abstract realm in which global forces interact elicits fear of the shifting order of the world.

3. See Richard W. Garnett, "The Worms and the Octopus: Religious Freedom, Pluralism, and Conservatism," this volume.

4. See for example the work of Rodney Stark, who advanced a rational-choice theory of religious choice, arguing that competition for religious believers increased the religiosity of American society.

5. Emphasis added. Garnett states again, at the beginning of section IV, that the separation must be "correctly understood" and that we must

not use "a mistaken version of the idea"—terminology that implies one solution to the meaning of the church-state separation. It is hard to imagine the long-term viability of this essential conception if there were one "correct" way to carve up political-social-religious space!

6. Robert Bellah's term for religious faith as a form of self-expression.

7. Noah Feldman, "A Church-State Solution," *New York Times Magazine* (July 3, 2005): 32.

8. Lewis Coser, *The Functions of Social Conflict* (New York: Free Press, 1956), 151–152.

9. As this chapter was being prepared for submission, I read David Brooks's column "Movement on the Right," *New York Times* (January 10, 2014), which holds out promise for a different and less hostile approach to the idea of government.

6

CONSTITUTIVE STORIES ABOUT THE COMMON LAW IN MODERN AMERICAN CONSERVATISM

KEN I. KERSCH

It is a commonplace to describe modern American conservatism as comprised of diverse—and, apparently, theoretically incompatible—ideological strands.[1] Some have insisted that these strands—traditionalism, libertarianism, and neoconservatism—stand in such tension with each other that their centrifugal force would inevitably, and soon, pull the movement apart.[2] Others within the movement were impelled by the difficulties occasioned by the tensions to attempt to forge a theoretical synthesis.[3] I have argued, however, that placing too much emphasis on the philosophical tensions within the movement has led us to underplay the immense power of symbolism, emotions, and identity as a unifying force in contemporary conservative politics. The symbol of the U.S. Constitution as a document traduced, betrayed, and (potentially) redeemed has played a major role in forging an ecumenical conservative movement that transcends its logical, philosophical contradictions.[4]

In this chapter, I supplement my account of the role of the Constitution-as-symbol in forging an ecumenical conservative movement with the very important role that many on the right have accorded to the common law as an adjunct means of

motivating, unifying, and fortifying their ranks, while simultaneously distinguishing themselves sharply from their antagonists.
The commitment to the common law trumpeted by conservatives
is nearly as important to the movement as its commitment to the
Constitution itself.

After a brief introduction to the common law and its place in
American law, I provide an overview of the understandings of
the common law of three important—and quite philosophically
distinct—strands of the contemporary conservative movement:
(1) Christian conservatives; (2) Hayekian free-market advocates;
and (3) public choice theorists. I conclude with some reflections
on the significance of the commitment to the common law (as
each of these understands it) to the movement's ecumenicalism.
I argue, moreover, that within the movement, the commitment to
the *lex non scripta* of the common law serves ideological functions
that are distinct from, but complementary to, the movement's parallel commitment to the *lex scripta* of the Constitution, functions
for which the Constitution is, by its nature, ill-suited. The dual
commitment to the common law and the Constitution, forged and
conveyed not as matters of abstract political philosophy but rather
in the form of "constitutive stories," I contend, are foundational
to the political ideology of contemporary American conservatism.[5]

THE COMMON LAW IN AMERICA, BRIEFLY

The common law was the primary source of legal rules in the
Anglo-American legal tradition for private law (real property,
contracts, torts, for example) prior to the rise and routinization
of statutory law (legislation) in the mid- to late nineteenth century.[6] In contrast to legislation, common law rules are introduced,
accrue, and develop incrementally as a by-product of judges deciding bilateral disputes in concrete individual cases—that is, by case
law.[7] Although it incorporated elements of Roman and Canon law,
English common law is largely *sui generis*, with its origins in twelfth-
century rulings by judges dispatched by the king to the country-
side to resolve real-world disputes consistently and dispassionately,
with the aim of securing the king's peace against the disturbances
of the disputatious, while standing outside the deformations
wrought by local loyalties and prejudices—in the process, and not

incidentally, forging loyalty to the crown over potentially competing centers of political power. Over hundreds of years, these rulings generated a remarkably intricate and sophisticated body of law that, even today, serves as the foundation of much—indeed, probably most—of the private law structuring economic and social relations in Great Britain, the United States, and in common law countries worldwide.

Much of the operative private law in the American colonies (and some of its public law) was rooted in English common law. Many colonial assemblies passed reception statutes specifically declaring the English common law to also be their law. Other colonies—populated and presided over by Englishmen, of course—simply applied English common law in their courts as a matter of course.[8] Even after independence, and the fervent reaction by many against all things English, the common law was understood to be, in many respects, indispensible. Some states enacted reception statutes after independence. Most others simply assumed that, unless otherwise stated, common law principles remained in effect. English common law also informed the new nation's public law.[9] In its assimilation of common law writs, like habeas corpus, with other criminal process protections in the Bill of Rights (most explicitly in the Seventh Amendment, which mentions the common law expressly), the Constitution is clearly the outgrowth of the English common law culture.[10]

In the early republic into the first half of the nineteenth century, with little access to law books, Americans availed themselves of William Blackstone's lucid and magisterial four-volume summary of the (otherwise famously arcane) English Common law (1765), which had been published fortuitously on the eve of the American Revolution. With the early-nineteenth-century appearance of indigenous American law, reports compiling the case decisions of domestic courts and the publication of learned legal treatises by homegrown giants of legal scholarship like James Kent of Columbia University and Joseph Story of Harvard, both of whom venerated the common law inheritance, American law remained strongly influenced by its starting point in the centuries-old English common law tradition.[11]

From the beginning—and, indeed, even before Independence—however, Americans, while often starting from English common law, frequently (and often subtly) innovated within it in ways that took account of the country's unique situation, needs, and political principles. Over the course of the nineteenth century, many of these adaptations helped promote the country's rapid economic development. As such, the common law in the United States was a modernizing force that responded flexibly to changing conditions in the service of important economic and social objectives.[12]

Although it has in parts been remade in America (and, in many cases, re-enacted through statutes), the fundamentals of English common law remain the basis of American private law. The center of gravity in American legal education—now via the case method of instruction developed by Christopher Columbus Langdell at Harvard Law School, rather than through apprenticeship in a law office—continues to be instruction in common law methods, with the still-standard first-year curriculum focusing on honing common law reasoning skills as applied to traditional common law subjects.

This is not to say that the predominance of the common law as a source of law has not been repeatedly challenged, at least in some subject areas, over the course of American history. In the period immediately after independence, some vociferously objected on nationalistic and patriotic grounds to the reception in the United States of English common law. The Codification Movement of the late early- to mid-nineteenth century, led by figures like Robert Rantoul, Jr., and David Dudley Field, was of more practical significance. While retaining the nationalistic and patriotic elements of the post-Independence reaction against the transplantation of English common law, the Codification Movement was also driven by characteristically Jacksonian political concerns. The common law, after all, was made by judges not by the people (through their elected representatives) and was, hence, undemocratic. Its intricacies were so arcane, and its innovations so obscure, that, in a very real sense, the content of the law was accessible only by and through lawyers, whom many regarded as elitist and, as such, unsuited to a republic.[13]

In the late nineteenth and early twentieth centuries, common law doctrines—most prominently, perhaps, as they governed the relationship between employer and employee—came under assault from populist and progressive reformers (as did the judges and the legal profession more generally, the body of which remained tribunes of the common law tradition).[14] The rise of the modern administrative ("statutory") state succeeded in replacing common law rules with modern statutory and administrative regimes anchored in the new social sciences and theories of interest group liberalism.[15] Today, American law is suffused by both statutes and the common law, in a mixed system in which the common law heritage and influence remains clear.

THE STORIES OF LAW AND ECONOMICS AND PUBLIC CHOICE

Although "originalism" is the public face of contemporary conservative legalism,[16] attentive scholars understand that the law and economics movement and public choice analysis have played an equally, if not more, important role in contemporary American legal conservatism. Arguments about the common law are at the heart of the law and economics, and (by implication) play a significant part in the public choice movement as well. Law and economics scholars hold that law is best understood in a positive sense—and, for many, is best assessed normatively—through economic analysis. Public choice scholarship studies the nature and effects of rules through the prism of the rational, individualistic actor pursuing his own self-interest; it is radically skeptical of any concepts that assume broader, more collective, social actors or interests (such as "society," "the community," or "the public interest"). A simultaneous commitment to the Founders, originalism, law and economics, and public choice is instantiated institutionally in conservative law schools like George Mason University Law School, in the work of seminal public choice scholars like James Buchanan, and promoted by educative conservative foundations like the Liberty Fund.[17]

The nineteenth century stands as a touchstone for conservative law and economics scholars, because, prior to the rise of the statutory state, the country was largely governed by common law rules. These rules, both in England and the United States, these scholars argue, performed their regulatory function remarkably well, promoting efficiency and underwriting the creation of wealth on a scale unique in human history. That Great Britain was able to "take off" and develop industrially without an active legislature is remarkable, and a puzzle to be explained. Many, and not just conservatives, have long credited the common law for this uniquely successful "release of energy."[18]

The virtues of the common law as a system of regulation are best appreciated, for conservatives, by looking beyond what the common law is, and does, to what it is not, and does not do. An affinity for regulation by common law is the other side of the coin of conservative hostility to regulation by legislation. Public choice scholars have emphasized that legislation is a relatively new (read: alien) innovation in the Anglo-American legal-political tradition. Before the late nineteenth century—before progressivism—the English and the Americans lived the (Edenic) dream of governance without government. In this prelapsarian world, the seemingly timeless problem animating liberalism—how to reap the benefits of law without having to submit to the will of another—had been all but solved. A world without legislatures was a world without politicians imposing their personal views on how individuals should act and officiously instructing them on what was best for them. These the individual was free to determine for himself.

In England, prior to its ascendency as a regular lawmaking body, Parliament was called into session primarily, and periodically, to raise revenue—to levy taxes (public choice scholars have observed that, historically in England, the consolidation of the constitutional doctrine of parliamentary supremacy was a recipe for the rapid growth of government expenditure and debt).[19] In the United States too, before the rise of the (progressive) statutory state (that is, during the classical or formalist period of American constitutional law), common law governance was largely the rule. Although legislatures were present in the United States from its inception, the judicial review power was wielded by judges to void any legislation contaminated by rent-seeking—one of judicial review's major purposes (here, rent-seeking came in the form of what American lawyers called "class legislation," or redistributionist legislation, designed to advance the interest of one class of people or interests at the expense of others—or, put otherwise, that served private rather than public interests).[20] Common law, and, by derivation, constitutional law, thus served as a veto upon redistributionist public policy, holding such policies to violate the due process clauses of the Fifth and the Fourteenth Amendments, and, later, the Fourteenth Amendment's equal protection clause, because redistributionist laws transgressed the rule of law principles holding that only rules aimed at advancing the public interest (as opposed to special or particular interests) are worthy of the title "law."[21]

Conservatives observe that the United States prospered under the guidance of only a minimal state (in the European sense)—that is, with almost no centralized, rationalist bureaucracy.[22] We in the present, the story goes, are thus confronted with a monumental, existential question: are we better off under a statutory law system, with an active, governing, problem-solving legislature, or a common law system, where the government—the legislature and the bureaucracy—do little? Evidence from the nineteenth century, many conservatives insist, clearly suggests the latter.[23]

Seminal work in law and economics by Richard Posner and his successors surveyed and analyzed a range of common law rules, contrasting them to hypothetical rules which (it was claimed), from the standpoint of modern economics, would be the most efficient means of allocating resources. They claimed to find a remarkable level of correspondence between the two, underlining the wonder of common law governance. These findings were held to reinforce Lord Mansfield's dictum that a glory of the common law was that, over time, it "works itself pure": parties will litigate inefficient common law rules until they get the (efficient) rules they seek.[24] The more recent "origins" debate amongst law and economics scholars considers the question of whether societies with English common law origins are more prosperous, or wealthier, than those anchored in (statutory, legislative) civil law tradition. Law and economics scholars have found that indeed they are.[25]

The culmination of this story about governance in prelapsarian nineteenth-century America is the legend of the fall. Beginning in the late nineteenth century, statist progressivism (with its legal adjunct, sociological jurisprudence) inspired a transfer of governing authority out of the de-centralized courts and into Congress and centralized bureaucracies. To make matters worse, this transfer of institutional authority also corrupted the thinking of the judges, prying them away from their traditional common law moorings and tutoring them in a novel redistributionist ethos. These modern judges, now a part of the New Class knowledge elite, conversant in social science, statism, and a redistributionist ethos, transformed the areas of law ostensibly remaining under common law governance into engines of redistributionism and inefficiency.[26]

Contemporary law and economics scholars, like George Mason's Todd Zywicki, compare the traditional to the new common law and detail the ways in which the latter differs from the former.[27] Is contemporary common law now infested with the same interest group pressures that typically corrupt legislation? "In recent years . . . this process of self-correction [noted by Lord Mansfield]," Zywicki has argued, "seems to have gone awry, leading to increased concerns about inefficiency in many areas of the common law and heightened calls for legislative tort reform and restoration of freedom of contract."[28] Zywicki laments:

> The historic system of weak precedent, a competitive legal order, freedom of contract, and customary law insured that judges would be unable to pursue their personal preferences at the expense of the public. As these factors changed over time, however, the legal system became more vulnerable to influence by judges' ideological preferences, thereby creating opportunities for greater judicial control over the path of the law.[29]

Stated in the language of public choice, twentieth-century common law, unlike its nineteenth-century progenitor, is more susceptible to the sort of rent-seeking that has typically been associated (in anti-statutory public choice literature) with legislation. Now, as has long been the case through legislative lobbying, private parties are able to leverage the process of common law adjudication to redistribute wealth to themselves at the expense of overall efficiency.[30]

The seminal public choice critique of the post–common law state is James Buchanan and Gordon Tullock's *The Calculus of Consent: Logical Foundations of Constitutional Democracy*.[31] For Buchanan and Tullock, legislation, far from representing the apotheosis of democracy (the perspective which animated both the Jacksonian Codification Movement and the progressive model), is often little more than legalized theft. To the extent that there is a state (worst of all centralized) or a legislature, there is a readily accessible tap at which self/rent-seekers can position themselves to draw down the resources provided by others, through taxes, to advance their personal, as opposed to the public, good.

Buchanan animadverted against "the normative delusion, stemming from Hegelian idealism . . . [that] the state was . . . a benevolent entity and those who made decisions on behalf of the state were guided by consideration of the general or the public interest."[32] Indeed, the term "public interest" is, for public choice theorists, a *bête noire*: the concept (along with the related concepts of "social welfare" and the "general welfare") is not only chimerical but founded upon dangerous assumptions. "The public" or "society" is not "organismic," Buchanan insists. It is not a unified entity, with a readily identifiable "interest."[33] Public choice theorists insist that an "individualistic" as opposed to an "organismic" perspective must be the starting point for all future considerations of constitutions and the state.[34]

For public choice theorists like Buchanan, then, drawing and building upon the work of their predecessors including Anthony Downs's *An Economic Theory of Democracy* and Kenneth Arrow's work in social choice, the study of politics is an individualistic science aimed at the study of self-interested individuals pursuing their own self-seeking objectives.[35] Positioning themselves squarely in the liberal contractarian tradition, Buchanan and Tullock proceed from the position that constitutions are constructed by individuals to advance their individual interests. Significantly, they insist, moreover, that this understanding was inherent in the theory of the American founding as advanced, for instance, in *The Federalist Papers*, the Constitution itself, and other key founding texts.[36] As such, later developments in the trajectory of the American constitutional tradition—crucially, the nationalization of politics, policy, and rights occasioned by the Civil War Amendments and the subsequent construction of the modern administrative state (whether properly authorized or not)—corrupted original constitutional design and moved the nation away from its foundational individualism and toward socialism. In S. M. Amadae's words, Buchanan and Tullock's book is "an unprecedented contribution to political theory that reinvents the logical foundations of constitutional theory so that it resembles the logic of the marketplace."[37]

Notably, public choice theory positions itself as non-normative and scientific. Against the charges of its critics, it does not see itself as especially pro-business; rather, public choice scholars are preoccupied with the perils of regulatory capture, a focus that lends it interesting affinities with critiques from the left of the modern liberal state.[38] That said, the temperament of many, if not most, public choice theorists is decidedly conservative. Typically tagged as libertarians, seminal public choice scholars could not resist the temptation to tie a story of moral decline to their critique of the modern statutory/administrative state. James Buchanan, for instance, has speculated about the connection between the growth of the state (and the decline of the concept of a disinterested state) and the rise of the sort of lax political thinking that can lead to moral latitudinarianism (ostensibly) yielding a decline in the work ethic and rampant sexual promiscuity.[39]

FRIEDRICH HAYEK'S STORY OF "GROWN LAW"

While often characterized as both a libertarian and a neo-classical economist, Friedrich von Hayek's understanding of the nature of law is anchored neither in a theory of self-interest, as is the public choice paradigm, nor in a theory of economic efficiency, as with law and economics.[40] It is rather, distinctively, rooted in a theory of knowledge.[41]

This understanding was richly informed by Hayek's reading of English legal and political history, particularly his appreciation for the uniquely successful way that the English had grappled with what Hayek considered the central fact of the social condition— "the fragmentation of knowledge."[42] Hayek's work consistently emphasized "the fact of the necessary and irremediable ignorance on everyone's part of most of the particular facts which determine the actions of all the several members of human society."[43]

Hayek's appreciation for the dynamic by which "[the] structure of human activities constantly adapts itself, and functions through adapting itself, to millions of facts which in their entirety are not known to anybody," was informed by his appreciation for the development of English common law, an influence shared by both Mandeville and Hume, Hayek noted (via the exposition of that development by Matthew Hale, written in opposition of Thomas Hobbes's (statist) legal positivism).[44]

The fragmentation of knowledge has implications for the exercise of our reason in legal and political life:

> Complete rationality of action in the Cartesian sense demands complete knowledge of all the relevant facts. A designer or engineer needs all the data and full power to control or manipulate them if he is to organize the material objects to produce the intended result. But the success of action in society depends on more particular facts than anyone can possibly know. And our whole civilization in consequence rests, and must rest, on our believing much of what we cannot know to be true in the Cartesian sense.[45]

"The fact of our irremediable ignorance of most of the particular facts which determine the processes of society is . . . the reason why most social institutions," like the common law, "have taken the form they actually have," Hayek continued. "To talk about a society about which either the observer or any of its members knows all the particular facts is to talk about something wholly different from anything which has ever existed—a society in which most of what we find in our society would not and could not exist and which, if it ever occurred, would possess properties we cannot even imagine."[46]

Common law governance, Hayek explained, did not presume the accessibility of relevant knowledge that it didn't have. Relatedly, it did not propose to create new laws but rather proposed to find the law that was already extant—that had emerged. It involved "discovering something which exists, not . . . creating something new." As such, it "was not conceived as the product of anyone's will but rather as a barrier to all power, including that of the king." In this way, Hayek observed, "the common law jurists [in England] had developed conceptions somewhat similar to those of the natural law tradition but not couched in the misleading terminology of that school."[47] Thus, he observed, the doctrines of legal positivism were developed "in direct opposition to a tradition which, though it has for two thousand years provided the framework within which our central problems have been mainly discussed . . . the conception of a law of nature."[48] Elsewhere, Hayek specifically notes the affinities between these features of the common law and the medieval religious view that the state cannot be the ultimate source of law.[49] He adds:

What all the schools of natural law agree upon is the existence of rules which are not of the deliberate making of any lawgiver. They agree that all positive law derives its validity from some rules that have not in this sense been made by men but which can be "found" and that these rules provide both the criterion for the justice of positive law and the ground for men's obedience to it. Whether they seek the answer in divine inspiration or in the inherent powers of human reason but constitute non-rational factors that govern the working of the human intellect, or whether they conceive of the natural law as permanent and immutable or as variable in content, they all seek to answer a question which positivism does not recognize. For the latter, law by definition consists largely of deliberate commands of the human will.[50]

The found nature of the common law, moreover, underwrites its predictability. "[J]udicial decisions," Hayek observed, "may in fact be more predictable if the judge is also bound by generally held views of what is just, even when they are not supported by the letter of the law, than when he is restricted to deriving his decisions only from those among accepted beliefs which have found expression in written law."[51]

By contrast, legal positivism amounts to a return to the concept of a "police state."[52] This renders common law, which typically involves the transposition of custom into law, "without deliberate organization by a commanding intelligence." As such, it intimates the possibility of Law without command—law without Leviathan.[53]

Hayek's work, like that of public choice and law and economics scholars (and, we shall see, the thought of prominent conservative evangelical Christians), repeatedly emphasizes the novelty and modernity of legislation.[54] "Unlike law itself, which has never been 'invented' . . . the invention of legislation came relatively late in the history of mankind," he wrote in *Law, Legislation, and Liberty*.[55] "[L]aw is older than law-making," he underlined. It "existed for ages before it occurred to man that he could make or alter it. . . . It is," moreover, "no accident that we still use the same word 'law' for the invariable rules which govern nature and for the rules which govern men's conduct. They were both conceived at first as something existing independently of human will."[56] In England, Parliament was first understood as a law-finding, not a law-making, body. With the birth of the modern state in the fifteenth and sixteenth centuries, however, came the notion that states (Leviathans) make policy.[57]

One of the defining features of the common law was its purposelessness. In contradistinction to French étatism, Hayek explained, the history of the development of the English common law demonstrates that "purposive institutions might grow up which owed little to design, which were not invented but arose from the separate actions of many men who did not know what they were doing."[58] Progressive critics of the common law insisted that it substituted the will of the judge for the will of the legislature. Hayek, however, defended common law judges, citing their unique position as government officials learned in law, but ruling without "particular aims."[59] "The judge," Hayek explained, "serves, or tries to maintain and improve, a going order which nobody has designed, an order that has formed itself without the knowledge, and often against the will of authority, that extends beyond the range of deliberate organization on the part of anybody, and that is not based on the individuals doing anybody's will, but on their expectations becoming mutually adjusted." In so doing, he is "not a creator of a new order but a servant endeavoring to maintain and improve the functioning of an existing order."[60] He aims not at a particular state of things, but rather at "the regularity of a process which rests on some of the expectations of the acting persons being protected from interference by others." In a common law order, the developmental process is one of gradual adaptation by which "[t]he parts of a legal system are not so much adjusted to each other according to a comprehensive overall view, as gradually adapted to each other by the successive application of general principles to particular problems—principles, that is, which are often not even explicitly known but merely implicit in the particular measures that are taken."[61] "[T]he spontaneous formation of a 'polycentric order' . . . involving an adjustment to circumstances, knowledge of which is dispersed among a great many people, cannot be established by central direction. It can only arise from the mutual adjustment of the elements and their response to events that act immediately upon them."[62]

In his thinking on these matters, Hayek explained that he was anti-rationalist, but not anti-reason. He expressly rejected "the rationalist tradition [which] assumes that man was originally endowed with both the intellectual and the moral attributes that enabled him to fashion civilization deliberately."[63] He, in contradistinction, is an "evolutionist" who insists that "civilization was the accumulated hard-earned result of trial and error; that it was sum of experience, in part handed down from generation to generation as explicit knowledge, but to a larger extent embodied in tools and institutions which had proved themselves superior—institutions whose significance we might discover by analysis but which will also serve men's ends without men's understanding them."[64] While "rationalistic design theories were necessarily based on the assumption of the individual man's propensity for rational action and his natural intelligence and goodness . . . evolutionary theory . . . showed how certain institutional arrangements would induce man to use his intelligence to the best effect and how institutions could be framed so that bad people could do the least harm." Once again, pointing out the affinities between his atheological outlook and religious perspectives, Hayek emphasized that, "[t]he antirationalist tradition is here closer to the Christian tradition of the fallibility and sinfulness of man, while the perfectionism of the rationalist is in irreconcilable conflict with it."[65] That said, his antirationalism is not an appeal to mysticism or irrationalism. "What is advocated here is not an abdication of reason but a rational examination of the field where reason is appropriately put in control."[66]

Hayek's "evolutionary empiricist" perspective harnesses reason in the only way that it is sensible—in its full social context:

> The first condition for . . . an intelligent use of reason in the ordering of human affairs is that we can learn to understand what role it does in fact play in the working of any society based on the cooperation of many separate minds. This means that, before we can try to remold society intelligently, we must understand its functioning; we must realize that, even when we believe that we understand it, we may be mistaken. What we must learn to understand is that human civilization has a life of its own, that all our efforts to improve things must operate within a working whole which we cannot entirely control, and the operation of whose forces we can hope merely to facilitate and to assist so far as we understand them. Our attitude ought to be similar to that of the physician toward a living organism: like him, we have to deal with a self-maintaining whole which is kept going by forces which we cannot replace and which

we must therefore use in all we try to achieve. What can be done to improve it must be done by working with these forces rather than against them. In all our endeavors at improvement we must always work inside this given whole, aim at piecemeal, rather than total, construction, and use at each stage the historical material at hand and improve details step by step rather than attempt to redesign the whole.[67]

(Progressive) historicism, by contrast, "claimed to recognize necessary laws of historical development and to be able to derive from such insight knowledge of what institutions were appropriate to the existing situation." That tradition, which underwrites welfare state liberalism, rejects all rules that cannot be rationally justified, or that were not deliberately designed. In this way, he argues, it is fueled by its positivist presuppositions.[68]

Hayek's opposition to historicism and positivism has constitutional implications. He explained that:

> From this it follows that no person or body of persons has complete freedom to impose upon the rest whatever laws it likes. The contrary view that underlies the Hobbesian conception of sovereignty (and the legal positivism deriving from it) springs from a false rationalism that conceives of an autonomous and self-determining reason and overlooks the fact that all rational thought moves within a non-rational framework of beliefs and institutions. Constitutionalism means that all power rests on the understanding that it will be exercised according to commonly accepted principles, that the persons on whom power is conferred are selected because it is thought that they are most likely to do what is right, not in order that whatever they do should be right. It rests, in the last resort, on the understanding that power is ultimately not a physical fact but a state of opinion which makes people obey.[69]

Once a bastion of the common law and constitutionalism, in the early-twentieth-century United States the rationalist, positivist "public administration movement," buttressed by support of "progressives," "directed their heaviest attack against the traditional safeguards on individual liberty, such as the rule of law, constitutional restraints, judicial review, and the conception of a 'fundamental law.'"[70] This culminated in the 1920s and 1930s in "a flood of anti-rule-of-law literature" associated with the legal realist movement. "It was the young men brought up on such ideas," in turn, "who became the ready instruments of the paternalistic policies of the New Deal."[71]

Though staunchly anti-socialist, anti-progressive, and anti–New Deal, Hayek was quick to insist that he was not a proponent of laissez-faire, or a worshipper of unregulated markets. It "is important not to confuse opposition against this kind of planning with a dogmatic laissez-faire attitude," he insisted. "It does not deny, but even emphasizes, that, in order that competition should work beneficially, a carefully thought-out legal framework is required and that neither the existing nor the past legal rules are free from grave defects."[72] He denied that *homo economicus* constituted an indigenous part of his much-admired British evolutionary tradition. Indeed, he considered laissez-faire doctrine to be a paradigmatic example of rationalism, introduced as a foreign element into the tradition by such figures as John Stuart Mill. Hayek favored, rather, a respect—but never a blind respect—for traditions and customs.[73]

Although a hero to libertarians, and a staunch opponent of positivistic statism, Hayek believed it was the proper business of the state to regulate morality.[74] He held moral rules to be "the most important" of society's customs and traditions.[75]

> Next to language, [moral rules of conduct] are perhaps the most important instance of an undesigned growth, of a set of rules which govern our lives but of which we can say neither why they are what they are nor what they do to us; we do not know what the consequences of observing them are for us as individuals and as a group. And it is against the demand for submission to such rules that the rationalistic spirit is in constant revolt.[76]

"Like all other values," he explained, "our morals are not a product but a presupposition of reason, part of the ends which the instrument of our intellect has been developed to serve."[77] He challenged the "rationalistic" attack on the moral rules as set out by religion as mere "superstition." "That we ought not to believe anything which has been shown to be false does not mean that we ought to believe only what has been demonstrated to be true," he argued. "There are good reasons why any person who wants to live and act successfully in society must accept many common beliefs, though the value of these reasons may have little to do with their demonstrable truth." Moral restraint, for him, was both socially useful and sensible in light of the underlying theory of knowledge and information upon which his political and legal theories are premised.[78]

<h2 style="text-align:center">EVANGELICAL CHRISTIAN CONSERVATIVE STORIES ABOUT THE COMMON LAW</h2>

For many contemporary social conservatives, the commitment to the common law stems from their understanding of it as inherently, and foundationally, Christian. Since, as most conservatives acknowledge, the Constitution does not mention God, and is thus to all appearances secular, this understanding of the common law, while rarely discussed, is an indispensible component of social conservatism's ideology of law and its peculiar form of Christian constitutional nationalism.[79]

The belief in the inherent Christianity of the common law is long-standing in the United States, advanced across the nineteenth century not only by countless evangelicals, but also by a handful of leading conservative legal scholars like Chancellor James Kent and Justice Joseph Story.[80] Current articulations of this understanding fit neatly into this history and are simply a reiteration of its familiar (if, nevertheless, consistently contested) claims. Within the contemporary conservative movement, one of the most influential purveyors of this view has been John W. Whitehead, a leading evangelical Christian conservative author, activist, and litigator, whose views I survey here as illustrative.

In 1982, Whitehead founded The Rutherford Institute, a pioneering evangelical Christian litigation group designed to counteract the influence of liberal legal groups like the ACLU. Like many of the liberal public interest litigation groups that preceded it, The Rutherford Institute recruited evangelical Christian lawyers in private practice to donate their time to cases central to the group's mission: the advancement of (their understanding of) religious freedom. The Institute has been particularly active in cases involving religion and the schools.[81]

In the year he founded Rutherford, Whitehead published *The Second American Revolution* (1982), which has sold more than

100,000 copies and was also made into a documentary film. *The Second American Revolution,* along with Francis Schaeffer's *A Christian Manifesto,* played a signal role in igniting the constitutional activism of contemporary evangelical Christian conservatives.[82] Under the manifest influence of R. J. Rushdoony's *Christian Reconstructionism* (Rushdoony is cited repeatedly as a source), the book is an attack on the role that American courts have played in creating and advancing "the pagan state."[83]

In *The Second American Revolution*—which gives an account of American history and constitutionalism that, while powerfully presented, is highly idiosyncratic, selective, and distorted—Whitehead opens with the assertion that an absolute, eternal, and fixed foundation is indispensible to government.[84] "[M]an cannot escape his religiousness," Whitehead announced. "This principle is inherent in the Second Commandment, prohibiting idolatry. In it the concern is not with atheism but with the fact that all men, Christian or not, seek something outside themselves to deify."[85] Since man is a deifying animal, in forming a society he faces a stark and momentous decision: he can either deify and worship God or Man. To deify man (including under the guise of the separation of Church and State) is to commit the sin of idolatry. Thus, the state must be anchored in the belief in (a Christian) God. A state founded on the worship of God will be a Christian state. A state founded on the worship of man will be pagan.

There is no such thing as a religious pluralism (in its "new," modern sense) consistent with Christianity, Whitehead explains. Since the truth is absolute, uniform, and Christian, religious pluralism is a step backwards into pagan polytheism. At the time he wrote, he complained that in the United States, "a new polytheism exists: the state tolerates many religions and, therefore, many gods. . . . The position of the American state is increasingly that of pagan antiquity," he warned, "in which the state as god on earth provides the umbrella under which all institutions reside."[86] Whitehead insisted that the American Founders were clear about these matters, and that they intended to institute a Christian state. The First Amendment's prohibitions on the Establishment of religion and protection for religious liberty were added to the body of the Constitution for one reason only, he instructed: to ensure that the newly powerful national state would have no authority over the

Church and religion. The First Amendment's religion clauses were fashioned to protect "denominational pluralism—a healthy coexistence between the various Christian denominations." Whitehead explained, "[s]uch practical denominational pluralism is not to be confused with the new concept of pluralism, which commands complete acceptance of all views, even secular humanism."[87] "The principal religion to be protected by the First Amendment was Christian theism," he stated. Through its rulings, however, the Supreme Court has demoted Christianity from its historically preferred constitutional position.[88]

Although it forbade the establishment of a national church, the Constitution secured the "blessings of liberty" by licensing the states to be "openly Christian."[89] As evidence for this, Whitehead cited the preambles and bodies of the various state constitutions at the time of the Founding, which, he noted, all clearly manifested the theistic grounding of their governments—all sovereign under the American federal system. Thus, "when the federal constitution was drafted, the principle of faith in God was presumed to be a universal for healthy civil government."[90] The nation's Christian grounding was also evident in the text of the Seventh Amendment, which expressly incorporated the common law—"which applied biblical principles in judicial decisions"—into the constitutional system.[91] By incorporating the common law, Whitehead concluded, "the Constitution was acknowledging that a system of absolutes," accessible only through Biblical revelation, exists "upon which government and law can be founded."[92]

The American Founding, he explained, was a restoration of (Protestant) Christianity to its proper role in government after its influence had been attenuated through the corrosive effects of Roman Catholic theology. The modern crisis began with the work of Saint Thomas Aquinas, who had argued in error "that man could discover at least some truth without revelation." Fortunately, "the Reformation thinkers of the sixteenth century, notably Martin Luther and John Calvin, fought against Aquinas's concept of the Fall. They revived the old Christian suspicion of human reason and once again made the Bible the sole reference point for truth."[93]

The Second American Revolution explained that the "fundamental principles" of the Reformation were bequeathed to the American colonists "without significant alteration" through the influence of

Lex Rex, or the Law and the Prince (1644), written by the Scottish clergyman Samuel Rutherford. "Rutherford's assertion [was] that the basic premise of government and, therefore, of law must be the Bible, the Word of God rather than the word of any man." "All men, even the king," Rutherford argued, "were under the law and not above it." Whitehead (strangely) elevated the significance of Rutherford to American political thought, placing Rutherford's influence on the American Founding over and above that of John Locke (he treats Locke and John Witherspoon as mere conduits for Rutherford's views, though Witherspoon is an especially significant conduit in Whitehead's stations-of-the-Constitution iconography since he was the teacher of James Madison—"the Father of the Constitution"—at Princeton). Whitehead (oddly) insisted, moreover, that it was Rutherford who first "established the principle of equality and liberty among men, which was later written into the Declaration of Independence." Rutherford's influence on the Founding was thus, by Whitehead's account, pervasive.[94]

William Blackstone, whose study of the common law (genuinely) had a major influence on the Founders and on nineteenth-century American law, was, Whitehead emphasized, likewise "a Christian, [who] believed that the fear of the Lord was the beginning of wisdom"—as is evidenced by his decision to open his Commentaries "with a careful analysis of the law of God as revealed in the Bible."[95] As Blackstone and the American founders understood:

> Law in the Christian sense implies something more than form. Law has content in the eternal sense. It has a reference point. Like a ship that is anchored, law cannot stray far from its mooring. If the anchor chain breaks, however, the ship drifts to and fro. Such is the current state of law in our country. Law in the true sense is bibliocentric, concerned with justice in terms of the Creator's revelation.[96]

"[B]ecause law establishes and declares the meaning of justice and righteousness," he continued, "law is inescapably religious."[97] "Acts of the state that do not have a clear reference point in the Bible are . . . illegitimate and acts of tyranny."[98]

Like legislative power, properly understood, judicial power in its true sense consists of enacting into positive law principles that were already inherent in God's commands. Whitehead explained:

> Essentially, common law is an age-old doctrine that developed by way of court decisions that applied the principles of the Bible to everyday situations. Judges simply decided their cases, often by making explicit reference to the Bible, but virtually always within a framework of biblical values. Out of these cases rules were established that governed future cases.[99]

"To some extent," Whitehead instructed his readers, "the common law has been present with us ever since the teachings of Moses, in that common law is essentially biblical principles adapted to local usage. It was an application of biblical principles—essentially the Ten Commandments—to the problems of everyday life."[100]

The common law, moreover, is biblical not simply in substance, but in process as well. For instance, "[t]he doctrine of stare decisis," he insisted, "is clearly based upon biblical principles."[101] Whitehead continued:

> This precedent of precedents was based upon Christian principles as they had been expressed in judicial opinions. Past decisions provided a ground for deciding present cases because past decisions were developments of the implications of the basic principle that was based on biblical absolutes. Common law rules then were conceived as founded in principles that were permanent, uniform, and universal.[102]

The Second American Revolution detailed how the English common law arose out of:

> [John] Wycliffe's contention that the people themselves should read and know the law of the Bible (hitherto the province of the clergy) and that they should in some sense govern as well as be governed by it. From this thesis . . . emerged a set of principles based upon the Bible and applied by the courts that came to be known as the common law or the law of the people. The common law became established in the English courts, and when the Constitution was being drafted, much of it was incorporated as part of that document.[103]

Whitehead explained that, given that some of it was peculiar to the English system, English common law was not imported into the United States in its entirety. It was, however, "in its Christian form, substantially implanted in the American legal system."[104]

Whitehead argued that the United States is governed by three basic systems of law. The first is Fundamental Law, which is "clearly expressed in God's revelation as ultimately found in the Bible." The second is Constitutional Law, which provides "the form of civil government to protect the God-given rights of the people." The Constitution, he emphasized, "presupposes the Declaration and the higher, fundamental law to which the Declaration witnesses." Popular sovereignty governs in the sense that "[t]he people can base their institutions upon constitutional law, in conjunction with the higher or fundamental law. . . . Such biblical principles as federalism, separation of powers, limited authority, and liberty of conscience found in the Constitution" make sense only if we understand that the Constitution rests on the foundation of Fundamental Law. "They did not arise in a vacuum."[105] The same is true for rights, which Whitehead defines as "a benefit or lawful claim recognized by the law itself in recognition of principles of the biblical higher law."[106]

The third kind of law is comprised of "laws enacted by the political body having legislative power"—positive law. Legislators, in Whitehead's account (as in Hayek's), do not make law; they pronounce it. "The very term legislator," he notes, means "not one who makes laws but one who moves them—from the divine law written in nature or in the Bible into the statutes and law codes of a particular society. Just as a translator is supposed to faithfully move the meaning from the original language into the new one so the legislator is to translate laws, not make new ones." Democracy and freedom are consistent with each other for Whitehead only in the sense that true freedom consists in enacting laws consistent with God's will. "In the last analysis," he insists, "we would be far freer under an absolute monarch who saw his authority as subject to God's law in the Bible and in nature than under a democratically elected assembly that took the arbitrary will of the majority as its highest value."[107]

Whitehead condemned "[m]odern legal scholars" who "have rejected the views of Blackstone because they have rejected his faith in God and his reliance upon the Genesis account of creation and the origin of man and the universe."[108] The seminal act of treachery in this regard was committed by Christopher Columbus Langdell, who, through his invention of the case method of

law teaching at Harvard in the 1870s, re-imagined law along evolutionary scientific lines. "Langdell's real impact on law education," Whitehead wrote, "was his belief that basic principles and
doctrines of the law were the products of an evolving and growing process over many years. Langdell believed that this evolution
was taking place in opinions written by judges. This meant that
what a judge said was law, and not what the Constitution said."[109]
In prelapsarian America:

> Before Langdell's influence became dominant in the legal educa-
> tion system, the law had primarily been taught by practicing lawyers
> in law offices throughout the country. William Blackstone's *Com-
> mentaries* were often the basic legal treatise. The prevailing opinion
> was that the principles and doctrines of the law were unchanging;
> law was based on absolutes in the biblical sense. All the student had
> to learn was to apply those legal principles and doctrines. Begin-
> ning with Langdell, however, law education shifted to the class-
> room, where students were taught that the principles and doctrines
> of the law were being developed in the appellate courts by judges
> across America. Justice Hughes was merely echoing Langdell's phi-
> losophy when he remarked that "the Constitution is what the judges
> say it is."[110]

Langdell's views were reinforced by the scholarship of Oliver Wendell Holmes, Jr.:

> In Holmes's theory—summed up in the expression that the law is
> not logic but experience—law was the product of man's opinion,
> supported by the absolute rights of the majority. Thus, the princi-
> ples of the common law, which had guided courts and governments
> for centuries before America was settled, were to be left in the dust
> of history for the concept of evolving law. As a consequence com-
> mon law is virtually ignored in legal education today.[111]

Whitehead explained to his readers that they were living under
a system ruined by the intellectual, moral, and historical corruptions of legal positivism. Such positivism, "unknown in early American law . . . has resulted in a decline of American liberties. . . .
Justice itself has become a remote concept, which is the esoteric
concern of a group of legal technicians and professionals who cod-
ify the concerns of almost every area of life in some form of state

or bureaucratic regulation."[112] Moreover, "with the rise of legal positivism and sociological law, the flexibility once reserved to the common law judge is given over to the legal technician—or the modern judge who sits without the Bible as his guide and who, in fact, is often openly hostile to the Bible and Christian principles."[113]

Today, law schools hide the truth from their students: "Very few attorneys even have an understanding of what the common law is."[114] Whitehead called upon Christian law students to study the "true law." They had a duty to remind their professors "that much of law is still based on the Bible," and to demand courses on Blackstone and the common law, and to commit themselves to the study of "the true legal roots of American society."[115]

The Second American Revolution called for a renewed commitment by judges as well. Whitehead reminded them, and us, that, as the apostle Paul declares in Romans 13: 1–4, "all civil authorities are ministers of God."[116] As civil authorities, judges must employ higher law as their ultimate reference point. Courts must act as ministers of God, and, in this sense, are religious establishments.[117]

At one time, American judges understood that the United States is a Christian nation. Today, however, they proceed in accord with the whims of man. They are humanists—devotees of a pagan religion "opposed to any other religious system."[118] It is the obligation of Christians to act now to reclaim their country for Christ. "When a [pagan] state claims divine honors, there will always be warfare between Christ and Caesar, for two rival gods claim the same jurisdiction over man. It is a conflict between two kingdoms, between two kings, each of whom claims ultimate and divine powers . . . [O]ur government has . . . become a religion and is . . . involved in a bitter conflict with the religion of Christ. Christianity and the new state religion of America cannot peacefully coexist." In a state with Christian foundations, Whitehead concluded, "man's law must have its origin in God's revelation. Any law that contradicts biblical revelation is illegitimate."[119]

DISCUSSION

The perspectives of the strands of conservative legalism I have briefly canvassed here—law and economics, public choice, Hayekian thought, and evangelical Christianity—are different in many ways, and take different positions on foundational issues that political theorists would characterize as fundamental. Hayek condemned understandings of law based on homo economicus—central to the law and economics movement—as a variety of the rationalism he consistently inveighed against. John Whitehead aggressively condemned (Gilded Age) laissez-faire capitalism for being "without compassion," adding apropos of the Supreme Court's late-nineteenth/early-twentieth-century, pro-business/anti-regulatory substantive due process decisions that "the so-called right to contract is not found in the Constitution or even the English common law."[120] Whitehead also provided an extended critique of *Lochner v. New York* (1905), a decision that has been aggressively defended in recent years by prominent libertarian and public choice scholars. There is no trace of theism either in Hayek or in law and economics or public choice scholarship.[121] Those writing from these diverse perspectives also take different positions and evince different sensibilities on matters that many legal and constitutional theorists would hold to be categorically defining. For many years, the category of legal "conservative" has been synonymous with an "old" originalism rooted in a positivist understanding of the Constitution as a binding contract, deriving its authority from the sovereign act of its ratification by "We the People," aimed at "politicized" judges and courts, and meant and understood as a theory and instrument of judicial restraint through an adherence to "law." Some of the conservatives I survey here carry on these preoccupations and commitments—evincing a positivism, I would note, that is actually derived from early-twentieth-century progressivism (rather than any philosophic conservatism).[122] Many conservatives, however (consistent with what has been called the "new" originalism), are neither preoccupied with courts and judges as problems, nor consistently committed to forging theories of judicial restraint—at least as defined by a general rule of deference to legislatures, as opposed to assessing the constitutionality of legislation by a yardstick of substantive, foundational "law."[123]

Many political and legal theorists would take it as their job to anatomize and critique these contrasts, tensions, and contradictions within the conservative movement, with legal scholars especially spotlighting their diverse attitudes toward judges and courts and a default rule of deference. My objective here is to do something different, if not the opposite: to focus instead on how, despite these tensions and disagreements, conservatives have come to find common ground, to the point where all came to see themselves—whatever their differences and disagreements—as part of a common intellectual and political endeavor. In different contexts, disagreement on issues that once might have marked someone as not a member of the group—that is, a disagreement that is a deal-breaker or sign of "exit"—might come to be considered a point of legitimate disagreement within the group.[124] So long as it is not considered a deal-breaker, the differences and disagreements—even about fundamentals—might ultimately benefit and reinforce the collective endeavor and the political movement associated with it. Far from being something that needs to be ultimately resolved, worked out, or made consistent, the manifest fact of ongoing disagreement allows the movement to understand itself collectively as an intellectual endeavor, operating according to scientific norms of cordial questioning, empirical inquiry, intellectual diversity, disagreement, and debate. The disagreement is, stated differently, constitutive of the movement's identity, and of the identity of its participant members. As such, what Cass Sunstein has called "incompletely theorized agreement" is more than a make-do, pragmatic concession to pluralism: it is constitutive of the very idea of a discursive community. In political parties and movements, which, if successful, are inevitably coalitions and alliances (at least in a two-party liberal democratic system like the United States), it is less acknowledged than it should be that the valorization of disagreement—and not agreement—is what makes politics possible. In the contemporary United States, where conservatives have been long criticized as "the stupid party," mired in emotions and prejudices as opposed to thought and reason—the construction of a collective political identity that valorizes disagreement will be of particular value—indeed, a matter of pride.[125] It goes without saying that this identity-forging, constitutive pride in incompletely theorized agreement is a commitment made not in the abstract, but to deliberation and disagreement within an historically constituted, discursive community, with many agreements already in place on matters of concrete public policy.[126]

The commitment to the American Constitution, properly understood, as law, symbol, and historical/mythic constitutive story about origins, fidelity, betrayal, and redemption, has long been apparent as a constitutive touchstone of modern American conservatism. This chapter has emphasized the degree to which a complementary commitment to the common law has served as its adjunct. Constituent parts of modern legal conservatism—law and economics, public choice, Hayekian thought, and evangelical Christianity—all afford the common law a prominent place in their understandings. The twin commitments to the common terrain of Constitution and common law work in tandem to provide an intellectual foundation that serves to simultaneously motivate, unify, and fortify the contemporary conservative movement.

What is that common ground's content? All of the perspectives surveyed here understand themselves to be tribunes of the American Founding and the U.S. Constitution. Many of their practitioners understand themselves as locked in an epic battle with their faithless, liberal/progressive antagonists (enemies?) who are committed to unmooring the American polity from its Founding commitments and traditions. All are preoccupied with the unique virtues of the pre–New Deal/nineteenth-century American form of governance, which, in many respects, came close to achieving the benefits of governance without the oppressions and coercions of government. For law and economics and public choice scholars, this prelapsarian America (in which the common law, as opposed to legislatures, governed) was unusually prosperous and efficient. Law and economics and public choice scholars emphasize the ways in which this era preserved the freedom of individuals to pursue their own self-interest, in the process advancing, additively, the collective good of society. Hayek, by contrast, emphasized the ways in which common law governance worked to coordinate local knowledge in a way that advanced social interests. For Christians, this was the order that consistently recognized God as the foundation of all law, and was thus anchored against drift into heresy and evil. Collectively and respectively, then, nineteenth-century American society—following the template as set out by the Founders—was efficient, knowledgeable, and grounded.

All of the perspectives I have presented here devote considerable attention to the fall of this Edenic phase of American life. All agree that the culprit was the corrupting influence of legal positivism, or the idea that it was up to society, acting collectively, and through legislation (worst of all, centralized legislation). The legal Constitution—as opposed to the Constitution read willfully—placed aggressive limits upon this sort of rule by positivism, and created an expansive space for governance through the common law.[127]

Both Hayek and conservative Christians placed a heavy emphasis on the nature of true law as *found* rather than *made* (Hayek famously distinguished the *law* from *command*). Each of these perspectives apprehended the dangers of a conception of law as made rather than found in a different way. Law and economics and public choice scholars assume that individuals are perpetually and aggressively self-seeking. If society hands selfish and self-seeking men the immense powers of a legislative and administrative state, they will inevitably use that power to advance themselves at the expense of others—that is, they will abuse it. Hayek emphasized the ignorance of man. If you hand society the powers of a legislative and administrative state, Hayek emphasizes that it will fly blind and coerce others, where these others would be best off availing themselves of local knowledge and law and governing themselves. Conservative Evangelical Christians, by contrast, root their profound concerns about a powerful state in Original Sin. Assuming—as legal positivism does—that government can rest on the desires and preferences of man will lead to moral decline, if not evil. Statist positivism, for conservative evangelicals, is more than bad policy or bad theory: it is idolatry and paganism. Hayek expressly recognized the affinities between his emphasis on man's inherently limited ken and Christian conceptions of Original Sin. He also observed the similarity of his understanding of law as found rather than made to religious understandings of natural law. It is, of course, relatively easy to see the homo economicus of law and economics, or the selfish, self-seeking man of public choice, as what Evangelical Christians take to be man-as-fallen—corrupted, that is, by Original Sin.

For public choice scholars, legislation introduced rent-seeking and rent-appropriation as the primary modus operandi of government. Individuals and groups leveraged the coercive powers of the state through legislation and regulation to take what belonged to others and forcibly redistribute it to themselves. For Hayek, the statutory state legislated in spite of its ignorance of the detailed knowledge it would need to advance the public interest (most) effectively. For conservative evangelical Christians, the statutory state represented the displacement of God by man, of the prideful notion of man-as-lawgiver. What's worse, the modern administrative state was staffed by a small, unrepresentative—and, indeed, alien—"new class": an administrative, governing elite comprised of professors, bureaucrats, and politicians. Law and economics and public choice scholars understood this elite as redistributionist, as partial, self-seeking, and inefficient. Hayek understood it as *dirigiste*, as ignorant and rationalist. Evangelical Christian conservatives understood it as Godless and secular.

The common law state, by contrast, minimized or avoided many of these pitfalls and corruptions. In the common law state, where judges instantiated and enforced the rule of law, if there is legislation (the United States, after all, has a Congress) it will be strictly confined through judicial review to a limited sphere that maximizes common law governance (in the United States, via a robust federalism). In addition, even where the national legislature is operating in its proper sphere, judges will aggressively wield their judicial review powers to void attempts at rent-seeking. Hayek explained that unlike the (rationalist) legislator, the common law judge was purposeless (in his role, properly understood, at least) without a politics or a theory, operating in the limited sphere of case-deciding to instantiate the rule of law. Unfortunately, with the rise of the statutory state, judges became infused, and corrupted, by the redistributionist, *dirigiste*, and secularist ethos of the new, elitist, governing class. These corrupted, unmoored judges now followed not the rule of law, but the inclinations of ideology and their personal biases and preferences.

All of these groups find common ground in their defense of the promotion of traditional morality. While the law and economics and public choice scholars—allegedly libertarian—often avoid or downplay the issue, seminal proponents of these views (like public choice scholar James Buchanan) take what (even) they see as the current moral laxity of society as, in some way, an outgrowth of the decline of a sense of individual duty and responsibility that is a consequence of the rise of the "nanny state." Hayek celebrates moral rules as a form of tradition, which instantiates, often unconsciously, deep, de-centered human knowledge and experience.

Christian conservatives find the law's origins in God's command, as set out in the Bible, the basis for all law.

It should be clear from this brief overview that, ostensible philosophical differences notwithstanding, there is an enormous amount of ideological and political common ground to be found amongst these diverse perspectives. Indeed, the commonalities of these supposedly divergent perspectives, if apprehended in the right spirit, all but dwarf the differences.

Appeals to the nation's common law heritage and practice serve certain ideological and symbolic functions that are not served by the parallel commitment to the Constitution. To the extent that the U.S. Constitution, written and ratified in a precisely identifiable time and place, takes its authority from an act of popular, democratic will, the document's authority stems in significant part from human action, understood positivistically.[128] The authority of the common law, by contrast, gained legitimacy from its antiquity, its "immemoriality." Its origins were unclear—indeed, mystical. It was not democratic per se (with all the "instability, unpredictability, violence, and dangerousness" that, especially to many of the Founding generation, democracy entailed), but nevertheless its rules were held to be rooted in the customs and traditions of the people. It was held to embody "the order of things itself." As Kunal Parker explains, it embodied a "sense that the world was, in crucial ways, beyond the power of the democratic subject to remake, that it was subject to laws not of its making." It was timeless, and suggested eternal constraints, but it was not abstractly universalistic. The common law, rather, was both eternal and rooted.[129]

Many modern conservatives—like many Americans before them—sought to integrate American common law thinking with American constitutional thinking.[130] This allowed them to claim both *lex scripta* and *lex non scripta* as law, to permit the exercise of democratic will while at the same time suggesting that there were deeper, real limits to that will, some of which were inherent in the nature of things, as had long been recognized in the (Christian) Anglo-American political and constitutional tradition. In this often ambiguously specified combination, "[n]ewer notions of contemporaneous consent mingle promiscuously with older notions of multigenerational and attributed consent." Whereas written law held out the promise of clarity, of self-evident meaning, the common law allowed for appeals to unarticulated truths, to the long-recognized benefits of mystification.[131] In this, of course, the common law suggested many of the attributes of natural law. Indeed, the relationship between the (positive) law of the Constitution and legislation passed pursuant to it, the common law, and natural law was extensively debated in the United States during the slavery controversy.[132] As such, stories about the common law have served as significant adjuncts to stories about the nation's constitutional founding within the modern American conservative movement.

CONCLUSION

Commentators tethered to the usual concepts and categories of political, legal, and constitutional theory will typically miss the grounds of agreement shared by these supposedly diverse groups, which are often found in the realms of history, culture, and symbolism—conveyed in the narrative form, as constitutive stories—as opposed to the categorical abstractions of theory. Indeed, disagreements over principle are often managed—if not superseded—by stories.

In *Stories of Peoplehood*, Rogers M. Smith sets out a framework to help us understand the way in which individuals come to—and (crucially) are led to—develop a sense of being, of membership, of identity, and intra-group trust through the telling of "people-making," "ethically constitutive stories." These stories are typically historical and interpretive: they are rooted in interpretations of the group's (or nation's) past, and offer a shared understanding of the group's mores, understood in light of where they have been and where they are going.

Smith places particular emphasis on the role of elites (of the sort I have canvassed here) in constructing such stories, and championing them in the political process against competing, rivalrous stories of peoplehood. Intergenerational stories about the nature of the nation's legal/constitutional order are often critical components of the stories of peoplehood. In the United States, they are, arguably, the preeminent stories of peoplehood. These stories are constructed interactively, discursively, across time, lending meaning to individuals' lives, associations, and identities.[133] Such stories rationalize, direct, motivate, and "provid[e] grounds or warrants" for political behavior.[134]

Despite their many disagreements and diverse preoccupations, all of the perspectives surveyed here understand themselves to be tribunes of the American Founding and the U.S. Constitution, and position themselves as locked in an epic battle with their faithless liberal/progressive antagonists who are committed to unmooring the American polity from its Founding commitments and traditions.[135] All are preoccupied with the unique virtues of the pre–New Deal/nineteenth-century American form of constitutional governance, which, in many respects, came close to achieving the benefits of *governance* without the oppressions and coercions of *government*. All are profoundly disturbed by the country's abandonment of this Edenic garden, and agree that it was the snake of willful (progressive/liberal) legal positivism that persuaded their countrymen to take the fateful bite of the apple. Each apprehends the dangers of a conception of law as made rather than found. While political, legal, and constitutional theorists may focus on differences in their attitudes toward individualism, the sources and nature of political authority, and rights and the role of courts and judges—points upon which these groups certainly differ—they implicitly downplay the fellow-feeling created by their sense of unity in their role in a common legal drama. In that, the conservative stories about the common law play an important part.

NOTES

1. In writing this chapter, the author benefited from discussions at the symposium on this volume at the University of Texas Law School (September 2012), the workshop at Yale Law School on the Processes of Legal and Constitutional Change sponsored by the New York Historical Society's Institute for Constitutional History (July 2010), and from discussions at the Schmooze on "Invisible Constitutions" hosted by Princeton University's Law and Public Affairs Program (December 2010). Thanks also to Clem Fatovic, Dan Geary, Lino Graglia, Sandy Levinson, and Joel Parker for helpful comments and criticism.

2. See Theodore J. Lowi, *The End of the Republican Era* (Norman: University of Oklahoma Press, 1995).

3. Most famous is Frank Meyer's "fusionism." See Frank S. Meyer, *In Defense of Freedom and Related Essays* (Indianapolis, IN: Liberty Fund, 1996).

4. Ken I. Kersch, "Ecumenicalism Through Constitutionalism: The Discursive Development of Constitutional Conservatism in *National Review*, 1955–1980," *Studies in American Political Development* 25 (April 2011): 86–116; Kersch, "Beyond Originalism: Conservative Declarationism and Constitutional Redemption," *Maryland Law Review* 71 (Issue 1, 2011): 229–282.

5. Rogers M. Smith, *Stories of Peoplehood: The Politics and Morals of Political Membership* (New York: Cambridge University Press, 2003).

6. Kunal M. Parker, *Common Law, History, and Democracy in America, 1790–1900: Legal Thought before Modernism* (Cambridge: Cambridge University Press, 2011), 1.

7. See Martin M. Shapiro, *Courts: A Comparative and Political Analysis* (Chicago: University of Chicago Press, 1981).

8. Parker, *Common Law, History, and Democracy in America*, 77–78; Ford W. Hall, "The Common Law: An Account of Its Reception in the United States," *Vanderbilt Law Review* 4 (June 1951): 791–825.

9. While private law governs the relationships between private parties in areas such as contracts, real property, and torts, public law governs those between individuals and the state, and within the state, such as criminal law, civil liberties, the separation of powers, and federalism.

10. "In suits at common law, where the value in controversy shall exceed twenty dollars, the right of trial by jury shall be preserved, and no fact tried by a jury, shall be otherwise re-examined in any Court of the United States, than according to the rules of the common law." U.S. Constitution, Amendment VII.

11. William Blackstone, *Commentaries on the Laws of England, Vols. 1–4* (Chicago: University of Chicago Press, 1979); James Kent, *Commentaries on American Law, Vols. 1–4*, 7th ed. (New York: W. Kent, 1851); Joseph Story, *Commentaries on the Constitution of the United States: With a Preliminary Review of the Constitutional History of the Colonies and States, Before the Adoption of the Constitution* (Boston: C.C. Little and J. Brown, 1851).

12. See William E. Nelson, *The Americanization of the Common Law: The Impact of Legal Change in Massachusetts, 1760–1830* (Cambridge, MA: Harvard University Press, 1975); Mary Bilder, Maeva Marcus, R. Kent Newmyer, eds., *Blackstone in America: Selected Essays of Kathryn Preyer* (New York: Cambridge University Press, 2009). See also J. Willard Hurst, *Law and the Conditions of Freedom in the Nineteenth Century United States* (Madison: University of Wisconsin Press, 1956); Leonard W. Levy, *The Law of the Commonwealth and Chief Justice Shaw; The Evolution of American Law, 1830–1860* (New York: Harper and Row, 1957); Morton J. Horwitz, *The Transformation*

of American Law, 1780–1860 (Cambridge, MA: Harvard University Press, 1977); Howard Schweber, *The Creation of American Common Law, 1850–1880: Technology, Politics, and the Construction of Citizenship* (New York: Cambridge University Press, 2004).

13. See, as examples, Robert Rantoul, Jr., *An Oration Delivered Before Democrats and Antimasons, of the County of Plymouth: At Scituate on the Fourth of July, 1836* (Boston: Beals and Greene, 1836); David Dudley Field, *Speeches, Arguments, and Miscellaneous Papers of David Dudley Field, Vols. 1 & 2* (New York: D. Appleton, 1884 and 1890).

14. See Victoria C. Hattam, *Labor Visions and State Power: The Origins of Business Unionism in the United States* (Princeton, NJ: Princeton University Press, 1993); Karen Orren, *Belated Feudalism: Labor, the Law, and Liberal Development in the United States* (Cambridge: Cambridge University Press, 1991). See also William G. Ross, *A Muted Fury: Populists, Progressives, and Labor Unions Confront the Courts, 1890–1937* (Princeton, NJ: Princeton University Press, 1994).

15. Orren, *Belated Feudalism*; Stephen Skowronek, *Building a New American State: The Expansion of National Administrative Capacities, 1877–1920* (Cambridge: Cambridge University Press, 1982); John Fabian Witt, *The Accidental Republic: Crippled Workingmen, Destitute Widows, and the Remaking of American Law* (Cambridge, MA: Harvard University Press, 2004); William J. Novak, "Making the Modern American Legislative State," in *Living Legislation: Durability, Change, and the Politics of American Lawmaking*, ed. Eric M. Patashnik and Jeffrey A. Jenkins (Chicago: University of Chicago Press, 2012), 20–45; William N. Eskridge, Jr. and John Ferejohn, *A Republic of Statutes: The New American Constitution* (New Haven, CT: Yale University Press, 2010); Arthur F. Bentley, *The Process of Government: A Study of Social Pressures* (Chicago: University of Chicago Press, 1908); Robert A. Dahl, *A Preface to Democratic Theory* (Chicago: University of Chicago Press, 1956); Theodore J. Lowi, *The End of Liberalism* (New York: W. W. Norton, 1979).

16. Originalists hold that, in interpreting the Constitution, judges are obligated to hew to its original meaning, as it was understood at the time of its ratification. See Sotirios A. Barber and James E. Fleming, *Constitutional Interpretation: The Basic Questions* (New York: Oxford University Press, 2007).

17. There is a liberal wing of the law and economics movement, which includes scholars like Guido Calabresi and Ian Ayres. My focus here is on that movement's conservative wing.

18. Hurst, *Law and the Conditions of Freedom*. See W. W. Rostow, *Stages of Economic Growth: A Non-Communist Manifesto* (Cambridge: Cambridge University Press, 1960). See Douglass C. North and Barry Weingast,

"Constitutions and Commitment: The Evolution of Institutions Governing Public Choice in Seventeenth-Century England," *Journal of Economic History* 49 (December 1989): 803–832.

19. See North and Weingast, "Constitutions and Commitment," 823–824.

20. See Howard Gillman, *The Constitution Besieged: The Rise and Demise of Lochner Era Police Powers Jurisprudence* (Durham, NC: Duke University Press, 1993). See also Theodore J. Lowi, "Four Systems of Politics, Policy, and Choice," *Public Administration Review* 32 (July/August 1972): 298–310.

21. See Lon L. Fuller, *The Morality of Law* (New Haven, CT: Yale University Press, 1969); Friedrich von Hayek, *The Constitution of Liberty* (Chicago: University of Chicago Press, 1960).

22. See Skowronek, *Building a New American State*.

23. See, for example, Paul H. Rubin, "Common Law and Statute Law," *Journal of Legal Studies* 11 (June 1982): 205–224.

24. See, as examples, Richard A. Posner, *Economic Analysis of Law* (Boston: Little, Brown, 1972); Paul H. Rubin, "Why Is the Common Law Efficient?" *Journal of Legal Studies* 6 (January 1977): 51–64.

24. For an overview of this "legal origins" scholarship, which used quantitative methods to demonstrate that societies with common law origins are more prosperous than those with civil law origins, see John Reitz, "Legal Origins, Comparative Law, and Political Economy," *American Journal of Comparative Law* 57 (Fall 2009): 847–862; Ralf Michaels, "Comparative Law by Numbers? Legal Origins Thesis, *Doing Business* Reports, and the Silence of Traditional Comparative Law," *American Journal of Comparative Law* 57 (Fall 2009): 765–796. See also Paul Mahoney, "The Common Law and Economic Growth: Hayek Might Be Right," *Journal of Legal Studies* 30 (June 2001): 503–526; Rafael La Porta, Florencio Lopez-de-Silanes, and Andrei Shleifer, "The Economic Consequences of Legal Origins," *Journal of Economic Literature* 46 (June 2008): 285–332.

26. For overviews, see Todd J. Zywicki and Edward Peter Stringham, "Common Law and Economic Efficiency," in *Law and Economics*, 2nd ed., ed. Francesco Parisi and Richard A. Posner (forthcoming), accessed online January 20, 2015, at: http://www.law.gmu.edu/assets/files/publications/working_papers/1043CommonLawandEconomicEfficiency.pdf; Peter H. Aranson, "Economic Efficiency and the Common Law: A Critical Survey," in *Law and Economics and the Economics of Legal Regulation*, ed. J.-Matthias Graf von der Schulenburg and Göran Skogh (Boston: Kluwer Academic, 1986); George L. Priest, "The Common Law Process and the Selection of Efficient Rules," *Journal of Legal Studies* 6 (January 1977): 65–82; Priest, "The Modern Expansion of Tort Liability: Its Sources, Its Effects, and Its Reform," *Journal of Economic Perspectives* 5 (Summer 1991): 31–50.

27. Todd J. Zywicki, "The Rise and Fall of Efficiency in the Common Law: A Supply-Side Analysis," *Northwestern University Law Review* 97 (Summer 2003): 1551–1633.

28. Ibid., 1552.

29. Ibid., 1633. According to this view, the critical fact is that common law judges, if they are doing it right, are not willful. This is the theme of Philip Hamburger, *Law and Judicial Duty* (Cambridge, MA: Harvard University Press, 2008).

30. Zywicki, "The Rise and Fall of Efficiency in the Common Law," 1553.

31. James M. Buchanan and Gordon Tullock, *The Calculus of Consent: Logical Foundations of Constitutional Democracy* (Ann Arbor: University of Michigan Press, 1962).

32. James M. Buchanan, "Socialism Is Dead but Leviathan Lives On," in James M. Buchanan, *Post-Socialist Political Economy* (Lyme, CT: Edward Elgar, 1997), 85, quoted in S. M. Amadae, *Rationalizing Capitalist Democracy: The Cold War Origins of Rational Choice Liberalism* (Chicago: University of Chicago Press, 2003). I draw extensively on Amadae's book in the overview that follows.

33. It is precisely this that Margaret Thatcher meant when she famously declared: "There is no such thing as society." "Margaret Thatcher in Quotes," *Spectator* (April 8, 2013).

34. Amadae, *Rationalizing Capitalist Democracy*, x, 143. On the role of the economic think tank in informing Thatcher's conservative thought and policy, see Kersch, "Ecumenicalism Through Constitutionalism."

35. Anthony Downs, *An Economic Theory of Democracy* (New York: Harper, 1957); Kenneth Arrow, *Social Choice and Individual Values* (New York: Wiley, 1951).

36. Amadae, *Rationalizing Capitalist Democracy*, 137–138.

37. Ibid., 139.

38. See Peter Bachrach and Morton S. Baratz, *Power and Poverty: Theory and Practice* (New York: Oxford University Press, 1970); Theodore J. Lowi, *The End of Liberalism: The Second Republic of the United States* (New York: W. W. Norton, 1969); Grant McConnell, *Private Power and American Democracy* (New York: Vintage Books, 1970). See generally Richard M. Merelman, *Pluralism at Yale: The Culture of Political Science in America* (Madison: University of Wisconsin Press, 2003); Ronald Kahn, *The Supreme Court and Democratic Theory: 1953–1993* (Lawrence: University Press of Kansas, 1994).

39. James M. Buchanan and Richard F. Wagner, *Democracy in Deficit: The Political Legacy of Lord Keynes* (San Diego, CA: Academic Press, 1977), 65, cited in Amadae, *Rationalizing Capitalist Democracy*, 144.

40. See Friedrich A. Hayek, *Law, Legislation and Liberty: A New Statement of the Liberal Principles of Justice and Political Economy, Volume 1—Rules and Order* (Chicago: University of Chicago Press, 1973), 88.

41. Friedrich A. Hayek, *The Road to Serfdom* (Chicago: University of Chicago Press, 1944), for instance—which was influentially serialized in *Reader's Digest* when it first appeared—is frequently cited as one of the top ten most influential "conservative" books of the twentieth century. Hayek, famously, did not consider himself to be a conservative, and wrote a prominent essay on precisely that point. He was, however, certainly a vehement anti-socialist. See Friedrich A. Hayek, "Why I Am Not a Conservative," in Hayek, *Constitution of Liberty* (Chicago: University of Chicago Press, 1960), 397–411.

42. Hayek, *Law, Legislation and Liberty*, 14.

43. Ibid., 12.

44. Ibid., 13, 22, 85. See also Hayek, *Constitution of Liberty*, 58, quoting "Sir Matthew Hale's Criticism on Hobbes's Dialogue on the Common Law," reprinted in W. S. Holdsworth, *A History of English Law, Vol. V: The Common Law and Its Rivals* (London: Methuen, 1924), 504–505. Kunal Parker underlines the degree to which nineteenth-century American "historical school" legal scholars like Christopher Tiedemann and Oliver Wendell Holmes emphasized the common law not as a backwards-anchored fixed restraint, but, like Hayek, as a form of dynamic, living law. For many of these historical school thinkers, it was legislation, with its rigidities, that was "anti-life." Parker, *Common Law, History, and Democracy in America*, 219–245, 291–292. See also Guido Calabresi, *A Common Law for the Age of Statutes* (Cambridge, MA: Harvard University Press, 1982).

45. Hayek, *Law, Legislation and Liberty*, 12.

46. Ibid., 13.

47. Ibid., 78, 84, 85.

48. Hayek, *Constitution of Liberty*, 236.

49. Ibid., 163.

50. Ibid., 236–237.

51. Hayek, *Law, Legislation and Liberty*, 115–116.

52. Hayek, *Constitution of Liberty*, 237. See also Noga Morag-Levine, *Chasing the Wind: Regulating Air Pollution in the Common Law State* (Princeton, NJ: Princeton University Press, 2003).

53. Hayek, *Constitution of Liberty*, 149, 151.

54. See, for example, Hayek, *Law, Legislation and Liberty*, 89–91.

55. Ibid., 72; emphasis added. I have added the emphasis to highlight that Hayek here specifically equates the concept of "law" exclusively with common law. He puts legislation in a hermetically different category, where it is, by definition, not "law" at all. Similarly—but taking

the opposed position—Thomas Paine sharply distinguished the obscuran-
tist "lawyer's law" (the common law) from (legitimate) "legislative law."
Parker, *Common Law, History, and Democracy in America*, 71–73, 80–83, 99.
See also Richard E. Ellis, *The Jeffersonian Crisis: Courts and Politics in the
Young Republic* (New York: Oxford University Press, 1971).

56. Hayek, *Law, Legislation and Liberty*, 73.

57. Hayek, *Constitution of Liberty*, 163.

58. Ibid., 59. He added: "This demonstration that something greater
than man's individual mind may grow from men's fumbling efforts represented in some ways an even greater challenge to all design theories
than even the later theory of biological evolution. For the first time it was
shown that an evident order which was not the product of a designing
human intelligence need not therefore be ascribed to the design of a
higher, supernatural intelligence, but that there was a third possibility—
the emergence of order as the result of adaptive evolution." Darwin borrowed from this, rather than the other way around: "It is unfortunate that
at a later date the social sciences, instead of building on these beginnings
in their own field, re-imported some of these ideas from biology and
with them brought in such conceptions as 'natural selection,' 'struggle
for existence,' and 'survival of the fittest,' which are not appropriate in
their field."

59. Ibid., 242.

60. Hayek, *Law, Legislation and Liberty*, 118–119.

61. Ibid., 65. See also Philip Hamburger, *Law and Judicial Duty* (Cambridge, MA: Harvard University Press, 2008).

62. Hayek, *Constitution of Liberty*, 160, citing Michael Polanyi, *The Logic
of Liberty: Reflections and Rejoinders* (London: Routledge, 1951), 159.

63. Hayek, *Constitution of Liberty*, 59.

64. Ibid., 60.

65. Ibid., 60–61.

66. Ibid., 69.

67. Ibid., 70.

68. Ibid., 236.

69. Ibid., 181.

70. Ibid., 244–245. In opposition to this trend was Roscoe Pound, a
pioneer of the sociological jurisprudence who later became a critic of
"administrative absolutism" and a champion of the common law. See John
Fabian Witt, *Patriots and Cosmopolitans: Hidden Histories of American Law*
(Cambridge, MA: Harvard University Press, 2007), 211–284.

71. Hayek, *Constitution of Liberty*, 247.

72. Hayek, *The Road to Serfdom*, 36. See also Juliet Williams, "The
Road Less Traveled: Reconsidering the Political Writings of Friedrich

von Hayek," in *American Capitalism: Social Thought and Political Economy in the Twentieth Century,* ed. Nelson Lichtenstein (Philadelphia: University of Pennsylvania Press, 2006), 213–227.

73. Hayek, *Constitution of Liberty,* 60–61, 67.

74. See also Angus Burgin, *The Great Persuasion: Reinventing Free Markets Since the Depression* (Cambridge, MA: Harvard University Press, 2012).

75. Hayek, *Constitution of Liberty,* 62.

76. Ibid., 65.

77. Ibid., 63.

78. Ibid., 64–66.

79. See Isaac Kramnick and R. Laurence Moore, *The Godless Constitution: A Moral Defense of the Secular State* (New York: W. W. Norton, 2005). Some conservatives nevertheless cite the notation in Article VII that the document was "done in Convention by the Unanimous Consent of the States present the Seventeenth Day of September *in the Year of our Lord* one thousand seven hundred and Eighty seven . . ." as evidence that the Constitution patently presupposed Christianity. U.S. Constitution, Article VII [emphasis added]. See, for example, Felix Morley, *Freedom and Federalism* (Indianapolis, IN: Liberty Fund, [1959] 1981), 302. Others hold the Constitution's godlessness—the result of which was the tolerance of the nation's original sin of slavery—was corrected by the constitutional thought of Abraham Lincoln, whose reading of the Constitution incorporated the Declaration of Independence, which expressly mentioned both "the Laws of Nature and Nature's God" and that "all Men are created equal" and "endowed by their Creator with certain unalienable Rights." See Ken I. Kersch, "Beyond Originalism: Conservative Declarationism and Constitutional Redemption," *Maryland Law Review* 71 (Issue 1, 2011): 229–282.

80. See Steven K. Green, *The Second Disestablishment: Church and State in Nineteenth-Century America* (New York: Oxford University Press, 2010); Parker, *Common Law, History, and Democracy in America.*

81. Whitehead himself was co-counsel for Paula Jones in her sexual harassment lawsuit against President Bill Clinton. Francis A. Schaeffer, *A Christian Manifesto* (Westchester, IL: Crossway Books, 1982). See Ann Southworth, *Lawyers of the Right: Professionalizing the Conservative Coalition* (Chicago: University of Chicago Press, 2008), 16, 26, 32, 34. See www.rutherford.org/ (the site's banner trumpets the group as being "dedicated to the defense of civil liberties and human rights"). Within the movement, Whitehead's Rutherford model was soon followed by the Reverend Donald Wildman's American Family Association Center for Law and Policy, available online at: www.afa.net/; and Pat Robertson's American Center for Law and Justice, headed by Jay Sekulow, available online at:

www.aclj.org/. Whitehead is a prolific author. See John W. Whitehead, *The Separation Illusion: A Lawyer Examines the First Amendment* (Milford, MI: Mott Media, 1977); Whitehead, *Slaying Dragons: The Truth behind the Man Who Defended Paula Jones* (Nashville, TN: Thomas Nelson, 1999); Whitehead, *The Freedom of Religious Expression in Public Universities and High Schools*, 2nd ed. (Westchester, IL: Crossway Books, [1985] 1986); Whitehead, *Stand and Fight: It's Time for a Second American Revolution* (Tyler, MN: Glass Onion/TRI Press, 2009). See also R. Jonathan Moore, *Suing for America's Soul: John Whitehead, The Rutherford Institute, and Conservative Christians in the Courts* (Grand Rapids, MI: William B. Eerdmans, 2007). Moore observes that, of all his writings, Whitehead was proudest of *The Second American Revolution* (Westchester, IL: Crossway Books, 1982). In recent years, the Rutherford Institute has taken some seemingly surprising turns, opposing, for example, the Iraq War and the USA Patriot Act and defending the due process rights of War on Terror detainees Jose Padilla and Yaser Hamdi. Whitehead has, in some respects, turned away from politics, at least in its more statist ambitions. See Whitehead, *God Is a Four-Letter Word* (Tyler, MN: Glass Onion/TRI Press, 2007). See Rob Boston, "Theocracy Rejected: Former Christian Right Leaders 'Fess up': Frank Schaeffer, John Whitehead and Cal Thomas Have Repudiated the Theocratic Movement They Once Led. Here's Why," *Alternet* (March 10, 2008), accessed online January 20, 2015, at: http://www.alternet.org/story/78818/theocracy_rejected%3A_former_christian_right_leaders_%27fess_up/?page=2; Ted Olson, "The Dragon Slayer: He Fights for Religious Liberty, Defends the Civil Rights of Homosexuals, and Funded Paula Jones's Case against the President—the Enigmatic John Wayne Whitehead," *Christianity Today* 42 (December 7, 1998).

82. Whitehead, *The Second American Revolution*, 18. (Cover image: "The Spirit of '76," original painting in Selectmen's Room, Abbot Hall, Marblehead, Massachusetts.) At Franky Schaeffer's instigation, and in line with his conceptions, the book was also made into a film released by Franky Shaeffer V Productions (Acknowledgments, n.p.). In the Foreword to the book, the influential evangelical intellectual Francis Schaeffer explains that, "The government, the courts, the media, the law are all dominated to one degree or another by [the] elite. They have largely secularized our society by force, particularly using the courts. . . . If there is still an entity known as 'the Christian church' by the end of this century, operating with any semblance of liberty within our society here in the United States," he writes, "it will probably have John Whitehead and his book to thank," adding that this is "the most important book that I have read in a long, long time." See http://www.rutherford.org/.

83. See R. J. Rushdoony's *This Independent Republic: Studies in the Nature and Meaning of American History* (Nutley, NJ: Craig Press, 1964); *The Nature of the American System* (Nutley, NJ: Craig Press, 1965); *The Roots of Reconstruction, Law and Liberty* (Portland, OR: Ross House Books, 1971); and *Institutes of Biblical Law, Vols. 1–3* (Nutley, NJ: Craig Press, 1973). In 1965, Rushdoony founded the Chalcedon Institute, which is committed to the advancement of Reconstructionist Christianity. See http://chalcedon.edu/. "Post-Millennial" Reconstructionism calls for the rule here and now, on earth, by the literal word of God, as set out in the Bible—particularly in the Old Testament. See, generally, Walter Olson, "Invitation to a Stoning: Getting Cozy with Theocrats," *Reason* (November 1, 1998).

84. See Neal Devins, "Book Review: *The Second American Revolution* by John W. Whitehead," *Hastings Constitutional Law Quarterly* 11 (Spring 1984): 505–522, concluding that Whitehead's thinking as expressed in the book "is alien to the values underlying American jurisprudence," that his history is "inaccurate," and that *The Second American Revolution* in the end is little more than "normative advocacy of the virtues of and the necessity for Christian life in a Christian state."

85. Whitehead, *The Second American Revolution*, 86.

86. Ibid., 113.

87. Ibid., 96.

88. Ibid., 101, 103. See also Robert T. Handy, *A Christian America: Protestant Hopes and Historical Realities* (New York: Oxford University Press, 1984); Green, *Second Disestablishment*.

89. Whitehead, *The Second American Revolution*, 95.

90. Ibid., 96.

91. Ibid., 76.

92. Ibid., 21.

93. Ibid.

94. Ibid., 28–30. Hayek alludes to Rutherford's *Lex Rex* in *The Constitution of Liberty* as "one of the polemical tracts of the period." Hayek, *Constitution of Liberty*, 169.

95. Whitehead, *The Second American Revolution*, 31.

96. Ibid., 73.

97. Ibid., 111.

98. Ibid., 153.

99. Ibid., 76.

100. Ibid., 77, 194. This lends a special symbolic importance to the Supreme Court's recent decisions holding that the Establishment Clause limits the public display of the Ten Commandments. *McCreary County v. American Civil Liberties Union*, 545 U.S. 844 (2005); *Van Orden v. Perry*, 545

U.S. 677 (2005). From the ideological perspective set out here, this is evidence of major corruption on the Supreme Court. Such decisions are "the false dictum of the absolute separation of church and state." Whitehead, *The Second American Revolution*, 78.

101. Whitehead, *The Second American Revolution*, 195.

102. Ibid., 195–196.

103. Ibid., 193.

104. Ibid., 197.

105. Ibid., 75.

106. Ibid., 116. For this reason, there can be no such thing as "gay rights" or a right to an abortion. Because they are inconsistent with God's law, they are not "rights." "Vice—homosexuality, prostitution—represents idolatry and can never be justified even if 'legalized' by the state. Attempts to do so repudiate the Second Commandment," at 79.

107. Ibid., 75–76.

108. Ibid., 47.

109. Ibid.

110. Ibid.

111. Ibid., 193.

112. Ibid., 196.

113. Ibid., 200.

114. Ibid., 193.

115. Ibid., 170, 171.

116. Ibid., 85–86.

117. Ibid. This theme is emphasized by Hamburger as well. Hamburger, *Law and Judicial Duty*.

118. Whitehead, *The Second American Revolution*, 40, 106. This is a major theme on the Right. See, for example, Robert P. George, *The Clash of Orthodoxies: Law, Religion, and Morality in Crisis* (Wilmington, DE: ISI Books, 2001).

119. Whitehead, *The Second American Revolution*, 18, 74.

120. Ibid., 36–37. Prominent conservative thinkers put their shoulders to the wheel to reconcile religious views of people like Whitehead with a robust commitment to free market capitalism. Perhaps most prominent in this regard was the work done by Michael Novak to bring conservative Catholics around to a robust commitment to free markets. See Michael Novak, *The Spirit of Democratic Capitalism* (New York: American Enterprise Institute/Simon & Schuster, 1982).

121. Whitehead, *The Second American Revolution*, 119–20. *Lochner v. New York*, 198 U.S. 45 (1905). See, as examples, David E. Bernstein, *Rehabilitating Lochner: Defending Individual Rights against Progressive Reform* (Chicago: University of Chicago Press, 2011); Richard Epstein, *Principles for a Free*

Society: Reconciling Individual Liberty with the Common Good (New York: Perseus Books, 1998).

122. See Ken I. Kersch, "Constitutional Conservatives Remember the Progressive Era," in *The Progressives' Century: Democratic Reform and Constitutional Government in the United States,* ed. Stephen Skowronek, Stephen Engel, and Bruce Ackerman (New Haven, CT: Yale University Press, 2016); David E. Bernstein, "The Progressive Origins of Conservative Hostility to *Lochner v. New York,*" in *Toward an American Conservatism: Constitutional Conservatism During the Progressive Era,* ed. Joseph Postell and Johnathan O'Neill (New York: Palgrave Macmillan, 2013).

123. See, as examples, Robert H. Bork, *The Tempting of America: The Political Seduction of the Law* (New York: Simon & Schuster, 1991); Randy E. Barnett, *Restoring the Lost Constitution: The Presumption of Liberty* (Princeton, NJ: Princeton University Press, 2004); Antonin Scalia, "Originalism: The Lesser Evil," *University of Cincinnati Law Review* 57 (Issue 3, 1989): 849–866. See Keith E. Whittington, "The New Originalism," *Georgetown Journal of Law and Public Policy* 2 (Summer 2004): 599–613; Robert C. Post and Reva B. Siegel, "Democratic Constitutionalism," in *The Constitution in 2020,* ed. Jack M. Balkin and Reva B. Siegel (New York: Oxford University Press, 2009), 25–34; Robert Post and Reva Siegel, "*Roe* Rage: Democratic Constitutionalism and Backlash," *Harvard Civil Rights—Civil Liberties Law Review* 42 (Summer 2007): 373–434.

124. Albert O. Hirschman, *Exit, Voice, and Loyalty: Responses to Decline in Firms, Organizations, and States* (Cambridge, MA: Harvard University Press, 1970).

125. In a statement made during a May 1866 parliamentary debate, John Stuart Mill famously said: "Although it is not true that all conservatives are stupid people, it is true that most stupid people are conservatives." See Lionel Trilling, *The Liberal Imagination: Essays on Literature and Society* (New York: Harcourt Brace Jovanovich, 1950). "But the conservative impulse and the reactionary impulse . . . do not, with some isolated and some ecclesiastical exceptions, express themselves in ideas but only in action or in irritable mental gestures which seek to resemble ideas." See also: Richard Hofstadter, *The Paranoid Style in American Politics and Other Essays* (New York: Knopf, 1965); Chris Mooney, *The Republican Brain: The Science of Why They Deny Science—and Reality* (New York: Wiley, 2012); Patricia Cohen, "'Epistemic Closure'? Those Are Fighting Words," *New York Times* (April 27, 2010).

126. Cass R. Sunstein, "Incompletely Theorized Agreements in Constitutional Law," *Social Research* 74 (Spring 2007): 1–24. See also John S. Dryzek and Simon Niemeyer, "Reconciling Pluralism and Consensus Political Ideals," *American Journal of Political Science* 50 (July 2006): 634–649.

127. See Novak, "Making the Modern American Legislative State"; David R. Mayhew, "Lawmaking as a Cognitive Enterprise," in *Living Legislation: Durability, Change, and the Politics of American Lawmaking*, ed. Jeffrey A. Jenkins and Eric M. Patashnik (Chicago: University of Chicago Press, 2012), 255–264; Hamburger, *Law and Judicial Duty*.

128. See *Federalist* No. 1.

129. Parker, *Common Law, History, and Democracy in America*, 1–2, 7, 12–15, 29. Parker explains that early-seventeenth-century common law thinkers "reworked the medieval ideal that law could not be made, but only discovered and declared. Where medieval legal thinkers had argued on the basis of timeless, discoverable, universal, and rational principles, early seventeenth century common lawyers attributed a special non-historical temporality to the common law," at 29.

130. See James R. Stoner, Jr., *Common Law Liberty: Rethinking American Constitutionalism* (Lawrence: University Press of Kansas, 2003); Stoner, *Common Law and Liberal Theory: Coke, Hobbes and the Origins of American Constitutionalism* (Lawrence: University Press of Kansas, 1992); Robert Lowry Clinton, *God and Man in the Law* (Lawrence: University Press of Kansas, 1997). See also John Philip Reid, *The Ancient Constitution and the Origins of Anglo-American Liberty* (New York: New York University Press, 2005); Parker, *Common Law, History, and Democracy in America*, 2.

131. Parker, *Common Law, History, and Democracy in America*, 58, 68–69, 71–72, 77–79, 92–93,107.

132. Ibid., 176–193. See also Douglas Edlin, *Judges and Unjust Laws: Common Law Constitutionalism and the Foundations of Judicial Review* (Ann Arbor: University of Michigan Press, 2010).

133. Smith, *Stories of Peoplehood*. See also Rogers M. Smith, "Identities, Interests, and the Future of Political Science," *Perspectives on Politics* 2 (June 2004): 301–312; Peter A. Hall and Rosemary C. R. Taylor, "Political Science and the Three New Institutionalisms," *Political Studies* 44 (December 1996): 946–950; Jack M. Balkin, *Constitutional Redemption: Political Faith in an Unjust World* (Cambridge, MA: Harvard University Press, 2011); Murray Edelman, *Politics as Symbolic Action: Mass Arousal and Quiescence* (Chicago: Markham Publishing, 1971); Edelman, *Constructing the Political Spectacle* (Chicago: University of Chicago Press, 1988); Kersch, "Ecumenicalism Through Constitutionalism."

134. See Willard A. Mullins, "On the Concept of Ideology in Political Science," *American Political Science Review* 66 (June 1972): 498–510, arguing that ideologies are inherently structured by an historical consciousness and lend moral significance to human experience; Harold D. Lasswell and Abraham Kaplan, *Power and Society: A Framework for Political Inquiry* (New Haven, CT: Yale University Press, 1950), 116, claiming

"the *political myth* is the pattern of political symbols current in a society" [emphasis in original]. See also Pamela Brandwein, "Law and American Political Development," *Annual Review of Law and Social Science* 7 (December 2011): 187–216.

135. This is, of course, a classical "origins" or "founding" myth. See Mullins, "On the Concept of Ideology," 505: "In politics, some of the most important myths concern the founding of the polity. The founding myth often refers to heroic figures, real or imaginary, who created the political order. When persons invoke the name or recount the exploits of the founders, past and present are merged; the past is reviewed in the present, even as the present draws significance from the past. By such practices, political communities celebrate the essential identity between the original act of founding and the continuing actions that extend and preserve the polity. Hence in a society characterized by mythical consciousness, the social structure is not viewed as an arrangement that might be altered by each generation according to its perceptions of justice and convenience, but as a sacred and timeless order which is sanctified by the myths that explain its importance and its origin," citing Carl Friedrich, *Man and His Government: An Empirical Theory of Politics* (New York: McGraw Hill, 1963), 96, 393–396 and Bronislaw Malinowski, *Magic, Science, and Religion and Other Essays* (Garden City, NY: Doubleday/Anchor, 1954), 100–101. The call for a return to founding principles, from a place of corruption or decline, is, of course, a key theme of republican thought. See Niccolo Machiavelli, *Discourses,* in Niccolo Machiavelli, *The Prince and the Discourses* (New York: Modern Library, 1950); J. G. A. Pocock, *The Machiavellian Moment: Florentine Political Thought and the Atlantic Republican Tradition* (Princeton, NJ: Princeton University Press, 1975).

7

THE ROLE OF CONSERVATISM IN SECURING AND MAINTAINING JUST MORAL CONSTITUTIONS: TOWARD A THEORY OF COMPLEX NORMATIVE SYSTEMS

GERALD GAUS

Now let us say that a society is well-ordered when it not only is designed to advance the good of its members but when it also is effectively regulated by a public conception of justice. That is, it is a society in which (1) everyone accepts and knows that the others accept the same principles of justice, and (2) the basic social institutions generally satisfy and are generally known to satisfy these principles.

—John Rawls, *A Theory of Justice*

In politics, again, it is almost a commonplace, that a party of order or stability, and a party of progress or reform, are both necessary elements of a healthy state of political life; until the one or the other shall have so enlarged its mental grasp as to be a party equally of order and of progress, knowing and distinguishing what is fit to be preserved from what ought to be swept away. Each of these modes of thinking derives its utility from the deficiencies of the other; but it is in a great measure the opposition of the other that keeps each within the limits of reason and sanity.

—John Stuart Mill, *On Liberty*

1. Two Conceptions of a Well-Ordered Society

For the last 40 years—since John Rawls's *A Theory of Justice*[1]—the Holy Grail of mainstream political philosophy has been "the theory

256

of justice." Although political philosophers have paid lip service to diversity of ends and moral disagreement as the background for their quest, the aim has been to present *the* correct theory of justice that can provide *the* basis for the sort of moral homogeneity that Rawls described as "well-ordered." In a just society, it has been thought, all would endorse the very same principles of justice, to which social institutions would conform. Typically, these principles are described as "liberal," so a just liberal society is characterized by moral homogeneity about justice.[2] If liberalism, or a liberal order, is identified with a specific "theory of justice" in this way, it must set itself up in opposition to competing "political theories" such as conservatism. A successful, triumphant, just liberal order has no place for conservatism as a popular political program, for the conservative rejects "the liberal theory of justice" and so cannot be a part of a well-ordered society based on it. The existence of a viable conservative party must indicate an incomplete or imperfect "collective commitment to justice."[3] The enemy—a purveyor of injustice—has not yet been banished. Their electoral success would spell doom for a free and just order.

This philosophical quest for the liberal theory of justice, I believe, has been worse than a dead end—though it certainly has been a dead end—if there was ever an aspiration that the fruits of this 40-year quest would be some sort of consensus on the nature of a just, well-ordered society. Amartya Sen is quite right: no matter how well-informed and impartial, competent inquirers simply will not arrive at the same conclusions as to the most just social condition.[4] Much worse, however, is that fixation on the ideal of a morally homogeneous society committed to a specific conception of justice has rendered normative political philosophy itself an ideological activity. The argument for any specific "political vision"[5] is at best only suggestive; the many alternatives remain morally and intellectually viable.

Contrast this pursuit of homogeneity to the analysis of a free order implied by the nineteenth-century doctrine of the parties of order and progress (or, to employ the other contrast Mill provides, of stability and reform), as described in the epigraph.[6] In contrast to the currently dominant view, which identifies a successful liberalism with the victory of a sectarian theory of justice, this latter view depicts a free and just order as inherently one of deep moral and political diversity. Such a society could still be well-ordered in the sense that its participants endorse as normative the basic terms of their common life and so achieve a justified and stable order, but the shared terms would be grounded on diverse normative commitments, and they will not agree that these are the best or optimal terms. What is interesting about such moral and political systems is that their deep normative diversity, rather than being a barrier to a sustained public moral and political existence, is the grounds of it. A sustainable free order is not one that has banished the enemies of "liberalism," but a complex system that requires diverse moral and political views for its maintenance.

In this chapter I explore this latter conception of a moral and political order, and how political philosophy may study and evaluate it. In section 2, following a different idea of Rawls, I sketch a conception of a truly diversity-based normative political philosophy as a search for a "moral constitution" that can be endorsed by a variety of normative commitments. I show in section 3 how our current foci, American conservatives, are well-placed to be "wholehearted members" of this moral order.[7] However, conservatives are not simply committed to this order; in section 4 I argue that the conservative tradition has insights into the nature of such an order that are often resisted by liberal political philosophers, and so an adequate political philosophy of normatively diverse systems coheres with basic conservative ideas. Section 5 then turns directly to the way that diversity is required for a sustainable, justified moral constitution. I maintain that a division between conservatives and what I shall call "left-leaning liberals"[8] is conducive to a just and sustainable moral constitution. I conclude with a few remarks on the idea of a political theory for complex normative systems.

2. RETHINKING MORAL LIFE UNDER CONDITIONS OF DIVERSITY

2.1. Moral Theory and Moral Constitutions

Although I have pointed to Rawls's *Theory of Justice* as the fountainhead of the contemporary obsession with producing "the liberal theory of justice,"[9] there is good reason to think that Rawls was less enamored with this project than were his followers, and became increasingly skeptical as his work developed in the 1980s and 1990s. He came to stress that our society is confronted by irreconcilable conflicts of "absolute depth."[10] Thus, his regulative question became: "How is it possible for there to be a just and stable society of free and equal citizens who remain profoundly divided by reasonable religious, philosophical, *and moral* doctrines?"[11] Of the utmost importance is that, in contrast to his earlier work, Rawls did not restrict these deep conflicts to matters of "the good"—he explicitly recognized that the free use of reason among good-willed and reasonable people leads them to disagree about morality and the principles of political right.[12] Given this enduring and pervasive disagreement, the "real task" of "justifying a conception of justice" involves:

> The search for reasonable grounds for reaching agreement rooted in our conception of ourselves and our relation to society [which] replaces the search for moral truth interpreted as fixed by a prior and independent order of objects and relations, whether natural or divine, an order apart and distinct from how we conceive of ourselves. *The task is to articulate a public conception of justice that all can live with* . . . What justifies a conception of justice is not its being true to an order antecedent to and given to us, but its congruence with our deepest understanding of ourselves and our aspirations, and our realization that, given our history and the traditions embedded in our public life, it is the most reasonable doctrine for us. *We can find no better basic charter for our social world.*[13]

Rawls advanced a fruitful and radical proposal: We can conceive of the justification of a liberal conception of justice as the search for a "public moral constitution" that we all can live with.[14] Just as a political constitution is the basis of legitimate and mutually recognized political authority among those who favor competing political views—conservatives, democratic socialists, liberal egalitarians, greens, feminists, libertarians, and so on—a justified moral constitution articulates a shared, public, moral framework that all can live with. Now, to say that all can live with a certain moral constitution is not to say that it is (in some deep sense) the true, or morally best, constitution as judged from any particular moral, religious, or metaphysical perspective. In his American Philosophical Association presidential address, Rawls identifies a form of moral inquiry that he calls "moral theory," which is distinct from moral philosophy:

> Moral theory is the study of substantive moral conceptions, that is, the study of how basic notions of the right, the good, and moral worth may be arranged to form different moral structures. Moral theory tries to identify the chief similarities and differences between these structures and to characterize the way that they are related to our moral sensibilities and natural attitudes, and to determine the conditions they must satisfy if they are to play their expected role in human life.[15]

Rawls explicitly stressed that the perspective of the moral theorist must be divorced from that of one committed to a particular moral conception.[16] "One thinks of the moral theorist," wrote Rawls, "as an observer, so to speak, who seeks to set out the principles of *other people's* moral conceptions and attitudes."[17] As moral theorists, Rawls writes, "we are investigating an aspect of human psychology, the structure of our moral sensibility." Moreover, moral theory is necessarily concerned with social theory, and the feasibility of the sort of society a moral conception instructs us to seek.[18] In contrast, when taking up the perspective of an individual devoted to a moral conception, one may regard it as the correct theory, as that which provides the definitive account of normativity, justice, or the nature of objective right and wrong.[19] When advocating a moral conception one may find it puzzling that others can fail to grasp its insights, whereas Rawls repeatedly and approvingly cites Sidgwick's remark, in the preface to the first edition of *The Methods of Ethics*, that he sought "to put aside temporarily the urgent need which we all feel of finding and adopting the true method of determining what we ought to do; and to consider simply what conclusions can be rationally reached if we start with certain ethical premises." The aim, said Sidgwick, is to adopt "a neutral position" when evaluating the various methods of ethics.[20]

The moral theorist, then, stands back from his own deepest (sectarian) normative commitments, and seeks to discover a moral framework we all can live with—a framework that is socially feasible, psychologically workable, and resonates with each person's deepest normative commitments. Many are uncomfortable with this project (which perhaps explains why it has not been taken up). As many see it, it hovers uneasily between the normative and descriptive. If we take the normative as that which concerns what is, in some sense, truly and really moral and valuable, moral theory is agnostic about such normativity. And if, as some would have it, any concern with social and psychological feasibility, and what is warranted given bounded deliberation, are mere social scientific matters that lie outside the realm of the moral, then again moral theory will seem to be non-normative. Rawls challenges these narrow understandings of the normative realm. The moral constitution identifies an enduring framework that each of us, exercising her reason within the bounds of normal human competency, can reflectively endorse as providing moral grounds for interpersonal demands and the adjudication of claims. That is, it provides a shared conception of justice.

2.2. Deep Diversity and the Non-optimizing Stance

Here, then, is our problem: A cooperative social life that treats all as free and equal moral persons—one that is liberal in the widest sense—requires a common moral constitution. In far-flung cooperative social and economic orders, one needs to have a firm idea about the terms of intercourse with the undefined stranger. To know what you can expect—indeed, morally demand—of others, and what they can require of you is indispensible for social life. Within small, like-minded groups we may share a local moral constitution based on deep agreement in outlooks, but in our wider social interactions such agreement seems, at best, thin. We have irreconcilable disputes of absolute depth. What are we to do?

One response, which we can associate with much of the work of Rawls and many of his contemporary followers, sees our disagreements as ultimately shallow. If we can only abstract away from our disagreements, we will find that we share a common reasonable conception of the just moral constitution, and so, when abstracted to this common core we all really do agree on what is the best or optimal way to arrange the moral basis of our common life. Thus, when we take the view of the original position, we would all see that despite our disagreements, we all concur on justice as fairness. But clearly this procedure is not plausible if our disagreements are intractable, wide, and of absolute depth. Surely it is implausible to say that our disagreements are wide and deep, yet do not impact our judgment as to what constitutes an acceptable normative basis of our shared life. Rawls, I believe, ultimately came to this conclusion, and so relaxed his supposition that we would agree on the very same principles of justice.[21] In this sense, he abandoned his original search for a well-ordered society.[22] However, he never succeeded in building such disagreement into his deliberative model: How might we do so?

Suppose we take seriously the width and depth of our disagreements in our diverse society; in our deliberative model each person is well aware of the full extent of her normative commitments. For the sake of simplicity, let us assume that each person proposes a moral constitution (alternatively, and more plausibly, we might suppose that the deliberators consider different rules that could be elements of a constitution, see sections 3 through 5 below). Suppose that each deliberator, i, proposes her optimal or best constitution (C_i), based on her own deeply held convictions (let us call this her "overall evaluative outlook"); suppose further that she ranks all the others (we can even allow that she may come to the conclusion that her proposal was not, after all, the best from her perspective, and so ranks one of the alternatives as superior). In a five-person society, we thus might have the outcome shown in table 7.1.

We immediately see that a deliberator cannot insist on her optimal constitution and still share a commonly endorsed framework for moral life. If they are to share a constitution, each must renounce the optimizing stance: one must accept that one could

TABLE 7.1

A	B	C	D	E
C_A	C_B	C_C	C_D	C_E
C_B	C_A	C_D	C_B	C_B
C_D	C_C	C_B	C_A	C_A
C_C	C_D	C_A	$[C_C]$	C_D
$[C_E]$	$[C_E]$	$[C_E]$	$[C_E]$	C_C

grant normative authority to a public moral constitution that falls short of what is best by one's own lights.

A common moral life is a great benefit, a benefit that everyone's overall evaluative standards endorse.[23] When you and I confront each other, recognizing the same moral constitution as possessing normative authority, we have shared grounds for the adjudication of moral claims and a shared recognition of the moral demands that we can make on each other. And, importantly, we will both experience guilt at their violation. This, in turn, means that the reactive attitudes of resentment and indignation are well-grounded: not only are we making demands on each other, but they are demands that we are justified in supposing the other has adequate reason to acknowledge and act upon. As P. F. Strawson stressed, the reactive attitudes are based on a supposition that the other has acted toward one with ill will; I feel resentment and indignation when I understand your action toward me as manifesting contempt or disregard for me.[24] However, if you can see no reason to acknowledge my demand (it is based on a constitution you cannot see as providing you with normative reasons to endorse), your violation is not a manifestation of contempt or ill will, but an indication that you cannot see how my demand has the force I attribute to it. Typically, when I realize this, my resentment and indignation will be undermined.[25]

Of course even though I see great value in sharing a moral constitution with others, the constitution must sufficiently cohere with my evaluative outlook for me to see it as giving adequate normative reasons to comply. No matter how important it is to share a social-moral life with others, if a moral constitution does not draw on my evaluative outlook, I cannot see it as sufficiently normative. My evaluative outlook, after all, defines what I can see as normative; my recognition of the normativity of the moral constitution, as it were, flows from it. This is the heart of Rawls's claim that "full justification" only occurs when the constitution is embedded into one's overall evaluative outlook.[26] It follows from this that in some cases full justification fails: the constitution may be rejected "once all the values are tallied up."[27] In this case, the person cannot endorse some proposed constitution C_x as sufficiently normative; claims based on it do not cohere with her overall evaluative outlook.[28]

We might say, then, that given the overall evaluative outlook of such a person C_i, some possible constitutions are not normatively eligible for her. In table 7.1, we may suppose that C_E is not eligible for persons A–C, that neither C_C nor C_E is eligible for person D, and all are eligible for person E. In this case, then, moral constitutions C_A, C_B, and C_D could be endorsed by all as providing a mutually recognized normative basis for their social life—one that sustains the reactive attitudes. I shall call constitutions that all can endorse "socially eligible." To paraphrase Rawls, all three provide public conceptions of justice that all can live with. We can find no better basic charters for our social world.[29]

3. Claim 1: American Conservatives Share Eligible Constitutions with Left-Leaning Liberals

The current partisan climate in both politics and political philosophy appears to assume that left-leaning liberals and conservatives cannot embrace the same charter for their social world. The left-leaning-liberal, we are told, has a secular and scientific outlook, the conservative a religious view that is sometimes hostile to, or at least skeptical about, certain scientific claims. Or, to be more philosophical, the academic liberal is said to base her political philosophy on the supposition of equal concern and respect, while conservatism is said to be premised on a conception of virtue or the good.[30] I set aside these disputes here. Some are deeper than we need to go (such as whether conservatism, but not liberalism, is based on a conception of virtue), while others are too close to policy (such as the teaching of evolution). Our concern is whether left-leaning liberals and conservatives have common eligible moral constitutions—whether, in Rawls's terms, they can concur on "a conception of justice" or a basic moral charter for their social world. To make progress on this question, it will help to replace the general idea of sharing a moral constitution with the various elements that comprise such a constitution. Fundamental to all contemporary versions of liberalism, including left-leaning liberalism, are four commitments: a robust regime of equal basic personal liberties, a constitutional democracy, a private-property market order, and a commitment to state provision of basic needs and services.

3.1. Equal Basic Liberties

In specifying the core of all liberalisms, Rawls gives pride of place to a regime of equal basic liberties, and in this he speaks for the liberal tradition. "By definition," Maurice Cranston wrote, "a liberal . . . believes in liberty."[31] A recurring worry of liberals is that conservatives have, at best, a hesitant commitment to equal basic liberties. In the European tradition conservatism has often stood for a natural hierarchical authority and class privilege—recall that Filmer explicitly focused his attack on the "dangerous" opinion of the natural freedom and equality of mankind, arguing instead for a natural hierarchy of authority.[32] The American conservative tradition has not been free of this anti-liberal strain. Ralph Adams Cram, writing in 1918, proclaimed that:

> "[T]he hungry sheep look up and are not fed," for the soul of sane man demands leadership and in spite of academic aphorisms on Equality, a dim consciousness survives of the fundamental truth that without strong leadership democracy is a menace; without strong leadership culture and even civilization will pass away.[33]

Indeed, to Cram most of us do not even "measure up to the standard" of human beings.[34]

Far more important to American conservative thinking in the twentieth century was Russell Kirk's revival of traditionalism, most importantly in his 1953 classic *The Conservative Mind*.[35] Although Kirk too is a critic of most forms of equality, his version of traditionalism endorsed the moral equality of all. In his influential statement of the canons of conservative thought, Kirk proclaimed "[t]he only true equality is moral equality,"[36] and he clearly upholds equal basic rights.[37] While we see definite movement in Kirk's conservatism to an insistence on basic equality and a defense of a certain form of individuality,[38] he remains anchored in the conservative traditionalism that dominated the first part of the twentieth century.[39] What is most remarkable about American conservatism in the 1950s is the emergence of the so-called fusion of conservative traditionalism with classical liberalism, most notably in the work of Frank S. Meyer.[40] A fierce critic of Kirk, Meyer insisted that traditional conservatism "was far too cavalier to the claims of freedom, far too ready to subordinate the individual person to the authority of the state."[41] Whereas Kirk upheld James Fitzjames Stephen's critique of Mill's defense of liberty, Meyer defends Mill:

> The only alternative to the moral rule of liberty is to enthrone the sad tendency of human history as right, to glorify with James Stephen "the man of genius who rules by persuading an efficient minority to coerce an indifferent and self-indulgent majority" . . . Liberty is the political end of man's existence because liberty is the condition of his being. It is for this reason that conservatism, which in preserving the tradition of this truth, is only constant with itself when it is libertarian.[42]

It was not only Mill, but Adam Smith and the Austrian economists such as Menger, von Mises, and Hayek, who Meyer insisted must be integrated into an adequate American conservatism for the twentieth century.[43]

"Fusion" conservatism had a profound effect on American conservatism in the latter part of the twentieth century and continues to this day. "Extremism in the defense of liberty is no vice. . . . moderation in the pursuit of justice is no virtue!"[44] It is neither the rallying cry of the traditionalist of the first part of the century nor of Kirk. To be sure, in policy debates, and on issues of specific interpretation of individual rights, American left-leaning liberals and conservatives have intense disagreements. It is because so much of politics is focused on these debates—from school prayer to gay marriage—that American left-leaning liberals are convinced that conservatives are not strongly committed to freedom, just as American left-leaning liberals' embrace of the expansion of government convinces American conservatives that left-leaning liberals have forsaken liberty by embracing the security of Leviathan.[45] But these are not disputes about the fundamental place of equal liberty in the basic terms of social interaction.

3.2. Constitutional Democracy

European history reveals periodic attractions of conservative parties and followers to the anti-democratic radical right. The most infamous cases are the support of conservatives for the Nazis in the legislative elections of 1932 and Hindenburg's naming of Hitler as Chancellor in 1933. Now to be sure, the history of American conservatism is not entirely free of such cases. Seward Collins, a publisher of some influence in the 1920s and 1930s who advocated a "revolutionary conservatism," eventually embraced fascism, praising Franco and Mussolini.[46] American left-leaning liberals, however, have tended to wildly exaggerate anti-constitutionalism among conservatives; the 1963 movie *Seven Days in May* (which, I must admit, is a favorite of mine), roughly inspired by General Edwin Walker, depicts a right-wing military plot to overthrow an obviously Democratic, peace-loving, president.[47] (The hero, Kirk Douglas, defends democracy and the constitution against the rabid anti-communist, Chairman of the Joint Chiefs, Burt Lancaster.) In the American tradition, however, these are extremely rare outliers—a veneration of the constitution and its form of government is one of the core commitments running through practically the entire gamut of American conservative thinking.[48] Barry Goldwater insisted that the conservative's task was to uphold constitutional limits on power against the tendency of the left to conceive of the "*federal government as the whole people organized to do what had to be done.*"[49] Under the Constitution, the federal government, he argued, was not an all-purpose mechanism designed to legislate for whatever problems arose, but a system of defined powers under restraints that "make it possible for men to follow their chosen pursuits with maximum freedom."[50] Although this understanding of the Constitution is characteristic of the more libertarian strains of American conservatism, it certainly is not a definitive feature; Robert Bork, deemed as a proponent of the "New Right," argued for much greater majoritarian, legislative, leeway.[51] We cannot identify a particular theory of constitutional democracy with American conservatism in general. What we can say is that a devotion to the constitution is indeed characteristic of it.

3.3. The Market Order

All conservatives uphold private property; to Robert Nisbett, the defense of private property is a "dogmatic" of conservatism.[52] "The true rights of man," wrote Kirk, "are equal justice, security of labor and property, the amenities of civilized institutions and the benefits of an ordered society."[53] However, in the twentieth century, the threat of communism to private property too often drove conservatives into the arms of the far right and authoritarian regimes (as in the German elections of 1932). Various forms of corporatism and state direction are consistent with the privileges of property. Moreover, defending property is consistent with attacking the modern economic order. Traditional conservatives have often bemoaned international economic activity, industrialization, mass production, and consumerism, "the grand end which justifies the evil of modern labor."[54]

Distinctive of American conservatism in the latter half of the twentieth century and into this century has been not simply a strong defense of private property, but of the market. According to Meyer, conservatives:

> [S]tand for a free economic order for two reasons. In the first place, they believe that the modern state is politically so strong, even without controls over the economy, that it concentrates power to a degree that is incompatible with the freedom of its citizens. When to that power is added control over the economy, such massive power is created that the last defenses against the state becoming a monstrous Leviathan begin to crack. Second—though this is subsidiary in the conservative outlook to the danger to freedom—conservatives in general believe, on the basis of classical and neoclassical economic theory, that a free economy is much more productive of material wealth than an economy controlled directly or indirectly by the state.[55]

To Irving Kristol, "The United States is the capitalist nation par excellence . . . the Founding Fathers *intended* this nation to be capitalist and regarded it as the *only* set of economic arrangements consistent with the democracy they had established."[56]

An objection immediately arises: Surely this devotion to a capitalist market order shows a significant disjuncture between the conservative's and the left-leaning liberal's understanding of eligible moral constitutions. In his most detailed discussion of eligible economic systems in *Justice as Fairness*, Rawls appears to dismiss capitalism, including welfare-state capitalism, as inherently unjust (a view that might have surprised readers of *A Theory of Justice*).[57] More generally, hostility to capitalism is, if not quite characteristic of left-leaning-liberal political philosophers, certainly common enough. There is considerable confusion, however, over what is meant by "capitalism."[58] To many, the rejection of capitalism is tantamount to the rejection of largely unregulated markets or extreme inequalities of wealth and income. And to some, "capitalism" is simply employed as a general term of criticism for aspects of modern markets and business of which they disapprove. It is probably best to set the term "capitalism" aside. What we can say with confidence, I think, is that a market economy based on nonpublic ownership of a wide variety of assets and investment instruments, with strong protection of property rights including shareholder rights, extensive freedom to start businesses and hire employees, along with widespread use of the hierarchically organized firm, remains the focus of all plausible proposals for economic reform and policy.[59]

To be sure, insofar as one is occupying the role of political philosopher, expounding personal visions of a "perfectly just" society,[60] one may well hold that no version of such a system could possibly fill the bill. If, however, our concern is moral theory, such a position is tantamount to a declaration that no feasible reform of property or trade relations could render economic life morally legitimate; left-leaning liberalism is thus transformed into a radical, revolutionary doctrine holding that this basic aspect of human existence (involving exchange, savings, production, and the pursuit of careers) is nowhere even in the neighborhood of moral legitimacy, and can only be made legitimate by instituting a type of economic order that has never existed, the operation of which would be highly conjectural. If we take the task of a moral theorist as speaking to a certain historical social and political situation, seeking to discover a basic charter for the social world that all reasonable people can live with and so performs the necessary social role of a conception of justice,[61] this radical utopian vision is inapposite. When left-leaning-liberal political philosophy becomes a conversation restricted to those who share similar revolutionary aspirations, it becomes irrelevant to—or, worse, a threat to—the search for a basic moral framework that we all, here and now, can live with. As is so often the case, the practical implication of an uncompromising utopianism is a practical nihilism. Happily, very few left-leaning-liberal political philosophers take this route, consistently claiming that all or most existing property and trade relations are morally illegitimate.[62] They, themselves, ground moral claims on existing property and trade relations—they buy and sell real property, invest in corporations for their retirements, call on the courts if they have been swindled, and experience resentment and indignation at being burgled.

3.4. The Welfare State

But surely the shoe is on the other foot when we consider the conservative's attitude toward the welfare state. "The welfare state is not inevitable," Goldwater wrote.[63] Isn't *this* an uncompromising utopian position? Hayek long ago insisted that he was not a conservative because conservatives end up endorsing the proposals advanced by their victorious opponents in the previous generation's political struggles, whatever they may be.[64] American conservatism has been accused of doing precisely this, moving ever leftward.[65] By 1993, Kristol was sketching a conservative view of the welfare state.[66] Conservative policy analysts such as James Q. Wilson had already been doing so, though in a more piecemeal and careful manner.[67] Conservative analyses of good public policy in a welfare state certainly conflict with mainstream Democrats. There is, for example, a much stronger emphasis on the relation of the welfare state's incentive structure to character, more worry about an expansive federal government, and far more readiness to enlist religious organizations as providers in government-sanctioned schemes. Interestingly, however, Wilson defined the core of the "neoconservative" approach to public policy not in terms of specific value commitments, but a lively appreciation of the law of unintended consequences: "Things almost never work out quite as you hope; in particular, government programs often do not achieve their objectives or do achieve them but with high or unexpected costs."[68]

To be sure, the last few years have witnessed a more populist conservative opposition to certain existing and proposed programs of the welfare state, as well as taxation policies. In the current, overheated, ideological political environment, it is tempting to rush to the view that we are witnessing a radical break with postwar American conservatism. I am deeply skeptical. Almost all these elements have been a part of "fusion" conservatism since the 1950s—evaluation of public policy in terms of the "Judeo-Christian tradition,"[69] a defense of markets, and deep reservations about expansive state policies. Overwhelmingly, this political program has evolved into a debate within the welfare state, about its appropriate tasks and limits, not its legitimacy. In his first inaugural address, Ronald Reagan proclaimed:

> It is my intention to curb the size and influence of the Federal establishment and to demand recognition of the distinction between the powers granted to the Federal Government and those reserved to the States or to the people. . . . Now, so that there will be no misunderstanding, it's not my intention to do away with government. It's rather to make it work—work with us, not over us; to stand at our side, not ride our back. Government can and must provide opportunity, not smother it; foster productivity, not stifle it.[70]

4. Claim 2: Conservatism Shows Us How to Achieve a Justified Moral Constitution

4.1. A Lacuna in the Liberal Philosopher's Quest for Determinacy

Looking at these four fundamental aspects of (to use the term in its broadest sense) a liberal moral constitution, I conclude that American conservatism not only can endorse them (as, say, something they can live with, but without great enthusiasm), but "wholeheartedly" embrace them, for they also express their cherished ideals. This is not to say, of course, that they and left-liberals agree on their interpretations of these ideals; we know that we have continuing and often deep political disputes about the "true meaning" of these commitments (I shall argue in section 5 that this lack of agreement is a source of moral strength in a social and political order). But, because both left-leaning liberals and conservatives have an enduring interest in shared terms of moral life that both can see as grounding legitimate claims—and so avoiding a social life based simply on power, force, and indoctrination—they have compelling reasons to embrace the non-optimizing stance, and accept that articulations of these basic commitments that fall considerably short of their ideal are eligible (section 2.2). In terms of the model presented in section 2, we can say that they concur on some eligible constitutions (that is to say, ones that adequately articulate these four general commitments), but they deeply disagree on which is best. American conservatives, for example, tend to stress a different interpretation of the basic liberties; they are apt to join libertarians in seeing economic liberties as very important, a view with which left-leaning (more traditional Rawlsian) liberals disagree.[71] Similarly, the commitments of American conservatives and left-leaning liberals favor different understandings of the constitution, the market, and the size and responsibilities of the welfare state.

Supposing, then, that on each of these issues (and no doubt any other elements we would wish to add to the moral constitution) left-leaning liberals and conservatives disagree on the ordering of the eligible options; what are we to do? The liberal tradition in political philosophy tends to two responses. On one hand, academic liberalism has sought to push beyond the claim that basic constraints on acceptable moral constitutions can be justified to everyone to the much more controversial claim that a single, best moral constitution or "theory of justice" can be. Trotting out heavy and controversial philosophical machinery—the original position, or bargaining theory, or (much worse) proclaiming moral intuitions about what is "true basic liberty"—the liberal philosopher has often declared that she has justified one unique moral constitution (or, somewhat more modestly, a set of very similar constitutions) that, remarkably enough, wonderfully align with her controversial political opinions. Only one already committed to the political conclusions generated is convinced by these devices; their suppositions are controversial, their conclusions uncertain. We are left with a plethora of deeply controversial theories of justice.

When the liberal philosopher finally admits that her philosophical machinery has cranked out all it can (we might, as in *Frankenstein*, picture sparks flying and the rafters shaking as the devices reach the limit of their capacity), the only recourse is to leave the rest to democratic politics. And there is a deep truth here: In the end many of our disputes about the proper interpretation of our fundamental commitments must be left to the political arena. It is because this is so that those who most focus on politics and legislation are most impressed by our disagreements; rather than being the realm of deliberative consensus, politics is the adjudication of our disputes so that those who continue to disagree can engage in coordinated action.[72] The strength of the political is that it can give us some answer to just about any question; but there is no guarantee that this answer is one that falls into the eligible arrangements of all citizens.[73] The legislature can legislate as to the shape of the economic system, but this will reflect the views of only a part of the population, and of course may override those of others. Political adjudication is a powerful tool; it can help us identify a specific coordinative arrangement that we all see as acceptable, but it can also enforce a system that many find deeply objectionable.

4.2. The Moral Constitution and How We Can Arrive at One

Conservatives have long recognized that between the individual's private moral judgment and the political lies the social. Indeed, the insight that there is a social-moral constitution that underlies the political constitution has been viewed as a characteristic theme in conservative thinking.[74] Many liberals (including Rawls) have also recognized this. As T. H. Green observed, "A state presupposes other forms of community, with the rights that arise out of them. . . . In order to make a state there must have been families of which the members recognized rights in each other . . . there must further have been intercourse between families, or between tribes that have grown out of families, of which each in the same sense recognized rights in the other[]."[75] Green's insight is that between the individual's private judgment about what is right and the public authority of the state lies the moral authority of social practices, which I have been calling the moral constitution.

From Hume to Hayek (both of whom are sometimes seen as liberals, sometimes as conservatives), the selection of one among many eligible moral constitutions is understood as a matter of history and the evolution of tradition.[76] As I have shown elsewhere, we can understand the evolution of such a constitution as an iterated, multi-person impure coordination game.[77] To see the basic point, take the simplest case; suppose that we have simply two socially eligible constitutions (x,y) and two parties (Left-leaning Liberal and Conservative) and a one-play game as shown in table 7.2. The numbers represent each party's rankings of the outcomes given their fundamental values and moral principles, with higher numbers indicating better outcomes.

TABLE 7.2

| | | Left-leaning Liberal | |
| | | x | y |

		x		y	
Conservative	x		1		0
		2		0	
	y		0		2
		0		1	

The important point is that, if *x* and *y* are both socially eligible moral constitutions, both the Left-leaning-liberal and Conservative think it is better to coordinate on either than neither, though they will disagree on which is the best. Both are Nash equilibria; should the Left-leaning Liberal become convinced that the Conservative will act on *x*, also abiding by *x* is her best response. Recall that Rawls's aim was to show this—namely that a stably just society is one in which acting justly is each person's "best reply" to others acting justly.[78] That is, Rawls sought a society in which acting on the rules of justice is a Nash equilibrium.[79] Coordination on any moral constitution in the socially eligible set—and only ones in the set—fulfills this requirement. Experimental evidence in many-generational iterated impure coordination games indicates that, indeed, people settle on a tradition of playing one or the other equilibrium, despite their disagreement on which is best. In deciding what equilibrium to play, the current generation draws on both the history of play and, more importantly, "socialization in which present generations teach and pass on current conventions of behavior to the next generation."[80]

From the social perspective, ex ante, there is no way to choose *x* over *y* or vice versa. We disagree on this matter and there is no ordering that all good-willed and rational members of our society accept. However, once we have, largely though historical accident, settled on one, it uniquely fulfills Rawls's Nash requirement. What philosophical reflection could not do, tradition accomplishes for us. However, as Meyer stressed, this appreciation of tradition must be combined with critical reflection. Meyer criticized the sanctification of tradition as such:

> The philosophical position upon which the American constitutional settlement was based had already brought into a common synthesis concepts which were placed in radical opposition by the European conservative-liberal struggle: a respect for the tradition together with a respect for reason, the acceptance of the authority of an organic moral order with a fierce concern for the freedom of the individual.[81]

Only if our tradition is viewed by each as eligible can its authority be freely endorsed by each; as Meyer put it, only then can we combine "freedom and moral authority."[82]

4.3. Localism: A Diversity of Constitutions Between Groups

Consider a simple case: the selection of a moral constitution composed of our four core elements: basic liberties (L), constitutional democracy (D), a private-property market economy (M), and a welfare state (W). And let us make a further radical simplifying assumption that for each element there are two, mutually exclusive, eligible interpretations (say, a left-leaning-liberal and a conservative one). Supposing that these issues are relatively separable, even in this highly simplified case we have sixteen eligible constitutions. Now (using uppercase for the left-leaning-liberal alternative and lower case for the conservative), even with identical eligible sets we could have, through convention, one group having a *LDMW* moral constitution while another has *ldmw*. It would look like these groups have fundamental moral disagreements, but this difference, impressive as it is, would be entirely within the bounds of what can be reflectively justified—the socially eligible set. Once we accept that reflection on moral matters does not yield a single, unequivocal, understanding of the best moral constitution, we must accept the quintessential conservative claim that morality depends on local conventions and can differ from place to place. We thus witness an important relation of coordination and diversity that can be observed across a variety of domains: *The value of coordination simultaneously decreases diversity (of moral constitutions) within a group, leading members to converge, while increasing diversity (of moral constitutions) between groups.*[83]

Liberal philosophers often recoil at this, disparaging such views as advocating "parochialism," and insisting that true moral objectivity must imply that the moral rules that are justified for one group must be justified for all.[84] The conservative certainly need not be claiming that morality is *only* a matter of tradition and convention; but to refuse to make that extreme claim does not mean that morality is not significantly shaped by convention. As Meyer put it, tradition is not a weapon that should be employed to suppress reason: it is a "guide to the operation of reason."[85]

5. CLAIM 3: DIVERSITY (THAT INCLUDES CONSERVATIVES) ENHANCES THE SUSTAINABILITY OF A MORAL CONSTITUTION

5.1. A Benefit of Moral Diversity: Multiple Eligible Constitutions

The traditional liberal political philosopher is apt to view this as a deeply disappointing result. Asking what justice requires of us, we find that its demands vary in significant ways from place to place and from time to time—and perhaps simply because of historical contingency. Our shared moral framework is, to some extent, an accident. Perhaps we should go back and reconsider our reasoning. That the liberal project of justifying a moral framework to all could end up with such a "conservative conclusion" surely is a matter for concern. Shouldn't we revise our analysis so that we rescue Rawls's early vision of a well-ordered society, in which all accept the best (left-liberal) theory of justice, and will not settle for less?[86]

An attraction of a return to the ideal of a morally homogeneous liberal order may appear to be its ability to achieve stability. Although traditional moral and political philosophy may intelligibly insist that stability is not itself a desideratum of morality or a theory of justice,[87] when we take up the perspective of moral theory, something like stability is of critical importance.[88] Stability is the tendency of a moral constitution to return to a just equilibrium (in which acting on a moral constitution is the best reply to others doing so) in the face of both internal and external shocks that induce deviation from it.[89] If we are seeking to evaluate a moral framework, we need to know whether it provides the basis for a just social framework in a narrow or a wide range of conditions; if the former, we may well doubt that the constitution can perform its expected function given the vicissitudes of human life. Now Rawls and almost all other political philosophers who have considered the matter have supposed that stability is induced by homogeneity and endangered by diversity. A society that shares the same basic outlook on justice, it is thought, can weather storms better than one in which people have diverse perspectives on justice. Rawls's proposed solution to the problem of stability in *A Theory of Justice* was to show a surprising degree of homogeneity not only concerning justice but in our understanding of the good, which would lead us to remain faithful to justice as fairness, even in the face of injustice by others; his later work, acknowledging greater diversity, struggled to show how such a deeply divided society could nevertheless be stably just.[90]

The idea of a society that is apt to maintain just social relations in the face of endogenous and exogenous disruptions can be understood in two ways: stability and robustness. Let us call "stability" the tendency of a system to return to the *same* equilibrium given some dynamic, and "robustness" the tendency of a system to maintain an equilibrium (on a just constitution)—a robust system returns to *an* equilibrium, but not necessarily the same one.[91] To better see the contrast, compare two societies, A and B. In A, the Holy Grail of contemporary political philosophy has been achieved: There is one, and only one, moral constitution that is eligible and so can be justified to all, *LDMW* (section 4.3). Everyone accepts this, and knows that others accept it, as *the one and only correct view* (it is in this sense that A is homogeneous). B, in contrast, has not achieved moral agreement on one and only one constitution as eligible. Suppose all sixteen constitutions that can be generated from left-leaning-liberal and conservative views on each of our four core elements are socially eligible in B. Let us suppose, however, that it too has, because of convention, gravitated to the *LDMW* constitution, so it too is in this sense a thoroughly left-leaning-liberal society. Suppose that *W* (the left-leaning-liberal view of the welfare state) comes under strain; people begin to question it, its rules are violated. To make the case more vivid, suppose that considerable parts of the population begin to dodge high taxes or resent beneficiaries of the welfare state. Perhaps many start to question whether this version of the welfare state is justified at all. Now society A can sustain a basic moral charter that all can live with only if it returns to the *LDMW* constitution; it must somehow induce people to return to *W*. It must be *stable*. In contrast, B has two routes by which it can return to justice: a return to *W* or a switch to *w*. We can model B (which, recall, is also a thoroughly left-leaning-liberal *LDMW* society) as carrying a "conservative gene" that allows it to adapt to a changed environment; it is *robust* as it can maintain its justification either by returning to the *LDMW* equilibrium or through moving to *LDMw*. The first society has fewer ("genetic") resources to achieve a justified moral constitution in the new environment. Justice is more fragile in A; it has fewer moral resources to adapt. A society that has significant moral disagreement *within an eligible set* has greater resources to maintain a basic charter for their social world that all can live with.[92]

5.2. Is Instability the Price of Robustness?

A society that has coordinated on a moral constitution from a wide eligible set thus is more apt to be robust in the face of disruptions. The worry arises, however, whether this robustness invites instability. Consider a simple model, with representative persons A and B in, respectively, societies A and B, both of which are currently at the *LDMW* constitution. Suppose at some point in society A people are generally acting according to the *LDMW* constitution; person A will act on it so long as his commitment to maintain justified moral relations with his fellows and his fear of being punished outweighs his temptation to cheat in order to better pursue his values. Radically simplifying, then, for A to continue acting justly it must be the case that (letting p indicate the relevant probability):

$$(\text{EQ 1}) \ p[\text{benefits}(\text{moral relations})] \geq$$
$$p[\text{benefits}(\text{defection})] - p[\text{costs}(\text{punishment})]$$

The probable benefits of continued moral relations based on *LDMW* only need outweigh the probable benefits of defection discounted by probable punishment. Contrast this to person B in society B. She has an additional incentive to defect on the moral constitution—the expected payoff that her defection might drive

B to, say, her favored *LDMw* constitution. So for her to have reason to conform to the *LDMW* constitution, it must be the case that:

$$(\text{EQ 2}) \ p[\text{benefits(moral relations under } LDMW)] \geq$$
$$p[\text{benefits(defection)}] + p[\text{benefits(of moral relations having}$$
$$\text{achieved } LDMw)] - p[\text{costs(punishment)}]$$

The probable benefits of moving society to what she sees as a better moral constitution gives her a type of *moral* reason to defect. Of course, if $p[\text{benefits(of getting } LDMw)]$ is very low, this will not much matter, but if B thinks there are enough like-minded others such that they could actually move to *LDMw*, and so that the probable benefits of moving to the new constitution become significant, then unless $p[\text{benefits(moral relations under } LDMW)]$ is greater in B (why would that be?) or the threat of punishment is greater in society B than in A, even though they may have the same value systems and are living under the same constitution (*LDMW*), B may defect while A does not. We face the prospect that the very possibility of change to another eligible constitution, which is required for robustness, will tend to destabilize the current moral constitution, inducing people to defect in order to achieve a constitution they consider superior. Here then, is our problem: how do we achieve sufficient stability while also allowing us to exploit the moral resources that promote robustness?

5.3. More Benefits of Diversity: The Parties of Stability and Reform

As equation 2 shows, increasing punishment certainly can induce stability on a specific equilibrium by discouraging those who would seek to move to another moral constitution in the eligible set. Although recent analysis shows that punishment is indispensible in maintaining equilibrium on norms and moral rules,[93] the problem with punishment is that it can stabilize any equilibrium, in or out of the eligible set.[94] And, of course, liberals recoil at the prospect of a social order that can only be sustained by high levels of force.

A moral constitution requires significant *stability* if it is to perform its coordinating task, helping to settle expectations about future interactions, while at the same time it should possess sufficient flexibility to be capable of responding to disruptions by switching to a new equilibrium. Now we can imagine ideal members of a moral order that have precisely the right trade-off rate between valuing stability and inducing change, but of course we do not know at any particular time what this trade-off rate is. In environments with a low rate of change, stability is generally appropriate; in times of storm and stress, flexibility is apt to be more valuable. And, in any event, we should no more expect homogeneity on this value than on any other. But that is not a worry, for we do not need individuals to agree on the optimal trade-off rate. Recent work in cultural evolution, the philosophy of science, organizational theory, and democratic theory converge in showing that diverse populations—those that are divided between different values or behavior—often arrive at better collective outcomes than those characterized by a single type.[95] This, of course, was precisely Mill's claim about a population divided between a party of reform and a party of stability in our epigraph.

Consider a society such as B_{DIV}, divided between those who are critical of the existing constitution, searching for ways to improve it, and those who place high value on stability and so are very reluctant to move to a new equilibrium. Contrast this to societies B_{CON}, an orderly society whose members all value stability, and B_{LIB}, a society of reformists whose members all place high value on achieving what they see as the best constitution. There is strong reason to think that under a range of environmental conditions, B_{DIV} will outperform B_{CON} and B_{LIB} in the sense of better maintaining justified social relations over a sustained period. As Scott E. Page demonstrates, there are two lines of analyses that support this: averaging performance and decreasing returns to type.[96] A homogeneous B_{CON} population will perform very well (that is, keep us in the eligible set while providing settled moral expectations) in (a) an environment with minimal disruptions, (b) assuming that it has initially achieved a justified equilibrium. B_{CON} will perform badly when (c) there are severe and regular disruptions that render the current equilibrium difficult to maintain, and (d) the current equilibrium is not in the eligible set. On the other hand, B_{LIB} does well under (c) and/or (d), but worse than B_{CON} under conditions (a) and (b). In a range of environments, B_{CON} and B_{LIB} will thus experience wide variation in their ability to maintain a justified constitution; in contrast, the diverse B_{DIV} is almost certain to have less variation in its performance, and it can be shown that systems such as B_{DIV}, with less variation, generally outperform less diverse systems such as B_{CON} and B_{LIB}.[97]

A similar result can be shown by appealing to decreasing returns to type.[98] Suppose we start out with B_{CON} and replace n conservative members with reformist members, where n constitutes a small proportion of the society. This new group, $B_{CON}{}^*$, will almost certainly outperform B_{CON}; given that there is still a large proportion of conservative members, the small n conservatives lost will not much reduce the impact of the pro-stability perspective, but the small n of reformist citizens will make contributions that otherwise would not exist, alerting the other citizens to new possibilities and problems (for example, that the current equilibrium is flawed in ways not previously appreciated). If we think in terms of one's marginal value to achieving long-term, just social life, the new n reformist members have a higher marginal value than the conservative members they replaced.[99]

5.4. Two Levels of Conservatism: Diversity within Conservatism

At this point it becomes clear that American conservatism has two distinct aspects. On the one hand, it constitutes an ordering of constitutions that institutionalize the basic elements of a free constitution—liberty, democracy, the market, and the welfare state. We might call these the conservative's *first-level moral-political commitments.* Understood in terms of first-level commitments, conservatives can be reformist; if a society is at a left-leaning-liberal equilibrium, conservatives can agitate for change. We have seen how a population that possesses such conservative policy preferences can improve the moral performance of a society (in comparison to a homogeneous society). Some American conservatives, such as Barry Goldwater, stressed their first-level moral commitments: they agitated for major reforms in order to institute them.

On the other hand, conservatism is also a *second-level moral perspective (a perspective on altering constitutions),* one that generally is skeptical about the benefits of altering the status quo and more sensitive to the possibilities implicit in the status quo. To put the point in terms of organizational theory, any group that employs a routine, yet is also searching for better ways of doing things, must trade off the benefits of *exploiting* the routine that has been arrived at and *exploring* for better solutions.[100] At this second level, left-liberals have a lively appreciation of the benefits of exploration; but if we are constantly exploring for better solutions, we do not sufficiently exploit the solutions we have already found. As Jonathan Haidt observes:

> [I]f you are trying to change an organization or society and you do not consider the effects of your changes on moral capital, you're asking for trouble. This, I believe, is *the fundamental blind spot of the left*. . . . It tends to overreach, change too many things too quickly, and reduce the stock of moral capital inadvertently. Conversely, while conservatives do a better job of preserving moral capital, they often fail to notice certain classes of victims, fail to limit the predation of powerful interests, and fail to see the need to change or update institutions as times change.[101]

In this second-level sense, conservatives have a deep appreciation of what Haidt calls "moral capital"; such second-level conservatives may well oppose challenges mounted to the features of the welfare state by their first-level cousins. Of course most actual conservatives combine first- and second-level commitments, so their overall view is an amalgamation of both, as is the view of left-leaning liberals (as we see with recent debates about Social Security in America, left-leaning liberals can be quite averse to change). It is important for a society to have diversity at both the first and second levels. First-level diversity generates different proposals about how we can live together, while second-level diversity divides society into those who seek ways to change society by moving to new arrangements and those who seek to exploit the current one. As I have stressed, getting the precise trade-off rate correct is a complicated matter. Here, as elsewhere, a diverse population, which disagrees on the right trade-off rate, can often outperform a homogeneous one that gets it almost perfect.

6. CONCLUSION: TOWARD A THEORY OF COMPLEX NORMATIVE SYSTEMS

Political philosophers are accustomed to conceiving of their activity as a philosophical elaboration and defense of specific theories of justice. We are left-leaning-liberal political philosophers or conservative political philosophers. Like Plato, who continues to cast a spell over our profession, the deep conviction is that the best state would, in a deep sense, be a morally homogeneous one. Our current, real-world communities, characterized by disagreement and moral dispute, may be the best we can attain, but fall far short of the ideal or perfection. Like Plato, we see the moral community as a person writ large; if a just person is moved by a well-thought-out and consistent theory of justice, so too must a just community be. And the most just community would be one that is moved by the best theory of justice. Societies, however, are far better understood as normative systems of a very different type: complex moral systems in which the very diversity and disagreements of the participants sustain the community's moral life.

This is not to say that diversity and conflict are always healthy for a justified moral constitution. Conflict, like homogeneity, can undermine the ability of our moral order to function. Too much diversity leads to chaos. In section 3, I was at pains to cast doubt on the supposition that the differences between American conservatives and left-leaning liberals are so wide and deep that there are no mutually satisfactory equilibria. My claim one, that left-leaning liberals and conservatives can endorse a common moral constitution, may seem incredible in our current shrill, often nasty, partisan environment. Political philosophers (as well as more influential academics) cannot simply wash their hands of this; through our teaching, public pronouncements, and participation in various ideological gatherings and centers, we have too often shrilly maintained that an acceptable society is one that must conform to our (many) blueprints. A political philosophy of complex normative systems sets aside the ancient aim of describing the just, well-ordered society where we all agree what justice is and conform to its dictates. Instead, it aims to investigate the benefits, costs, and limits of sustainable moral diversity, enlightening us about the conditions under which we can achieve and maintain what in the end Rawls sought—a basic charter for our social world that we all can live with.

NOTES

I am indebted to John Thrasher for encouraging me to think about these matters, and for pointing me in the right directions. Thanks also to Fred D'Agostino, John Holbo, and Chad Van Schoelandt for their help. I am especially grateful for the comments and suggestions of Melissa Williams.

1. John Rawls, *A Theory of Justice*, Rev. ed. (Cambridge, MA: Belknap Press of Harvard University Press, 1999).

2. The back cover of *Justice as Fairness* proclaims that Rawls's theory is about "the meaning and theoretical viability of liberalism." John Rawls, *Justice as Fairness: A Restatement* (Cambridge, MA: Harvard University Press, 2001).

3. Again, the back cover of *Justice as Fairness*: "Rawls is well aware that since the publication of *A Theory of Justice* in 1971 American society has moved further away from the idea of justice as farness. Yet his ideas retain their power and relevance to debates in a pluralistic society about the meaning and theoretical viability of liberalism. This book demonstrates that moral clarity can be achieved even when a collective commitment to justice is uncertain."

4. Amartya Sen, *The Idea of Justice* (Cambridge, MA: Harvard University Press, 2009), 12, 45, 56–58, 89, 103. See further my "Social Contract and Social Choice," *Rutgers Law Journal* 43 (Spring/Summer 2012): 243–276.

5. Ronald Dworkin, *Sovereign Virtue* (Cambridge, MA: Harvard University Press, 2000), 236.

6. Compare Mill's discussion in *Considerations on Representative Government*, in *The Collected Works of John Stuart Mill, Vol. 19*, ed. J. M. Robson (Toronto: University of Toronto Press, 1977), chapter 3.

7. See Rawls, *Political Liberalism*, Paperback ed. (New York: Columbia University Press, 1996), xl.

8. To stress that this is a sectarian, ideological position, I shall contrast this to simple "liberalism," which is a wider tradition in political thought and to "academic liberalism" (or "liberal political philosophy"), which refers to a variety of political philosophy. I apologize for these awkward locutions, but it is required by the tendency in America for "liberalism" to refer to: (i) a type of philosophy (what Michael Freeden, the leading contemporary scholar of ideologies, calls "American philosophical liberalism"); (ii) a wide tradition in political thought that stresses the moral freedom and equality of individuals, individual freedom, and the rule of law; and (iii) a political ideology that tends to the left. Freeden, *Ideologies and Political Theory: A Conceptual Approach* (Oxford: Clarendon Press, 1996), chapter 6, argues that "American philosophical liberalism" is itself

ideological; I question his analysis in "Ideology, Political Philosophy, and the Interpretive Enterprise: A View from the Other Side," in *Liberalism as Ideology: Essays for Michael Freeden,* ed. Ben Jackson and Marc Stears (Oxford: Oxford University Press, 2012), 178–198.

9. The name Brian Barry gave to Rawls's theory: *The Liberal Theory of Justice: A Critical Examination of the Principal Doctrines in* A Theory of Justice *by John Rawls* (Oxford: Oxford University Press, 1973). Although in 1973 Barry sought to distance himself from liberal justice, by the end of his career he seems to relent, and offers his own theory of liberal justice. *Justice as Impartiality* (Oxford: Oxford University Press, 1995).

10. Rawls, *Political Liberalism,* xxviii.

11. Ibid., xxxix. Emphasis added.

12. I stress this point in "The Turn to a Political Liberalism," in *A Companion to Rawls,* ed. Jon Mandle and David A. Reidy (Hoboken, NJ: Wiley-Blackwell, 2014), 235–250.

13. John Rawls, "Kantian Constructivism in Moral Theory," in *John Rawls: Collected Papers,* ed. Samuel Freeman (Cambridge, MA: Harvard University Press, 1999), 306–307. Emphasis added.

14. Ibid., 326. This idea is explored in greater depth in my "On the Appropriate Mode of Justifying a Public Moral Constitution," *Harvard Review of Philosophy* 19 (2013): 4–22.

15. John Rawls, "The Independence of Moral Theory," in *John Rawls: Collected Papers,* 286.

16. Ibid., 288.

17. Ibid. Emphasis added.

18. Ibid., 296.

19. Ibid., 288.

20. Henry Sidgwick, *The Methods of Ethics,* 7th ed. (Chicago: University of Chicago Press, [1907] 1962), vi. See Rawls, "The Independence of Moral Theory," 290; Rawls, "Kantian Constructivism in Moral Theory," 341.

21. See my "Turn to a Political Liberalism."

22. As Samuel Freeman suggests in "Public Reason and Political Justification," in his *Justice and the Social Contract* (Oxford: Oxford University Press, 2007), 255–256.

23. Of course there are the problems of the psychopath and the fanatic. Before working out what we wish to say to those not interested in sharing a moral life with us, let us think harder about what we shall say to those who do.

24. P. F. Strawson, "Freedom and Resentment," *Proceedings of the British Academy* 48 (1962): 187–211.

25. See further my *The Order of Public Reason* (Cambridge: Cambridge University Press, 2011), 205–225.

26. See Rawls, *Political Liberalism*, 386. Rawls is here restricting himself to the political, not the moral, constitution. The major change from Rawls's original Dewey Lectures ("Kantian Constructivism in Moral Theory") to the revised Dewey Lectures (*Political Liberalism*) was a change from the justification of a moral constitution to principles governing the political.

27. Rawls, *Political Liberalism*, 386.

28. I consider the distinction between eligible and ineligible rules in much more depth in *The Order of Public Reason*, 310–321. Here I rely on the intuitive idea that some constitutions would not gain sufficient support from one's evaluative standards to endorse them.

29. Rawls, "Kantian Constructivism in Moral Theory," 306–307.

30. Ronald Dworkin, "Liberalism," in *Public and Private Morality*, ed. Stuart Hampshire (Cambridge: Cambridge University Press, 1978), 113–143.

31. Rawls, *Political Liberalism*, xlviii; Maurice Cranston, "Liberalism," in *The Encyclopedia of Philosophy*, ed. Paul Edwards (New York: Macmillan and Free Press, 1976): 458–461.

32. Robert Filmer, "Patriarcha," in *Patriarcha and Other Writings*, ed. Johann P. Sommerville (Cambridge: Cambridge University Press, 1991), 2 and generally.

33. Ralph Adams Cram, *The Nemeses of Mediocrity* (Boston: Marshall Jones, 1918), 6.

34. Ralph Adams Cram, "Why We Do Not Behave Like Human Beings," *American Mercury* (February 1956), 131.

35. See Gregory L. Schneider, *The Conservative Century: From Reaction to Revolution* (Lanham, MD: Rowman & Littlefield, 2009), 53–55.

36. Russell Kirk, *The Conservative Mind: From Burke to Eliot* (BN Publishing, 2008), 8; see also 82.

37. Ibid., 82. In contrast, at 139, John Randolph, speaking for the Southern "aristocracy," followed Filmer in denying that all are born free and equal.

38. Ibid., 90.

39. Which includes the southern agrarians. See Twelve Southerners, *I'll Take My Stand: The South and the Agrarian Tradition* (Baton Rouge: Louisiana State University Press, [1930] 1977).

40. See Schneider, *The Conservative Century*, 54–60.

41. Frank S. Meyer, "Freedom, Tradition, and Conservatism," in *Defense of Freedom and Related Essays*, ed. William C. Dennis (Indianapolis, IN: Liberty Fund, 1996), 22.

42. Meyer, "In Defense of John Stuart Mill," in *Defense of Freedom*, 168. Compare Kirk, *The Conservative Mind*, 265–275.

43. Meyer, "Freedom, Tradition, and Conservatism," 26–27.

44. These words, of course, are from Barry Goldwater's acceptance address at the 1964 Republican convention. "Extremism in the Defense of Liberty," in *Conservatism in America Since 1930*, ed. Gregory L. Schneider (New York: New York University Press, 2003), 245. In *The Conscience of a Conservative* (Bottom of the Hill Publishing, 2010), at 13, Goldwater insists: "The Conservative's first concern will always be: Are we maximizing freedom?" Meyer agrees: The principles of political right require "a state capable of maintaining order while at the same time guaranteeing to each person in its area of government the maximum liberty possible to him short of his interference with the liberty of other persons." Frank S. Meyer, "In Defense of Freedom: A Conservative Credo," in *Defense of Freedom*, 98.

45. Meyer, "In Defense of Freedom," 149–151.

46. Schneider considers the cases of Collins and Lawrence Dennis in *The Conservative Century*, 20–24. At one point, on the way to fascism, Collins advocated monarchy. "Monarchy as Alternative," in *Conservatism in America Since 1930*, 16–28.

47. Schneider mentions this case in *The Conservative Century*, 103.

48. See Schneider's "Introduction" to *Conservatism in America Since 1930*, 3.

49. Quoting Dean Acheson, emphasis in original. Goldwater, *The Conscience of a Conservative*, 14.

50. Ibid., 15.

51. See Robert H. Bork, *The Tempting of America: The Political Seduction of the Law* (New York: Simon & Schuster, 1990). For a criticism from the libertarian direction, see Stephen Macedo, *The New Right v. the Constitution* (Washington, DC: Cato Institute, 1987).

52. Robert Nisbett, *Conservatism: Dream and Reality* (London: Open University Press, 1986), 55–68.

53. Kirk, *The Conservative Mind*, 49. Kirk is discussing Burke in this passage.

54. Twelve Southerners, "Introduction: A Statement of Principles," in *I'll Take My Stand*, xlii. Compare John Gray, *False Dawn* (New York: New Press, 2000).

55. Meyer, "Conservatism," in *Defense of Freedom*, 194.

56. Irving Kristol, "Why Big Business Is Good for America," in *Conservatism in America Since 1930*, 318.

57. Rawls, *Justice as Fairness*, 8 note 7, 135–140. Note the first entry of the index under "capitalism": "conflicts with justice as fairness."

58. I seek to characterize it in "The Idea and Ideal of Capitalism," in *The Oxford Handbook of Business Ethics*, ed. George G. Brenkert and Tom L. Beauchamp (Oxford: Oxford University Press, 2009), 73–99.

59. All OECD countries meet these criteria, including those some deem "democratic socialist." See my *The Order of Public Reason*, appendix B.

60. See Rawls, *A Theory of Justice*, 7–8.

61. Rawls, "Kantian Constructivism in Moral Theory," 305.

62. Many so-called critics of capitalism see themselves as Keynesians, though Keynes himself thought that, despite his criticisms of great inequalities, in many ways his view was "moderately conservative in its implications." His aim was to preserve freedom, efficiency, and an adequate social existence for all—something that he believed capitalism could best deliver. See John Maynard Keynes, *The General Theory of Employment, Interest and Money* (Cambridge: Cambridge University Press, 1973), 377, 381; Keynes, "The End of Laissez-Faire," in his *Essays in Persuasion* (London: Macmillan, 1972), 294.

63. Goldwater, *The Conscience of a Conservative*, 52.

64. Friedrich A. Hayek, "Why I Am Not a Conservative," in his *The Constitution of Liberty* (London: Routledge and Kegan Paul, 1960), 397–411.

65. See Paul Edward Gottfried, *Conservatism in America* (New York: Palgrave-Macmillan, 2007).

66. Irving Kristol, "A Conservative Welfare State," in *The Essential Neoconservative Reader*, ed. Mark Gerson (New York: Addison-Wesley, 1996), 283–287.

67. For a useful summary, see James Q. Wilson, "The Rediscovery of Character: Private Virtue and Public Policy," in *The Essential Neoconservative Reader*, 291–304.

68. James Q. Wilson, "Foreword" to *The Essential Neoconservative Reader*, viii. For an excellent, accessible survey of this feature of public policy, see Edward Tanner, *Why Things Bite Back* (London: Fourth Estate, 1996). Tanner sums up his review of public policy: "[w]hat is almost a constant, though, is that the real benefits usually are not the ones we expected, and the real perils are not the ones we feared," 272.

69. See Ronald Reagan's "Remarks at the Annual Convention of the National Association of Evangelicals in Orlando, Florida, March 8, 1983," in *Conservatism in America Since 1930*, 352–361.

70. Ronald Reagan, "Inaugural Address, January 20, 1981," in *Conservatism in America Since 1930*, 343. Paragraph break deleted.

71. See, for example, Samuel Freeman's dissent from John Tomasi's claim, in *Free Market Fairness* (Princeton, NJ: Princeton University Press, 2012), that economic liberties are basic. "Can Economic Liberties Be Basic Liberties?" available online at: http://bleedingheartlibertarians.com/2012/06/can-economic-liberties-be-basic-liberties/.

72. This is the important insight of Jeremy Waldron's analysis of politics and law. See his *Law and Disagreement* (Oxford: Oxford University

Press, 1999), especially 102 and thereafter. What Waldron misses is the deeper underlying agreement on what is eligible. See my *Contemporary Theories of Liberalism* (London: SAGE, 2003), 84–99.

73. I make this point more fully in *Contemporary Theories of Liberalism*, 97–99.

74. Jerry Z. Muller, "Introduction" to *Conservatism: An Anthology of Social and Political Thought from David Hume to the Present* (Princeton, NJ: Princeton University Press, 1997), 18.

75. T. H. Green, "Lectures on the Principles of Political Obligation," in *Lectures on the Principles of Political Obligation and Other Writings*, ed. Paul Harris and John Morrow (Cambridge: Cambridge University Press, 1986), section 134.

76. Readings from Hayek are almost always included in anthologies of conservatism, including his "Why I Am Not a Conservative," [!] in *Conservatism in America Since 1930*, 180–194. Michael Freeden insists that Hayek is a conservative, but Freeden has a resolutely rationalistic view of liberalism. *Ideologies and Political Theory*, 373 and thereafter. Compare my "Liberalism at the End of the Century," *Journal of Political Ideologies* 5 (Issue 2, 2000): 186–189.

77. Gaus, *The Order of Public Reason*, 391–409.

78. See Rawls, *A Theory of Justice*, 497.

79. This is the core claim of Paul Weithman's *Why Political Liberalism? On John Rawls's Political Turn* (Oxford: Oxford University Press, 2010). See, for example, 48 and thereafter.

80. Andrew Schotter and Barry Sopher, "Social Learning and Coordination Conventions in Intergenerational Games: An Experimental Study," *Journal of Political Economy* 111 (June 2003): 507.

81. Meyer, "Conservatism," 198. Meyer criticized Kirk for reaffirming nineteenth-century conservatism, stressing tradition to the neglect of freedom. See also Meyer, "Collectivism Rebaptized," in *Defense of Freedom*, 3–13.

82. Meyer, "In Defense of Freedom," 36.

83. For a general analysis, see Scott E. Page, *Diversity and Complexity* (Princeton, NJ: Princeton University Press, 2011), 109–110, 138–140.

84. See, for example, Amartya Sen, *The Idea of Justice* (Cambridge, MA: Belknap Press of Harvard University Press, 2009), chapter 6. That Rawls did not embrace the necessity of such universality is another way in which, while being held up as the quintessential liberal philosopher, his work is more complex, and tends to straddle traditions. The unenthusiastic reception of most of his followers to *The Law of Peoples* was not surprising; it rejects the sort of universalistic cosmopolitanism most characteristic of contemporary academic liberal thought.

85. Meyer, "Freedom, Convention, and Conservatism," 24.

86. I am not being facetious; this seems to be one aim of Robert S. Taylor, *Reconstructing Rawls: The Kantian Foundations of Justice as Fairness* (University Park, PA: Pennsylvania State University Press, 2011), for example, 279 and thereafter.

87. This is a fairly widespread view today. See, for example, G. A. Cohen, *Rescuing Justice and Equality* (Cambridge, MA: Harvard University Press, 2008), part II; David Estlund, "Human Nature and the Limits (if Any) of Political Philosophy," *Philosophy and Public Affairs* 39 (Summer 2011): 207–237.

88. "Other things equal, persons in the original position will adopt the most stable scheme of principles." Although the "criterion of stability is not decisive," if the parties find that a conception is unworkable, this would force a reconsideration of their initial choice. Rawls, *A Theory of Justice*, 398–399, 472, 505.

89. Ibid., 401; Weithman, *Why Political Liberalism?*, 45. On the idea of a justice equilibrium, see also my "A Tale of Two Sets: Public Reason in Equilibrium, *Public Affairs Quarterly* 25 (October 2011): 305–325.

90. See my "The Turn to a Political Liberalism."

91. I am following Page, *Diversity and Complexity*, 149–150.

92. We might say that such a society will exhibit punctuated equilibrium, converging on an equilibrium for a period and then, after disruption, gravitating to a new one. In experiments on many-generational impure coordination games, this was observed. Schotter and Sopher, "Social Learning and Coordination Conventions," 501.

93. See my "Retributive Justice and Social Cooperation," in *Retributivism: Essays on Theory and Practice*, ed. Mark D. White (Oxford: Oxford University Press, 2011), 73–90.

94. See *The Order of Public Reason*, 438 and thereafter.

95. See Scott E. Page, *The Difference* (Princeton, NJ: Princeton University Press, 2007); Fred D'Agostino, "From the Organization to the Division of Cognitive Labor," *Politics, Philosophy & Economics* 8 (January 2009): 101–129; and his *Naturalizing Epistemology* (New York: Palgrave Macmillan, 2010); Michael Weisberg and Ryan Muldoon, "Epistemic Landscapes and the Division of Cognitive Labor," *Philosophy of Science* 76 (April 2009): 225–252.

96. Page, *Diversity and Complexity*, chapters 6 and 7.

97. This result relies on several theorems, which show the benefits of averaging performance over a wide variety of circumstances. See ibid., chapter 6.

98. Ibid., chapter 7.

99. Various caveats are necessary here, of course: if critical and conservative citizens tend to come into conflict and so destabilize the constitution, then the benefits of diversity may be swamped. See Page, *Diversity and Complexity*, 194 and thereafter.

100. See, for example, James G. March, "Exploration and Exploitation in Organizational Learning," *Organization Science* 2 (Organizational Learning: Papers in Honor of (and by) James G. March, May 1991): 71–87.

101. Jonathan Haidt, *The Righteous Mind: Why Good People Are Divided by Politics and Religion* (New York: Pantheon, 2012), 294. Emphasis in original. Haidt cites Mill on the parties of progress and stability, at 305.

8

CONSTITUTIONAL CONSERVATISM AND AMERICAN CONSERVATISM

JOHNATHAN O'NEILL

Have American conservatives been constitutional conservatives? The intense study of American conservatism in recent decades has all but ignored its relationship to constitutionalism and how it is conserved or maintained.[1] Lately scholars have more often asked the related question of how established constitutional systems adjust to change. But, as Aristotle's political science reminds us, too much or too rapid constitutional change undermines the constitution, or indicates that some kind of constitutional revolution has occurred. From this perspective, constitutionalism is properly understood as a conservative approach to political life. But the famously contentious components of American conservatism have not always or simply opted for conserving the Constitution (or maintaining or preserving it, here the terms are used interchangeably). Constitutional conservatism and political conservatism are not necessarily or always the same thing. This chapter addresses these issues by first taking a broad view of what advocates of constitutionalism have said is required for it to endure. It then examines how the different types of post–World War II American conservatives assessed their relationships to American constitutionalism, and its preservation, in light of the challenge of modern progressive liberalism.

CONSTITUTIONAL CONSERVATISM

Attempts to preserve constitutionalism proceed from some definition of it, and its defenders are driven to articulate the substantive components of constitutionalism they think are most in need of support. Since the time of Plato and Aristotle, defining constitutionalism has generated a wealth of literature, as have the related contests and ambiguities involved in its development.[2] Rather than again recounting this long history and fully restating the contrasts between ancient and modern constitutionalism, the following analysis aims to articulate, with the help of recent scholars, a rather abstract statement of what might be termed the "methods" or "modalities" of constitutional maintenance.[3] Of course on some level this endeavor must observe what constitutionalists have said constitutionalism is, but the goal is better to describe the kinds of arguments or practices typically used by those aiming to preserve or maintain it.

At the outset it should be noted that though constitutionalism seeks to limit, order, and constrain politics, it does so for political reasons. Thus the project of constitutional maintenance remains inside politics. Ultimately, one who would preserve or defend constitutionalism defends its irreducibly political commitments.[4] In an immediate sense, attempts to maintain constitutionalism remain inside politics because they are typically advanced by those who have an interest (against their opponents) in seeing constitutionalism, or their favored vision of it, entrenched over time.[5] In a broader sense political contests over constitutional meaning preserve constitutionalism when citizens debate what is required or prohibited by their shared commitment to constitutional norms.[6] With these considerations in mind, we turn to the types of arguments constitutionalism induces from those who would maintain it and pursue their political projects within it. This discussion draws heavily from the American case and somewhat elides important differences between ancients and moderns, though from its origins America was a modern regime that always understood itself as maintaining some connection to ancient constitutionalism.[7] One more point by way of introduction: the components of constitutionalism are interrelated, so any analytic parsing is inevitably heuristic and thus somewhat artificial.[8] This also is true of the interdependent and mutually reinforcing modes of argument and practice by which constitutionalism is maintained.

Balance

Those who define and defend constitutionalism speak of balance. It was central to the ancients' understanding of a well-designed "mixed" constitution (or regime), and remains so in the modern understanding of the "separation of powers." The modern idea was not simply or straightforwardly derived from the ancient one: though there are connections, there are also differences and discontinuities.[9] One of the central continuities is that exponents of both theories, as well as contemporary scholars, find it all but impossible to make sense of constitutionalism without the idea of balance.[10] Since the eighteenth century, discussions also have used the well-known formulation of "checks and balances."[11] Likewise, scholars have often used the modern checks and balances to describe the ancient mixed regime. More recent and less common is the description of a mixed constitution and a separation of powers constitution with such expressions as "countervailing institutions" or "countervailing powers."[12]

In the mixed constitutions of Plato and Aristotle, society's monarchical, aristocratic, and democratic components (or classes) were seen as naturally and permanently antagonistic. Each had differing views of justice and the common good and pursued them at the expense of the others. A good constitution involved these classes in offices and in ruling so that no one part could oppress or be oppressed. Their clashing principles and interests were to be accounted, moderated, and harmonized—balanced—to make the regime stable and enduring. This political task belonged to prudent founders and statesmen.[13] In ancient constitutionalism, maintaining the balance among the elements of the constitution helped to preserve it.

As the separation of powers developed in English constitutional history, the theories of Locke and Montesquieu, and the American founding, it detached from the primary basis of the mixed constitution in the classes or orders of society. It became increasingly oriented around the division and interaction of governmental functions, without wholly abandoning the ancient idea that some elements of society had characteristics that made them better at some functions.[14] The mixed constitution remained a referent for the American founders, but their modern political science relied more fundamentally on self-interest channeled through institutions than on virtue and deliberation about justice.[15] Accordingly, checks and balances had a central place in the separation of powers constitution, a development that owed something to the Enlightenment idea of mechanics but cannot be reduced to it.

The interaction of institutions, as they checked and balanced one another, was a major theme of *The Federalist Papers'* defense of the Constitution. Publius famously offered, as one of the modern improvements in the "science of politics," the "regular distribution of power into distinct departments [and] the introduction of legislative balances and checks." The Constitution aimed to contrive "the interior structure of the government, as that its several constituent parts may, by their mutual relations, be the means of keeping each other in their proper places." This goal required "giving to those who administer each department, the necessary constitutional means, and personal motives, to resist the encroachments of the others."[16] Publius also quoted Thomas Jefferson to the same effect: Americans had fought for a government whose powers "should be so divided and balanced among several bodies of magistracy, as that no one could transcend their legal limits, without being effectually checked and restrained by the others."[17] American constitutionalism made balance among the institutions of government central to its political science—the design aimed to make it possible for the "members of the government to maintain the balance of the Constitution."[18]

When one asks what ends balance serves (or checks and balances via the separation of powers), we encounter the substantive goods sought by constitutionalism. Both ancient and modern constitutionalism favored balance because it brought order and stability to political interaction, thereby preventing the concentration of power, which led to tyranny.[19] The balance in the ancient mixed constitution likewise encouraged moderation and deliberation because it required the ever-contending social orders to acknowledge one another's claims to justice.[20] The separation of powers in modern constitutionalism similarly created delay and compelled compromise because personal and political interests arrayed in institutions had to confront one another. In the famous words of *Federalist No. 51*, "the constant aim is to divide and arrange the several offices in such a manner as that each may be a check on the other; that the private interest of every individual, may be a centinel over the public rights."[21] It was hoped that this method would enable refinement of the popular will into the nation's "cool and deliberate sense," giving reason and justice an opportunity to rule over immediate desire.[22] Additionally, the balance resulting from government institutions, which were themselves based on different constituencies yet required to negotiate, was intended to secure government by consent and individual liberty—the twin bases of legitimacy in modern times.[23] An appeal to balance in constitutional politics thus involves the claim that some action or development unbalances the constitution: imbalance threatens the political ends constitutionalism seeks to secure, or else it has allowed one element in society to benefit at the expense of others.

In America, the separation of powers among branches and levels of government structures political interactions that have always been rich in appeals to balance. Here we might instance the perennial discussion about the "balance of federalism," or the recent struggles between Congress and the Executive over such things as the Independent Counsel statute or the War Powers Act. Additionally, appeals to balance realigned as most political liberals in the twentieth century moved from criticizing judicial review to embracing it, and likewise as most political conservatives moved from criticizing expanded executive power to embracing it.[24] In such disputes about what should be done or halted, political actors claimed that a proper constitutional balance was at stake and must be preserved, or indeed restored. Thus, arguments aiming to conserve constitutionalism appeal to balance, though over time these arguments may refer to and result in a balance different from what it once was.

Restraint and the Rule of Law

Any attempt to understand constitutionalism and how it is preserved must involve the notion of restraint or limitation. Most authorities put this idea very near the core of constitutionalism, often in tandem with the rule of law in both its ancient and modern versions.[25] In the ancient view, the restraint of law was the best alternative to the absolute and particularistic rule of the wise, which was better but not readily available. Limitation by law was second-best: it could never dispense with the need for discretion and inevitably would fall short of perfect justice according to nature. Yet it was good for several reasons. Its generality, relative permanence, and constraints on rulers accounted for human limitations, helped reason control the passions, and conduced to natural justice (or at least the regime's inevitably partial approach to it). Further, in a well-balanced constitution, the limitations imposed by the law treated citizens equally and provided for their participation in self-government, leaving them free to do whatever the law did not prohibit.[26] The restraint of law thus ordered and stabilized the regime, fostering its endurance over time. Preservation of the regime required abiding by the restraints imposed by its laws—those who ranged beyond them endangered its future.

The idea of restraint endured as modern politics narrowed from the cultivation of virtue or the salvation of souls to the protection of individual liberty. Restraint became inextricably intertwined with the liberal ideas of natural rights, limited government, and the rule of law; and with a written fundamental law as the best way to secure them. In this sense restraint on behalf of liberty was a defining purpose of modern limited government, rule of law constitutionalism.[27] The operating procedures of government were fixed and its overall purposes constrained, thereby impeding arbitrary rule and securing liberty for individuals and their voluntary cooperation in civil society. Moreover, in the estimation of many, a written constitution that limited government for the sake of liberty was the major American contribution to constitutional development.[28] Efforts to maintain modern written constitutionalism are often manifested in claims that restraints or limits have been breached.

In America, from *The Federalist Papers* onward, it was recognized that a constitution as written fundamental law implied interpretation by courts in concrete cases. The preservation of American constitutionalism both assumed and required judicial review as enforcement of the limitations inscribed in the text.[29] Indeed, throughout American history, adverting to the U.S. Supreme Court as the guardian and preserver of the Constitution has been a reliable way of quelling attacks on judicial review. As a corollary, judicial interpretation mandates claims, even when general or abstract, about what the constitutional text meant to those who wrote and authorized it as law. This imperative has come to be called originalism, and it is intrinsic to the preservation of a constitution as written fundamental law. Consequently, originalism in varying forms has had a continuing presence in American constitutional law and politics, particularly as an attempt to constrain what courts legitimately can say in the name of the Constitution.[30] Since the rapid ascendance of originalism in the 1980s, neither the onslaught of postmodern literary hermeneutics, nor attempts to co-opt originalism for the further expansion of modern judicial review, nor dueling appeals to history by justices of the Supreme Court (as in *District of Columbia v. Heller*[31]) has succeeded in eradicating its fundamental orientation toward limited government. Originalists have refined the theory's historical and epistemological claims, and it continues to develop as a forceful expression of the idea that a written constitution can limit government and instantiate the rule of law only if it has fixed meaning that constrains interpreters.[32] This is not to say originalism as a manifestation of these principles reliably generates "judicial restraint" or "deference" by a court to the constitutional judgment of a legislature (a point taken up in more detail below). Nor is originalism somehow outside the irreducibly political contest over constitutional meaning, which is always "won within politics." But if we grant that under any acceptable definition "constitutionalism seeks to bind politics to a set of constraints,"[33] supporters of a constitutional regime based on a written text will logically and unavoidably gravitate toward arguments about the limitations imposed on interpreters by the document's original meaning.

Education, Recurrence to First Principles, and Reverence

Advocates of constitutionalism have long adopted the Aristotelian teaching that any enduring regime must make, through education, the kind of citizens who support it. Preservation requires citizens whose character and culture are formed toward the regime's virtues and principles of justice, via both tutored choice and habituation.[34] For the ancients, "recurrence to first principles" was in essence this broad moral, civic, and political education. For the moderns, beginning with Machiavelli, it became one's recollection of the need for protection and desire for ease amid the viciousness and insecurity that was said to be the natural condition of humanity. Over time, these modern first principles were increasingly invoked, in the idiom of natural rights, to judge the legitimacy of governments during periods of revolutionary upheaval and political foundation, as in seventeenth-century England and eighteenth-century America. Many early American state constitutions held that frequent "recurrence to first principles," understood as those of liberal constitutionalism rather than those of Machiavelli, was necessary for their preservation.[35]

As a formal matter the American Constitution made no provision for an education that would foster this recurrence. But throughout American history, concerns about the health and longevity of constitutionalism have been expressed as calls for education in its first principles and for renewed dedication to them. Calls for such a return, and more broadly for understanding the political and institutional logic of constitutionalism, have frequently appeared in both political and scholarly discourse. This idea was famously expressed in George Washington's Farewell Address (1796) and Abraham Lincoln's Lyceum Address (1838). It was readily evident in the desire of Washington and others for a national university, and in the writing and educational schemes of Noah Webster and Thomas Jefferson. In the twentieth century, politicians and scholars again called for a return to and broader understanding of constitutional first principles. It was part of the response to the challenges of legal realism and Progressivism, and then to World War II and the Cold War. The idea currently persists in intensifying discussions about improving civic and historical education.[36]

Though modern constitutionalism emphasized institutional design over the formation of citizens, it still accepted that longevity required both education in first principles and "reverence" for them. To be sure, there is some tension between reverence and frequent recurrence to first principles. In the context of intense political conflict, such recurrence could involve the passions of the polity more than its reason. As *The Federalist* observed, politics at the level of fundamentals might produce too frequent alterations of government and deprive it "of that veneration, which time bestows on every thing, and without which perhaps even the wisest and freest of governments would not possess the requisite stability." This needed "reverence for the laws" could not be guaranteed solely by an appeal to reason or philosophy, and therefore the "most rational government will not find it a superfluous advantage, to have the prejudices of the community on its side."[37] Reverence or prejudice, as a species of passion, could serve constitutional maintenance. Opinion in favor of the Constitution need not be blind or ignorant: those who grasped its political theory could venerate it with a "thinking man's prejudice."[38] Still, constitutional maintenance would require the devotion of citizens who could not and need not be able in every instance to articulate fully its political theory. In American political culture, reverence for the Constitution has long been associated with its endurance. This idea was expressed perhaps most famously in Lincoln's Lyceum Address, and it has recurred at various other times throughout the nation's history.[39] Concomitantly, any attempt at fundamental constitutional change must challenge reverence for the Constitution.[40]

Preservation in an Emergency

Politics can present hard problems that lay beyond the horizons of constitutionalism. Since Aristotle, constitutionalists have known that a regime of laws, limits, and procedures can never wholly elude fundamental challenges from those who reject this approach to government. Moreover, if such challenges are violent and immediate, perhaps only if they are well-laid conspiracies, they present the prospect of a constitutional regime violating its own laws or principles to preserve its very existence. Such situations are unique and cannot be foreseen any more than a regime of law can anticipate the particulars of every dispute. Accordingly, constitutionalists usually accept that there must be some allowance in emergencies for actions that preserve the regime even though they are beyond or against its laws. In modern times, this recognition has often been expressed by the Lockean idea of "prerogative" and housed in the "executive" branch of government.[41] Inherent in the general tension between executive power and constitutionalism is the possibility of tyranny—the person or institution with the power to save constitutionalism necessarily has the power to destroy it. Another risk is that the routinization or legalization of emergency powers might atrophy and wither the polity's appetite and capacity for self-government.

How to preserve constitutionalism in the face of an existential challenge, without giving in to tyranny or lawlessness, has been an ongoing practical and theoretical concern. This was especially true during the development, since Machiavelli, of the modern idea of executive power.[42] In American constitutional history, the general problem has periodically recurred—from the Pacificus-Helvidius debates in the 1790s, to Lincoln's actions during the Civil War, to the Japanese relocations in World War II, to mid-twentieth-century fears of communist subversion, to the War on Terror. The topic has recently received renewed attention in the aftermath of the latter development. One general theoretical approach has been to state fairly specific rules or thresholds for declaring an emergency—and then delimiting its duration and regulating the response—in order to avert or minimize violation of constitutionalist principles, especially the legal rights of individuals.[43] This approach tends toward what might be called a type of constitutionalist deontology—let us act as constitutionalists though the heavens may fall. A more political approach, and therefore a more contingent one, accepts forthrightly the possibility of tyranny or lawlessness, because it sees more clearly that no limits can be set in advance on what might be necessary for survival. How to judge the measures taken to preserve constitutionalism, and whether what is preserved emerges as the same constitutional system that was threatened with destruction, are eminently political considerations for the polity as a whole. In this approach the preservation of constitutionalism depends on the character and virtue of whoever exercises the preservative (executive) power, as well as on the ability and willingness of the people to judge politically the exercise of that power.[44]

Political Limits, Effective Government, and Preservation by Adaptation

From its Aristotelian beginnings constitutionalism was conservative, aiming to preserve the regime by regulating its politics and averting decay into its corrupt form or a tyranny. Moderns hoped that individual liberty would endure when constitutions put some things beyond the reach of government and carefully delineated its operations. In these ways, constitutionalism seeks stability and order by holding political interaction to prescribed patterns. "Constitutions tame politics," establishing that not all possibilities are available at all times. Modern liberal constitutionalism especially sought "escape from the hardships of a politics where everything could be on the table."[45] This approach proceeds from a certain pessimism about human nature and "tries to lower the stakes of politics, to restrict the risks to liberty and dignity of being a member of a political society."[46] Some political programs are fenced out entirely, and those pursued are held to preordained methods and ends.[47] Written constitutionalism also constrains and configures politics by requiring that it occur with reference to the text and norms of the constitution, which comes to be understood as both a source of authority and standard of legitimacy.[48] Much of constitutional politics consists of "efforts to entrench favored constitutional understandings," so that victories in past contests about constitutional meaning are sustained over time.[49] Accordingly, scholars of varying perspectives often have observed that American constitutionalism is both a cause and effect of the nation's political stability, as well as the marked continuity in its core values and, some would insist, its basic conservatism.[50]

However, the constitutionalist preference for stability, diffusion of power, and incremental change opens it to the charge of being overly biased toward the status quo and prone to ineffectual government. Constitutionalism must contend with this challenge. No regime will last if it fails to address problems that people think the government should confront. Charles Howard McIlwain influentially sounded this alarm during the Great Depression and the rise of fascism. He went so far as to attack the separation of powers and checks and balances as a "figment of the imagination of eighteenth century doctrinaires." These doctrines wrongly had been conflated with the principle of limited government. The result was a "dissipation of governmental power with its consequent irresponsibility," tending in America toward "government for private interests or groups instead of government for the whole people."[51] McIlwain feared that enfeebled and irresponsible government would generate a backlash that destroyed all hard-won constitutional limitations, as was then happening in Europe. He surely overstated his case, but any fair assessment of constitutional development over the past several centuries must acknowledge that, in preventing tyranny and protecting liberty, it also has hampered attempts at large-scale government intervention in economic and social affairs.[52] That fact will be praised by some and condemned by others. Yet a key challenge for those who would preserve constitutionalism, as McIlwain underscored, will always be to assure that limited government can still be effective and responsible government.

Despite constitutionalism's fundamentally conservative orientation, constitutional thought has always understood that preservation requires adaptation and change. Much of Aristotle's teaching concerned how statesmen could exercise wisdom and discretion to apply and preserve a regime's principles in altered conditions— even reforming them—to make politics as reasonable and just as circumstances permitted.[53] Edmund Burke, a founder of modern conservatism, famously observed that, "A state without the means of some change is without the means of its conservation. Without such means it might even risque the loss of that part of the constitution which it wished most religiously to preserve."[54] Similarly, John Marshall, undeniably a constitutional conservative, recognized the necessity of adaptation. His court held that, through the "necessary and proper clause" of the Constitution, Congress had discretion in the choice of legislative means to reach constitutional ends. In one of the most-quoted lines in all of American constitutional law, Marshall wrote that Congress was given this power as part of the "constitution, intended to endure for ages to come, and consequently, to be adapted to the various *crises* of human affairs."[55] Of course modern written constitutions typically acknowledge the fact of change by providing for their own amendment, as in Article V of the American Constitution. Nevertheless, Article V has been criticized as being overly obstructionist by observers who think American constitutionalism has changed insufficiently or responded too slowly to majorities.[56] As this observation suggests, it is a fundamental question how much a constitutional order should change, and how it properly does so. This is because at some point there must be a judgment about the validity or legitimacy of change. As Walter Murphy asked, "what if some changes subvert the very nature of the constitutional order?"[57]

His response, the constitutionalist one, is that such change is illegitimate within the terms of the constitutional order and would amount to its replacement or re-creation.[58] Here again we see the reappearance of constitutionalism's conservative orientation even amid its acknowledgment of change.

AMERICAN CONSERVATIVES AND AMERICAN CONSTITUTIONALISM

The preceding analysis suggests that it could be shown that, across the span of American history, conservatives defended constitutionalism with the argumentative themes and practices just described. So too did other political actors who were not conservative, again reminding us that constitutional conservatism and political conservatism are not simply identical. That inquiry cannot be pursued here. Rather, I would like to sketch a portion of it by briefly restating the core principles of differing types of post–World War II American conservatism, and then considering the major points of approbation and tension between them and American constitutionalism. American conservatives have always confronted American constitutionalism as a form of political order that made its own demands on them—a point the now large literature on conservatism has not fully appreciated. Accordingly, I will conclude by observing that, just as American conservatism ascended through coalitions and alliances among its contending components, so too did conservatives increasingly accept that rallying to the Constitution served their favored principles, despite some enduring disagreements with it and with one another.

Traditionalists

Traditionalist conservatives hold that any civilization is defined more by culture and custom than by politics or a constitution.[59] Primary are the morals and virtues taught and honored by family, tradition, and religion. A constitution emerges to protect and facilitate a society's understanding of the good and virtuous life as experienced in local communities. Sometimes this view is announced by saying that the written constitution of governmental forms and procedures expresses, and is ultimately subservient to, the unwritten constitution of culture and custom. Most traditionalists are deeply indebted to Edmund Burke. They typically emphasize the English and Christian roots of American civilization, as well as its ties to the natural law tradition of the West. Burkean conservatism was central to Russell Kirk's influential *The Conservative Mind* and subsequently was applied more specifically to American constitutionalism in a book he subtitled *Reflections on Our Conservative Constitution*. In addition to Kirk, probably the most sustained expression of the traditionalist approach to American constitutionalism is the work of George W. Carey (who is less Burkean), followed by Bruce P. Frohnen (who is very much so).[60] Additionally, Southern Agrarianism is properly understood as a form of traditionalist conservatism. Originally a literary and cultural defense of Southern distinctiveness, its most pronounced intervention in postwar constitutional politics was the work of M. E. Bradford in the 1980s and 1990s.[61]

Since constitutionalism grows from culture, and despite the War for Independence, traditionalists often emphasize the continuities between colonial America and the newly independent nation.[62] The rebellious colonists fought to continue their practice of local self-government and to defend the traditional, common law rights of Englishmen from a distant but meddling empire. Indeed, following Burke, traditionalists insist that 1776 was "a revolution not made, but prevented." Both the Declaration of Independence and the Constitution were outgrowths and articulations of a long-established understanding of politics and government. The founding of America was a conservative act, and by no means a revolutionary upheaval. While not wholly denying the relevance of John Locke, natural rights, and social contract theory, traditionalists downplay their significance and subsume them into their larger narrative of continuity. The Declaration especially is read against the background of the common law and natural law traditions, diminishing the innovation and universality others associate with it.[63] The result, often quite explicit, is rejection of the claim that natural rights and human equality were the definitive American ends that the Constitution was meant to secure. Traditionalists argue that that view is a historically inaccurate account of the American founding. Especially since Abraham Lincoln, they say, it has unleashed a messianic, ideological politics of individualism

and egalitarianism that has all but effaced the proper understanding of American constitutionalism.[64]

The traditionalist vision of the constitutional order holds that
its aims were less modern and more circumspect than what has
become of it. Originally constitutionalism was structural and pro-
cedural, establishing only the methods by which a religious and
republican people deliberated and governed itself under God. To
distinguish this view from the mistaken one that elevated the Declaration, Carey and Bradford used Michael Oakeshott's distinction
between "nomocratic" and "teleocratic" political orders.[65] A nomocratic order establishes modes of operation for conducting official
business in accord with the established customs of society, while
a teleocratic order seeks the ever-fuller realization of an abstract
end or goal. The Constitution originally had been nomocratic—
encouraging moderation and deliberation about common concerns according to set procedures and limits—but it had become
increasingly teleocratic, transformed by the crusade for greater
equality and more rights, often in the name of the Declaration.[66]
The move from a nomocratic to a teleocratic regime was the fundamental "derailment" of the American tradition, which traditionalists regard as the source of the nation's constitutional and political ills, and which was prefigured in Lincoln's understanding of
the Declaration before the Civil War.

For traditionalists, this transformation is the error that has politicized all social interaction. A debasing, incomplete modern
politics of rights and equality has become sovereign over what was
once a Christian humanist culture, necessarily miscasting the original purpose of American constitutionalism and skewing its subsequent development. Understood in this way, the gravamen of the
traditionalist argument is that American constitutionalism, at least
originally, was not fundamentally modern and liberal, not the first
instantiation of a new universalism of natural rights and equality.[67] Rather, it was the humble attempt of a people to sustain their
established mode of deliberative and consensual self-government,
under the ultimate judgment of their God.[68] From this perspective, it is fair to observe, as have others, that traditionalist conservatism has no positive political program other than " 'containing liberalism' [or] 'boxing in' liberal justice."[69] What traditionalists have
most wanted from American constitutionalism is what they insist

the founding had achieved: a limited federal government that intrudes only minimally into state and local affairs, so that families, churches, and communities can foster the good life according to inherited conceptions of morality, virtue, and justice.[70]

At the level of concrete constitutional commentary, traditionalists revile the centralization of power and evisceration of federalism that resulted from the New Deal's reinterpretation of the commerce clause. The modern bureaucratic, regulatory, and welfare state established by the New Deal destroys communities by undermining both their capacity for self-government and the teaching of virtue and morality that sustain them. Modern judicial review, especially in the form of the "rights revolution," has further undermined traditional cultural norms. It enforces liberalism's norm of the autonomous, self-creating individual, undermining the ability of states and local communities to teach anything deemed illiberal by the Supreme Court. Consequently, the Court has fostered evergreater vulgarization of the culture by steadily erasing standards of common decency and restraint.[71] Sounding the traditionalist emphasis on the primacy of culture, George Carey has long argued that such developments fundamentally endanger constitutionalism itself. The continual breakdown of general cultural norms, including the particular virtues constitutionalism needs but does not create, leads to a breakdown of "constitutional morality." This term describes the willingness of citizens and officeholders to deliberate and persuade, and their orientation toward compromise and consensus, without which a constitutional system of diffused power and multiple veto points cannot govern or endure.[72]

It also should be noted that traditionalist conservatives have consistently opposed the modern "rhetorical" or "plebiscitary" presidency and its favoring of an interventionist foreign policy based on America's supposed destiny to advance democracy and human rights. Traditionalists see this kind of executive power as a corruption of constitutionalism, part of the self-delusional derailment of American politics whereby "we, God's own people, can get down to our proper business, which is building the New Jerusalem and spreading it over the face of the entire earth." This development displaced the legislative deliberation that should properly lead the constitutional system, orienting politics away from the concerns of American society and toward the remaking of others in its supposed self-image. Among traditionalists, these criticisms were largely in abeyance during the Cold War, but have since reemerged in response to America's ongoing, undeclared wars and the sweeping assertions of executive power accompanying them.[73]

Traditionalist assessments of American constitutionalism, as of American culture, often convey a certain resignation in the face of irretrievable loss. Modern judicial review constitutes a "new regime" while the old order is "dying." Continued centralization means that communities face "the prospect of extinction." We can no longer avoid the question of whether the original constitutional order is gone, and some traditionalists conclude that now it only "survives in memory" to be recollected by a "remnant."[74] To be sure, on some level the sense of loss inheres in the conservative cast of mind.[75] But the traditionalist judgment raises hard questions that never quite disappear: about the human cost of the changes they bemoan, and the lack of accepted constitutional standards that might legitimate them.

Libertarians

Libertarianism is built on the principles of maximizing individual liberty and "spontaneous order."[76] The latter idea is derived most directly from the Scottish Enlightenment. It holds that as individuals pursue their own ends and interact with one another, a coordinated and evolving order arises—one that is patterned without being designed or directed. The market is a spontaneous order. It efficiently coordinates production and distribution through mutually beneficial, voluntary exchanges that reflect individual self-interest as pursued in light of the information contained in the price mechanism. It is a key tenet of libertarianism, as developed especially in the work of Ludwig von Mises and Friedrich von Hayek, that a centrally planned (socialist) economy is impossible: no single entity can process the widely dispersed knowledge necessary for economic efficiency.

In nearly all situations, libertarians privilege human freedom and the absence of coercion. This dedication to individual liberty is sometimes rooted forthrightly in the theory of natural rights, especially John Locke. Sometimes liberty is treated in a utilitarian and consequentialist fashion, as a social construction or inherited custom that has proven attractive and efficient over time. Liberty and the market as a spontaneous order reinforce one another because the latter is based on freely chosen exchanges. Another hallmark of libertarianism is tolerance of others' self-regarding and "victimless" activities or associations, most saliently in the realms of drug use and sexuality. Likewise, libertarians favor a foreign policy based on the proposition that free trade brings prosperity and peace, and they oppose mercantilism, colonial conquest, and most armed intervention that is not directly related to self-defense.

In its moderate form, libertarianism advocates the minimal state and the large sphere of individual liberty broadly characteristic of the nineteenth-century American polity. The term "libertarian" is now often used interchangeably with "classical liberal"—both emerged in contradistinction to the larger and more interventionist state of twentieth-century "progressive liberalism." Moderate libertarians accept that there is a small range of "public goods" which are the legitimate subjects of state provision or regulation. More radical or pure libertarians deny the very concept. In its more radical form, libertarianism tends toward anarchism, or perhaps "anarcho-capitalism." On this view, market exchanges can satisfy all or nearly all human needs, and to the extent that government exists it is responsible for enforcing property rights and the principles of tort and contract. Some radical libertarians even suggest that roadways, policing, and national defense could be contracted to private corporations.

Whether moderate or extreme, libertarians are confident that they know the truth about political things, and they have a very certain positive program. Politics is about "liberty versus power" and "man versus the state." The libertarian goal is always to defend the first from the inevitable depredations of the second. This understanding has sometimes distanced libertarianism from American constitutionalism, as in the case of Albert Jay Nock (1870–1945), a journalist and author who remains a foundational figure for the libertarian movement. In his journal *The Freeman* (1920–1924), and the elaboration of its perspective in *Our Enemy, the State,* Nock described himself as a "philosophical anarchist." While "government" had always existed in some form to manage the concerns natural to any community, brigands founded the "state" in conquest and confiscation to seize the land and exploit the production of others. The state was in essence a criminal enterprise, the "political means" for expropriation from honest folk who made their living by productive "economic" means. This was as true in America as anywhere else, and Nock did not think much of the Constitution or any claim of a principled politics in defense of it. Early in his career, he observed that *The Freeman* was "never very strong for the Constitution. . . . We sometimes think that it is the appointed function of the United States to clear the way for a regime of philosophical anarchism elsewhere in the world."[77] The doctrines of natural rights and popular sovereignty announced in the Declaration of Independence quickly had come to justify merely "an unlimited economic pseudo-individualism on the part of the State's beneficiaries," who served themselves while only appearing to act in the name of the public.[78] Especially fraudulent was any politics "put on show as 'constitutional principles.'" Such constitution talk was only "an elaborate system of fetishes," so much "sophistry" and "agonized fustian" which hid the "only actual principle of party action—the principle of keeping open the channels of access to the political means."[79]

Nock inspired Murray Rothbard, an influential post-War libertarian. Although always willing to advance his views by alliances of convenience with everyone from anti-Vietnam hippies to Patrick Buchanan, Rothbard's libertarianism-cum-anarchism pronounced the Constitution a failure. Perhaps unsurprisingly, in his self-described "extremist" vision, the New Deal would go. But so too would the Federal Reserve and Internal Revenue Service. Rothbard would "not stop until we repealed the Federal Judiciary Act of 1789, and maybe even think the unthinkable and restore the good old Articles of Confederation."[80]

Over time this rejectionist extremism became less typical among libertarians who more carefully considered American constitutionalism. To use one influential early example, Hayek found much in it to admire and advocate. The Constitution's division of powers, its substantive limits on government, and its guarantees of individual rights were major achievements. So was judicial review, though Hayek lamented the desuetude of both the Ninth Amendment and the Privileges or Immunities Clause of the Fourteenth Amendment. Beyond these points, he repeatedly underscored that

American constitutionalism secured liberty because it embodied the rule of law: it compelled government to act according to previously announced, general principles that could not be suspended by those in power. This crucial fact was what gave Americans "a constitution of liberty, a constitution that would protect the individual against all arbitrary coercion." Consequently, Americans had "been able to defend freedom by defending their Constitution."[81] America was not merely a pilfering state as corrupt as any other, but rather an exemplar of how to protect liberty.

A more positive view of the Constitution also was evident in the second series of *The Freeman*, which provided a focal point for the early post-War libertarian movement. A noted article by Charles Hull Wolfe counseled libertarians not to forsake the Constitution. It was undeniable that "as currently amended and interpreted [the Constitution] expresses the libertarian ideal only to a minimum degree. It has been twisted and bent to serve the purposes of collectivism." Though the Constitution had been "mutilated," libertarians still should not abandon it. In fact, it contained provisions that were "a legal anchor to which we can tie our idealism." Though the original Constitution did not limit government "as severely as we might like," Wolfe asked rhetorically, "is that reason to dismiss it, especially at a time when the original document is still much nearer the libertarian standard than is popular opinion?" The goal was to get the country to "live up to the governmental restrictions imposed by the Constitution" as a first step toward a more libertarian future.[82] Another author in *The Freeman* also lamented that "the American people have abandoned the system of government which made their nation outstanding." The solution was for the Constitution to "be restored to its original purity and strength."[83]

Libertarian constitutional commentary generally developed on this template, rather than that of Nock or Rothbard. Indeed, libertarian calls to "preserve" the Constitution or "restore" its original meaning from the statist corruption of progressive liberalism became particularly salient among major figures in the 1980s and thereafter. Richard A. Epstein, for example, consistently urged interpreters to seek "the standard meanings of ordinary language as embodied in constitutional text" because "the mission of constitutional government must soon founder if judges can decide cases as freely with the Constitution in place as without it."[84] In America, there had been a "systematic repudiation of the basic principles of limited government which informed the original constitutional structure," so libertarians now must "resurrect a lost tradition."[85] This theme also was central to the often-overlooked work of Bernard Siegan, an early libertarian voice in the legal academy.[86] It reached its greatest prominence in Randy E. Barnett's *Restoring the Lost Constitution* (2004). Barnett labored mightily to present "evidence of original meaning" which showed that "the entire Constitution, as amended, is much more libertarian than the one selectively enforced by the Supreme Court." This "lost Constitution" had not been repealed: "it remains before our eyes and its restoration within our grasp."[87]

Libertarians have established a strong presence in American law schools and seek to influence the development of legal doctrine. One of their major targets has been the expansion of federal economic regulation under the commerce clause, especially since Progressivism and the New Deal. They complain that the Supreme Court has acted in a manner contrary to the limited original meaning of the commerce clause by upholding regulation of virtually any activity which Congress says has some effect on interstate commerce, however remote.[88] This "massive expansion of federal power" is in many respects the libertarians' worst nightmare, because "courts have granted Congress a near plenary power to do anything it wills and thus have nearly destroyed the system of limited enumerated powers."[89] Similarly, the administrative agencies created to effectuate the modern regulatory state are another object of libertarians' ire. In Epstein's view, "they are flatly unconstitutional—there is no Article IIIA." Indeed, he added, "the modern regulatory state is quite unthinkable without independent administrative agencies, and that is the way it should be."[90]

Libertarians' positive program often attempts to revive pre–New Deal economic doctrines in American constitutional law. One example is the call to return to the older, more constrained conception of the "police power," the state's traditional authority to protect health, safety, morals, or the public welfare. The limited regulatory authority of the traditional police power, when combined with robust enforcement of contracts, is seen as the best way to hold government to libertarian ends: the protection of "individual liberty and private property against all manifestations of force and fraud." Government should uphold voluntary agreements, punish criminal and tortious harms, and forbid monopoly—but not much more.[91] Likewise, most libertarians regard *Lochner v. New York* (1905) as rightly decided, and there are increasing calls to rehabilitate its liberty of contract jurisprudence. For libertarians, *Lochner* represents the proper corrective to illegitimate, overly expansive use of the police power.[92] The broad scope for free choice afforded by this understanding of the police power and liberty of contract tolerates a wide range of consensual human relationships, and Barnett has lauded *Lawrence v. Texas* (2004) for striking down a state law that criminalized consensual homosexual conduct.[93]

Libertarians also seek to reinvigorate heretofore "lost" or "neglected" constitutional provisions that explicitly protect persons and property. The most prominent of these efforts has been Richard Epstein's work on the takings clause of the Fifth Amendment. It argues that the original meaning of the clause is broad enough to require that government compensate owners for regulations that diminish the value of property and not only for actual physical expropriations. Epstein also insists that a taking must be for a truly public use—and not merely for a public purpose, which would hardly be any limit at all. Led by Epstein, libertarians have made these ideas part of serious scholarly and policy discussions, and have had some success in bringing them to the Supreme Court on behalf of individual property owners. Likewise, Randy Barnett has sought to retrieve the Ninth Amendment and the Privileges or Immunities Clause of the Fourteenth Amendment as the bases for judicial defense of unenumerated natural rights against state encroachment.[94] It is worth observing that both Epstein and Barnett advocate active judicial protection for individual liberties, not the traditional conservative position of judicial restraint and deference to the legislature.[95]

In sum, though libertarians sometimes pine for the Articles of Confederation or side with the Anti-Federalists, aside from a small coterie of purist-rejectionists, most want to claim that the "United States was founded on libertarian principles." "Overall," they conclude that, "the modern American libertarian, if so inclined, can feel unambiguous stirrings of patriotic fervor when

contemplating the covenantal purpose of this nation."[96] Though
they might let it be known that they have a list of proposed constitutional amendments to advance their views (examples include:
requiring a balanced budget; forbidding delegation of legislative
authority to administrative agencies; requiring rotation in office;
and the line item veto), libertarians now typically affirm that
"enforcing the Constitution as it stands would be a big step in the
libertarian direction."[97]

Straussians (and Neoconservatives?)

Leo Strauss (1899–1973) was a German-Jewish émigré scholar of
the history of political thought and a central figure in post–World
War II conservative intellectual history. He led a return to the
"Great Books" of Western civilization to reencounter their teachings about reason, nature, God, and morality. His influence has
steadily increased, and studies of his thought and legacy have been
appearing at a rapid pace.[98]

Strauss said that a reconsideration of Western political thought
was urgent because Western civilization was in crisis. It had come
to doubt or disbelieve its own claims of justice and right. No
longer did revealed religion set the moral standard of society.
Enlightenment rationalism had not only failed to bring universal
prosperity, freedom, and justice, but was no longer sure what was
right by nature. The modern crisis was the inability to "know what
is good and bad, what is right and wrong."[99] Moderns had become
convinced that neither reason nor revelation could answer the
fundamental human question of Socrates: "What is the best way
of life?"

Strauss traced this crisis to "three waves of modernity," the
trend in political thought that had displaced ancient political
philosophy and biblical morality with historicism, positivism, and
nihilism.[100] From Machiavelli to Hobbes and Locke, on through
Rousseau, and finally to Nietzsche and Heidegger, Western
thought had steadily abandoned its traditional attempt to discern universal truths and then to live by them. Instead it had endorsed materialism, appetite, and the claim that all standards were
time- and culture-bound, and hence meaningless. Finally, modern
thought had arrived at the conscious construction of "values" to

govern one's self, and perhaps others—self-creation and the will to power. Strauss thought that in this way modern rationalism had self-destructed. There was now a grave danger in the absence of standards by which to condemn, say, the Nazis. There was also an opportunity, which Strauss pursued: a way out of the crisis via recovery of the confrontation between the conceptions of morality and human excellence found in the Bible and the ancient idea of natural right. This project, in turn, required the conservation of modern regimes that permitted such a recovery, such as America. As a refugee from the Nazis, Strauss keenly appreciated this point, though he remained a friendly critic of American shortcomings as he understood them.[101] Indeed, he stated more emphatically than was typical of him that an education in the great ideas of Western civilization, particularly after communism and fascism, taught that "wisdom cannot be separated from moderation" and hence that "wisdom requires unhesitating loyalty to a decent constitution and even to the cause of constitutionalism."[102]

Strauss's teaching enabled his students to take seriously the political theory of America's founding and its Constitution. His diagnosis of the ills of modern politics and his recovery of the ancient study of political regimes also pushed them to consider how America and its principles might endure. But in doing so they faced a problem. As one recent study put it, for Strauss modernity was "bad" because it was low. Basing politics on passions-cum-rights, modern regimes built on and perpetuated an impoverished vision of humanity. And America was modern. It was derived most fundamentally from Locke's theories of rights, consent, and social contract. America as a regime had not attempted to cultivate virtue or defer to the rule of the wise. Moreover, America's basis in modern natural right had made it susceptible to the next destructive waves of modernity, thus endangering its once stable, though flawed or incomplete, foundation. Yet Strauss's students, who saw the critique of America inherent in his teaching, still wanted to affirm that America was "good" and that its constitutionalism was worthy of defense and preservation.[103] The solution to this problem, recently described by James W. Ceaser as "the core of 'Straussianism' insofar as it has become a project of American political thought," was to try "to restore the possibility of the idea of natural right," but in a way that "takes into account the shortcomings of the modern doctrine of natural rights and that seeks to modify or correct it."[104]

Approaches differed on how best to advance this effort. But in general, Straussians consider the origin, development, and current tendency of American politics and constitutionalism from the perspectives of Platonic political philosophy and Aristotelian political science. Their objective was to call on the ancients for help in "modifying" or "correcting" America in the light of the older, better understanding of human beings, philosophy, and politics. These efforts produced protracted and occasionally vehement disagreements among those who differently elaborated the apparently conflicting aspects of Strauss's designedly veiled and ambiguous teaching. The full substance of these debates cannot be engaged here, though appreciating their basic contours clarifies the differing versions of the Straussian approach to American constitutionalism.

"West Coast" Straussians, led by Harry V. Jaffa, probably have had the most direct and visible effect on American constitutional discourse. They defend the philosophy of natural rights and social contract as America's definitive political commitment, but in a way that seeks to exempt or insulate America from the ensuing destructive waves of modernity. This move depends on the contested claim that the founders understood only Locke's surface teaching, which was compatible with Aristotle and Christianity, or else that Locke's true teaching was in fact so compatible. (Despite Strauss's apparent view that Locke's doctrine of rights and consent rested on the Hobbesian ground of materialism and atheism.) Jaffa and his students hold that "nature and nature's God," as announced in the Declaration of Independence and further explicated by Abraham Lincoln, established human equality and natural rights. "All men are created equal" in being above mere animals but beneath perfection or god. Human equality is thus an abstract truth applicable in all times and places, though it can be described in either Aristotelian or Christian terms. Either description generates the duty to respect other people as expressed in the language of rights, which in turn justifies limited government based on consent.[105] On this view, Lincoln had recalled America to the Aristotelian politics and Christian morality embodied in the proper understanding of its founding principles—he had not needed to "refound" the nation to correct its modern errors (as Jaffa's earlier work had suggested). Therefore, the way to combat modern decline was with "a straightforward and patriotic return to the founders" and to Lincoln's unsurpassed defense of their achievement.[106]

West Coast Straussians offer this understanding of natural rights and limited government as the basis for and the original purpose of American constitutionalism. Evaluating subsequent constitutional developments by this standard, they attack various American manifestations of the second and third waves of modernity. A consistent target of theirs is Progressivism, because its historicist attack on the natural right principles of the founding enabled the centralized, regulatory state of the New Deal and Great Society. Another is the modern Supreme Court, for basing constitutional law on a corrupt, relativist understanding of rights and the illegitimate doctrine of judicial supremacy. Other conservatives are also roundly criticized. These include many constitutional originalists, such as William Rehnquist and Robert Bork, for their legal positivism; as well as Southern agrarians and traditionalists for their criticism of Lincoln's natural rights arguments against slavery and his related rejection of secession.[107]

"East Coast" Straussians, once led by Allan Bloom, have been more often intransigently Platonic in doubting that any appeal to nature in politics ultimately can be justified by reason. Consequently this group has intervened less directly in political affairs. Indeed, some Easterners incline toward a detached philosophical contemplation that quietly accepts its tension with claims of moral virtue or political right.[108] Likewise, the East characteristically holds that since Strauss's basic negative judgment on modernity clearly applies to America, it has always needed modification and elevation by principles from outside modern natural right.[109] One result of that view is an emphasis on education, in particular an inquiry into the great contest of ideas in Western civilization and consideration of where America stands in light of them. Such an education could produce "a renewed, thoughtful, and therefore undogmatic or reasonably qualified appreciation for the strength and validity of the principles underlying our Constitution."[110] Nevertheless, another important result of such an inquiry, in the estimation of

Thomas Pangle, is that the American founders' emphasis on individual rights and institutional architecture slighted the education of citizens. They must be taught the virtues and morals proper to republican self-government if it is to endure.[111] In a similar vein, East Coast Straussians frequently draw on the Aristotelianism of Alexis de Tocqueville's *Democracy in America*. It offered the best statement of the pre-modern elements in the United States that foster the virtues and morals necessary to sustain it against mass democracy's individualism and relativism—especially the ethic of moral self-restraint derived from Christianity and sustained in local government and civic association.[112]

Another Eastern approach, central to the work of Harvey Mansfield, has been to argue that American constitutionalism contains opportunities within itself to be better than its modern elements. It "calls forth virtue" without ensuring the practice of it, and fosters reasoned deliberation about the public good without guaranteeing it will happen. For example, the office of president invites prudence in emergencies and leadership toward long-term policy goals. Yet, the imprecise definition of "executive power" in the Constitution creates only the opportunity, not the certainty, that in these endeavors a president will act virtuously or reasonably. Mansfield similarly argues that institutional features of American constitutionalism, such as representation, federalism, and the separation of powers, provide opportunities to moderate and elevate public opinion toward reason and the common good. This "constitutional space" between popular will and government action facilitates (again, without guaranteeing) deliberative and informed self-government.[113] Constitutionalism, on this view, requires more of its citizens than American conservatives often ask. Mansfield has written that:

> [C]onservatives need to be taught that mere release from government is not enough to make people capable of self-government. The people also need a well-made constitution enabling them to elevate their will into an intention and calling for the virtues necessary to the task . . . Constitutional government must make its people aware of the demands as well as the pleasures of freedom and not leave the impression that when government is limited, things will take care of themselves.[114]

Straussians are thus conservative defenders of American constitutionalism who nevertheless think it has weaknesses or blind spots, which must be actively addressed. In this way, they echo and elaborate Strauss's own statement, itself an application of ancient political science, that "we are not permitted to be flatterers of democracy precisely because we are friends and allies of democracy."[115] Moreover, despite the differences captured in the "East versus West" labels, as James Ceaser has recently concluded, Straussians "agree on the need for a political foundation in America based on a regulating idea of natural right that combines the substance of modern right with the appreciation of certain classical virtues."[116] For Straussians this need is so pressing because of the self-destruction of modern rationalism and consequent absence of standards capable of distinguishing right from wrong, or legitimate government from tyranny—what Strauss diagnosed as the "crisis of modernity." Prepared by Strauss to consider America anew in light of the ancients, Straussians aim to preserve, supplement, and improve American constitutionalism as the best possible regime under modern conditions. This goal accounts for their consistent and lively efforts to sustain it against both its own problematic tendencies and the more direct challenges of modern progressive liberalism.

Finally, a word is in order regarding the much discussed and much confused topic of Straussians and neoconservatism. The first point is that these are not convertible categories. Neoconservatism was and is a multifaceted political orientation that moved through several stages from the mid-1960s to the present. However we might understand neoconservatism—a careful recent study concludes that it "is such a diverse thing that the term has always been close to meaningless"—it is too variegated and its development too contingent to be attributed to the thought of Strauss. To do so is "fundamentally erroneous" and simply "does not work."[117] Moreover, the condition of American constitutionalism as such was not one of the initial motivations for neoconservatism. The movement's attention to legal-constitutional issues in its formative years was the purview of frustrated liberal social scientific policy analysts with no connection to Strauss or the way his students thought about American constitutionalism. To the extent that Straussian constitutional theory and its concern with nature as a standard of right became associated with neoconservatism, it did so by displacing the original neoconservative approach to the topic, not by inspiring it.[118]

This is not to deny that there has been some overlap or affinity between particular neoconservatives and Straussians. Neoconservatives who had contact with Strauss or his students were part of the George W. Bush administration, and some helped formulate and apply its interventionist, neo-Wilsonian foreign policy. And after all, Irving Kristol, a founder of neoconservatism, sometimes acknowledged the influence of Strauss (and one of his students, Martin Diamond). Kristol also once described his overriding political concern in rather Straussian terms, as the "tendency of democratic republics to depart from . . . their original, animating principles, and as a consequence to precipitate grave crises in the moral and political order."[119] That thought, along with the appeal to natural right, fairly describes much of the overlap between Straussians and contemporary neoconservatism.[120] But Kristol was also a realist in foreign policy, not a neo-Wilsonian. He denied that America could or should export democracy through armed intervention. For example, he defended the limited objectives of the first Gulf War, stating that "no civilized person in his right mind wants to govern Iraq" and that America's national interest had "never implied a commitment to bring the blessings of liberty to the Arab world."[121] One must either read Irving Kristol out of neoconservatism or acknowledge that engagement with Strauss's ideas did not necessarily produce advocacy of America's recent invasions and attempts at remaking foreign nations.

CONCLUSION: CONSTITUTIONAL CONSERVATISM, ORIGINALISM, AND THE CONSERVATIVE POLITICAL COALITION

From the foregoing, it is apparent that major variants of post–World War II American conservatism were never entirely satisfied with American constitutionalism at the level of principle, and certainly not with its trajectory since the dawn of Progressivism and the victory of the New Deal (or perhaps even since Lincoln). Additionally, conservatives continue routinely to disagree about the meaning of American principles and history, and heatedly to debate issues such as abortion, foreign affairs, and the proper extent of economic regulation. Yet, despite these tensions, conservatives also have consistently recognized that their opposition to modern liberalism required compromise and cooperation with one another. After World War II they welded themselves into a coalition that ascended politically and remained stable until quite recently. This coalition was possible because the differing types of American conservatives thought that defending their principles required defending American constitutionalism, at least in part. Just this ecumenical function of the Constitution was displayed in the pages of *National Review* throughout the middle decades of the twentieth century, as a recent study has shown. There, the Constitution helped conservatives come together in recognition of their affinities and their common cause against modern liberalism. Such practical accord was always one of William F. Buckley, Jr.'s goals for the publication, and defense of the Constitution cohered the conservative coalition as it advanced through the decades.[122]

A significant aspect of conservative constitutional coherence from the 1960s through the 1980s was the idea of originalism. It emerged initially in response to the Warren Court and was understood primarily as a way to effectuate judicial restraint and judicial deference to legislatures.[123] Originalism thus accorded with conservatism insofar as it favored stability, or constitutional change that was formal and slow, rather than innovative judicial decisions that revised existing law in the direction of modern liberalism. But since the last decade of the twentieth century, originalism moved beyond this reactive opposition to a judiciary dominated by liberalism. Indeed, it has gained significant influence on the Supreme Court and in the legal academy. Along the way it has become more intellectually sophisticated and less inclined simply to insist on judicial restraint or deference.[124] At the jurisprudential level, de-emphasizing restraint was based on the proposition that, if the Constitution is indeed a written fundamental law whose original meaning can be known, judges should actively enforce it. "The primary virtue claimed by the new originalism is one of constitutional fidelity, not of judicial restraint or democratic majoritarianism."[125]

Another major development in originalist theory has been emphasis on the "public meaning" of the constitutional text rather than the older idea of "intent." It remains a matter of disagreement whether this shift is a slight refinement or a major departure. But in combination with various other moves in the ongoing evolution of originalism, this change indicates a theoretical enterprise that is both fertile and increasingly diffuse. Some observers now claim that originalism has become a "smorgasbord of distinct constitutional theories that share little in common except a misleading reliance on a single label."[126] It is said to have morphed into mutually conflicting variants that are incapable of delivering on the initial originalist promise of constraining judicial interpretive discretion, and which may have become nothing more than a rationalization of desired results.[127] On this view, the major problem is "internal incoherence" and a capaciousness, perhaps even a "scholasticism," which may make it difficult to distinguish originalism from the "living constitutionalism" it first attempted to combat.[128] One response to these developments, most closely associated with the work of Lawrence Solum, is to acknowledge the variation in originalist theories while attempting to delineate the core claims on which all types seem to agree.[129] Another is to forthrightly acknowledge that originalism as a method of constitutional interpretation cannot be expected always to produce results that conservatives like. There has always been a gap between the Constitution and the political desires of various kinds of conservatism.[130]

Many of the issues involved in the relationship between conservatism, constitutionalism, and originalism were embodied in the landmark decision of *District of Columbia v. Heller* (2008). Justice Antonin Scalia's majority opinion invoked and practiced "public meaning" originalism, appealing primarily to historical evidence in overturning a gun control law that was reviled by most contemporary political conservatives. In this instance, originalism was the jurisprudential tool of conservatives in power rather than the doctrine of resistance to judicial "activism" it was when it emerged several decades ago.

Evaluation of *Heller* necessarily involves consideration of whether Scalia got the history right in claiming that the original meaning of the Second Amendment was to recognize a pre-existing individual right of armed self-defense that need not be tied to militia service. This question cannot be fully plumbed here, but unsurprisingly, Scalia has been relentlessly attacked for reaching the wrong historical conclusion,[131] and for reaching the right historical conclusion despite inadequately presenting the available evidence.[132]

If Scalia's historical conclusions are deemed unpersuasive—a judgment which presumes that true knowledge of the past can be apprehended and restated—such "flawed practice" is not proof that originalism as a theory is a mere rationalization of conservative results. Rather, it is proof that the theory has been misused or abused, as any theory can be.[133] But, as a corollary, admitting that *Heller* contains bad history would "substantially undermine" the claim that the decision was made on the basis of originalism.[134]

Of course it was precisely Scalia's firm conviction of historical accuracy that was offered as the basis of the opinion. Originalism overcame ambiguity, or the notion of plausible but opposed interpretations, that earlier conservatives had insisted should mandate judicial restraint and deference to the legislature.[135] To be sure, when original meaning can be accurately known, few contemporary originalists would deny that it should be vigorously enforced. But the tumult surrounding *Heller* should remind originalists that they ought not to pretend that the historical record is clearer than it is. To do so substitutes a faux determinacy for the rational defense of discretion and judgment that can never be eliminated from jurisprudence.[136]

Just as Supreme Court Justices should be called to account for manipulating originalist method as much as any other, conservatives should not expect originalism honestly applied always to yield their favored outcome. Originalism aims to preserve the political choices embodied in the text of the Constitution, and if it produces results that are unpalatable to conservatives, that is what the Constitution requires. Still, originalism remains connected to conservatism at a more general level: it aims to abide by past political settlements and the ways that those settlements, as written into the Constitution, constrain the range of legitimate political action.

Notwithstanding the continued prominence of originalism and conservatism in constitutional discourse, and despite some conservative electoral victories, the liberal achievements of the New Deal and Great Society remain secure. It now seems plain that the conservative ascendance occurred within the parameters of the regulatory-welfare state, and that the conservative "victory" in American politics was decidedly incomplete or attenuated.[137] Additionally, commentators of all stripes have noted the increasing fractiousness of the conservative coalition in the post–Cold War

era, particularly during and since the George W. Bush administration. Many conservatives were dissatisfied with interventionist
domestic initiatives like the No Child Left Behind policy and international ones such as the War on Terror. Also readily apparent was
the disarray resulting from the loss of the 2008 and 2012 presidential elections and the reform agenda of the Obama administration.

In these challenging circumstances it is notable that conservatives are again emphasizing the Constitution. "Constitutional conservatism" is being offered as the basis for unity and as the best
way to oppose modern liberalism. In the words of one such statement, "having tried almost everything else, perhaps conservatives
should consider the Constitution again."[138] Another high-profile
effort says succinctly that: "A Constitutional conservatism unites
all conservatives through the natural fusion provided by American
principles."[139] If conservative political influence still depends on
ecumenism and coalition building, as it did in the past, the Constitution might again foster them.[140] In light of the evidence presented here, however, there are limits to how much conservatives
can reconcile themselves to the original meaning of the Constitution, to the changes it underwent in the twentieth century, and to
one another.

NOTES

The support of the Earhart Foundation during the preparation of this
chapter is gratefully acknowledged.

1. This topic is not mentioned in a helpful recent overview of the literature; Julian E. Zelizer, "Rethinking the History of American Conservatism," *Reviews in American History* 38 (June 2010): 367–392. An important exception called on below is Ken I. Kersch, "Ecumenicalism Through
Constitutionalism: The Discursive Development of Constitutional Conservatism in *National Review,* 1955–1980," *Studies in American Political Development* 25 (April 2011): 86–116.

2. Gordon J. Schochet, "Constitutionalism, Liberalism and the Study
of Politics," in *NOMOS XX: Constitutionalism,* ed. J. Roland Pennock and
John W. Chapman (New York: New York University Press, 1979), 14 note
11, says constitutionalism is very nearly an "essentially contested concept."
See also David T. ButleRitchie, "The Confines of Modern Constitutionalism," *Pierce Law Review* 3 (Issue 1, 2004): 1–6.

3. In this sense I have been influenced by Philip Bobbitt, *Constitutional Fate: Theory of the Constitution* (New York: Oxford University Press, 1984).

4. Steven Kautz, Arthur Melzer, Jerry Weinberger, and M. Richard Zinman, "Introduction: The Idea of Constitutionalism," in *The Supreme Court and the Idea of Constitutionalism,* ed. Steven Kautz, Arthur Melzer, Jerry Weinberger, and M. Richard Zinman (Philadelphia: University of Pennsylvania Press, 2009), 4; Keith E. Whittington, "Constitutional Constraints in Politics," same volume, 233.

5. Whittington, "Constitutional Constraints," 225, 232.

6. Herman Belz, *A Living Constitution or Fundamental Law? American Constitutionalism in Historical Perspective* (Lanham, MD: Rowman & Littlefield, 1998), 33–34; see also Benjamin F. Wright, "Traditionalism in American Political Thought," *International Journal of Ethics* 48 (October 1937): 86–97.

7. A similar point is made in Nathan Tarcov, "Ideas of Constitutionalism Ancient and Modern," in *The Supreme Court,* 11–29, which has been of much help.

8. Walter F. Murphy, *Constitutional Democracy: Creating and Maintaining a Just Constitutional Order* (Baltimore, MD: Johns Hopkins University Press, 2006), ix–x, 536.

9. M. J. C. Vile, *Constitutionalism and the Separation of Powers,* 2nd ed. (Indianapolis, IN: Liberty Fund, 1998), 1–41; Gordon S. Wood, *The Creation of the American Republic, 1776–1787* (New York: Norton, 1972), 574–592; Martin Diamond, *As Far As Republican Principles Will Admit,* ed. William A. Schambra (Washington, DC: AEI, 1992), 58–67; Scott Gordon, *Controlling the State: Constitutionalism from Ancient Athens to Today* (Cambridge, MA: Harvard University Press, 1999), 80–84; Harvey C. Mansfield, Jr., *America's Constitutional Soul* (Baltimore, MD: Johns Hopkins University Press, 1991), 115–116.

10. For example, Paul A. Rahe, *Republics Ancient and Modern, Vol. I* (Chapel Hill: University of North Carolina Press, 1994), 152; Mansfied, *Soul,* 119; Vile, *Constitutionalism,* 16, 19–20, 37–40; Wood, *Creation,* 602–604; Mary P. Nichols, *Citizens and Statesmen: A Study of Aristotle's Politics* (Lanham, MD: Rowman & Littlefield, 1992), 102; Jan-Erik Lane, *Constitutions and Political Theory* (Manchester: Manchester University Press, 1996), 23–24.

11. David Wootton, "Liberty, Metaphor, and Mechanism: 'Checks and Balances' and the Origins of Modern Constitutionalism," in *Liberty and American Experience in the Eighteenth Century,* ed. David Womersley (Indianapolis, IN: Liberty Fund, 2006), 209–274.

12. Tarcov, "Ideas of Constitutionalism," 13, 14, 16, 29; Gordon, *Controlling the State,* 16–18, 79–80, 276–283, 307–312. Gordon sometimes used "countervailance" interchangeably with "checks and balances."

13. Vile, *Constitutionalism*, 38–40; Sotirios A. Barber, "Notes on Constitutional Maintenance," in *Constitutional Politics: Essays on Constitution Making, Maintenance, and Change*, ed. Sotirios A. Barber and Robert P. George (Princeton, NJ: Princeton University Press, 2001), 163; Diamond, *Republican Principles*, 60–61; Tarcov, "Ideas of Constitutionalism," 11–18; Nichols, *Citizens and Statesmen*, 100–104, 119, 123.

14. This is a major theme of Vile, *Constitutionalism*, esp. 40–41; Wood, *Creation*, 604; Mansfield, *Soul*, 122, 124.

15. Fred D. Miller, Jr., "Aristotle and American Classical Republicanism," in *Justice v. Law in Greek Political Thought*, ed. Leslie G. Rubin (Lanham, MD: Rowman & Littlefield, 1997), 183–194; Rahe, *Republics, Vol. II*, 181–182, 207–213; Diamond, *Republican Principles*, 58–63.

16. Jacob E. Cook, ed., *The Federalist* (Hanover, NH: Wesleyan University Press, 1961): No. 9, 51; No. 51, 347–348, 349.

17. *Federalist* No. 48, 335. See also No. 45, 310, where Publius writes of "balance" in the context of the relations between the states and the federal government.

18. *Federalist* No. 71, 484. See also *Federalist* No. 49, 341, which adverts to "maintaining the constitutional equilibrium of the government."

19. Thus, to some extent balance among components that are defined in the constitution is inseparable from the idea of restraint, as discussed in more detail below. Vile, *Constitutionalism*, 15; Alfred H. Kelly, Winfred A. Harbison, and Herman Belz, *The American Constitution: Its Origins and Development*, 7th ed. (New York: Norton, 1991), xx.

20. Tarcov, "Ideas of Constitutionalism," 16–18.

21. *Federalist* No. 51, 349.

22. *Federalist* No. 63, 425; *Federalist* No. 71, 482; Mansfield, *Soul*, 16, 212–213.

23. Diamond, *Republican Principles*, 63–67.

24. Helpful overviews of these realignments (though not focused on the idea of balance) are Barry Friedman, "The Cycles of Constitutional Theory," *Law and Contemporary Problems* 67 (Summer 2004): 149–174; and Raymond Tatalovich, Travis Cook, and Scott Yenor, "The Constitutional Presidency: Conservative Scholarship and Energy in the Executive," in *The Presidency Then and Now*, ed. Phillip G. Henderson (Lanham, MD: Rowman & Littlefield, 2000), 95–113.

25. Carl J. Friedrich, "Constitutions and Constitutionalism," in *International Encyclopedia of the Social Sciences, Vol. 3*, ed. David L. Sills (New York: Macmillan/Free Press, 1968), 318, 319–320; Whittington, "Constitutional Constraints," 221; Charles Howard McIlwain, *Constitutionalism: Ancient and Modern*, Rev. ed. (Ithaca, NY: Cornell University Press, 1947),

21–22; Giovanni Sartori, "Constitutionalism: A Preliminary Discussion," *American Political Science Review* 56 (December 1962): 853–864; Graham Maddox, "Constitutions," in *Political Innovation and Conceptual Change*, ed. Terrence Ball, James Farr, and Russell L. Hanson (Cambridge: Cambridge University Press, 1989), 51–52, 57; Brian Z. Tamanaha, *On the Rule of Law: History, Politics, Theory* (Cambridge: Cambridge University Press, 2004), 114–126.

26. Tarcov, "Ideas of Constitutionalism," 13, 14–16, 18; Judith N. Shklar, "Political Theory and the Rule of Law," in *The Rule of Law: Ideal or Ideology*, ed. Allan C. Hutchinson and Patrick Monahan (Toronto: Carswell, 1987), 3–4; Judith A. Swanson, "Aristotle on How to Preserve a Regime," in *Justice v. Law*, 154–159, 168–169; Tamanaha, *On the Rule of Law*, 7–10; Nichols, *Citizens and Statesmen*, 8, 71–72, 78–79.

27. Steven Kautz, "On Liberal Constitutionalism," in *The Supreme Court*, 30–51; Schochet, "Constitutionalism," 1; Shklar, "Political Theory," 12, 16; Diamond, *Republican Principles*, 232; Lane, *Constitutions*, 50, 58.

28. Schochet, "Constitutionalism," 4, 13 note 6, and 10–11; Gerald Stourzh, "Constitution: Changing Meanings of the Term from the Early Seventeenth to the Late Eighteenth Century," in *Conceptual Change and the Constitution*, ed. Terrence Ball and J. G. A. Pocock (Lawrence: University Press of Kansas, 1988), 46–48; Belz, *Living Constitution*, 1–3; Tamanaha, *On the Rule of Law*, 55–56.

29. Tarcov, "Ideas of Constitutionalism," 27–28; Whittington, "Constitutional Constraints," 230–231; Barber, "Constitutional Maintenance," 164; Mansfield, *Soul*, 125–126.

30. See generally, Johnathan O'Neill, *Originalism in American Law and Politics: A Constitutional History* (Baltimore, MD: Johns Hopkins University Press, 2005); see also Belz, *Living Constitution*, 2–3, 9–12, 34–36, 229–230; Schochet, "Constitutionalism," 10–11.

31. *District of Columbia v. Heller*, 128 S. Ct. 2783 (2008).

32. Robert W. Bennett and Lawrence B. Solum, *Constitutional Originalism: A Debate* (Ithaca, NY: Cornell University Press, 2011), esp. 2–4, 18–20, 36–40. See also Lawrence B. Solum, "What Is Originalism? The Evolution of Contemporary Originalist Theory," in *The Challenge of Originalism: Essays in Constitutional Theory*, ed. Grant E. Huscroft and Bradley W. Miller (Cambridge: Cambridge University Press, 2011), 12–41. These two volumes illustrate the ongoing development of originalism and its continued influence, and Solum's contributions are among the very best recent work on originalism.

33. Whittington, "Constitutional Constraints," 232, 233.

34. Tarcov, "Ideas of Constitutionalism," 18–19, 28, 29; Rahe, *Republics, Vol. I*, 10 and generally. See also, Nichols, *Citizens and Statesmen*, 160–163.

35. Rahe, *Republics, Vol. II*, 36, 248–249; *Vol. III*, 236.

36. Rahe, *Republics, Vol. III*, 236–237, 240; Lorraine Smith Pangle and Thomas Pangle, *The Learning of Liberty: The Educational Ideas of the American Founders* (Lawrence: University Press of Kansas, 1993), generally; Johnathan O'Neill, "Constitutional Maintenance and Religious Sensibility in the 1920s: Rethinking the Constitutionalist Response to Progressivism," *Journal of Church and State* 51 (Winter 2009): 24–51; Belz, *Living Constitution*, 77–127; Susan Jacoby, *The Age of American Unreason* (New York: Pantheon, 2008), 298–301.

37. *Federalist* No. 49, 340.

38. C. Bradley Thompson, "James Madison and the Idea of Fundamental Law," in *America and Enlightenment Constitutionalism*, ed. Gary L. McDowell and Johnathan O'Neill (New York: Palgrave Macmillan, 2006), 261. A fine analysis of this issue is Charles R. Kesler, "Natural Law and the Constitution: *The Federalist's* View," in *Constitutionalism in Perspective: The United States Constitution in Twentieth Century Politics*, ed. Sarah Baumgartner Thurow (Lanham, MD: University Press of America, 1988), 166, 172–173, 178.

39. In addition to *Federalist* No. 49 and Lincoln, see W. Y. Elliot, "The Constitution as the American Social Myth," in *The Constitution Reconsidered*, ed. Conyers Read (New York: Columbia University Press, 1938), 209–224; O'Neill, "Constitutional Maintenance and Religious Sensibility."

40. Sanford Levinson, *Our Undemocratic Constitution* (New York: Oxford University Press, 2006), 16–20.

41. The best recent treatment is Ross J. Corbett, *The Lockean Commonwealth* (Albany: State University of New York Press, 2009).

42. Harvey C. Mansfield, Jr., *Taming the Prince: The Ambivalence of Modern Executive Power*, Paper ed. (Baltimore, MD: Johns Hopkins University Press, 1999).

43. Clinton Rossiter, *Constitutional Dictatorship: Crisis Government in Modern Democracies* (Princeton, NJ: Princeton University Press, 1948); John E. Finn, *Constitutions in Crisis: Political Violence and the Rule of Law* (New York: Oxford University Press, 1991). See also Carl J. Friedrich, *Constitutional Reason of State: The Survival of the Constitutional Order* (Providence, RI: Brown University Press, 1957).

44. Mansfield's seminal *Taming the Prince* outlined these key issues. See also Benjamin A. Kleinerman, *The Discretionary President: The Promise and Peril of Executive Power* (Lawrence: University Press of Kansas, 2009); Clement Fatovic, *Outside the Law: Emergency and Executive Power* (Baltimore, MD: Johns Hopkins University Press, 2009).

45. Kautz et al., "Introduction: The Idea of Constitutionalism," 3, 4.

46. Quote from Walter F. Murphy, "Constitutions, Constitutionalism, and Democracy," in *Constitutionalism and Democracy: Transitions in the Contemporary World*, ed. Douglas Greenberg, Stanley N. Katz, Melanie Beth Oliviero, and Steven C. Wheatley (New York: Oxford University Press, 1993), 6; see also Wright, "Traditionalism," 87.

47. Paul Sigmund, "Carl Friedrich's Contribution to the Theory of Constitutionalism—Comparative Government," in *NOMOS XX: Constitutionalism*, 41; O'Neill, *Originalism*, 215–216.

48. Belz, *Living Constitution*, 10–11, 33–34, 154.

49. Whittington, "Constitutional Constraints," 232.

50. Wright, "Traditionalism," 86–87, 88–89; Claude S. Fischer, *Made in America: A Social History of American Culture and Character* (Chicago: University of Chicago Press, 2010), 241–242; Leo P. Ribuffo, "Rediscovering American Conservatism Again," History News Network (May 21, 2007), available online at: http://hnn.us/; Russell Kirk, *The Conservative Mind, from Burke to Eliot*, 3rd rev. ed., 6th printing (Chicago: H. Regnery, [1960] 1964), 96, 98. Originally published as Kirk, *The Conservative Mind, from Burke to Santayana* (Chicago: H. Regnery, 1953).

51. McIlwain, *Constitutionalism*, 143.

52. Maddox, "Constitutions," 62–64; ButleRitchie, "Confines," generally. See also Murphy, "Constitutions, Constitutionalism," 6.

53. Nichols, *Citizens and Statesmen*, 85–123. See also Swanson, "Aristotle," 168.

54. Edmund Burke, *Reflections on the Revolution in France: A Critical Edition*, ed. J. C. D. Clark (Stanford, CA: Stanford University Press, 2001), 170.

55. *McCulloch v. Maryland*, 17 U.S. 615, 415 (1819).

56. Carl J. Friedrich, *Limited Government: A Comparison* (Englewood Cliffs, NJ: Prentice Hall, 1974), 47; and Levinson, *Our Undemocratic*, 20–22, 159–166.

57. Murphy, *Constitutional Democracy*, 333.

58. Ibid., 505–508, 523–524.

59. Two histories of recent American conservatism from the traditionalist perspective are Paul Edward Gottfried, *Conservatism in America: Making Sense of the American Right* (New York: Palgrave Macmillan, 2007) and Joseph Scotchie, *Revolt from the Heartland: The Struggle for an Authentic Conservatism* (New Brunswick, NJ: Transaction, 2002).

60. Russell Kirk, *Rights and Duties: Reflections on Our Conservative Constitution* (Dallas, TX: Spence, 1997). For an overview of Carey's work, see Bruce P. Frohnen and Kenneth L. Grasso, eds., *Defending the Republic: Constitutional Morality in a Time of Crisis* (Wilmington, DE: ISI, 2008); Bruce P. Frohnen, *Virtue and the Promise of Conservatism: The Legacy of Burke and Tocqueville* (Lawrence: University Press of Kansas, 1993).

61. M. E. Bradford, *Remembering Who We Are: Observations of a Southern Conservative* (Athens: University of Georgia Press, 1985). See also Eugene D. Genovese, *The Southern Tradition: The Achievements and Limitations of an American Conservatism* (Cambridge, MA: Harvard University Press, 1994).

62. For this argument see especially Russell Kirk, *The Roots of American Order*, 3rd ed. (Washington, DC: Regnery Gateway, 1991). See also Donald S. Lutz, *The Origins of American Constitutionalism* (Baton Rouge: Louisiana State University Press, 1988).

63. For example, Kirk, *Rights and Duties*, 95–109, 119–120; Bruce P. Frohnen, "George Carey on Constitutions, Constitutionalism, and Tradition," in *Defending the Republic*, 27, 28; Bradford, *Remembering*, 41–42.

64. M. E. Bradford, "The Heresy of Equality: Bradford Replies to Jaffa," *Modern Age* 20 (Winter 1976): 62–77; Willmoore Kendall and George W. Carey, *The Basic Symbols of the American Political Tradition* (Washington, DC: Catholic University Press, [1970] 1995), generally; Bruce P. Frohnen and Kenneth L. Grasso, "Editors' Introduction," in *Defending the Republic*, xi–xii, xxi–xxii.

65. Willmoore Kendall and George W. Carey, "Preface," in *The Basic Symbols*, xxii–xxiii; M. E. Bradford, *Original Intentions: On the Making and Ratification of the United States Constitution* (Athens: University of Georgia Press, 1993), 33, 104–105; Frohnen, "George Carey on Constitutions," 19–20.

66. This same basic idea, sans the reference to Oakeshott, was central to Kirk's understanding of American constitutionalism. See, for example, Kirk, *Rights and Duties*, 15–16.

67. For example, Frohnen, "George Carey on Constitutions," 34–35.

68. This is a primary theme of Kendall and Carey, *Basic Symbols*.

69. Mark C. Henrie, "Traditionalism," in *American Conservatism: An Encyclopedia*, ed. Bruce P. Frohnen, Jeremy Beer, and Jeffrey O. Nelson (Wilmington, DE: ISI, 2006), 873.

70. Bruce P. Frohnen, "Law's Culture: Conservatism and the American Constitutional Order," *Harvard Journal of Law and Public Policy* 27 (Spring 2004): 459–488.

71. George W. Carey, "The Constitution and Community," in *Community and Tradition: Conservative Perspectives on the American Experience*, ed. George W. Carey and Bruce P. Frohnen (Lanham, MD: Rowman & Littlefield, 1998), 63–84; George W. Carey, "The Philadelphia Constitution: Dead or Alive?" in *The End of Democracy II? A Crisis of Legitimacy*, ed. Mitchell S. Muncy (Dallas, TX: Spence, 1999), 229–251; Kirk, *Rights and Duties*, 30–31, 136, 256; Frohnen, *Virtue*, 70, 211–212; Frohnen, "Law's Culture," 474–481, 487–488.

72. Kendall and Carey, *Basic Symbols*, 141–142, 147–150; Frohnen, "George Carey on Constitutions," 23, 29–31.

73. Kendall and Carey, *Basic Symbols*, 153 (quote) and Claes G. Ryn, "Neo-Jacobin Nationalism or Responsible Nationhood?" in *Defending the Republic*, 263–281; Gary L. Gregg II, "Whiggism and Presidentialism: American Ambivalence toward Executive Power," in *Presidency Then and Now*, 69–94; Scotchie, *Revolt from the Heartland*, chapter 6. See also Gottfried, *Conservatism in America*, and Bruce Fein, *Constitutional Peril: The Life and Death Struggle for Our Constitution and Democracy* (New York: Palgrave Macmillan, 2008).

74. Carey, "Philadelphia Constitution," 245, 250; Carey, "The Constitution and Community," 84; Paul Edward Gottfried, "Making Sense of Majoritarianism," in *Defending the Republic*, 15; Gary L. Gregg II, "No Presidential Republic: Representation, Deliberation, and Executive Power in The Federalist Papers," in *Defending the Republic*, 151.

75. Henrie, "Traditionalism," 872.

76. Helpful overviews of American libertarianism called on in the next two paragraphs are David Boaz, *Libertarianism: A Primer* (New York: Free Press, 1997) and Charles Murray, *What It Means To Be a Libertarian: A Personal Interpretation* (New York: Broadway Books, 1997). For a history, see Brian Doherty, *Radicals for Capitalism: A Freewheeling History of the Modern Libertarian Movement* (New York: Public Affairs, 2007).

77. Quoted in Michael Wreszin, *The Superfluous Anarchist: Albert Jay Nock* (Providence, RI: Brown University Press, 1971), 59. This paragraph draws from my earlier treatment of Nock in "The First Conservatives: The Constitutional Challenge to Progressivism," *The Heritage Foundation First Principles Series* 39 (July 5, 2011), available online at: http://www.heritage.org/research/reports/2011/06/the-first-conservatives-the-constitutional-challenge-to-progressivism.

78. Albert Jay Nock, *Our Enemy, The State* (New York: Morrow, 1935), 130 (quote), 140, 142, 145, 173–174.

79. Ibid., 52 note 12, 176–177, 180.

80. Murray N. Rothbard, *The Betrayal of the American Right* (Auburn, AL: Ludwig von Mises Institute, 2007), xii.

81. Friedrich A. Hayek, *The Constitution of Liberty* (Chicago: University of Chicago Press, 1960), quotes at 182, 192.

82. Charles Wolfe, "Libertarians and the Constitution," *Freeman* 6 (September 1956), available online at: www.thefreemanonline.org.

83. *Palm Beach Times*, "Twilight of the Republic?" editorial reprinted in *Freeman* 8 (July 1958): 13–16, available online at: www.thefreemanonline.org. A similar analysis is offered in Kersch, "Ecumenicalism," 5.

84. Richard A. Epstein, *Takings: Private Property and the Power of Eminent Domain* (Cambridge, MA: Harvard University Press, 1985), 20, 29.

85. Richard A. Epstein, "Self-Interest and the Constitution," in *The Libertarian Reader*, ed. David Boaz (New York: Free Press, 1997), 42, 48. See also Richard A. Epstein, *How Progressives Rewrote the Constitution* (Washington, DC: Cato Institute, 2006), 134–136.

86. Bernard H. Siegan, *The Supreme Court's Constitution* (New Brunswick, NJ: Transaction, 1987), xi, 179–180.

87. Randy E. Barnett, *Restoring the Lost Constitution: The Presumption of Liberty* (Princeton, NJ: Princeton University Press, 2004), 5, 356.

88. Bernard H. Siegan, *Economic Liberties and the Constitution*, 2nd ed. (New Brunswick, NJ: Transaction, 2006), 204–225; Epstein, *How Progressives*, 66–77; Epstein, "Self-Interest," 44–45; Barnett, *Restoring*, 312–317.

89. Epstein, "Self-Interest," 45; Barnett, *Restoring*, 315.

90. Epstein, "Self-Interest," 45. See also Siegan, *Economic Liberties*, 81–82; Boaz, *Libertarianism*, 120–121.

91. Epstein, *Takings*, 112 (quote); Epstein, *How Progressives*, 44–51; Barnett, *Restoring*, 204–219, 319–334.

92. Barnett, *Restoring*, 211–215; Siegan, *Economic Liberties*, 108–109, 136–141; Epstein, "Self-Interest," 47; Epstein, *How Progressives*, 48. See also David E. Bernstein, *Rehabilitating Lochner: Defending Individual Rights against Progressive Reform* (Chicago: University of Chicago Press, 2011).

93. Barnett, *Restoring*, 334. See also Boaz, *Libertarianism*, 242.

94. Barnett, *Restoring*, 53–86.

95. Epstein, *Takings*, 30–31; Barnett, *Restoring*, 266–269.

96. Doherty, *Radicals*, 3, 21.

97. Boaz, *Libertarianism*, 125, 126 (quote).

98. Two helpful overviews are Thomas L. Pangle, *Leo Strauss: An Introduction to His Thought and Intellectual Legacy* (Baltimore, MD: Johns Hopkins University Press, 2006) and Catherine and Michael Zuckert, *The Truth about Leo Strauss: Political Philosophy and American Democracy* (Chicago: University of Chicago Press, 2006). See also Kenneth L. Deutsch and John A. Murley, eds., *Leo Strauss, the Straussians, and the American Regime* (Lanham, MD: Rowman & Littlefield, 1999). These and other recent works inform my treatment in Johnathan O'Neill, "Straussian Constitutional History and the Straussian Political Project," *Rethinking History: The Journal of Theory and Practice* 13 (Issue 4: Politics and History, 2009): 459–478, which I draw from in this section and which is available at the Journal's website: www.tandfonline.com.

99. Hilail Gildin, ed., *An Introduction to Political Philosophy: Ten Essays by Leo Strauss* (Detroit, MI: Wayne State University Press, 1989), 81.

100. Ibid., 81–98.

101. William A. Galston, "Leo Strauss's Qualified Embrace of Liberal Democracy," in *The Cambridge Companion to Leo Strauss*, ed. Steven B. Smith (Cambridge: Cambridge University Press, 2009), 193–214.

102. Leo Strauss, *Liberalism, Ancient and Modern* (New York: Basic, 1968), 24.

103. Zuckert and Zuckert, *Truth*, 58–79, 197–202.

104. James W. Ceaser, *Designing a Polity: America's Constitution in Theory and Practice* (Lanham, MD: Rowman & Littlefield, 2011), 49.

105. Charles R. Kesler, "A New Birth of Freedom: Harry V. Jaffa and the Study of America," in *Leo Strauss, the Straussians*, 276–277.

106. Zuckert and Zuckert, *Truth*, 239–252, quote at 251.

107. For example, Ronald J. Pestritto, *Woodrow Wilson and the Roots of Modern Liberalism* (Lanham, MD: Rowman & Littlefield, 2005); Christopher Wolfe, *The Rise of Modern Judicial Review: From Judicial Interpretation to Judge-Made Law*, Rev. ed. (Lanham, MD: Rowman & Littlefield, 1994); Thomas L. Krannawitter, *Vindicating Lincoln: Defending the Politics of Our Greatest President* (Lanham, MD: Rowman & Littlefield, 2008); Harry V. Jaffa, *Storm over the Constitution* (Lanham, MD: Lexington Books, 1999).

108. Michael Zuckert, "Straussians," in *Cambridge Companion*, 280–286.

109. Ceaser, *Designing a Polity*, 47–48.

110. Thomas L. Pangle, *The Ennobling of Democracy: The Challenge of the Postmodern Age* (Baltimore, MD: Johns Hopkins University Press, 1992), 216.

111. Ibid., 148–154. See also Pangle and Pangle, *Learning of Liberty*.

112. Ceaser also observes the Eastern emphasis on Tocqueville in *Designing a Polity*, 50. For example, Pangle, *Ennobling Democracy*, 206, 213–216; Mansfield, *Soul*, 177–192; Robert P. Kraynak, "Tocqueville's Constitutionalism," *American Political Science Review* 81 (December 1987): 1175–1195; James W. Ceaser, *Liberal Democracy and Political Science* (Baltimore, MD: Johns Hopkins University Press, 1990).

113. Mansfield, *Soul*, 16.

114. Ibid., 192.

115. Strauss, *Liberalism*, 24.

116. Ceaser, *Designing a Polity*, 50.

117. Justin Vaisse, *Neoconservatism: The Biography of a Movement* (Cambridge, MA: Belknap Press of Harvard University Press, 2010), 271.

118. Ken I. Kersch, "Neoconservatives and the Courts: The Public Interest, 1965–1980," in *Ourselves and Our Posterity: Essays in Constitutional Originalism*, ed. Bradley C. S. Watson (Lanham, MD: Lexington Books, 2009), 247–296, especially 292. Kersch points to the Straussian Martin Diamond,

whose work occasionally appeared in neoconservative publications, as the harbinger of this development. See also Kersch, "Ecumenicalism," 8.

119. Irving Kristol, *On the Democratic Idea in America* (New York: Harper and Row, 1972), vii (quote), ix.

120. Ceaser, *Designing a Polity*, 49, 143–144.

121. As quoted in Vaisse, *Neoconservatism*, 5. See also at 272 and Zuckert and Zuckert, *Truth*, 263–266.

122. Kersch, "Ecumenicalism," generally.

123. Keith E. Whittington, "The New Originalism," *Georgetown Journal of Law and Public Policy* 2 (Summer 2004): 602; O'Neill, *Originalism*, 192; Kersch, "Ecumenicalism," 18.

124. O'Neill, *Originalism*, 204.

125. Whittington, "New Originalism," 609.

126. Thomas B. Colby and Peter J. Smith, "Living Originalism," *Duke Law Journal* 59 (November 2009): 239, 244.

127. Ibid., 300, 305, 307.

128. Joel Alicea, "Forty Years of Originalism," *Policy Review* 173 (June/July 2012): 69, 76; Steven D. Smith, "That Old-Time Originalism," in *Challenge of Originalism*, 227, 230.

129. See Bennett and Solum, *Constitutional Originalism*, and Solum, "What Is Originalism?"

130. Keith E. Whittington, "Is Originalism Too Conservative?" *Harvard Journal of Law and Public Policy* 34 (Winter 2010): 29, 32–34, 37.

131. Saul Cornell, "*Heller*, New Originalism, and Law Office History: 'Meet the New Boss, Same as the Old Boss,'" *UCLA Law Review* 56 (June 2009): 1095–1125.

132. Nelson Lund, "The Second Amendment, *Heller*, and Originalist Jurisprudence," *UCLA Law Review* 56 (June 2009): 1343–1376.

133. Whittington, "Is Originalism," 31.

134. Mark Tushnet, "*Heller* and the New Originalism," *Ohio State Law Journal* 69 (Issue 4, 2008): 609, 611 note 13.

135. J. Harvie Wilkinson III, "Of Guns, Abortions, and the Unraveling Rule of Law," *Virginia Law Review* 95 (April 2009): 253, 265–272.

136. Whittington, "New Originalism," 611; Tushnet, "*Heller* and the New Originalism," 623.

137. Zelizer, "Rethinking"; Stephen Skowronek, "An Attenuated Reconstruction: The Conservative Turn in American Political Development," in *Conservatism and American Political Development*, ed. Brian J. Glenn and Steven M. Teles (New York: Oxford University Press, 2009), 348–363.

138. Charles R. Kesler, "The Constitution, At Last," *National Review* (Special Issue, "What Happened to the Constitution?": May 17, 2010): 24–28.

139. Edwin Meese et al., "The Mount Vernon Statement—Constitutional Conservatism: A Statement for the 21st Century" (February 17, 2010), available online at: www.themountvernonstatement.com.

140. George H. Nash, *Reappraising the Right: The Past and Future of American Conservatism* (Wilmington, DE: ISI, 2009), 336; Peter Berkowitz, "Constitutional Conservatism: A Way Forward for a Troubled Political Coalition," *Policy Review* 153 (February/March 2009): 3–23.

9

FIGHTING OVER THE CONSERVATIVE BANNER

CARL T. BOGUS

Whither Conservatism? It is a question everyone—conservative, liberal, or otherwise—is asking. For many, the question has taken on a sense of almost desperate urgency. Formed in the late 1950s and early 1960s, the modern American conservative movement has become so ideologically extreme, bellicose, and uncompromising, and—by virtue of having gradually but now effectively taken full control of one of the nation's two major political parties—also so powerful that the nation has become nearly ungovernable.[1] Although the public is often slow to recognize and react to challenges, even sober-minded conservatives hope that voters will demand a different kind of conservatism from the people they elect. Meanwhile, conservative intellectuals are beginning to debate what a new conservatism should look like.[2]

We are in such a state of disarray precisely because we are in a time of ideological transition. To a considerable degree, both conservatism and liberalism are victims of their own success. Conservatism saw a significant part of its raison d'être realized when the Cold War was won. It has tried substituting the so-called war on terror—or the war with Islamofascism, as some conservatives tried framing it—but that has not been entirely satisfactory.[3] Similarly, many of modern liberalism's greatest causes—the civil rights, feminist, environmental, and consumer movements—have largely succeeded. Meanwhile, one of its other causes, the war on poverty, has proved intractable. Thus liberalism is also entering a period of searching and redefinition. The transitional period is more convulsive for conservatism because conservatism is more consciously ideological. Liberals eschew ideology and focus on discrete issues of public policy, which, they believe, is more pragmatic and enlightened. Conservatives, by contrast, expend vast quantities of ink thinking about—and debating—what conservatism means. They categorize themselves not merely as conservatives but as particular kinds of conservative. There is no parallel taxonomy for liberals.

Modern American conservatism is a coalition of three main schools of thought: libertarianism, neoconservatism, and religious or social conservatism. These three schools have important commonalities, but they have significant differences as well. In the late 1950s and the 1960s, they were brought together as allies—and even more, to a degree intertwined—by William F. Buckley, Jr., and his colleagues at *National Review.* This came naturally to Buckley because he personally embraced all three ideologies, despite their inconsistencies. One of Buckley's strengths as a leader of a movement was that he lacked the disposition of a political philosopher and was relatively untroubled by ideological contradictions. He permitted debate and disagreement among the three schools of thought, but only within certain parameters. This integrated community of editors, writers, and readers—who acknowledged some differences but emphasized what they had in common— produced a unified movement. Moreover, Buckley became so personally popular and admired, and *National Review* so successful, that during the nascent period of the movement Buckley and the magazine became nearly synonymous with conservatism. Conservatism was pretty much the views that Buckley espoused and *National Review* published.

Over time, two things happened. First, as the conservative movement grew and became more successful, Buckley and *National Review*'s singular influence declined. This was not because they fell from favor; Buckley and his magazine remained respected voices, but they came to be surrounded by other thinkers, journals, and organizations. No longer was conservatism defined by a single magazine and united in a single community. No longer could Buckley set limits on debate or—and as we shall see, this will become important—excommunicate irresponsible groups from the movement. Second, the Berlin Wall fell and the Soviet Union dissolved. The three schools of conservatism had been held together by the powerful gravitational force of anticommunism. With surprising suddenness, that force was gone.

Now, as the three schools of conservative thought separate, the debate among them is becoming more intense and acrimonious. Each wishes to claim the conservative banner—to be recognized as the one, true conservatism—and to deny their rivals that recognition. Meanwhile, internal debates are taking place within each of the three schools as to whether and how it should redefine itself. It is a time of confusion and strife. Before attempting to peer into the future to discern how conservatism may change—and what that means for the nation—it is helpful to spend a little time reflecting on what conservatism was before Buckley, how Buckley and his colleagues reformulated it, and what is happening right now. That is how we shall proceed.

I.

At the risk of mixing political and intellectual history, it may make sense to begin with Calvin Coolidge. Coolidge, of course, served as president from 1923 to 1929. He was Warren G. Harding's vice president, and became president on August 2, 1923, when Harding unexpectedly died. History has not treated Coolidge kindly. According to one survey, historians rank him twenty-fifth among the first forty-four presidents.[4] Some argue that Coolidge's low ranking results from historians unfairly judging him in retrospect.[5] Coolidge sat idle while speculative investments and market bubbles in the economy of the Roaring Twenties set up the Great Depression. Coolidge, however, was following the mainstream economic thought of his day, and he did not have the benefit of Keynesian insights. John Maynard Keynes's *General Theory of Employment, Interest, and Money* was not published until 1936.[6] I am not going to take sides in this debate. What is important for our purposes is that Coolidge was extremely popular at the time. When he stood for election on his own in 1924, he captured 54 percent of the popular vote and 72 percent of the electoral vote in a three-way race against Democrat John W. Davis and Progressive Robert "Fighting Bob" La Follette. When Coolidge decided not to run again four years later, it was because he believed that if reelected he would wind up serving nearly ten years, which, he said, was "longer than any man has had it—too long!"[7] It appears that when he left office the consensus was that Coolidge had been a successful president.[8]

Coolidge was not the hardest-right conservative of his day. Warren G. Harding selected him as his vice-presidential running mate in 1920 because Coolidge was acceptable to both the progressive followers of Teddy Roosevelt and establishment, pro-business Republicans.[9] As governor of Massachusetts, he had been distinctly moderate. But regardless of what they thought of him when he assumed the presidency, because Coolidge governed conservatively and was deemed successful, conservatives surely became pleased with Coolidge's brand of conservatism.

Coolidge is interesting for another reason. Ronald Reagan claimed to have closely studied Coolidge and greatly admired him. One of Reagan's first acts as president was to hang Calvin Coolidge's portrait in the Cabinet Room.[10] It is not difficult to understand why Reagan liked Coolidge. Coolidge pursued a program of what we today would call trickle-down economics. He installed Andrew Mellon as his treasury secretary and generally followed Mellon's advice on economic policy. Through a series of reductions, the Coolidge administration lowered the effective tax rate on those with incomes exceeding $6,000 (the equivalent of about $75,000 today) from 70 percent to 40 percent.[11] Exemptions were also increased to the point that most Americans paid no federal income taxes at all. Federal spending was trimmed, business boomed, and by 1925 the federal budget was in surplus.[12] The Coolidge years were prosperous for most Americans, but the wealthy did particularly well and income inequality increased.[13] Still, Coolidge was hardly the hard-edged, anti-government libertarian of the present day. One of Coolidge's biographers, historian Daniel Greenberg of Rutgers University, argues that Coolidge's economic thinking was driven not by ideology, but by moral sentiments instilled by a New England upbringing that valued thrift, prudence, and fiscal responsibility. For Coolidge, this translated into an economic program of low spending, low taxes, and balanced budgets.[14]

With Mellon as his adviser, Coolidge was certainly pro-business. He preferred "welfare capitalism," as it was called at the time—that is, benefits supplied by employers—to government benefit programs. He cut back on enforcement by the antitrust agencies, the FDA, and the Interstate Commerce Commission. Professor Greenberg persuasively argues, however, that Coolidge followed a moderate laissez-faire vision, not a purist one.[15] He protected American business with import duties, for example, while laissez-faire absolutists believe in unfettered free trade.[16] Moreover, Coolidge supported the expenditure of federal monies for what were then large infrastructure projects, including the construction of the Boulder Dam (later renamed Hoover Dam) on the Colorado and federal buildings for government departments and agencies in Washington, DC, as well as the construction of roads financed by block grants to the states.[17]

Further, if Coolidge was not a modern-day doctrinaire libertarian, he was not what we would today call a religious conservative or a neoconservative either. The modern religious conservative finds religion to be a source not merely of inspiration and humility, but of certainty. For them, religious teachings often provide answers for questions of public policy. Some religious conservatives believe they have been called by God to seek public office. Coolidge was just the opposite. Greenberg writes that Coolidge subscribed to a social gospel Protestantism that filled him with a sense of humility and that he "never deployed Christian teachings as a political weapon."[18] Coolidge supported U.S. membership in the World Court, recognized the revolutionary Obregon government in Mexico (after Obregon agreed to compensate American companies for property seized by his government), vigorously pursued arms control negotiations, and signed the Kellogg-Briand Pact, in which states pledged not to use war to resolve disputes.[19] These policies are more than enough to disqualify Coolidge as a modern-day neoconservative, even if he also pursued other policies they would find more agreeable.

We next take up Herbert Hoover. Despite having become known to history as the ultimate champion of laissez-faire and the archenemy of Franklin Delano Roosevelt, Hoover wound up in that position more through egomania and narcissism than through ideological beliefs. Before becoming president, Hoover made his reputation as a brilliant administrator and a humanitarian. He happened to be in Britain when World War I broke out and took it upon himself to organize a relief effort to provide food for starving people in war-torn Belgium. Along with extraordinary administrative talent, Hoover possessed extreme self-confidence. He was never reluctant to take total command and do whatever he considered necessary, irrespective of whether he had any authority to do so. As he set himself up in this work he declared—in what seems to have become his life-long credo—"it has got to be recognized by everybody . . . that I am the boss, and that any attempts to minimize the importance of my leadership would do . . . infinite harm."[20] From this experience, Hoover also developed a strong belief in the power of private rather than government-directed relief efforts.

In 1917, during the war, Woodrow Wilson asked Congress to create the position of food administrator to provide for the production and distribution of food for both domestic consumption and American troops. Hoover was serving as food czar before Congress acted. When the war ended in 1918, Hoover sailed to Europe to head relief efforts.[21] Not only was he extraordinarily effective in all of these efforts, he was also adept in letting the world know just how extraordinary he had been. The then-assistant secretary of the navy remarked that Hoover "is certainly a wonder, and I wish we could make him President of the United States. There would not be a better one."[22] That man was named Franklin Delano Roosevelt.

Hoover certainly agreed. In 1920, he announced that he was a Republican, and declared that if the party "adopts a forward-looking, liberal, constructive platform on the Treaty [of Versailles, which included the creation of the League of Nations] . . . and is neither reactionary nor radical in its approach to our great domestic questions," he would give the party his entire support. He added that should the party demand that he become president, "I cannot refuse to serve."[23] Hoover entered the California presidential primary, but was trounced.

After Warren G. Harding was elected president later that year, he asked Hoover to be his secretary of commerce. Hoover agreed, but on certain conditions. Because the commerce department, as then constructed, did not offer Hoover adequate opportunities for "constructive national service," Hoover demanded that bureaus in other departments be relocated to Commerce. It was critical, Hoover later wrote in his memoirs, that his portfolio include "business, agriculture, labor, finance, and foreign affairs."[24] Harding reluctantly agreed, over the strenuous objections of other cabinet members who were losing bureaus to Commerce, and to the consternation of right-wing Republicans. "Hoover gives most of us gooseflesh," a Republican senator privately remarked.[25]

During his tenure in the Harding and Coolidge administrations, Hoover cemented his reputation as a progressive. To Andrew Mellon's horror, Hoover declared that he favored a progressive income tax and "a steeply graduated tax on legacies and gifts . . . for the deliberate purpose of disintegrating large fortunes."[26] He published a short book, in which he wrote: "We have long since abandoned the laissez-faire of the 18th Century—the notion that it is 'every man for himself and the devil take the hindmost.'. . . We have also learned that fair division can only be obtained by certain restrictions on the strong and the dominant."[27] Hoover, however, generally preferred that efforts be undertaken by private parties rather than government, and he was strongly supportive of business. He got into a tussle with the attorney general for applying the antitrust laws to trade associations, which Hoover decried as "a perversion of justice."[28]

In 1927, heavy rains caused the Mississippi River to swell, levees broke, and floods engulfed communities along more than a thousand miles of the Mississippi River Valley, causing a disaster of epic proportions. It was a crisis made for Hoover. President Coolidge dispatched him to oversee rescue and relief efforts. Hoover performed so well—and received so much credit for it—that the following year, notwithstanding reservations by the party's right wing, he captured the Republican presidential nomination on the first ballot.[29] The general election was a cakewalk. The nation, under Republicans Harding and Coolidge, seemed to be enjoying unprecedented prosperity. "Given a chance to go forward with the policies of the last eight years, we shall soon with the help of God be in sight of a day when poverty will be banished from the nation," Hoover declaimed at a campaign rally.[30] Hoover beat his Democratic opponent—New York Governor Al Smith—in a landslide.

Despite having made some right-wing appeals during the campaign, Hoover seemed to take office as a progressive.[31] In his first week as president, he remarked that "excessive fortunes are a menace to true liberty."[32] One of his first initiatives was to push though legislation providing federal loans to help small farmers develop alliances so that they could compete with large agricultural companies.[33] Hoover also supported establishing a national institute of health, proposed reforming the banking system, directed the census bureau to begin counting the number of unemployed workers in the country, called a White House conference on the health and protection of children, added two million acres to the national forest reserve, terminated oil exploration on federal lands, and persuaded insurance companies to underwrite pension policies as a precursor to a national system.[34]

Then came October 29, 1929—"Black Tuesday."[35] The stock market crashed and financial markets panicked. This was not a crisis, declared Hoover, but merely a "depression."[36] Though that turned out to be one of the most hapless word choices in history, for a while knowledgeable observers agreed with him. Hoover asked Congress to appropriate $150 million for public work projects (the equivalent of less than $2 billion today), and he asked governors to pursue "energetic but prudent" public work projects in their states.[37] To do more, suggested Hoover, would run up the federal debt and shake business confidence. As time wore on and the situation became increasingly dire—as businesses closed or laid off workers, breadlines formed on the streets, and people who found themselves homeless moved into "Hoovervilles"—the president refused to acknowledge that things were worse than his original diagnosis or that drastic federal action was necessary to reverse the downward spiral. He was acting not as much from an ideological commitment as from cognitive dissonance. He was, quite simply, certain that an approach he adopted could not possibly be wrong. He had already decided that the way to respond was to provide reassurance to business and the financial markets, so that had to be right. When six hundred banks failed during a two-month period at the end of 1931, Hoover responded by promising that federal spending would not exceed revenues. He thought that would be reassuring to business firms and investors. The nation, he explained, was "suffering . . . more from frozen confidence than . . . from frozen income."[38] As time wore on, Congress, economists, and even his own advisers told him that the government had to do more.[39] He refused to listen. In his State of the Union Message in December 1931, he said that it was not necessary to provide a "dole" to the unemployed because "our people have been protected from hunger and cold" by voluntary efforts and the nation's "sense of social responsibility."[40] That this was fatuously wrong did not stop Hoover from believing it.

As dismally as history evaluates Hoover's economic policy, his foreign policy is considered, if anything, even worse.[41] In 1931, Japan seized Manchuria from China. This was in direct violation of the Kellogg-Briand Pact, in which, only four years earlier, fifteen nations—including Japan—agreed not to use military force to resolve disputes. If this use of force was allowed to stand, the pact was as good as dead. Few people blame Hoover for not intervening militarily, but Hoover also nixed proposals to punish Japan with economic sanctions. His utterly flaccid response was to have Secretary of State Henry Stimson tell China and Japan that the United States would not recognize any "agreement"—a euphemism for acquisition of territory—that violated covenants of the Kellogg-Briand Pact. Many believe this emboldened Japan and was a contributing cause of World War II. At roughly the same time, Hoover urged parties at the World Disarmament Conference in Geneva to agree to large cuts in their defense budgets, oblivious to the concerns about rising Nazi political power in Germany. Against the advice of Andrew Mellon, who complained that the president was exceeding his constitutional authority, Hoover said that if European countries would grant an economically desperate Germany a one-year moratorium on war reparation payments, the United States would in turn grant them a one-year suspension on their debt payments to the United States. This initiative, albeit commendable, was inadequate. In all these initiatives, Hoover acted more like a Quaker (as Henry Stimson once noted) than a modern-day neoconservative.[42]

Hoover had come into office in a landslide, and in 1932 he was swept out of office in an even greater landslide. He did not, writes his biographer William E. Leuchtenburg, "go gently into the purgatory of the ex-presidency."[43] Surely all presidents who lose reelection are more than a little disappointed; but as an off-the-charts narcissist, Hoover was a special case. Poisonously embittered about Franklin D. Roosevelt's accomplishments and popularity, Hoover denounced his successor in increasingly virulent terms. Because he couldn't argue that Roosevelt's policies weren't working, Hoover joined extreme right-wingers in calling the New Deal socialist and a betrayal of American principles. "When the American people realize some ten years hence that it was on November 8, 1932, that they surrendered the freedom of mind and spirit for which their ancestors had fought and agonized for over 300 years, they will, I hope, recollect that I at least tried to save them," he said, for example.[44] More than that, Hoover even claimed that the New Deal was anti-Christian and anti-religious. Liberals "defame the Sermon on the Mount" and seek to "destroy our religious faiths."[45]

Hoover personifies something about the turning of the conservative mind. Hoover had his own reasons for disliking—indeed, hating—FDR, the New Deal, and the modern liberal era. His reasons were, at their root, personal. He came to adopt extreme right-wing views to provide salve for his wounded ego, so that he could see himself as a principled hero rather than an abject failure. Many conservatives detested FDR and the New Deal for more straightforward ideological reasons. Some opposed governmental intervention in the financial system because they considered social security and other programs "socialistic." Some were "America First" isolationists up until the attack at Pearl Harbor. Some considered FDR a "traitor to his class" because he was not sufficiently protective of business and the wealthy. But while these resentments were intensely felt by some conservatives, they were politically unsuccessful. Hoover could not have been more wrong when he predicted that Americans would recognize him as a hero and FDR as a villain in ten years' time. Putting aside Hoover himself—who few people have ever come to see as a hero—conservatism seemed utterly routed as a political philosophy for a very long time. In fact, in 1936, 1940, 1944, 1948, 1952, 1956, and 1960, even the Republican presidential nominees were, at least arguably, all liberals.[46]

The principal conservative standard bearer for much of this time was Senator Robert A. Taft of Ohio.[47] He had been the candidate conservatives favored for the Republican presidential

nomination in 1940, 1948, and 1952. Taft's conservatism was not
far from that of Calvin Coolidge. Taft believed in the free market,
but was not an absolutist. The free enterprise system "has certain
definite faults," he said.[48] He believed in balanced budgets and
preferred to achieve them by holding spending in check, but he
was willing to raise taxes when necessary. He was a pragmatist who
followed facts and data where they led him, even when they led
him to conclusions that were inconsistent with his general ideological preferences. He supported America's participation in the
United Nations, and especially in the International Court of Justice. He did not believe in projecting American values across the
globe through use of military force. He was worried that treating
the Soviet Union as an adversary might become a self-fulfilling
prophecy. Taft was an admirable (if not exciting) individual, but
his brand of conservatism—which stressed caution, prudence, fiscal responsibility, and a wariness about achieving foreign policy
objectives through the use or threat of force—was not competing
successfully with modern liberalism.[49]

II.

It is natural that during a long period in the political wilderness
different schools of conservative thought would develop—each
refining a message to appeal, first, to a community of readers, lis-
teners, and activists, and then ultimately to voters. These schools
undoubtedly embraced ideas that could be traced back to earlier
times, but it is during this period that they wove ideas into a full
philosophic fabric and built distinct followings.

The first people to call themselves "libertarians" were Albert
Jay Nock and H. L. Mencken. Nock and Mencken were journal-
ists, public intellectuals, social critics, essayists, and book authors.
They also both helped start and edit magazines—Mencken,
American Mercury, and Nock, *The Freeman*. Nock's book *Memoirs
of a Superfluous Man*, published in 1943, is considered a seminal
libertarian masterpiece. It became the favorite book of a high
school senior named William F. Buckley, Jr., who read it because
Nock was a friend of his father and an occasional guest at his
home.[50] Mencken, meanwhile, had become a fan of an author
who, despite denying she was a libertarian, ultimately became the

single most powerful magnet for libertarianism in history—Ayn Rand.[51] Mencken read the manuscript of Ayn Rand's autobiographical novel, *We the Living*, and helped recommend it to publishers. Thereafter, Mencken and Rand became mutual admirers who read and were influenced by each other's work.[52] Rand's two blockbuster novels, *The Fountainhead*, published in 1943, and *Atlas Shrugged*, published in 1957, have converted countless people to libertarianism. A couple of expatriate Austrian economists—F. A. Hayek and Ludwig von Mises—also became important influences on the growth of libertarianism.[53] When William F. Buckley, Jr., founded *National Review* in 1955, he recruited libertarian Frank S. Meyer, who served as an editor and wrote a regular column for the magazine titled "Principles & Heresies."

Modern libertarianism believes in an absolutist laissez-faire economic system and a government that maintains a police force, courts of law, and a military to protect citizens against foreign attack, but does little else. There are, of course, strong and weak libertarians. While some libertarians are purists about those beliefs, others are less rigid. Taken all together, libertarianism is today the largest, strongest, and most influential of all of the schools of conservative thought.

Religious conservatism combines fundamentalist religiosity with political conservatism. By religious conservatism, I generally mean fundamentalist views, including the belief that Scripture should be interpreted literally, or in Catholic circles, that the Church is the infallible interpreter of Scripture. Religious conservatives often believe that religion is under attack, both on the international and domestic fronts. In the formative period of religious conservatism, religious conservatives thought that religion was threatened by atheistic Communism. Today Islam, or radical Islam, may be seen as the principal international threat. Domestically, religious conservatives believe religion is under assault by liberals. For them, the terms "liberalism" and "secular liberalism" are synonymous. They believe that liberals threaten religion by promoting a secular society and squeezing religion out of public life. Some religious conservatives may believe that liberals are sidelining religion out of a mistaken but good faith belief in things such as the separation of church and state. However, other religious conservatives believe that liberals are engaged in a deliberate conspiracy to destroy religion in America. Hoover suggested something along these lines when he said that liberals were defaming Christ's Sermon on the Mount and seeking to destroy religion.

A number of fundamentalist Protestant preachers—notably, Carl McIntire in Collingswood, New Jersey, and Billy James Hargis in Tulsa, Oklahoma—developed large radio audiences in the 1950s and 1960s by, in the words of Professor Gary K. Clabaugh, marrying the "fundamentalism of the cross" with the "fundamentalism of the flag."[54] The fundamentalism of the cross involved a literal interpretation of the Bible; the fundamentalism of the flag involved ostentatious patriotism and alarmist anticommunism. The two were deemed not merely inseparable but the very same thing.

But it was not only fundamentalist preachers who made this argument. In *God and Man at Yale*, William F. Buckley, Jr., wrote: "I myself believe that the duel between Christianity and atheism is the most important in the world. I further believe that the struggle between individualism and collectivism is the same struggle reproduced on another level."[55] He was suggesting that America was in the midst of a struggle between good and evil—perhaps literally between God and Satan. On the side of good were Christianity and individualism. On the side of evil were atheism and collectivism in all its forms, which for Buckley included not only totalitarianism and Communism but also government intervention in the economy. Half of his book is devoted to criticizing Yale for teaching Keynesian economics, which Buckley saw as not merely the enemy of national prosperity but of "individual freedom" and "public morality" as well.[56] The other half is devoted to criticizing Yale for failing to "Christianize Yale."[57]

Buckley, it may be said, married religion and libertarianism. He saw the two as inextricably intertwined with truth and goodness. He argued that Christianity was "ultimate, irrefutable truth," and individualism was "if not truth, the nearest thing we have to truth."[58] This was the powerful message of *God and Man at Yale*, the book that propelled its twenty-four-year-old author to fame and ignited the modern conservative movement.[59] Buckley was Catholic, and his Catholicism was integral to his magazine's political views. In its early years, *National Review* ran many stories about Catholic theology and about the church, decrying liberalizations in Catholic doctrine and practice. A number of key editors wound up converting to Catholicism from other faiths.[60] When he was later presented with the question whether an atheist who was a staunch anticommunist could be a conservative, Buckley, upon reflection, answered no.[61]

Not only did Buckley help make the alliance between religious conservatism and libertarianism possible, he infused modern conservatism with a righteousness that became one of its fundamental features. Conservatives do not see themselves as engaged in a cheerful debate with fellow liberals about questions of governance. They do not believe that there is wisdom in both traditions, and that America benefits from a lively debate and a healthy tension between the two. Rather, they see the contest between conservatism and liberalism in stark and simple terms: Conservatism is true and just. Liberalism is fallacious and execrable. Liberals may be misguided rather than malicious, but they are doing the Devil's work nonetheless. When one sees the world through this lens, a debate over tax rates, stimulus spending, or health insurance mandates appears of Armageddon-type proportions.

This, of course, is more of a sentiment than an expressed view—but that makes it especially potent because it is embraced at a deep level without being presented for examination. It is this sentiment that often makes modern conservatives—as opposed to earlier conservatives such as Coolidge and Taft—so zealous. The sentiment suffuses the movement.[62] Although its origins are distinctly religious, even non-devout adherents see the conservative movement as a crusade against darkness. In conservative circles, words such as "liberty" and "freedom" can operate at two levels. In addition to the standard meaning of not being subject to governmental coercion, they often connote goodness and light. When Barry Goldwater captured the 1964 Republican presidential nomination, most observers thought his first job was to persuade American voters that the charge leveled against him by his liberal opponents—namely, that he was an extremist—was overblown. They were stunned when, during his acceptance speech at the Republican National Convention, Goldwater delivered the lines that simultaneously sent conservatives at the convention into wild ecstasy and extinguished whatever chance Goldwater may have had of winning the election. "I would remind you that extremism in the defense of liberty is no vice," Goldwater defiantly declared. The cheers were so long and loud that Goldwater had to wait a full forty seconds before uttering his next sentence: "And let me remind you that moderation in the pursuit of justice is no virtue!" Conservative delegates at the Cow Palace leapt to their feet.[63]

The third leg of the modern conservative stool is neoconservatism. Irving Kristol, who was known as "the godfather of neoconservatism," famously defined the term by saying, "A neoconservative is a liberal who has been mugged by reality."[64] The hard truth, he thought, was that some people are bad, some people are slothful, and it is a mistake to coddle them. Crime must be deterred by swift and certain punishment. People must be made to walk on their own; government handouts only make them dependent. The same was true in the international arena. Some nations are our enemies, and they must be deterred by superior military might. The Soviet Union, he believed, was bent upon world domination, and it was not going to be dissuaded from that goal through diplomacy and mutual understanding. It did not pay to be overly idealistic in this dangerous world. In a famous neoconservative article, Jeane Kirkpatrick argued that America should not be squeamish about befriending dictatorial regimes.[65] If it was in America's interest to ally itself with an anticommunist dictator, it should do so.

Although the term "neoconservatism" was not coined until the 1970s, some historians argue that the first neoconservative was James Burnham, whom Buckley recruited in 1955 to serve as *National Review*'s foreign policy guru.[66] In a series of books and feature articles, and most especially a regular column for the magazine titled "The Third World War," Burnham argued that American strategy for dealing with international Communism—the containment doctrine—was inadequate. He proposed adopting what he called a "rollback" doctrine. Burnham argued that Communism expansion should not merely be stopped but reversed through political warfare, or "polwar," which would employ propaganda, psychological warfare, sabotage, subversion, and guerrilla warfare. Although his main beat was foreign affairs, Burnham also argued for hard-nosed approaches for social problems at home. Liberals, he believed, were naïve in their desire to solve the problem of homelessness, or of "skid row" as it was then called. "Skid row is the end of the line; and there must be an end of the line somewhere," he wrote. It was "part of the normal order of things" that people "who by destiny or choice drop out of normal society" wind up there.[67]

Although Burnham and other writers, including Buckley, articulated what we today call neoconservative ideas, they attached no separate label to them. They considered those ideas conservative and nothing more. But in the late 1960s and 1970s, a group of formerly liberal and mostly Jewish intellectuals from New York City—notably including Kristol, Norman Podhoretz, Nathan Glazer, Daniel Bell, and Seymour Lipset—began elaborating on Burnham's thinking and giving something of a distinct flavor in the pages of the new journal, *The Public Interest*. For one thing, this group was cosmopolitan and pretty much secular, and not in accord with the social issues so important to religious conservatives. For another, because neoconservatives were the most ardent supporters of large defense expenditures and of using military might, overtly and covertly, to protect and project American interests abroad, they were befriended and supported by big business. As a result, neoconservatism grew in power and prestige within conservative circles, especially within the Republican establishment.

One very important Republican who never became a full convert, however, was Ronald Reagan. To neoconservative horror, Reagan vigorously pursued arms control negotiations with Soviet Premier Mikhail Gorbachev, even to the point of seeking the total abolition of nuclear weapons. While Reagan never got that far, in 1986 he—over strong neoconservative protest—reached an agreement with Gorbachev to drastically reduce intermediate-range nuclear missiles.[68] Nor was George H. W. Bush a neoconservative. However, neoconservatives came more fully into power in George W. Bush's administration. Indeed, the invasion of Iraq—fueled by neoconservative beliefs that the prior policy of containing Saddam Hussein was too weak, and that America could export democracy to Iraq and the wider Middle East through military means—was the ultimate neoconservative project.[69]

Neoconservatism was discredited along with the rationales for that invasion. It may be many years before we learn whether Iraq develops into a stable democracy, but it is clear that neoconservative predictions that American soldiers would be welcomed as liberators with "flowers in the streets"—not unlike the administration's statement that Saddam Hussein had weapons of mass destruction—turned out to be terribly wrong.[70] The jolt was so great that one prominent neoconservative, Francis Fukuyama, wrote a book to declare that he no longer supported that ideology.[71]

III.

Buckley braided a coalition consisting of three schools of conservatism, but he was not willing to include every philosophy. There were rivals that Buckley did not want to include in the coalition or, once in, decided to expel. We shall turn to the two most important examples of those now.

The first group was then called the New Conservatives, although it is better known today as traditional conservatism or Burkeanism. Its most influential voices came from four academics: Russell Kirk, a junior professor at what is now Michigan State University; Clinton Rossiter, a nationally prominent political scientist at Cornell University; Robert Nisbet, a young sociologist at the University of California-Berkeley; and Peter Viereck, an historian at Mount Holyoke who won a Pulitzer Prize for poetry. These were four unusual academics, however, because they could write evocatively for popular audiences. In addition to collectively writing many articles, between the years 1949 and 1955 each of these four men wrote a book championing Burkeanism as the true conservatism that was very widely read.[72]

For Buckley, the most dangerous was Russell Kirk. In 1953, when he was only thirty-five, Kirk published *The Conservative Mind: From Burke to Eliot*, in which he declared that Edmund Burke was "the greatest of modern conservative thinkers" and "Burke's is the true school of conservative thought."[3] Although the book was a revision of his doctoral dissertation, it became a popular sensation. The *Chronicle of Higher Education* hailed it as a "landmark study" that offered conservatism a "serious intellectual legacy," and *Time* magazine praised it effusively in an especially long and prominently featured review.[74] The book was so successful that Kirk resigned from his faculty position to pursue a career as an independent writer and speaker.

Not everyone within intellectual circles of the American right was pleased with Kirk's prominence, however. Many found Kirk's choice of Burke as the true exemplar of conservative thought to be off-putting since, as Kirk repeatedly stressed, Burke was both a conservative and a liberal.[75] Burke was, in fact, a reformer, though a particular kind of reformer. He believed that change is necessary. At the same time, he thought that our traditions, institutions, and culture are shaped through evolutionary processes. They come to be what they are because they serve us well; yet the reasons they serve us well are not always evident to us. Thus, when possible, change should be undertaken carefully and cautiously to avoid unforeseen consequences. This idea of caution, prudence, and a presumption that things have come to be what they are for good reasons did not appeal to Buckley, who considered himself a counterrevolutionary and was eager to radically change the liberal state and many of its institutions. Kirk also wrote: "Conservatism never is more admirable than when it accepts changes that it disapproves, with good grace, for the sake of a general conciliation; and the impetuous Burke, of all men, did most to establish that principle."[76] That was hardly the way Buckley saw things.

Even more importantly, Kirk was a fierce opponent of libertarianism. Burkeanism and libertarianism are almost diametrically opposed. Libertarianism places the individual first; Burkeanism places community first. Libertarians believe that human beings rationally pursue their own self-interest, and should be left unfettered to do so. They wish to radically throw off restraints on both individuals and the free market. Burke, by contrast, taught that the individual is foolish but the species is wise. Kirk considered libertarianism to be materialistic, decadent, and puerile. "We have obligations to mankind at large," he argued.[77] Life must not be merely about "another piece of pie and another pat of butter."[78] What matters, said Kirk, are "the permanent things," a phrase Kirk borrowed from T. S. Eliot.[79] For all these reasons, libertarianism and Burkeanism were then—and remain today—bitter foes.[80]

Buckley had harshly criticized Kirk in print, and had done so as part of what appeared to be a coordinated attack with other libertarians. But as he was getting ready to launch *National Review*, Buckley reversed course and embarked on an elaborate seduction to persuade Kirk to join the ranks of the forthcoming magazine. It was a brilliant maneuver. After giving up his faculty position, Kirk was finding it difficult to make ends meet. To earn a living on the speaker circuit and as an author, he needed to remain continually prominent within conservative circles, and being a regular columnist in what was likely to become the premier journal on the right would be of immeasurable help. Hat in hand, Buckley made the trek to Kirk's home in the remote village of Mecosta, Michigan, deployed his considerable charm, and persuaded Kirk to write for the magazine. It was, for Kirk, a bitter pill to swallow. Kirk refused to be listed as an associate or contributor to the magazine—"I won't be cheek by jowl with [libertarians] on the masthead," he rather angrily told Buckley—but he agreed to write a regular column. Kirk's column would be titled "From the Academy," and focus principally on educational policy, a subject that was dear to Kirk's heart, but would hardly be in the center ring of the debate over conservatism. Both parties got what they needed. Had he remained outside the magazine, Kirk could have been a formidable foe; but one does not bite the hand that feeds him. For the twenty-five years that he wrote for *National Review*, Kirk suspended his attacks on libertarianism. As measured by letters and other feedback, Kirk's column was one of the magazine's most popular regular features. He had been turned from enemy to asset. For his part, Kirk assured his constant visibility within conservative circles, and his association with *National Review* did, in fact, make it possible for him to earn a living by speaking and writing.

Each of the other three most prominent New Conservatives also left the field of battle. For a while, there was great interest in what they had to say, but this did not last long. After a while, the New Conservatives found themselves ignored by liberals and lambasted by conservatives. They were not having fun, and each drifted away from the debate over conservatism and into other things. Ironically, the New Conservatives were communitarians who acted as individuals—they never collaborated in any way—while Buckley and his colleagues were individualists who built a community. Ideas are vitally important, but they don't promote themselves.

If Buckley wanted to co-opt or marginalize the Burkeans out because, in part, they were too moderate, there were other conservatives he had to expel from the movement because they were too extreme. "Why is it our side is afflicted with all the loonies?" he was driven to ask.[81] In the early 1960s, Buckley found himself surrounded by members of the John Birch Society—a semisecret group that believed that Communists were taking over the United States from within. In his book, *The Politician*, which was originally circulated privately, Robert Welch, the Society's founder and absolute leader, had written that Communist agents included General George Marshall, Secretary of State John Foster Dulles, CIA Director Allen Dulles, Supreme Court Justice William J. Brennan, Jr., Supreme Court Chief Justice Earl Warren, and—if that weren't enough—President Dwight D. Eisenhower too. "Eisenhower and his Communist appointees are gradually taking over our whole government, right under the noses of the American people," wrote Welch.[82] By 1965, the John Birch Society's magazine, *American Opinion*, estimated that the United States was 60–80 percent under Communist control.[83]

Buckley faced two problems. The first was that he and Welch were not terribly far apart on the ideological spectrum. Buckley had been a prominent supporter of McCarthyism. Although he conceded that Senator Joseph McCarthy had often leveled erroneous and irresponsible attacks, he had defended his general approach nonetheless. "McCarthyism," Buckley had written, "is primarily the maintenance of a steady flow of criticism (raillery, the Liberals call it) calculated to pressure the President, Cabinet members, high officials, and above all the political party in power, to get on with the elimination of security risks in government."[84] So Buckley had himself argued, more or less, that the government was filled with Communist agents or fellow travelers. Nevertheless, there is a line, and Welch had stepped over it into zaniness. Buckley's second problem was that the John Birch Society was then powerful within right-wing circles; and because its membership was secret and many devoted members did not make their affiliation publicly known, no one—including Buckley—knew quite how powerful it was. When, in 1965, Buckley decided to launch an unequivocal attack on Robert Welch and the John Birch Society, observers estimated that the Society's membership was approximately 80,000, roughly the same size as *National Review*'s total paid circulation. The John Birch Society had a paid staff of 200, its own publishing company, and 350 bookstores nationwide. Its magazine, *American Opinion*, had a paid circulation of 40,000.[85] An unknown number of *National Review* subscribers were undoubtedly members of the Society, and even more disturbing, so were some of Buckley's largest financial backers. Buckley knew that some of his editors and writers were Birchers, but he did not know how many. In fact, at one point the *National Review* masthead included the names of at least five members of the John Birch Society, two of whom were members of the Society's national Council.[86]

The John Birch Society was a threat to the conservative movement precisely because it was so successful. Responsible people would not take conservatism seriously if the John Birch Society were taken seriously within conservative circles. Moreover, conservatism would not deserve to be taken seriously. And so, after previous false starts and pulled punches, Buckley decided to unequivocally denounce Robert Welch and the entire John Birch Society as grossly irresponsible and "a grave liability in the conservative and anti-Communist cause."[87] Buckley recruited a collection of conservative luminaries to join in or endorse his attack, including Frank S. Meyer, James Burnham, Russell Kirk, and Senator Barry Goldwater. The attack was successful. *National Review* survived, and the John Birch Society was successfully marginalized.

IV.

William F. Buckley, Jr. showed how to lead a successful coalition. *National Review* served as the hub of the conservative wheel, connecting three disparate schools of ideological thought and stressing their commonalities. Some inconsistencies were tolerated; others were not. Extremism—in the sense of succumbing to an alternative reality—was ultimately identified for what it is and denounced as unacceptable. But Buckley is no longer with us; *National Review*, while still important, is not the one main home of intellectual conservatism; the Soviet Union no longer exists; and the Cold War is over. As the three schools of conservatism separate, they will compete ever more vigorously in the realms of both ideas and electoral politics.

These dynamics were on full display during the 2012 election campaign. There were seven candidates for the Republican presidential nomination, and during some period of the primary contests five different candidates each spent some period of time as the frontrunner in national polls.[88] The seven candidates slugged it out over personal matters—accusing one another of being flip-floppers, grandiose, Washington insiders, out of touch with real people, and the like—but they also engaged in a less obvious struggle with ramifications beyond this election. They were fighting over the future of conservatism.

This somewhat under-the-surface debate showed up in the candidates' repeated claims about being the "real conservative," the "true conservative," or the "genuine conservative." A search in one electronic database reveals that those three phrases appeared more than 3,500 times in periodicals and news broadcasts during the battle for the Republican presidential nomination—and that's not counting "consistent conservative," which has a different meaning.[89]

There may be a tendency to assume this rhetoric was about who was *more* conservative—that is, further to the right on a one-dimensional ideological spectrum—but actually something else was going on. After all, "real," "true," and "genuine" mean something different than "more." At bottom, this was an argument about what conservatism means. The candidates were saying that their brand of conservatism is the one and true conservatism.

Though it is seldom articulated explicitly, this question may have been the most compelling of all to Republican voters. If God—or more appropriately, Ronald Reagan—had descended from heaven and declared a particular candidate to be the true conservative, much-relieved Republican voters would happily have fallen in line and propelled that candidate to victory at the Republican National Convention in Tampa. But there was no word from heaven. Instead, there was an often coded argument over who the real conservative was, and the fact that argument took place was evidence of uncertainty. Paradoxically, Republican voters may have considered being a true conservative a candidate's most important attribute, even though they were plagued by doubt and division about what being a true conservative meant.

I am by no means suggesting that the primary contest was just about ideology. It was about candidates—their personalities, competence, integrity, and electability. And it was about specific issues of public policy too. Yet in this particular election, questions of public policy seemed less important as ends-in-themselves than as examples of what conservatives should believe.

Michele Bachmann, Rick Perry, and Rick Santorum battled for the right to represent religious conservatism. I need to pause here to explain why I have listed Michele Bachmann as someone who sought to represent religious conservatives. After all, Bachmann was the founder of the Tea Party Caucus in the House of Representatives and was principally identified as a tea party conservative. So some observations about the tea party are in order.

The tea party movement traces its origins to February 19, 2009, when Rick Santelli, a reporter for CNBC, launched into an on-air rant that the new Obama administration (then less than one month in office) was subsidizing mortgages of irresponsible people who purchased homes for more than they could afford. "The government is rewarding bad behavior!" Santelli declaimed, and he called for "capitalists" to protest by staging a tea party in Chicago.[90] With lots of help from Fox News, right-wing talk radio hosts, some political operatives, and bloggers, the tea party movement was born, giving rise to both genuine grassroots organizations and ersatz-grassroots organizations organized by Republican operatives. A great deal of energy flowed into the tea parties, and they grew in size and fervor following passage of the Affordable Care Act (popularly known as "Obamacare"). In November 2010, Republicans gained sixty-three seats in the House of Representatives, taking control of that chamber from the Democrats, and six seats in the U.S. Senate. Republicans also gained six governorships and about seven hundred seats in state legislatures. There is a great deal of academic debate about how influential the tea parties were to the Republican victories, but it is probably safe to say that they had significant influence and were popularly perceived as having an enormous impact.[91]

Consequently, candidates for the 2012 Republican presidential nomination were interested in getting tea party support. But who are the tea partiers? Are they libertarians, religious conservatives, or neoconservatives—or are they a separate force? Theda Skocpol and Vanessa Williamson, two scholars at the Department of Government and Social Policy at Harvard University who have probably done the most in-depth investigation of tea parties, report that while they found tea party membership to be composed of both libertarians and religious conservatives, religious conservatives dominated.[92] "In our fieldwork experience," they wrote, "the many rank-and-file members who hold heartfelt Christian conservative views set the tone for the Tea Party as a whole. Libertarian members tend to accommodate the social conservative view, at least to some degree."[93] Skocpol and Williamson found that conventional religious conservative literature—opposing abortion, for example—was often distributed at tea party meetings. They also report that national Republican operatives understood this and used religious language to try to appeal to tea party members.[94] The tea party movement was, therefore, largely composed of and controlled by religious conservatives, and may be best thought of as part of a school of religious conservatism. That is why I say that—along with Rick Perry and Rick Santorum—Michele Bachman was fighting to be the candidate of religious conservatives. It was Santorum who prevailed.

Many assumed that after winning that struggle, Santorum would soft-peddle social issues. Most committed religious conservatives knew Santorum was faithful to their cause; he didn't need to continue beating their drum to win them over. To win over other types of conservatives, Santorum needed to emphasize issues they care about. But Santorum doubled down on religious conservatism. He questioned whether public education should continue, or whether education should become the exclusive province of private, parochial, and home schools. He made contraception a campaign issue. He said John F. Kennedy's famous Houston speech about the separation of church and state made him want to "throw up." He seemed to relish a 2008 speech turning up, in which he warned that Satan is embarked on a scheme to destroy America, and that the first two institutions to fall to the Father of Lies were academia and mainline Protestantism.[95] Some commentators assumed that Santorum's strategists calculated that whipping up religious conservatives would be more effective than making a more broad-based appeal. But there is another possible explanation for Santorum's campaign choices: He was a true believer who thought that battling evil and promoting religious conservatism—which, as he saw it, is the same endeavor—was more important than becoming president. After all, he had to know that even if pushing those issues led to pluralities in some Republican primaries, it was a strategy doomed to disaster in the general election.

Discredited by the invasion of Iraq and the unpopularity of George W. Bush's administration, neoconservatives laid low during the primaries. While none of the primary candidates could be clearly classified as neoconservative, Romney and Santorum sought to make themselves acceptable to neoconservatives by vowing not to permit Iran to acquire nuclear weapons. Newt Gingrich tried to one-up them by suggesting he would also pursue regime change.

Ron Paul represented libertarianism expressly. His goal was not to become the Republican nominee but to increase the influence of libertarianism, especially among young voters. He was enormously successful, drawing large crowds on college campuses and doing extremely well with voters under age thirty. By contrast, social conservatives were in trouble with young voters. According to Gallup, most voters under thirty-five are pro-choice on abortion, and 70 percent support same-sex marriage. Paul's popularity flowed exclusively from his ideas, not from a scintillating personality. Although he made some concessions to the other schools of conservatism—he opposed abortion, for example—his concessions were few and far between. He rejected neoconservative foreign policy root and branch. In attacking Santorum for supporting earmarks, Paul called Santorum a "fake conservative." His message was that libertarians—who oppose government spending so ardently that they will not compromise by funding projects in their districts with government largesse—were the real conservatives.

Mitt Romney, the candidate who ultimately won the nomination, was not perceived as a libertarian, neoconservative, or religious conservative—and therein was both his weakness and his strength. Members of none of these three schools were confident that he represented their views. Moreover, because he was not an identifiable kind of conservative, people questioned whether he was a conservative at all. If Romney clearly belonged to one of the three schools, his compatriots would have cut him slack for having taken pragmatic stands on particular issues while he was governor of Massachusetts.

Romney's weakness was also his strength because no one school of conservative thought saw him as promoting a competing vision of conservatism. Each school of thought recognized that in the battle for the future of conservatism, he would not be their champion—but he would not be their enemy either. Had Romney been elected, the best guess would be that his administration would have included representatives of all three of the conservative schools, and the battle for the future of conservatism would have continued. The school of conservatism that mistrusted Romney the most was religious conservatives—Romney was both pro-choice and pro-gay rights as a Massachusetts politician—and it was not a surprise that a religious conservative, Rick Santorum, contested Romney most forcefully and was the last of Romney's competitors to finally concede the nomination.

However, religious conservatives are not powerful enough to capture the nomination when they face another Republican—whether a libertarian or a neoconservative or someone like Romney—in a two-person field. Once the contest boiled down to Santorum and Romney, the final result was preordained.

While politicians angle to be the favorite of one of the three main schools of conservatism, interesting action has begun taking place in the trenches. Each of the three main schools of conservative thought has its own journals,[96] advocacy groups, think tanks,[97] and in some cases even colleges and universities[98] dedicated to promoting their distinct schools of conservative thought. In some instances, organizations support a combination of philosophies. For example, some of the most influential think tanks—the American Enterprise Institute, the Heritage Foundation, and the Hoover Institution at Stanford University—have become libertarian on matters of economics and governmental structure, and neoconservative on social and foreign policy. Although they remain a far smaller and weaker group, Burkeans are showing some renewed life and beginning to enter the debate. In 2012, Jesse Norman, an up-and-coming member of British parliament and the Conservative Party, wrote a new biography of Burke that is getting attention on both sides of the Atlantic, in which Norman argues why Burke is needed more than ever today, and why libertarianism is leading us astray.[99] Burkeans now also have their own magazine—*The American Conservative*, which has both print and online versions— as well as a couple of exclusively online outlets.[100] Nevertheless, the organs supporting the Burkean way are puny compared to the rich infrastructures supporting each of the three main schools of conservatism.

The battles have generally been between institutes representing different schools of thought, but the usual battles are being fought to control, change, or redirect some of the most important institutes. For example, shock waves reverberated throughout the intellectual right when, in 2011, a fight broke out for control of the Cato Institute, which is the best known of the libertarian think tanks. The Koch brothers sought to wrest organizational control from Cato's long-time president, Edward Crane, and the organization's existing board of directors, led by Robert A. Levy.[101] Crane and Levy feared that the Koch brothers wanted to make Cato more "politically relevant"—that is, less devoted to promoting a pure version of libertarianism and more a part of the Republican political infrastructure—and they vigorously resisted the Koch brothers' efforts to seize control. Litigation was commenced and later settled. Although Cato's leadership and governing structure changed, both sides claimed the agreed-upon arrangement would preserve Cato as an independent advocate of libertarianism. But if so, why was the battle fought?

Conservatives were even more surprised when, in December 2012, Senator Jim DeMint of South Carolina resigned his Senate seat—with four years left on the term to which he had been elected—to become president of the Heritage Foundation. The Heritage Foundation is more eclectic than Cato; it has adopted the Republican establishment stance of combining libertarianism on economic policy with neoconservatism on foreign and social policy. But DeMint is not an establishment Republican but a tea party Republican—the founder of the Senate Tea Party Caucus, in fact.[102] Was this a sort of hostile takeover? Many immediately expressed the belief that DeMint would convert the Heritage Foundation from an independent think tank specializing in well-researched and carefully analyzed policy studies into a partisan political organization, and under the surface establishment conservatives were surely worried that DeMint would change Heritage's ideological position. DeMint is in for a rocky ride. He is being assaulted in writing from the likes of Jennifer Rubin, who recently authored a piece for her "Right Turn" blog at *Washington Post* that was titled "Jim DeMint's Destruction of the Heritage

Foundation."[103] "The Heritage Foundation is suffering a grievous slide in intellectual integrity" under DeMint, wrote Rubin. She accused Heritage of playing "an overtly political role" in the battle of the government shutdown in the fall of 2013, and of issuing an "embarrassingly shoddy report" in an attempt to support the proposition that immigration was bad for the U.S. economy—a report that became even more embarrassing when it turned out that its author had previously claimed that Hispanics have genetically low intelligence. Rubin also quoted Senator Orrin Hatch of Utah as saying that many Republicans were asking: "Is Heritage going to be so political that it doesn't really amount to anything anymore?" It's unusual (or at least used to be unusual) for a senator to criticize another senator—or even a former senator—in such personal terms. Hatch is too savvy a senator to do so gratuitously. The battle for control of the Heritage Foundation may not be over yet.

V.

What does the future hold? I am not a determinist who believes that the future is predictable if we can trace the trajectory of history with enough skill. I do not believe that certain ideas are fated to triumph over other ideas. Modern conservatism became a coalition among three schools of thought because a particular man with extraordinary personal assets—great charm, literary skill, leadership talent, and a father who made considerable money in oil—showed up at the right time and happened to embrace a certain ideological view. The future of conservatism will be determined in part by ideas, by the people who promote those ideas, by politicians who articulate particular visions, and by dumb luck. Nevertheless, here are a few predictions:

First, conservatism will not wither on the vine. It will change, however.

Second, as they separate, the three main schools of conservatism will fight ever more fiercely for the conservative banner, that is, the right to declare itself the one, true school of conservatism and deny that right to its rivals. These battles will be fought both openly in the realms of ideas and less visibly in the trenches. There will be battles over infrastructure, as one school seeks to alter or even steal important assets—such as journals and foundations—from another school.

Third, religious conservatism will become progressively weaker. Demography is against it. Its social issues—abortion, premarital and extramarital sex, and same-sex marriage, immigration, and its skepticism of science (including evolution and global warming)—do not play well with voters, including Republican voters, who are under thirty. Republicans have talked a lot about how the party needs to change its position on immigration to not write off Hispanic voters, also a growing group, but that is not enough. When the Pope says, "I am no one to judge" homosexuals, not to mention declaring "I have never been a right-winger," it is a sign of things to come.[104] This is the withering school of conservatism.

Fourth, libertarianism will increasingly resonate with young people if it opposes corporate cronyism and American imperialism—as Ron and Rand Paul urge—even though it offers a naïve and unworkable system of regulation in our complex society.

Fifth, neoconservatism will enjoy a slow but powerful resurgence. It is, after all, the conservatism favored by big business, which wants a strong military-industrial complex. Neoconservatism took a terrible blow when the nation discovered that George W. Bush took the nation to war under false pretenses, and the nation remains war-weary. But memories will fade as we get further from the wars in Iraq and Afghanistan. This is where the money is, and money is a great asset.

Sixth, the transcendence of the true believers will end. This last prediction takes a little explanation. The American right has always had its share of "loonies," true believers, and extremists, but they have generally been declared out of the mainstream, relegated to the margins, and kept away from the levers of power.[105] By "true believers" I mean people who do not appreciate that democracy involves choices and who grant their fellow citizens the right to make different choices.[106] True believers believe that they possess truth, and they deny legitimacy to political outcomes and candidates with whom they disagree. True believers search for explanations about why truth is being rejected, often succumbing to conspiracy theories and other dark suppositions. To them, compromise is—perhaps even literally—a bargain with the Devil. For reasons previously described, post-Buckley the American conservative movement has been particularly vulnerable to true believers, for which Buckley himself was partly responsible. Yet when push came to shove, Buckley took considerable risks to denounce the true believers of his day and purge them from the conservative movement.

That has not been the case for quite a while now. Instead, conservative and Republican leaders have stoked the flames of true believers who were ready to believe that a failed investment by Bill and Hillary in a project called Whitewater concealed dark secrets, that Hillary murdered Vincent Foster, and that Bill Clinton should be impeached. They stoked the flames of those who raised bizarre questions of illegitimacy concerning Barack Obama, questioning his place of birth and his religion. They stoked the flames of true believers to support a grossly irresponsible attempt to eliminate a law they did not like (the Affordable Care Act) by closing the government and threatening to cause the nation to default on its debt obligations.[107] This string has now run out. American voters will no longer let true believers have the ballot boxes to themselves during off-year congressional elections. And for American business, which sat idly during all of these things because it supported the Republican Party, threatening national default was the last straw. Business will fund neoconservatives and other tea party opponents, weakening both the tea parties and religious conservatism.[108] Once a few leading conservatives step forward to follow Buckley's example and denounce the true believers, others will quickly follow. Ending the transcendence of the true believers is the most important change that can come to American conservatism.

NOTES

1. How extreme and how powerful has the modern conservative movement become? One measure is the congressional votes on a bill to end a government shutdown and extend the federal government's borrowing authority to avoid a financial default on the national debt that were cast during the night of October 16, 2013. My premise is that voting against this legislation was indefensible from any sensible public policy standpoint and motivated solely by extremist ideology. Forty percent of the Republican members of the U.S. Senate and 61 percent of the Republican members of the House of Representatives voted against the legislation. See Lori Montgomery and Rosalind S. Helderman, "Shutdown Ends:

Obama Signs Debt, Spending Bill," *Washington Post* (October 17, 2013), A1, reporting that eighteen senators and 144 representatives—Republicans all—voted against the legislation.

2. See, for example, David Brooks, "The Conservative Future," *New York Times* (November 20, 2012), A27, identifying prominent debaters and briefly describing their differences.

3. Regarding "Islamofascism," see, for example, William Safire, "On Language: Islamofascism," *New York Times* (October 1, 2006), available online at: http://www.nytimes.com/2006/10/01/magazine/01wwln_safire .html. Conservatives are now also trying to use the rise of China as a world power as a substitute for the threat of what they used to call international Communism, but that too is likely to prove an inadequate substitute.

4. See Julia Edwards, "How Historians Rank the Presidents," *National Journal* (February 19, 2011), accessed online at: http://www.national journal.com/how-historians-rank-the-presidents-20110219.

5. Those holding this view include economist John Kenneth Galbraith and historian David Greenberg, *Calvin Coolidge*, 1st ed. (New York: Times, 2007), 147, 156.

6. Greenberg acknowledges that some proto-Keynesians were issuing warnings. At the same time, books with wide readerships were claiming that the business cycle had been conquered and there was no need for concern. Greenberg, *Coolidge*, 144–145.

7. Ibid., 138.

8. I know of no poll, but according to Greenberg this was the view of the press. Greenberg, *Coolidge*, 141.

9. Ibid., 23.

10. Ibid., 1.

11. Ibid., 71–80.

12. Coolidge does seem to presage modern conservative sentiment in that, while he cut federal spending in almost all programs, two exceptions were increased spending for immigration control and prisons. Greenberg, *Coolidge*, 77. Regarding budget surplus, see 77–78.

13. Ibid., 143.

14. Ibid., 70.

15. Ibid., 73, 75.

16. Ibid., 73.

17. Ibid., 74–75.

18. Ibid., 55–56.

19. Ibid., 114–117 (World Court), 117 (Obregon), 121 (arms control), 123 (Kellogg-Briand).

20. Quoted in William E. Leuchtenburg, *Herbert Hoover*, 1st ed. (New York: Times, 2009), 27–28.

21. It has been said that Hoover "fed more people and saved more lives than any other man in history." Leuchtenburg, *Hoover*, 161, quoting a Hoover associate.

22. Ibid., 47.

23. Ibid., 48.

24. Ibid., 52.

25. Ibid., 51.

26. Ibid., 59.

27. Ibid., 66, quoting Hoover's book *American Individualism* (Garden City, NY: Doubleday, Page & Co., 1922).

28. Leuchtenburg, *Hoover*, 65.

29. Ibid., 70–71.

30. Ibid., 72.

31. Ibid., 74, regarding right-wing statements during the campaign.

32. Ibid., 82.

33. Ibid., 83.

34. Ibid., 84.

35. I am not suggesting that Hoover took office as a genuine progressive or later became a consistent conservative. His record was mixed throughout his administration. For example, in March 1930 he nominated John J. Parker to the U.S. Supreme Court. Parker was considered a racist and a staunch opponent of organized labor. That nomination pleased only the extreme right wing, and the Senate—with Republicans joining Democrats—did not confirm Parker. In 1932, Hoover (though perhaps somewhat reluctantly) nominated the great liberal jurist Benjamin N. Cardozo to the Court. Ibid., 88, 99–100. Despite his mixed record throughout his four years, it is probably true in general that Hoover seemed to enter office as a progressive and moved right or seemed to move right. Leuchtenburg writes that, by maybe a year or a little more into Hoover's administration, "progressives came to believe that they had been hoodwinked—fools to ever think of Hoover as an enlightened statesman," 98.

36. Ibid., 104.

37. Ibid., 105.

38. Ibid., 113.

39. For example, Congress passed legislation to rehabilitate the U.S. Employment Service, but against the advice of his own advisers, the press, and economists, Hoover vetoed it. Ibid., 113.

40. Ibid., 130.

41. Hoover was rated the worst president of the twentieth century on foreign affairs in a 2007 poll of scholars of international relations. Ibid., 125.

42. Ibid., 122–127.

43. Ibid., 147.

44. Ibid., 150.

45. Ibid., 151.

46. These were Alfred M. Landon (1932), Wendell L. Willkie (1940), Thomas E. Dewey (1944 and 1948), Dwight D. Eisenhower (1952 and 1956), and Richard M. Nixon (1960).

47. For a brief summary about Robert A. Taft and his ideology, see Carl T. Bogus, *Buckley: William F. Buckley Jr. and the Rise of American Conservatism*, 1st U.S. ed. (New York: Bloomsbury, 2011), 25–38.

48. Ibid., 29–30.

49. Taft was, of course, a politician—not a political philosopher—and he was not always ideologically consistent.

50. Bogus, *Buckley*, 67–69.

51. Regarding Rand, see Bogus, *Buckley*, 198–218 and sources cited therein.

52. Jennifer Burns, *Goddess of the Market: Ayn Rand and the American Right* (New York: Oxford University Press, 2009), 33, 43, 48.

53. Bogus, *Buckley*, 118 notes 134–136.

54. Gary K. Clabaugh, *Thunder on the Right: The Protestant Fundamentalists* (Chicago: Nelson-Hall, 1974), 84.

55. William F. Buckley, Jr., *God and Man at Yale*, Fiftieth Anniversary ed. (Washington, DC: Regnery Publishing, [1951] 2002), lxvi.

56. Ibid., 58. Buckley characterizes Keynesian economics as "a doctrinaire collectivist program," 61.

57. Ibid., 39. For the statement that many considered Kristol the godfather of neoconservatism, see Barry Gewen, "Irving Kristol, Godfather of Modern Conservatism, Dies at 89," *New York Times* (September 18, 2009), available online at: http://www.nytimes.com/2009/09/19/us/politics/19kristol.html?pagewanted=all&_r=0. Notwithstanding the title, the article makes it clear that many considered Kristol the godfather of *neoconservatism*.

58. Buckley, *God and Man*, 138–139.

59. In his foreword to the fiftieth-anniversary edition, for example, Austin W. Bramwell wrote that without *God and Man at Yale* "one could fairly say, the modern conservative movement would not exist today." Ibid., xi.

60. Three editors who converted were Jeffrey Hart, Russell Kirk, and Frank S. Meyer. Bogus, *Buckley*, 15–16. For more about *National Review* and Catholicism, see Bogus, *Buckley*, 98–100, 118–122.

61. See Bogus, *Buckley*, 120–121.

62. Although the sentiment has distinctly religious origins, the intensity with which it is held is not always related to a conservative's personal religiosity. Goldwater was neither devout nor a religious conservative, and although he expressed himself in secular terms, he presented conservatism as a crusade against evil. By contrast, Mike Huckabee, who is very much a religious conservative, leans the other way when he says, "I'm a conservative, but I am not angry about it." See, for example, Michael Medved, "Mike Huckabee Missed His Moment in Bowing Out of the 2012 Race," *Daily Beast* (January 16, 2012), available online at: http://www.the dailybeast.com/articles/2012/01/16/mike-huckabee-missed-his-moment -in-bowing-out-of-the-2012-race.html.

63. Bogus, *Buckley*, 194–195.

64. Ibid., 19, quoting Kristol.

65. Ibid., 20, quoting Kirkpatrick.

66. H. W. Brands and Richard Brookhiser have called Burnham the original neoconservative. For a summary of Burnham's work and influence, see Bogus, *Buckley*, 17–21, 222–244, 308–319.

67. James Burnham, *Suicide of the West: An Essay on the Meaning and Destiny of Liberalism* (Washington, DC: Regnery Gateway, 1985), 106.

68. Bogus, *Buckley*, 340–343.

69. Thomas E. Ricks, for example, writes that neoconservatives in George W. Bush's administration were "essentially idealistic interventionists who believed in using American power to spread democracy." Thomas E. Ricks, *Fiasco: The American Military Adventure in Iraq* (New York: Penguin, 2006), 22. This view was colorfully reflected by former CIA Director James Woolsey, who argued that the invasion of Iraq would get "the Arab world plus Iran" moving in the direction of democracy. "It's not Americanizing the world. It's Athenizing it. And it's doable," Woolsey said. James Fallows, *Blind into Baghdad: America's War in Iraq* (New York: Vintage, 2006), 40. Influential neoconservatives with the high councils of the Bush-43 administration included Paul D. Wolfowitz, Richard Perle, John R. Bolton, Douglas J. Feith, and Elliot Abrams. Even if George W. Bush, Richard Cheney, and Donald Rumsfeld did not come into office as committed neoconservatives, following the attacks on the United States on September 11, 2001, and surrounded by top neoconservative advisers, they governed like neoconservatives.

70. Regarding predictions of flowers in the streets, literally and figuratively, see Fallows, *Blind into Baghdad*, 64 notes 79–80, 99; Ricks, *Fiasco*, 96, 98, 111.

71. Francis Fukuyama, *America at the Crossroads: Democracy, Power, and the Neoconservative Legacy* (New Haven, CT: Yale University Press, 2006).

72. Russell Kirk, *The Conservative Mind, from Burke to Santayana* (Chicago: Regnery, 1953); Robert Nisbet, *The Quest for Community: A Study in the Ethics of Order and Freedom* (New York: Oxford University Press, 1953); Clinton Rossiter, *Conservatism in America* (New York: Knopf, 1955); Peter Viereck, *Conservatism Revisited: The Revolt against Revolt, 1815–1949* (New York: C. Scribner, 1949). All of these works have gone through multiple editions, in some instances involving a modification in subtitle. I list original dates of publication and titles, except where noted.

73. Kirk, *Conservative Mind*, 1, 4.

74. See Bogus, *Buckley*, 14—which references Kirk, *Conservative Mind*—and 354 note 17, which also cites Scott McLemee, "A Conservative of the Old School," *Chronicle of Higher Education* (May 7, 2004): A18 and Henry Regnery, "The Making of *The Conservative Mind*," in Russell Kirk, *The Conservative Mind from Burke to Eliot*, 7th revised ed. (Washington, DC: Regnery, 2001), i–xii.

75. Kirk, *The Conservative Mind*, 13, 19, 21, 316–317. See also Russell Kirk, *Edmund Burke: A Genius Reconsidered*, Revised and updated ed. (Wilmington, DE: Intercollegiate Studies Institute, 1997), 161.

76. Kirk, *The Conservative Mind*, 47.

77. Kirk, *The Conservative Mind*, 4th revised ed. (New York: Avon, 1968), 31.

78. W. Wesley McDonald, *Russell Kirk and the Age of Ideology* (Columbia: University of Missouri Press, 2004), 178.

79. See Bogus, *Buckley*, 117 and 365 note 66, which cites Russell Kirk, *The Sword of Imagination: Memoirs of a Half-Century of Literary Conflict* (Grand Rapids, MI: William B. Eerdmans, 1995), 214.

80. See, for example, Jesse Norman, *Edmund Burke: The First Conservative* (New York: Basic, 2013). See also the book review of same by Carl T. Bogus, "Burke Versus the Economists," *American Conservative* 12 (September/October 2013): 47.

81. See Bogus, *Buckley*, 8.

82. Ibid., 176.

83. Ibid., 196.

84. Ibid., 103, quoting Buckley and his co-author, L. Brent Bozell.

85. Ibid., 194.

86. Ibid., 182.

87. Ibid., 197.

88. The seven major candidates for the Republican nomination were: Michele Bachmann, Herman Cain, Newt Gingrich, Jon Huntsman, Jr., Tim Pawlenty, Mitt Romney, and Rick Santorum. For at least some time during the race, each of those candidates—with the sole exception of Jon Huntsman—led in the polls.

89. I ran the three phrases through the Westlaw "all news" database to see how often each appeared between July 1, 2011, by which time the campaign was unofficially well under way, and May 30, 2012, when Romney captured enough delegates to secure the nomination. The numbers are "genuine conservative," 147; "real conservative," 770; and "true conservative," 2,654.

90. Theda Skocpol and Vanessa Williamson, *The Tea Party and the Remaking of Republican Conservatism* (Oxford: Oxford University Press, 2012), 7.

91. Ibid., 157–168.

92. Ibid., 37.

93. Ibid.

94. Ibid., 38.

95. "Romney, Santorum Take Widely Divergent Tacks," *Boston Globe* (February 21, 2012), 6; Ronald Brownstein, "Santorum's Legacy," *National Journal* (April 14, 2012): 15; Mitchell Landsberg, "Santorum, Under Fire for Satan Comments, Recalls Reagan's 'Courage,'" *Los Angeles Times* (February 22, 2012), available online at: http://articles.latimes.com/2012/feb/22/news/la-pn-santorum-satan-20120222.

96. Libertarian journals include the *Cato Journal, City Journal, Reason,* and the *Journal of Libertarian Studies.* Neoconservative journals include *Commentary, National Interest, New Criterion, Weekly Standard,* and, famously, until it stopped publishing in 2005, *Public Interest.* Religious conservative journals include *Faith & Reason, First Things,* and *Human Life Review.*

97. Besides Cato, libertarian advocacy groups and think tanks include the Goldwater Institute, Independent Institute, Manhattan Institute, National Center for Policy Analysis, Pacific Research Institute, Reason Foundation, Young Americans for Liberty, and many others. In addition, both the Atlas Society and the Ayn Rand Institute promote Ayn Rand's philosophy of objectivism, which is a libertarian philosophy even if Rand herself claimed it was not and her acolytes prefer to call themselves objectivists. And, of course, the Libertarian Party USA is a political party dedicated to promoting libertarianism. Neoconservative advocacy and think tanks include the Center for Security Policy, Hudson Institute, Project for the New American Century, and the Jewish Institute for National Security Affairs. Religious conservative organizations include the Christian Coalition, the Faith and Freedom Coalition, and Focus on the Family.

98. Many colleges and universities are religiously affiliated, of course, but some schools consider conservative religious and political views to be inextricably intertwined and believe their mission includes providing conservative leadership for the nation. Pat Robertson reflected this sentiment

when he said that "there is no way that government can operate successfully unless led by godly men and women" and that Regent's mission is
to train "God's representatives on the face of the earth." See Kevin Phillips, *American Theocracy* (New York: Viking, 2006), 215, quoting Robertson. These schools include: Ave Maria University, supported by Domino's
Pizza CEO Thomas Monahan; Bob Jones University, which, according
to its website, defends and teaches "the inerrancy of Scripture"; Liberty
University, founded by Rev. Jerry Farwell, Sr.; Pepperdine University; and
Regent University, founded by Rev. M. G. "Pat" Robertson. There are different perspectives among religious conservative colleges. Ave Maria, for
example, is a Catholic college while the others listed above are all affiliated with Protestant sects. Pepperdine spans all three schools of conservative thought and may also be the most establishment-oriented university
on the list. Its faculty has included prominent neoconservatives, including
Daniel Pipes and James Q. Wilson, libertarian Arthur Laffer, and religious
conservative Douglas Kmiec. A flap occurred when Pepperdine University
offered Kenneth W. Starr (who may span all three schools of conservatism) dual deanships of both its law and public policy schools while he
was independent counsel for the so-called Whitewater investigation. Arch-
conservative donor Richard Mellon Scaife, who contributed $1.35 mil-
lion to Pepperdine's new school of public policy, also gave $2.3 million
to right-wing magazine *American Spectator* to conduct its own Whitewater
investigation. Many thought this raised the appearance of impropriety.
See Susan Schmidt, "Starr Declines Pepperdine Because of Investigation,"
Washington Post (April 17, 1998), A1; and Kenneth Reich, "Pepperdine's
Million-Dollar Club: University Releases List of Donors After Controversy Erupts on Contributions by Supporter of Whitewater Probe," *Los
Angeles Times* (March 9, 1997), available online at: http://articles.latimes
.com/1997-03-09/local/me-36476_1_pepperdine-university. By contrast,
the least establishment-oriented college on the list may be Bob Jones University, which has had a notoriously segregationist past. It was considered
an act of important political symbolism when, during his campaign for
the 2000 Republican presidential nomination, George W. Bush held his
first event in South Carolina at Bob Jones University. Phillips, *American
Theocracy*, 357. Hillsdale College in Hillsdale, Michigan, is nondenomina-
tional and may be most firmly planted in libertarian soil. It is so opposed
to what it regards as governmental interference that it accepts no subsi-
dies from federal or state governments.

    99. Norman, *Edmund Burke.*

    100. Full disclosure: I have written two articles for *American Conserva-
tive.* The other Burkean groups are the Russell Kirk Center—located in
Mecosta, Michigan and headed by Russell Kirk's widow, Annette Kirk—

which is in significant part devoted to preserving Russell Kirk's legacy. Its quarterly publication, *University Bookman*, is published exclusively online. Another journal with a Burkean viewpoint is *The Imaginative Conservative*, also available exclusively online.

101. Somewhat unusually for a nonprofit corporation, Cato was organized as a stockholder company. Over time there came to be four shareholders with equal shares of stock, one of whom was Cato's CEO, Edward H. Crane III, and two of whom were Charles and David Koch. After the fourth shareholder died in October 2011, the Koch brothers filed suit in Kansas state court, demanding that the deceased shareholder's stock either be repurchased by the corporation or distributed pro rata to the remaining shareholders, either of which would give them two-thirds of the stock and control of the organization. Crane and the Cato board of directors vigorously resisted this lawsuit. See Luke Mullins, "The Battle for Cato," *Washingtonian* (June 2012): 64. Settlement of the litigation included Ed Crane resigning both as CEO and as a director, Charles Koch resigning as a director, and John Allison—a self-described objectivist—becoming CEO. The stockholder structure was also replaced with a self-perpetuating board of directors. The settlement was portrayed as preserving Cato as an independent advocate of libertarianism. See as examples: Kenneth P. Vogel, "Cato, Koch Brothers Settle Ownership Fight," *Politico* (June 25, 2012), available online at: http://www.politico.com/news/stories/0612/77809.html; Allen McDuffee, "Koch Brothers, Cato Institute Announce Terms of Settlement," *ThinkTanked*, a blog of the *Washington Post* (June 25, 2012), available online at: http://www.washingtonpost.com/blogs/think-tanked/post/koch-brothers-cato-institute-announce-terms-of-settlement/2012/06/25/gJQAQEJJ2V_blog.html. Whether that, in fact, turns out to be the case depends upon the loyalties and alliances of the board of directors, which is difficult for outsiders to gage.

102. Skocpol and Williamson, *The Tea Party*, 38.

103. Jennifer Rubin, "Jim DeMint's Destruction of the Heritage Foundation," *Right Turn*, a blog of the *Washington Post* (October 21, 2013), available online at: http://www.washingtonpost.com/blogs/right-turn/wp/2013/10/21/jim-demints-destruction-of-the-heritage-foundation.

104. See Laurie Goodstein, "An Interview with Pope Francis," *New York Times* (September 19, 2013), available online at: http://www.nytimes.com/2013/09/20/world/europe/an-interview-with-pope-francis.html?pagewanted=all&_r=0.

105. E. J. Dionne, Jr. is right when he says that the tea party "crowd is simply the old far-right minority that has always existed, with a larger media megaphone." E. J. Dionne, Jr., "Obama Must Seize the Day," *Washington Post* (October 14, 2013): A19.

106. "True believer" is defined as "One who is deeply, sometimes fanatically devoted to a cause, organization, or person: 'a band of true believers bonded together against all those who did not agree with them' (Theodore Draper)." *American Heritage Dictionary of the English Language*, 4th ed. (Boston: Houghton Mifflin, 2000), 1850. Eric Hoffer's classic work, *The True Believer: Thoughts on the Nature of Mass Movements*, 1st ed. (New York: Harper, 1951), remains an insightful examination of the psychology of true believers.

107. See for example Sheryl Gay Stolberg and Mike McIntire, "A Crisis Months in the Planning," *New York Times* (October 6, 2013): A1.

108. Eric Lipton, Nicholas Confessore, and Nelson D. Schwartz, "Business Groups See Loss of Sway over House G.O.P.," *New York Times* (October 9, 2013), available online at: http://www.nytimes.com/2013/10/10/us/business-groups-see-loss-of-sway-over-house-gop.html.

10

UNITING CONSERVATIVES:
COMMENTS ON BOGUS'S
TRIFURCATED CONSERVATISM

ELDON EISENACH

The historical reach of "Fighting Over the Conservative Banner" is an important contribution to our understanding of contemporary political and ideological conservatism. Bogus reminds us that contemporary conservatism, in all of its three major iterations, has deep roots in opposition to the New Deal—and not, as is so often assumed, in the overreach and incompetence of the Great Society. Most of the canonical conservative books cited predate not only LBJ but JFK as well. Put differently, one might say that the conservative critique of liberalism has as its benchmark the overwhelming political and economic success of Republican Party conservatism in the 1920s, an era that saw an incredible expansion of and investment in consumer goods, housing, our major cities, our research universities, and our major corporations. The institutional foundations of what has been called "the American century" were principally laid here,[1] during the presidencies of Harding, Coolidge, and, until the crash, Herbert Hoover.

I offer four sets of reflections to give a slightly different reading of the chapter's main themes. Political scientists would first ask of Bogus: Where is Theodore Lowi's *End of Liberalism?*[2] He argued that interest group liberalism and its "empirical theory of

democracy" premised on "the end of ideology" became an unac-
knowledged ideology that was normatively bankrupt and dangerous for our politics. Lowi articulated what was already a major
theme of the New Left (I was particularly aware of this as a graduate student at Berkeley in the 1960s). Establishment liberalism was
politically and morally bankrupt because it could not *rank* any set
of policies or values, or even distinguish between necessary acts
of governance and using the government as a vast and coercive
patronage network of the powerful. Lowi wanted something called
"juridical democracy" anchored in the Constitution. But where
now is the New Left critique of "the liberal establishment" to be
found? Certainly not in today's progressive electoral discourse. But
many of these same themes, especially the critique of the inherent
elitism of the liberal establishment, were picked up by the New
Right, giving its appeal a populist cast. We might be sobered to
be reminded that Young Americans for Freedom (YAF) had more
members in the 1960s and '70s than Students for a Democratic
Society (SDS). Without something like this critique, today's Democratic Party lacks, in the words of Paul Pierson and Theda Skocpol
of Harvard, "ideational infrastructure."[3] Or, as Bogus declares at
the start: "[Today's] liberals eschew ideology and focus on discrete
issues of public policy, which, they believe, is more pragmatic and
enlightened." But how do liberals counter conservative *ideas* and
values? If they don't, they not only lose by default (even if they
win elections), they open themselves up to the charge that they
are merely creating a new patronage network of "victims" that
they can electorally mobilize as a negative majority for, at most,
presidential elections.

Put in terms of programs and ideas, Democratic majorities in
the House during the entire Presidencies of Nixon/Ford, Reagan,
and H. W. Bush, and in the Senate during the entire Presidencies
of Nixon/Ford and H. W. Bush, could slow down but not stop the
advance of a *conservative* presidential agenda, including tax cuts,
deregulation, and privatization. Why under Clinton and then
Obama were Democrats unable (with the exception of health care
reform) to enact a liberal agenda? Why couldn't these Democratic
majorities in Congress generate the motivation, support, and political will to block this partial dismantling of the policies and values
of the New Deal and the later liberal establishment? Unless the

Democratic Party can create as disciplined a majority (or minority) as the Republicans have during the previous twelve years, President Obama will be unable to implement a coherent liberal political agenda. But, lacking a coherent set of ideas/ideology/ values, how can a disciplined majority be created and a coherent and positive agenda be enacted?

What Bogus has given us is a contrast between conservatism as an uneasy and unstable alliance of ideologically committed economic, religious, and foreign policy conservatives and—nothing. Liberal pundits and the media seem to join Bogus in whistling in the dark to think that conservatism must be committing political suicide, but have given no evidence of coherent political and intellectual life on the left. This whistling continues by changing the term liberal to "progressive." Just try, however, to identify progressive *politics* today: Occupy Wall Street? Anti-globalization parades? Countless ephemeral media protest events staged as if a real political movement actually exists on the ground? The last liberal *policy* initiatives were those of the Great Society, a huge, incoherent, and disruptive expansion of federal money and power. But its failures and legacy are legendary—so much so that the term liberalism became the kiss of death: the "L" word. In short, the exhaustion of liberal ideology and the failure of the last great liberal agenda should not be covered over, as Bogus does, by calling it public policy/pragmatism. In this vacuum conservative ideas and values thrived as never before. But this was in the 1970s and onward, not the 1950s, and in response to the crime and social breakdown associated with the Great Society. And, as Bogus demonstrates, this is when most conservative publications, organizations, and think tanks began to blossom.

My second reflection is to ask: If conservatism, given its inner tensions, does not self-destruct, might it be weakened and even destroyed from the outside, by counter organizations and ideas? Who or what are the enemies of Conservatism? On one level, the answer is that the enemies are not only everywhere, but they seem to have the resources and organizational infrastructure to rout conservatives. Let us assess their bases of power: most of the federal judiciary and federal bureaucracy, along with almost all law school faculty; the major universities and high status colleges; the recipients of the billions of dollars in federal research grants; the national press and national professional organizations; the many environmental organizations; mainline Protestant churches and Catholic bishops; Hollywood; and all public and quasi-public sector unions. What is missing here? Most obviously is a coherent national political party organized from the ground up. But even if the Democratic Party were to become ideologically coherent, where would they get the ideas that would motivate local and state party organizations to engage actual friends and neighbors (not paid or unpaid volunteers from the outside) of citizens whose votes they seek?

A natural place to look would be the universities and among the huge army of liberal intellectuals and their influential books, journals, and reviews. Alas, these sources do not articulate a political left but only a cultural one—a pseudo-political left that Richard Rorty railed against in *Achieving Our Country*.[4] These are the only standing ideological shock troops on offer from the American left and the Democratic Party. Against this opponent, the answer to "whither conservatism," no matter how divided Professor Bogus says it is, is either to go from electoral victory to victory at all levels of government, or, when losing national elections and congressional majorities, to watch their liberal/progressive counterparts flail hopelessly in the face of serious or hard choices. To speak the *political* language of the *cultural* left is to speak through various ephemeral and symbolic "movements" that have the illusion of serious politics. How would the Democratic Party fare with its leading ideas from Occupy Wall Street? Or with the programs of various anti-globalization movements calling for American withdrawal from the G-7, the G-20, the WTO, and/or the IMF and an end to national borders? A coalition of Green soft-Marxists, radical feminists, gays and lesbians, and various people of color might effect some policy changes, but mostly in the distribution of symbolic rewards. David Bromwich, reviewing David Maraniss's biography of Obama, put it succinctly, "The right won the political wars of the last two generations, the left won the culture wars."[5] But victories in culture wars do not seriously address overall governing ideas and comprehensive governing policies. Policing intolerance, for example, by multiplying rules or by hiring more diversity experts for our major corporate, financial, philanthropic, and educational institutions is not serious governing. A coalition of identity tribes led by a culturally left over-class is not capable of governing—as even some progressives admit. And to glory in the fact that some areas of the country are "majority minority" and that stable two-parent families are rapidly becoming the *bourgeoisie* preserve of white and Asian college graduates hardly tells us what to do or where to go.[6]

My third reflection is to suggest that one value—the family— does unite the three fractious elements of American conservatism. As a font of values that contribute to self-sufficiency, self-respect, and economic success, the stable family is essential to all three strands of conservative programs and values. Neoconservatism (remember the Moynihan Report) practically began here; some of the largest and most effective conservative religious organizations focus on the family; and, whether they like it or not, even libertarians have as an unstated premise the continued effectiveness of personal values that can only be sustained in families. Michael Lind, a sharp critic of American conservatism and one of the more historically astute progressives, suggests that even the "next American nation" will require, like all American regimes before it, an effective shared sacred bond—his proposal is "civic familism"—as its civil religion.[7]

Lastly, I might have expected from a law professor at least a passing acknowledgment of the rise of conservative ideas in American law and jurisprudence, represented by the importance of the political theory behind the law and economics movement and by neoconservative theories of constitutional law.[8] This influence is already evident in the U.S. Supreme Court. Conservative constitutional gurus are neither libertarian, nor religious, nor neocons, but they are very busy reestablishing much stricter constitutional understandings of the extent and reach of federal power. Whether under the sign of originalism, natural rights, or simply the priority of the Declaration of Independence, law professors who have taught the living constitution for decades, and proclaimed principled constitutional jurisprudence dead when Roscoe Pound became dean of Harvard Law School, are now challenged—at least in the courts.

If conservatives can claim the mantle of "rule of law" and pit it against administrative bodies, regulatory czars, and executive prerogative to kill-by-drone, liberals will have lost a momentous rhetorical battle. Is liberalism's only redoubt bureaucratic power allied to policy expertise? Justice Breyer and an army of administrative mandarins[9] is hardly an adequate defense against the storms of democratic politics and the appeals of popular sovereignty. Conservatives, no matter their internal divisions, currently seem to have a significant rhetorical advantage over contemporary liberals because their rhetoric is anchored in long-standing theories of man, politics, society, and, more significantly, in a larger American national narrative.[10]

NOTES

1. Olivier Zunz, *Why the American Century?* (Chicago: University of Chicago Press, 1998). On the sudden growth in the competence of the federal government at the beginning of this period, see Stephen Skowronek, *Building a New American State: The Expansion of National Administrative Capacities, 1877–1920* (Cambridge: Cambridge University Press, 1982).

2. Theodore Lowi, *The End of Liberalism* (New York: Norton, 1969).

3. Paul Pierson and Theda Skocpol, eds., *The Transformation of American Politics: Activist Government and the Rise of Conservatism* (Princeton, NJ: Princeton University Press, 2007), 290.

4. Richard Rorty, *Achieving Our Country: Leftist Thought in Twentieth-Century America* (Cambridge, MA: Harvard University Press, 1998).

5. David Bromwich, "Diary: A Bad President," *London Review of Books* 34 (July 5, 2012): 42–43.

6. We might also be reminded that college graduates represent the *largest* percentage of church goers and provide through their children the vast majority of college and professional school graduates.

7. Michael Lind, *The Next American Nation: The New Nationalism and the Fourth American Revolution* (New York: Free, 1995), 277–285.

8. Steven M. Teles, *The Rise of the Conservative Legal Movement: The Battle for Control of the Law* (Princeton, NJ: Princeton University Press, 2008); and the collection in Ellen Frankel Paul, Fred D. Miller, Jr., and Jeffrey Paul, eds., *Natural Rights Individualism and Progressivism in American Political Philosophy* (New York: Cambridge University Press, 2012); also Ken I. Kersch, "Beyond Originalism: Conservative Declarationism and Constitutional Redemption," *Maryland Law Review* 71 (2011): 229–282, and Kersch's chapter in this collection.

9. See Ken I. Kersch, "Justice Breyer's Mandarin Liberty," *University of Chicago Law Review* 73 (Spring 2006): 759–822.

10. Eldon J. Eisenach, *Sacred Discourse and American Nationality* (Lanham, MD: Rowman & Littlefield, 2012).

11

LEO STRAUSS AND AMERICAN
CONSERVATIVE THOUGHT AND POLITICS

NATHAN TARCOV

In recent years Leo Strauss has been identified as one of the chief
sources of contemporary American conservative thought and
politics.[1] I must leave it to intellectual historians to determine the
degree of influence that various understandings and misunder-
standings of Strauss's thought have had on the diverse strands of
American conservative thought and politics. I will limit myself to
trying to determine Strauss's own stance toward American conservative thought and politics and some of the possible implications
of his thought for American conservative thought and politics.

I. POLITICAL PHILOSOPHY AND PRACTICAL POLITICS

To assess the bearing of Strauss's thought on American conservative thought and politics, one must first consider his understanding of the general relation of thought and politics. To be more
precise, one must consider his understanding of the relation of
political philosophy to practical politics, and therefore of his own
attempted recovery of classical political philosophy to practical politics. For Strauss, political philosophy in its original sense (which
for him was above all Platonic political philosophy) was "the
attempt to replace opinion about the nature of political things by
knowledge of the nature of political things." As *philosophy*, it goes

to the roots and is comprehensive. As *political* philosophy, it "deals with political matters in a manner that is meant to be relevant to political life"; it is directed toward knowledge of the good life or of the good society; it strives for knowledge of the true standards of goodness or justice by which political phenomena explicitly or implicitly demand to be judged.[2] But because political action is guided not by knowledge but by questionable opinion, "the element in which society breathes," for Strauss there is a permanent and fundamental tension between thought in its highest sense as philosophy—even and especially political philosophy—and politics.[3] Since this tension was fundamental for Strauss, it is safe to assume that the classical political philosophy he taught and studied must be in some tension with politics, including American conservative politics.

Strauss distinguishes political philosophy from political thought, by which he means any reflection on or exposition of ideas concerning political fundamentals. But unlike political philosophy, political thought as such is "indifferent to the distinction between opinion and knowledge"; it may be no more than "the expounding or the defense of a firmly held conviction or of an invigorating myth."[4] A political thinker who is not a political philosopher is primarily interested in or attached to establishing or defending a specific order or policy rather than in discovering the truth. Strauss distinguishes political philosophy not only from political thought in general but also from political theory or "comprehensive reflections on the political situation which lead up to the suggestion of a broad policy."[5] It is clear to me that Strauss understood himself to be engaged in political philosophy rather than in political thought or political theory, that he was interested in clarifying the standards by which societies and policies are judged, not in suggesting a broad policy. He probably would have considered American conservatism, in contrast, to be political thought or political theory.

The tension between political philosophy and politics that Strauss emphasizes does not necessarily imply that political philosophy is apolitical or antipolitical or that it plays no role in politics. On the contrary, as already noted, it "deals with political matters in a manner that is meant to be relevant to political life."

Strauss offers a perplexing variety of accounts of the political role of the philosopher based on his understanding of classical political philosophy. According to the first account, which might loosely be called Aristotelian, the political philosopher looks at politics from the perspective of the enlightened citizen or states-man, speaks the language of the citizens or statesmen, accepts "the basic distinctions made in political life exactly in the sense and with the orientation in which they are made in political life," and serves as an umpire trying to settle political controversies of paramount and permanent importance.[6] He thus performs the duty of a good citizen to make civil strife cease and create agreement among the citizens by persuasion. On a higher level (one that Strauss himself does not seem to me to occupy), he is the teacher of legislators or founders, "the umpire par excellence."[7] The political philosopher who aspires to the role of impartial umpire adopts a perspective that "encompasses the partisan perspectives," that sees the partial truths in the partisan perspectives (as Aristotle does, for example, with the oligarchs and the democrats),[8] rather than siding with one of the parties. One would expect such an umpire not simply to side with American conservatives against liberals or vice versa but to bring out the partial truths, which is to say also the errors, of each side, as we will see Strauss does in the preface to *Liberalism, Ancient and Modern.*

The second account Strauss offers of the role of the political philosopher in practical politics is that of the defender of autono-mous prudence from theoretical errors. This is a much more occa-sional and marginal role than that of umpire. Strauss explains:

> The sphere governed by prudence is then in principle self-sufficient or closed. Yet prudence is always endangered by false doctrines about the whole of which man is a part, by false theoretical opin-ions; prudence is therefore always in need of defense against such opinions, and that defense is necessarily theoretical. The theory defending prudence is, however, misunderstood if it is taken to be the basis of prudence.[9]

Strauss thus distinguishes philosophy from the prudence needed by statesmen and makes no claim on behalf of the superior pru-dence of philosophers. He was not an advocate of the rule of philosophers, contrary to some assertions. At most, according to Strauss, philosophy can protect the prudence of nonphilosophic citizens and statesmen from both utopianism and complacency by reminding them of permanent features of human nature and the problematic character of all practical solutions to human problems.

Strauss gives his fullest explanation of this view in a lecture titled "What Can We Learn from Political Theory?" delivered at the General Seminar Summer Course at the New School in July 1942.[10] Despite the mention of "political theory" in the title, which was not of Strauss's own choosing, the lecture is about what we can learn from *classical political philosophy* that can guide political practice. He first presents the negative case, that "we can learn *nothing* from political philosophy," on three grounds: (1) political philosophy is at best knowledge of the problems, not the solutions, and so cannot be a guide to action; (2) not political philosophy but practical wisdom is needed to guide political action; and (3) political philosophy merely reflects political practice, since all significant political ideas come from political practitioners. Strauss then makes his positive case, which concedes the force of the first two negative claims, but, using the example of foreign policy during and after World War II, argues that political philosophy is needed to defend reasonable political action, discovered by prudent statesmen like Churchill without the aid of political philosophy, when it is challenged by erroneous political teachings. Strauss also denies that all significant political concepts are the work of political men: the politically influential concept of natural law or natural right, by which classical political philosophy judges all actual political orders to be imperfect, is of philosophic origin even though implicit in some prephilosophic political arguments. He contrasts this ancient utopianism with the modern utopianism that he claims disastrously lowered the standards of conduct to guarantee their realization. Far from expecting political philosophy to provide the guidelines for foreign policy, Strauss claims that reasonable foreign policy could be arrived at and defended against other commonsense views without the assistance of political philosophy, though it might need the aid of political philosophy to defend itself against utopian or other erroneous political doctrines in light of the natural limits set to all human hopes and wishes. Reasonable policy needs to be protected in particular, he argues, from present-day utopianism, which tends to forget that "forces of evil" always exist or to think they can be countered by institutional and economic changes, replacing the equally illusory reliance on enlightenment of its early modern predecessors.[11] Political philosophy, Strauss argues, is needed to protect against the smugness of the philistine who thinks our own society is perfect, though the more urgent danger comes from the modern utopianism that believes it is achieving a future perfect society. Strauss soberly remarks, "political philosophy teaches us how terribly difficult it is to secure those minimums of decency, humanity, [and] justice, which have been taken for granted, and are still being taken for granted in the few free countries. By enlightening us about the value of those apparently negligible achievements, it teaches us not to expect too much from the future." It teaches that the "so-called perfect order on earth is bound to be a delusion."[12]

Closely related to the political philosopher's role of umpire between the parties or defender of prudence is that of teacher of moderation. According to Strauss, classical political philosophy is "free from all fanaticism because it knows that evil cannot be eradicated and therefore that one's expectations from politics must be moderate,"[13] a lesson that needs to be learned by conservatives as well as liberals or radicals.

Last but far from least, Strauss describes the political philosopher in politics as a defender of philosophy itself, of philosophy understood as it is by Strauss as a way of life rather than a set of doctrines. The political philosopher attempts "to supply a political justification for philosophy by showing that the well-being of the political community depends decisively on the study of philosophy" and at the same time "to lead the qualified citizens, or rather their qualified sons, from the political life to the philosophic life."[14] While such attempts may start by appealing to conservatism as well as liberalism, they are meant to lead to something different from and higher than either.

II. CONSERVATISM AND LIBERALISM

Strauss addresses American conservatism most explicitly and extensively in his preface to *Liberalism, Ancient and Modern*. Though, as one would expect from the preface to a book so titled, it focuses more on liberalism than on conservatism, it starts by noting that "Liberalism is understood here and now in contradistinction to conservatism."[15] The context makes clear that "here and

now" refers to the United States in the late 1960s: "Here and now
a man who is in favor of the war on poverty and opposed to the
war in Vietnam is generally regarded as doubtlessly a liberal, and
a man who is in favor of the war in Vietnam and opposed to the
war on poverty is generally regarded as doubtlessly a conservative." Although Strauss concedes that this distinction made "here
and now" is "sufficient for most present practical purposes,"[16]
he proves more interested in its theoretical difficulties and their
practical consequences.

Strauss notes that liberalism and conservatism have a common
basis in liberal democracy and therefore share an antagonism to
Communism. Elsewhere in that book, Strauss affirms that the most
important concern for political scientists in his time who would
take their bearings by classical political philosophy would be not
the opposition between liberalism and conservatism but "the
qualitative difference which amounts to a conflict, between liberal
democracy and Communism."[17] Nonetheless he discerns a profound difference between liberal and conservative opposition to
Communism. According to Strauss, present-day liberalism shares
with Communism the ultimate goal of a universal and homogeneous state, or at least its approximation in a universal federation,[18] with the important difference that it regards as sacred the
right to criticize the government, but liberalism prefers democratic or peaceful means and rejects foreign wars (though not necessarily revolutions with the sympathy of or for the interests of the
majority) as the means to that goal. Liberals believe the tension
between liberal democracy and Communism will disappear "as a
consequence of the ever increasing welfarism of the former and
the ever increasing liberalism, due to the overwhelming demand
for consumer goods of all kinds, of the latter."[19]

In contrast, conservatives, according to Strauss, "regard the
universal and homogeneous state as either undesirable, though
possible, or as both undesirable and impossible."[20] They do so
not because they are nationalists, for he says they do not deny the
necessity or desirability of larger units than the nation-state; they
do not necessarily oppose, for example, a united free Europe.
Nor is it because they are imperialists, which "for good or ill," he
says without further explanation, they can no longer be (contrary
to the notion that Strauss was the progenitor of a nationalist or

imperialist American conservatism). Conservatives, Strauss writes, reject the universal and homogeneous state to which both liberals and Communists in their different ways aspire because they "look with greater sympathy than liberals on the particular or particular-ist and the heterogeneous," or at least are more willing "to respect and perpetuate a more fundamental diversity" than liberals are. It then went without saying that conservatives like liberals rejected foreign wars as a means to a universal and homogeneous society since they did not share that goal. I would say that since Strauss wrote this in 1968, some liberals and conservatives have switched sympathies, at least rhetorically, with those liberals appearing to celebrate diversity and those conservatives affirming the universal-ity of liberty and democracy and even approving of foreign wars as a means to spread liberal democracy. If Strauss had lived to see this development, he might have continued to argue that the diversity liberals respect is not so fundamental, or he might have concluded instead that some liberals have come to surpass conservatives in their distrust of universal reason while some conservatives have come to surpass liberals in their political universalism. For Strauss traced conservatives' sympathy for particularism to their distrust of reason or trust in tradition.[21] His remark here that tradition "as such is necessarily this or that tradition" suggests the paradox involved in a universal principle of adherence to tradition, and the radical difference between traditional*ism* and tradition. Strauss therefore concludes that conservatism is "exposed to criticism guided by the notion of the unity of truth."[22] In this fundamen-tal respect, philosophy as rational pursuit of the universal truth was for Strauss at odds with conservatism. For Strauss, philosophy originates in the questioning of the authority of tradition or of the primeval identification of the good with the ancestral.[23] In *Natu-ral Right and History* he criticizes "the eminent conservatives who founded the historical school" for "denying the significance, if not the existence, of universal norms" and thereby destroying "the only solid basis of all efforts to transcend the actual." He argues in con-trast that "particular or historical standards can become authorita-tive only on the basis of a universal principle," and that to conform with tradition "is not obviously better, and it is certainly not always better than to burn what one has worshipped."[24] And the section on Burke in that work charges that that eminent conservative was not content with defending practice or prudence against the encroachments of theoretical science but prepared the way for the turn to history of the historical school and even of Hegel.[25] For Strauss it was "the shaking of all traditions" in his time that offered the accidental advantage of making possible the untraditional and genuine understanding of classical political philosophy.[26]

This opposition between conservatism's distrust of reason and trust in tradition, on the one hand, and philosophy's reliance on reason or questioning of tradition, on the other hand, does not necessarily imply that the conservative stance is inappropriate to politics. Strauss asks, "Is the conservatism which is generally speaking the wise maxim of practice the sacred law of theory?"[27] Although Strauss does not answer that question there, it is safe to conclude that for him theory recognized no such sacred law. For our purposes, however, the relevant portion of the question is rather the concession that conservatism is, generally speaking, the wise maxim of practice. It is also necessary to note, first of all, that Strauss says that conservatism is the wise maxim of practice only "generally speaking," and second, that the conservatism he is discussing is not "literalist traditionalism" but rather "the loyal and loving reshaping or reinterpretation of the inherited." Strauss seems sympathetic to Aristotle's reservations about the virtue of innovation on the grounds that law owes its power to command obedience, not to reason but to custom that comes into being over a long time, yet Aristotle concedes that laws sometimes have to be changed.[28] As the wise maxim of practice "generally speaking," such conservatism is only a rule of thumb that occasionally needs to be corrected. Strauss warns that "maxims which were justified by the uncontested experience of decades, and even of centuries or millenniums, may have to be revised because of unforeseen changes." In support of this warning he quotes Burke: "that the generality of people are fifty years, at least, behind hand in their politics."[29] Conservatism as adherence to tradition in general or a particular tradition needs to be supplemented and corrected by prudence or universal reason.

From Strauss's initial suggestion in the preface that conservative distrust of the universal and homogeneous state is rooted in distrust of reason and trust in tradition, he moves "closer to the surface" to say that it is rooted in distrust of change, whereas liberals believe in progress.[30] Insofar as conservatism is aversion to change, Strauss indicates, its substantive principles will vary with the status quo of its time and place. American conservatism as aversion to change is in the awkward position of opposing change in a country that "came into being through a revolution, a violent change or break with the past." Strauss goes on to add with evident amusement that, "one of the most conservative groups here calls itself the Daughters of the American Revolution." He notes that when the opposition between conservatives and liberals first arose (presumably in early nineteenth-century Europe) the substance was very different: conservatives stood for "throne and altar," liberals for popular sovereignty and the private character of religion. He adds: "conservatism in this sense is no longer politically important" (contrary to the notion that Strauss proposed a practical project of doing away with democracy or reestablishing religion). The conservatism of our age, in contrast, Strauss writes, is "identical with what originally was liberalism, more or less modified by changes in the direction of present-day liberalism."[31]

Strauss even suggests that conservatism, liberalism, and Communism share a common root in the modern break with the premodern tradition. Characteristically, he thus ascends from the contemporary opposition between liberals and conservatives to what he regards as the more fundamental quarrel between the ancients and the moderns.[32] He starts by invoking the original meaning of "liberal" as practicing the virtue of liberality or practicing the virtues more generally, and then turns to the liberalism of classical political philosophy.[33] The elaboration of this movement in Strauss's chapter "Liberal Education and Responsibility" makes clear that the original meaning of liberal is that of the gentleman of the prephilosophic premodern world, not yet the liberalism of classical political philosophy.[34] This distinction may help us to understand the relation between the following possibly confusing sentences in this portion of Strauss's preface to *Liberalism, Ancient and Modern*: "Being liberal in the original sense is so little incompatible with being conservative that generally speaking it goes with a conservative posture. Premodern political philosophy, and in particular classical political philosophy, is liberal in the original sense of the term. It cannot be simply conservative since all men seek by nature, not the ancestral or traditional, but the good."[35]

The premodern gentleman, the exemplar of Aristotle's moral virtues, was conservative in the sense of trusting in tradition, whereas classical political philosophy could not be conservative in that sense. Although classical political philosophy could not be "simply conservative," it could adopt "a conservative posture" by showing respect for tradition while understanding the need prudently and rationally to transcend, reshape, and depart from tradition.

Rather than conservatism's formal principles of trust in tradition and distrust of change, classical political philosophy opposes "a substantive principle" to the universal homogeneous state. It asserts that a closed society is natural to man, one that "rests on a particular fundamental opinion which cannot be replaced by knowledge and hence is of necessity a particular or particularist society."[36] Similarly, in the introduction to *The City and Man* Strauss writes that the West should learn a "practical particularism" from the experience of Communism. By this he means the acceptance that "for the foreseeable future, political society remains what it always has been: a partial or particular society whose most urgent and primary task is its self-preservation and whose highest task is its self-improvement."[37] Thus, Strauss combines a theoretical or philosophic universalism with a practical or political particularism. Strauss warns that Kojève's universal and homogeneous state would in fact be the rule of the "Universal and Final Tyrant" and "the end of philosophy on earth."[38] In *Natural Right and History*, Strauss explains that classical natural right opposed a universal society, because "political freedom, and especially that political freedom that justifies itself by the pursuit of human excellence, is not a gift of heaven; it becomes actual only through the efforts of many generations, and its preservation always requires the highest degree of vigilance."[39] The "practical particularism" Strauss teaches is based not on trust in tradition and distrust of reason but on recognition of the fragility of freedom and of the pursuit of excellence it makes possible. Although Strauss claims it would not be difficult to show that "liberal or constitutional democracy comes closer to what the classics demanded than any alternative that is viable in our age,"[40] he was far from teaching that it was viable and therefore the only legitimate form of government in every time and place.

Only late in the preface to *Liberalism, Ancient and Modern* does Strauss indicate that the book is intended as a "critical study of liberalism."[41] In the light of this indication, we can see that for the purpose of such critical study, conservatism does not provide a sufficient point of reference. Instead, Strauss contrasts liberalism here and now with liberalism where and when the opposition between liberalism and conservatism first arose in early nineteenth-century Europe,[42] then with what it meant to be liberal in its premodern sense,[43] then with the liberalism of classical political philosophy,[44] and finally with Judaism.[45] Conservatism is hardly discussed in the preface's last paragraphs: Strauss's primary concern there both as critic and as friend is, as we would expect from the book's title, with liberalism.

III. Strauss's Political Actions in America

My concern so far has been primarily with the political implications of Strauss's thought, by which I mean above all his turn to classical political philosophy,[46] as distinguished from whatever opinions he expressed about the politics of his day. Presumably his political opinions were not inconsistent with the possible political implications of his turn to classical political philosophy (though that possibility cannot simply be ruled out), but they need not have been the necessary consequences or the only possible implications of his political philosophy.

As far as I know, Leo Strauss publicly engaged in American political life on only three occasions.[47] The first was his participation in a panel on the reeducation of the Axis countries concerning the Jews at the public session of the annual meeting of the Conference on Jewish Relations, November 7, 1943, at the New School.[48] Strauss narrowed the topic to Germany but broadened it to include the reeducation of Germany concerning Nazism and liberal democracy. He claimed the mass of the Germans had been moved not by Nazi doctrines but by the prospect of a solution of all German problems by a short and decisive war, and he therefore concluded that the reeducation of Germany would take place not in postwar classrooms but through defeat followed by a just, stern, and stable peace, culminating in trials of the war criminals. He doubted liberal democracy would appeal to the Germans given its historical weakness in Germany and warned that "a form of government which is merely imposed by a victorious enemy, will not last."

Only Germans who remained in Germany could do the reeducating because of German pride, differences between the German and Anglo-American intellectual climates, and German awareness of the differences between Anglo-American doctrine and Anglo-American practice (such as racial segregation in the United States and British rule in India), which led Germans to regard the Atlantic Charter as hypocrisy.

As to German reeducation concerning the Jews, Strauss said that until the Germans purified themselves by spontaneously giving satisfaction for what they had done, "no self-respecting Jew can, and no Jew ought to, be interested in Germany." He said not returning German Jews, nor Jewish Americans, but only Germans could educate the Germans concerning the Jews. He suggested that the German Catholic clergy, and a part of the Catholic intelligentsia, and perhaps the Lutheran clergy might become significant agents of German reeducation concerning the Jews.

In retrospect, we are bound to think that Strauss was too pessimistic about the prospects for liberal democracy in postwar Germany. His skepticism about the ability of the Allies to reeducate the Germans may have been reasonable, but he was too skeptical about the inclination of the Germans themselves to take the British and American liberal democracies as models, and he was wrong in thinking that the German tendency to regard those democracies' principles as hypocrisy would prevent the Germans from adopting those principles. He seems to have erred in the direction of underestimating, not overestimating, the prospects for the spread of liberal democracy as the result of military conquest, exactly the opposite fault from that which he has sometimes been charged with encouraging.

Strauss's second act of public political engagement in America was his publication of a letter to the editor of *National Review*, originally written as a letter to his friend, the prominent conservative Willmoore Kendall. He began the letter by admitting that he agreed with many articles in the conservative publication but then went on to take it to task severely for its then hostility to Israel.[49] Strauss defended Israel as "an outpost of the West in the East," characterized by "heroic austerity supported by the nearness of biblical antiquity." He explained that the role of trade unions in Israel had to be understood in light of circumstances and excused the absence of civil marriage in Israel on the grounds that he was "not so certain that civil marriage is under all circumstances an unmitigated blessing." He concluded by praising political Zionism, despite its being "problematic for obvious reasons," for fulfilling a "conservative function" in restoring the dignity of the Jewish people and stemming the tide of leveling of ancestral differences. Although this letter was meant to appeal to the convictions of a conservative readership, Werner Dannhauser argues persuasively that it contained the "seeds of a possible critique of the kind of conservatism to be found in *National Review*" for its thoughtless attachment to heritage, its excessive concern with success, its tendency to be "ill-tempered and mean-spirited," and its dogmatic indifference to circumstance.[50]

Strauss's final public political engagement was his signing of a statement, along with forty-four other prominent academics, that appeared as an advertisement in the *New York Times* on October 15, 1972. It read in full: "Of the two major candidates for the Presidency of the United States, we believe that Richard Nixon has demonstrated the superior capacity for prudent and responsible leadership. Consequently, we intend to vote for President Nixon on November 7th and we urge our fellow citizens to do the same."[51] This endorsement did not address any specific policies or principles. Endorsing Nixon over McGovern in 1972, unlike, say, endorsing Goldwater over Johnson in 1964, did not necessarily identify one as a conservative. McGovern was seen by many liberals as having strayed from the defining policies of liberalism. Recalling Strauss's rough definition that "a man who is in favor of the war on poverty and opposed to the war in Vietnam is generally regarded as doubtlessly a liberal, and a man who is in favor of the war in Vietnam and opposed to the war on poverty is generally regarded as doubtlessly a conservative," we may note that Nixon, after all, moved to end the war in Vietnam, not the war on poverty.

IV. LEO STRAUSS AND CONTEMPORARY AMERICAN CONSERVATISM

The traditionalism discussed above is, of course, only one of several major strands of contemporary American conservative thought and politics, sometimes intertwined and sometimes running separately, such as cultural conservatism; free market or libertarian conservatism; social conservatism; populist conservatism; and "hardline" or "neoconservative" foreign policy. I will hazard a few cursory and tentative remarks about the relation of Strauss's thought to each of these. While I believe he might have some sympathy for each of these as antidotes to their opposites, it would be a critical sympathy.

Strauss is often not unreasonably associated with those conservatives who see themselves as defending Western culture or the Western tradition. In the preface to *Liberalism, Ancient and Modern,* Strauss warns that liberals, "especially those who know that their aspirations have their roots in the Western tradition, are not sufficiently concerned with the fact that that tradition is ever more being eroded by the very changes in the direction of One World which they demand or applaud."[52] He presents the replacement of the philosophic question of the right way of life by the historical question of "the ideals of Western civilization," however, as characteristic of the historicism of which he is so critical.[53] Though Strauss defends liberal education, which had become "almost synonymous with the reading in common of the Great Books," he advocates reading them not as the sources of our tradition but as reminders of human greatness, and he adds, "the greatest minds to whom we ought to listen are by no means exclusively those of the West."[54] Strauss does not call for a return to our tradition as such because our tradition contains contradictory elements that require us to find our own bearings and think for ourselves.[55]

Although as far as I know Strauss never publicly addressed any specific issues of economic policy, his famous characterization of Locke's vision of the rational life as "the joyless quest for joy" and his dictum that "economism is Machiavellianism come of age" sufficiently establish his critical distance from free-market conservatism.[56] He might regard the reliance on the automatic working of the market mechanism by free-market conservatives as another modern effort to replace the statesman's prudence and citizen's virtue. More broadly, he seems to agree with the classics "that the aim of human life, and hence of social life, is not freedom but virtue" and that political freedom "justifies itself by the pursuit of human excellence."[57] He does not sound like a libertarian.[58]

For some of the same reasons that Strauss seems to have kept a critical distance from free-market or libertarian conservatism, he would seem sympathetic to social conservatism's concerns for virtue and religion. Strauss suggested that concern for liberty should not preclude concern for virtue, but it is far from clear that what he meant by virtue had much to do with the preoccupations of social conservatives. It is possible that he would regard their preoccupations as dictated by religious rather than strictly political concerns. I see no way, however, of unequivocally determining the implications of Strauss's work for such central issues of the social conservative agenda as restricting or prohibiting homosexuality and abortion. It would be as silly, for example, to infer from the acceptance of gender equality, homosexual activity, and infanticide in Plato's *Republic* that Strauss's conception of Platonic political philosophy would demand their acceptance in twenty-first-century America as it would be to draw the opposite conclusion from the limitations on gender equality and on homosexual activity in Plato's *Laws*.

The practical implications of Strauss's lifelong theme of the theological-political problem are equally indefinite. The utility of religion for morality and hence for politics and the permanence of religion as an expression of deep human longings and fears suggest that policy should not and cannot aim to extirpate religion or even expel it from the public square. In that respect Strauss might be sympathetic to some of the complaints of social conservatives and critical of the secularizing policies of some liberals. Strauss, however, was far from arguing for the acceptance of religion on the grounds of its utility.[59] The hostility of revealed religion to reason and philosophy that Strauss stresses and the occasional disutility of religion for politics that he mentions suggest that politics should enjoy autonomy from religion.[60]

Some conservatives are as prone to bouts of populism as some liberals, though the people they invoke and the elites they rail against are quite different. Strauss's critique of "mass democracy" leaves no doubt that he was not a populist of either Left or Right.[61] He speaks highly of "a civil service properly so called, the specific difference between the bureaucrat and the civil servant being that the civil servant is a liberally educated man whose liberal education affects him decisively in the performance of his duties," and of "the true liberalism which is only the reverse side of constitutional democracy adorned by an exemplary judiciary."[62] His castigation of "creeping conformism and the ever-increasing invasion of privacy which it fosters" and his praise for "non-conformists" are far from populist and resemble instead the social criticism of his time found on both the Left and the Right.[63]

An adequate sketch of the implications of Strauss's work for foreign policy would require another study.[64] One should hardly expect his turn to classical political philosophy to yield specific guidance for foreign policy, since he claims classical political philosophy is guided by questions concerning the inner structure of the political community, not its external relations.[65] The reason he gives for this, that "the ultimate aim of foreign policy [the survival and independence of the political community] is not essentially controversial," along with his view that political society is "a partial or particular society whose most urgent and primary task is its self-preservation and whose highest task is its self-improvement," his recognition that military power matters and sometimes has to be used, and his distrust of a universal federation along the lines of the United Nations, all suggest kinship with foreign policy "realists," found among both conservatives and liberals, as well as with "unilateralists," found mostly among conservatives. But he also suggests that regimes matter, and he addressed the foreign policy not of the United States alone but of the Allies during World War II and of the West during the Cold War, as if the United States, as a society accustomed to understanding itself in relation to a universal purpose, had to think of itself as a part of a larger whole concerned with the survival of that whole.[66] Strauss's acceptance of the coexistence of opposed regimes rather than universal liberal democracy and his skepticism about the possibility of imposing liberal democracy on postwar Germany make me doubt he would have shared the sanguine views of some neoconservatives of the prospects for spreading liberal democracy through military conquest. He argues that civic morality necessarily suffers from the contradiction between warlike habits and the requirements of justice, so we must ignore neither the requirements of justice nor the exigencies of war.[67]

It would be a strain to extrapolate what Strauss might have considered reasonable policies for our particular circumstances from his recovery of classical political philosophy and critique of modern political philosophy. However edifying this attempt might prove to be, it is more important to notice that Strauss did not himself attempt to derive particular policies from his reflections on political philosophy, even on those few occasions when he did propose particular policies. He warns, "We cannot reasonably expect that a fresh understanding of classical political philosophy will supply us with recipes for today's use."[68] For Strauss, circumstances are crucial, and the application of principles to circumstances is the work of prudence, not philosophy. Strauss ventures to express the classical view that there is "a universally valid hierarchy of ends," but it is not sufficient for guiding our actions: one may have to prefer an end that is lower in rank as more urgent "here and now."[69]

I would venture to suggest that for Strauss these strands of contemporary American conservatism might reflect characteristically modern theoretical errors: a historicist version of the preference for the traditional over the good and the rational in cultural conservatism; the effort to find substitutes for prudence and virtue in free-market conservatism; the subordination of politics or prudence to religion in social conservatism; egalitarianism in populist conservatism; and universalism in neoconservative foreign policy.

Leo Strauss's understanding of political philosophy and its role in the political community was very different from that of political theorists who understand their task precisely as deriving particular policies from philosophical principles.[70] If one tries to turn Strauss into a political theorist of that sort, one has missed the point. Leo Strauss was neither simply a conservative nor simply a liberal, and he can remind both conservatives and liberals of the need for prudence and moderation and of the permanence of human nature and the permanent problems they may be tempted to ignore.

Notes

I am grateful for the comments and suggestions of Robert Devigne, Kenneth Hart Green, John Holbo, Arthur Jacobson, David Janssens, Ralph Lerner, Sanford Levinson, John McCormick, Robert Pippin, Steven B. Smith, and Melissa Williams, though I suspect none of them would agree with everything written here.

1. On Strauss and American conservatism, see: Robert Devigne, *Recasting Conservatism: Oakeshott, Strauss, and the Response to Postmodernism* (New Haven, CT: Yale University Press, 1994); Shadia B. Drury, *Leo Strauss and the American Right* (New York: St. Martin's Press, 1997); Steven Lenzner, "Leo Strauss and the Conservatives," *Policy Review* (April/May 2003): 75–82; Anne Norton, *Leo Strauss and the Politics of American Empire* (New Haven, CT: Yale University Press, 2004); Kenneth R. Weinstein, "Philosophic Roots, the Role of Leo Strauss, and the War in Iraq," in *The Neocon Reader*, ed. Irwin Stelzer (New York: Grove Press, 2004), 203–212; Douglas Murray, *Neoconservatism: Why We Need It* (New York: Encounter Books, 2006), 1–21; Francis Fukuyama, *America at the Crossroads: Democracy, Power, and the Neoconservative Legacy* (New Haven, CT: Yale University Press, 2006), 21–31; Andrew Sullivan, *The Conservative Soul: How We Lost It, How to Get It Back* (New York: HarperCollins, 2006), 256–265; Thomas L. Pangle, *Leo Strauss: An Introduction to His Thought and Intellectual Legacy* (Baltimore, MD: Johns Hopkins University Press, 2006), 83–86; Tony Burns and James Connelly, eds., *The Legacy of Leo Strauss* (Exeter, UK: Imprint Academic, 2010), 197–275; C. Bradley Thompson and Yaron Brook, *Neoconservatism: An Obituary for an Idea* (Boulder, CO: Paradigm, 2010); and Robert Howse, *Leo Strauss: Man of Peace* (Cambridge: Cambridge University Press, 2014).

2. Leo Strauss, *What Is Political Philosophy? and Other Studies* (New York: Free Press, 1959), 10–12.

3. Ibid., 10, 221.

4. Ibid., 12.

5. Ibid., 13.

6. Ibid., 27–28, 79–81.

7. Ibid., 83–84.

8. Aristotle, *Politics*, 1280a7–1281a10.

9. Leo Strauss, *Liberalism, Ancient and Modern* (Ithaca, NY: Cornell University Press, 1968), 206.

10. Leo Strauss, "What Can We Learn from Political Theory?" *Review of Politics* 69 (Fall 2007): 515–529. See my "Introduction to Two Unpublished Lectures by Leo Strauss," same issue: 513–514; also my "Will the Real Leo Strauss Please Stand Up?" *American Interest* 2 (September/October 2006): 121–123.

11. Strauss, "What Can We Learn," 523–526.

12. Ibid., 527.

13. Strauss, *What Is Political Philosophy*, 28.

14. Ibid., 93–94. See also at 125; Leo Strauss, *Persecution and the Art of Writing* (Glencoe, IL: Free Press, 1952), 17–18, 36–37; and my "Leo Strauss's 'On Classical Political Philosophy,'" in *Leo Strauss's Defense of the*

Philosophic Life: Reading What Is Political Philosophy?, ed. Rafael Major (Chicago: University of Chicago Press, 2013), 65–79.

15. Strauss, *Liberalism*, vii.

16. Ibid.

17. Ibid., 214. See also 209, 215, 223.

18. I wonder whether Strauss took Robert Hutchins's World Federalism as typical of liberalism in a way that no longer sounds familiar.

19. Strauss, *Liberalism*, vii–viii.

20. Ibid., viii.

21. Already in his 1921 doctoral dissertation, Strauss identified "the principle of conservatism" with "the principle of traditionalism," the recognition of tradition as such rather than of one particular tradition. *Gesammelte Schriften, Vol. 2*, ed. Heinrich Meier (Stuttgart: J. B. Metzler, 1997), 282 note 135.

22. Strauss, *Liberalism*, viii–ix.

23. Leo Strauss, *Natural Right and History* (Chicago: University of Chicago Press, 1953), 83–86.

24. Ibid., 14–17.

25. Ibid., 304, 311–319.

26. Leo Strauss, *The City and Man* (Chicago: Rand McNally, 1964), 9.

27. Strauss, *Liberalism*, 250; see also 14.

28. Strauss, *City and Man*, 21–22, discussing Aristotle, *Politics*, 1269a12–24.

29. Strauss, *Liberalism*, 213, quoting Edmund Burke, *Thoughts on the Cause of the Present Discontents* (London: J. Dodsley, 1770).

30. Strauss, *Liberalism*, ix.

31. Ibid.

32. This movement can be seen already at the end of Strauss's 1931 lecture "Cohen and Maimonides," where he calls for acquiring "a horizon beyond the opposition progress/conservatism, Left/Right, Enlightenment/Romanticism," in *Leo Strauss on Maimonides: The Complete Writings*, ed. Kenneth Hart Green (Chicago: University of Chicago Press, 2013), 222. Compare Steven B. Smith, *Reading Leo Strauss: Politics, Philosophy, Judaism* (Chicago: University of Chicago Press, 2006), 179: Strauss "saw politics neither from the Right nor from the Left but from above. . . . Strauss was neither a conservative nor a liberal in any of the standard uses of those terms."

33. Strauss, *Liberalism*, ix–x.

34. Ibid., 10–15.

35. Ibid., x. The second sentence starts a new paragraph. I have corrected "man" to "men" in the third sentence, which alludes to Aristotle, *Politics*, 1169a3–4.

36. Strauss, *Liberalism*, x.

37. Strauss, *City and Man*, 6. See my "Will the Real Leo Strauss," 125–128.

38. Strauss, *What Is Political Philosophy*, 132–133.

39. Strauss, *Natural Right and History*, 131.

40. Strauss, *What Is Political Philosophy*, 113. See also Leo Strauss, "The Three Waves of Modernity," in *An Introduction to Political Philosophy: Ten Essays by Leo Strauss*, ed. Hilail Gildin (Detroit, MI: Wayne State University Press, 1989), 98.

41. Strauss, *Liberalism*, x.

42. Ibid., ix.

43. Ibid., ix–x.

44. Ibid., x.

45. Ibid., x–xi.

46. Various claims have been made that Strauss's manifest turn to classical political philosophy masks his true adherence to the thought of such modern thinkers as Machiavelli, Nietzsche, Schmitt, and Heidegger, claims made most extensively by Shadia Drury in *The Political Ideas of Leo Strauss* (New York: St. Martin's Press, 1988). It is beyond the scope of this chapter to respond to this view or to give my reasons for taking my bearings by Strauss's evident turn to classical political philosophy, however "tentative and experimental" that turn may be. Strauss, *City and Man*, 11. See Catherine Zuckert and Michael Zuckert, *The Truth about Leo Strauss: Political Philosophy and American Democracy* (Chicago: University of Chicago Press, 2006).

47. As distinguished from brief published remarks, such as his reference to the dangers to intellectual freedom caused by "men like Senator McCarthy," Strauss, *What Is Political Philosophy*, 223, or opinions he expressed privately, such as his reported support for Adlai Stevenson for president. See Clifford Orwin, "The Straussians Are Coming! A Review of *Leo Strauss and the Politics of American Empire* by Anne Norton," *Claremont Review of Books* V (Spring 2005); and Smith, *Reading Leo Strauss*, 235 note 102.

48. Leo Strauss, "The Re-education of Axis Countries Concerning the Jews," *Review of Politics* 69 (Fall 2007): 530–538; my "Will the Real Leo Strauss," 123–125.

49. Leo Strauss, "Letter to the Editor," *National Review* (January 5, 1957): 23; John A. Murley and John E. Alvis, eds., *Willmoore Kendall: Maverick of American Conservatives* (Lanham, MD: Lexington Books, 2002), 192–199.

50. Werner J. Dannhauser, "The Achievement of Leo Strauss IV," *National Review* (December 7, 1973): 1355–1357.

51. *New York Times* (October 15, 1972): E7. Other signers included

Edward Banfield, Robert Bork, Martin Diamond, Milton Friedman, Oscar Handlin, Gertrude Himmelfarb, Sidney Hook, Morton Kaplan, Irving Kristol, Robert Nisbet, W. V. Quine, William Riker, Edward Shils, George Stigler, and Thomas Szasz.

52. Strauss, *Liberalism*, ix. See also Leo Strauss, "Progress or Return?" in *Jewish Philosophy and the Crisis of Modernity: Essays and Lectures in Modern Jewish Thought*, ed. Kenneth Hart Green (Albany: State University of New York Press, 1997), 101.

53. Strauss, *What Is Political Philosophy*, 59.

54. Strauss, *Liberalism, Ancient and Modern*, 3, 6, 7, 24.

55. Ibid., 7–8; Strauss, "Progress or Return," 104, 113; Leo Strauss, "German Nihilism," *Interpretation* 26 (Spring 1999): 367.

56. Strauss, *Natural Right and History*, 251; Strauss, *What Is Political Philosophy*, 49.

57. Strauss, *What Is Political Philosophy*, 36; Strauss, *Liberalism, Ancient and Modern*, 24, 64; Strauss, *Natural Right and History*, 131.

58. Compare Smith, *Reading Leo Strauss*, 171.

59. "I shall not waste words on the most popular argument [in favor of revelation] which is taken from the needs of present-day civilization, the present-day crisis, which would simply amount to this: that we need today, in order to compete with communism, revelation as a myth. Now this argument is either stupid or blasphemous." Strauss, "Progress or Return," 123. Strauss's ultimate concern is with the challenge to philosophy posed by the truth claims of religion, rather than with its political utility or disutility: see Heinrich Meier, *Leo Strauss and the Theologico-Political Problem*, trans. Marcus Brainard (New York: Cambridge University Press, 2006).

60. Strauss, *Natural Right and History*, 164; Strauss, *What Is Political Philosophy*, 44.

61. Strauss, *Liberalism, Ancient and Modern*, 5.

62. Ibid., 18; Strauss, "Letter to the Editor," 23.

63. Strauss, *What Is Political Philosophy*, 37–38.

64. See Thomas G. West, "Leo Strauss and American Foreign Policy," *Claremont Review of Books* IV (Summer 2004): 13–16; Smith, *Reading Leo Strauss*, 184–201; Howse, *Leo Strauss: Man of Peace*; and my "Will the Real Leo Strauss."

65. Strauss, *What Is Political Philosophy*, 84–85.

66. Strauss, *City and Man*, 2–6; Strauss, "What Can We Learn," 518; Strauss, "Re–education," 532, 534.

67. Strauss, *Natural Right and History*, 149, also 160–161.

68. Strauss, *City and Man*, 11.

69. Strauss, *Natural Right and History*, 162–163.

70. Compare Meier, *Leo Strauss and the Theologico-Political Problem*, 14–15.

12

WHAT FASCISM TEACHES US

ARTHUR J. JACOBSON

I want to begin by drawing your attention to a curious omission in Nathan Tarcov's presentation of the bearing of Leo Strauss's thought on American conservative thought and politics.[1] Actually, it is an omission in the text that provides Tarcov with the core of his presentation, not in his admirably thorough account of it. The text is the preface to Strauss's *Liberalism, Ancient and Modern*.[2] Tarcov remains faithful to the text, patiently expounding its argument. He does not, however, report or repair the omission. It therefore becomes his omission as well.

In that preface, Strauss musters three of the dominant political positions in the West today for inspection. These are liberalism, conservatism, and communism. He utters not a single word about a political position that had very much been on view during Strauss's life and caused it not a little disruption. It is still very much on view today. I refer, of course, to fascism. One would have expected some mention of it in Strauss's text, not only because fascism is an extremely important creature of modernity, but also because Strauss's own formulation of the relationship between liberalism and conservatism, on the one hand, and communism, on the other, begs for completion by the fascist paradigm, and Strauss's understanding of conservatism would, I believe, be strengthened by an appreciation of the fascist challenge to both liberalism and conservatism.

In an oddly distanced formulation, Strauss describes conservatism as "frequently characterized by distrust of reason or by trust in tradition."[3] Though he by no means explicitly says so in his text, Strauss would not disagree, I think, that liberalism may be characterized the opposite way, by trust in reason and distrust of tradition. And though he also by no means says so in the text, I think a fair characterization of communism would be as the perversion of liberalism. It would be the carrying of liberalism to an extreme, so that communism does not simply trust reason, as does liberalism, but has absolute certainty about reason, and does not simply distrust tradition, as does liberalism, but wants to eliminate tradition altogether from a role in human existence. But then fascism, by the same token, could be seen as the perversion of conservatism. It could be seen as the carrying of conservatism to an extreme, so that fascism does not simply trust tradition, as does conservatism, but gives tradition a biological foundation and sacred residence; it does not simply distrust reason, as does conservatism, but recoils from reason and abandons it as a regulator of and limitation on human affairs.

Fascism has a critique of conservatism. It is that mistrust of reason isn't enough to stop it from destroying tradition. Reason can't be cabined or regulated. Once you even admit the possibility of reason as a measure of behavior, it will take over every nook and cranny of life. A touch of reason is impossible. The fascist intuitively understands the communist and agrees with him that reason must always dominate tradition, and tradition will wither away. The conservative is naïve to think that one can kiss reason good night and send it on its way. The conservative is a liberal in waiting. The liberal, on the other hand, is just a sloppy communist who hasn't rigorously thought through the consequences of what he believes and does. The only difference between the fascist and the communist is that the fascist believes the life of reason is not worth living, that the irrational and the community sustaining the irrational are what mark off humans from the soulless equations of nature. If reason rules, then humanity becomes a sacrifice to Spinoza's cold and lonely God.

The fascist knows that in a world where reason is always a temptation, tradition must be merciless and hard. If it is not, then reason, which is always merciless and hard, will triumph and humanity will be destroyed. The fascist knows that sustaining a tradition in the face of reason requires discipline and violence. It requires total immersion in the texts and ways of the tradition. It requires intolerance. It requires keeping the strange, the different, the other at bay.

Fascism thus has a defensive strategy to survive against reason. But it also has an offensive strategy, a faith. It has the faith that human beings by nature—in their biological nature—experience the life of reason as loveless and not worth living, as inhuman and dead. It has the faith that reason as the basis for community cannot sustain itself, that at best reason can organize episodic bursts of terror, taking the steel to traditional structures as boys kill flies. Fascism has the faith, in other words, that reason cannot organize a tradition, either to maintain itself as reason or to construct a lasting community. Fascism's argument with reason in any of its iterations—communist, liberal, or conservative—is that reason can only be accepted on its own terms, as reason, and not on the irrational terms that must, according to fascism, be at the root of every successful civilization.

The difficulty with fascism—the fatal difficulty—is that it always comes on the scene only after reason is already well on its way toward destroying a tradition. Fascism is a *recoiling from* reason into tradition; it is not traditionalism. It is an afterthought to communism and parasitic upon it. It is the dread of communism, not a freestanding political doctrine. The fascist feels communism in his bones. The tradition that the fascist defends with blood and honor is thus always, without exception, an invented tradition. It is not in fact a tradition but rather nostalgia for a tradition. The fascist tradition is bogus, fake, or, more charitably, a work of art. The fascist regime mobilizes its resources through theater, through music and the visual arts. Fascist emotions are theatrical emotions. The love the fascist thinks he engenders is the love of an audience for its diva, the love of the moment, in a crowd, not real love. And the fascist knows it. This only increases his rage. His regime is as loveless as the communist's. The discipline and violence of his regime are no different from the discipline and violence of the communist regime. Neither can sustain loyalty beyond the romantic fervor of a founding cohort. The fascist is, in the end, a brute, not a defender of the faith; the communist, but an artless fascist, not the cynosure of reason; their regimes, the same regime.

Fascism nonetheless presents a very great challenge to the non-fascist politics of modernity based one way or the other on reason. Can reason organize a tradition? Can reason permit itself to be accepted for reasons other than reason? Strauss saw both components of the challenge at most moments in his work. He saw that the failure of Socrates to persuade Plato not to write, the failure of Plato to persuade Aristotle that reason must always be critical reason and may never simply be assumed as fact—that these are all telling indictments of the powers of reason, at least Athenian reason, to form an intellectual tradition, no less a world. He saw that the play of reason in society is rare and at risk. I suppose he could not bring himself to say, at least in his preface to *Liberalism, Ancient and Modern*, that these are the difficulties that fascism predicts.

The fact is, reason *can* organize a tradition. It *can* permit itself to be accepted for reasons other than reason. Strauss knew this and studied the great historical example of it intensively. This is the tradition of rabbinic Judaism. It is, for Strauss, the counter-model to the Athenian model of reason based solely upon reason. The rather relaxed and ill-fitting term commonly used to describe this counter-model is revelation. Revelation is precisely the acceptance of reason for reasons other than reason. It makes the claim that accepting reason for reasons other than reason must ultimately always be so, that the Athenian model of reason accepted solely because it is reason is childish fantasy. Plato, toward the end of his life, did not disagree. That is why Strauss was attracted to the last of Plato's dialogues, *The Laws*, the most pious and lawful of his dialogues, which explored the irrational acceptance of the rational—the necessity of drunkenness for political success, the requirement of piety for knowledge.

It would take far more time than I now have to describe adequately the rabbinic tradition of reason and to compare it as a sort of reason both with and against Athenian reason. Needless to say, it has a way of "handing over" tradition in both its senses. Rabbinic Judaism knows what is necessary for maintaining the educational institutions, family structures, and values that put the highest validation on perpetuating the cult of rabbinic reason. It knows what it must know in order to form the foundation for the institutions of a long-standing and sophisticated community based on reason. None of this would be possible were the reason at stake in the community not also revelation. The importance of rabbinic Judaism for Leo Strauss, one of its twentieth-century acolytes, is that it understood and responded to the fascist challenge, even before it got to be made.

So, yes, Tarcov is correct that Strauss in the preface at issue analyzes liberalism and conservatism as at best half truths, that liberalism and conservatism, acting in concert with communism, constitute a fully accepting approach towards the activity of reason in politics. Yet he is wrong—or implicitly wrong, or passively wrong—that liberalism and conservatism, acting in concert with communism, are the only possible instantiations of reason. And Strauss, though he did not say so in the preface, knew so as well.

Nathan Tarcov works and teaches at the Athens of America. I work and teach at its Jerusalem. Little wonder then that Tarcov, like Leo Strauss before him, is disinclined to pursue this kind of answer to fascism. That was what Strauss did while he was in Germany. When he came here, he began to work with the American model. That was all understandable and worthy of praise. It is what we must do. It is what Sanford Levinson has done in his book on constitutional faith.[4] But let us be clear. Finding an irrational basis for the rational, answering the fascist in some way other than through the intellectual tradition of revelation, is no easy task. Perhaps constitutional faith or constitutional patriotism accomplishes it. Perhaps not. I don't know yet. We shall see.

NOTES

1. Nathan Tarcov, "Leo Strauss and American Conservative Thought and Politics," this volume.

2. Leo Strauss, *Liberalism, Ancient and Modern* (Chicago: University of Chicago Press, 1968).

3. Ibid., viii.

4. Sanford Levinson, *Constitutional Faith* (Princeton, NJ: Princeton University Press, 1989).

13

SEGREGATION, AGGRESSION, AND EXECUTIVE POWER: LEO STRAUSS AND 'THE BOYS'

ALAN GILBERT

Dick [Cheney] remembers Bob [Goldwin] from the Ford years, when he became a resident scholar at the White House. Bob had worked for Don Rumsfeld at NATO, and after Don became White House Chief of Staff, Bob organized a series of seminars for President Ford and the senior staff. He'd get together a small number of people, always including the president, and bring in a speaker to enlighten the group. Dick particularly remembers one Saturday when Bob put together a gathering up in the solarium on the top floor of the White House. The speaker that day was Daniel Patrick Moynihan, and he talked about his book *Beyond the Melting Pot*, in which he and Nathan Glazer wrote about the persistence of ethnicity in America and the consequences of it. *Beyond the Melting Pot* was a controversial book at the time. All these years later, we know it was very prescient.

Dick says that he does not recall in all his years in Washington events like the ones Bob organized. Bob didn't advertise what he was doing and didn't talk about it much in the years after, which was part of his essential modesty, part of what made him so admirable. We will miss him very much.

—Lynne V. Cheney[1]

Few individuals had as much influence on the thinking of conservative American policy makers and yet were as little known to the public as Bob Goldwin. Bob was a man of sweeping, ambitious ideas, but personal modesty and quiet competence. He had the rare talent of asking the right questions at the right time, and gently nudging discussions toward the "eureka" moment. Every conversation with Bob left you with a perspective you hadn't considered before.

Bob and I had known each other since his days at the University of Chicago. In 1972, I lured away my friend from his position as dean of St. John's College in Annapolis, Maryland to join me at NATO, where I served as U.S. ambassador. Two years later, I was called back to Washington to help the newly sworn-in President Gerald Ford, and one of the first people I recruited to the White House staff was Bob. Bob led seminars for President Ford in the White House solarium, bringing in some of the finest minds in America, not least his own, to discuss the toughest issues of the time.

Bob Goldwin was the Ford administration's one-man think tank, its intellectual compass, and bridge to a new conservatism—a conservatism that was unashamed to be conservative. He helped provide the intellectual underpinning that convinced many Republicans that they didn't have to apologize when they stood for lower taxes or suggested that our strategy against the Soviet Union ought not be placation.

The ideas he corralled and the causes he championed—from opposing the creation of a new international bureaucracy with the Law of the Seas Treaty in 1982 to offering wise counsel on a new Iraqi constitution as recently as 2003—were without match. Bob was a valuable counselor and a dear friend.

I considered myself one of his many students, and I know I will miss him. So too will America, but perhaps without fully realizing what is being missed.

—Donald Rumsfeld[2]

On another occasion Antiphon asked him [Socrates]: "How can you suppose that you make politicians of others, when you yourself avoid politics even if you understand them?"

"How now, Antiphon," he retorted, "should I play a more important part in politics by engaging in them alone or by taking pains to turn out as many competent politicians as possible?"

—Xenophon, *Memorabilia*[3]

Nathan Tarcov insists that Strauss was apolitical, a man interested primarily in ancient texts and not in current problems. He is not alone in this assertion; Francis Fukuyama and Michael and Catherine Zuckert offer a similar argument. There is obviously some truth in this notion; Strauss *did* devote himself to scholarship, much of it quite esoteric and unlikely to be accessible to politicians or the punditry, and he did not invest himself directly in politics. Yet I think this portrait is incomplete; he was scarcely completely detached from contemporary politics, and one can certainly argue that he sought influence for his ideas, which have, after all, earned the label "Straussian." Still, with regard to a discussion of "American conservatism," the topic of this volume—and of what are now two conferences held five years apart—Strauss presents a difficult set of intellectual and conceptual issues. After all, he arrived in this country in 1937 as a quite fully formed scholar and intellectual; to put it mildly, he could not then be described as an "American thinker," and some might argue, with justice, that he had an orthogonal relationship to "American" thought thereafter. Even with regard to "conservatism," his was a distinctive variety, having little in common with some "standard" sources of American conservatism in Edmund Burke, misty-eyed Southern agrarianism (though we will see that he allied with its racism), or the teachings of Catholic natural law, however much, like partisans of all of these views, he made his reputation as a caustic critic of liberalism. But criticism of liberalism is obviously not enough to earn one's stripes as a "conservative." Not only could Marx or Nietzsche serve as exhibit A; one must recall that Hayek wrote a famous essay on why he was not a conservative.

Fortunately, for purposes of the limited space available to me in this volume, it is possible to avoid a full-scale analysis of Strauss by focusing instead on several of his students, including Robert Goldwin, the subject of the eulogies that preface this chapter. Whatever Leo Strauss's status as an exemplar of American conservatism, there can be no doubt that Goldwin—and Walter Berns and Harvey Mansfield, to name only two other prominent figures who will appear below—qualify both as American by any available criteria and, more to the point, as men of influence on a host of important political figures who would be proud to assert their own conservative credentials. To be sure, there are Straussians who are not so conservative (let alone influential). Still, any serious analysis of American conservatism over the past half century—and, perhaps, into the future—must contend with the fact that certain

Straussians were indeed involved both in the conservative movement—think only of Allan Bloom's manifesto against American
culture and higher education—and in conservative politics.

As mention of Bloom suggests, one could write an extended
chapter on the role played by Strauss and Straussians in the educational culture wars of the past several decades. But in this chapter, I want to emphasize other aspects of the Straussian corpus.
The first involves a debate from quite long ago that nonetheless
continues to have relevance for contemporary American politics;
it focuses on the claim of the civil rights movement to full inclusion in American life and a concomitant use of national power to
limit state autonomy committed to maintaining the exclusion associated with segregation. As we shall see, Strauss and Goldwin displayed a remarkable antagonism to *Brown v. Board of Education*. For
many readers, no doubt, even more important is the stance taken
by a number of important Straussians on the specifics of executive
power—including quasi-tyrannical "prerogative" powers—that
have challenged, if not indeed undermined, traditional conceptions of American constitutional checks and balances. During the
Bush-Cheney regime, the "commander in chief power" served as a
justification for systematic violations of the United Nations Conv-
enant Against Torture and Other Inhumane and Degrading Acts,
one of the few international human rights treaties that the United
States has in fact ratified.

One might say that it is a calumny against conservatives to link
them to segregation or to defenses of torture. Many people identified with conservatism, including Richard Epstein and Bruce
Fein, joined with liberals to denounce exalted claims made by the
Bush-Cheney administration—and, in many important ways, continued into the Obama administration. Perhaps we should draw
a distinction between conservatives and reactionaries. A conservative defends habeas corpus—the right of each prisoner to a day in
court and not to be indefinitely detained or tortured as vital, since
the Magna Carta, to the rule of law. By this standard—the Anglo-
American standard—those who dismiss the importance of habeas
corpus are no conservatives. In Europe, "conservatives" were often
defenders of Throne and Altar, frequently Catholic, authoritar-
ians; in the person of Carl Schmitt, a strong influence on Strauss,
such views could slide easily into fascism.

Strauss sometimes expressed amusement at what (or who) was called conservative in the United States. In lectures, Strauss would often use the expression "what a conservative *or a reactionary* would say."[4] With precision, a reflection of esoteric or hidden writing, he would often distance himself from conservatives, for instance, by saying that conservatism is a good "rule of thumb," or in his 1957 letter rightly critical of the *National Review*'s anti-semitism, invoking repetitively "what a conservative might think," as if he almost—but not quite—was an example of the breed. One can imagine his being sympathetic with Hayek's similar disdain for many American conservatives. Still, as Donald Rumsfeld has taught us, just as one fights wars with the army one has, instead of the army one wishes one had, one takes part in politics with the people and movements who are available, not the ones one might wish in an ideal political world. And if we look at decisions made by Strauss—and, more to the point, Straussians like Goldwin, especially, we find some extraordinarily unattractive material.

1. Strauss's Activism and Caution

An exile, a German Jew, and darkly reactionary, Strauss was rightly wary of American xenophobia. He was not by temperament inclined to devote himself simply to politics. Nonetheless, following Xenophon, he devoted remarkable care and attention to shaping American politics. His political activism was strategic and, in the long run, influential. Paralleling his twin roles, Strauss's letters to his American students divide into two types.[5] The first letters, reflected in correspondence with Seth Benardete and a few others, center on Strauss's love of scholarship and are sometimes striking. His relationship with Benardete probed the subtleties of Greek texts.

The second type, however, underlines Strauss's reactionary activism. For instance, Strauss worked with the Public Affairs Conference Center at the University of Chicago, run by his student Robert Goldwin, to connect with political and military leaders around a particular agenda: (1) defense of segregation and hostility to the Supreme Court's *Brown v. Board of Education* decision and the civil rights movement; (2) advocacy of aggression to intimidate the Soviet Union, including the conquest of Cuba, even after the Cuban missile crisis; and (3) urging of authoritarianism and untrammeled executive action, coupled with scorn for parliamentary politics or the separation and balance of powers. Steven Teles, in his own history of American conservatism, has emphasized the importance of think tanks and similar institutions in creating networks of like-minded individuals empowered to fight against their intellectual adversaries. The Public Affairs Conferences are pioneering in this regard.

Through the Public Affairs Conferences, Strauss indirectly engaged Senator Charles Percy, Republican keynoter in 1960 and a potential Republican presidential nominee. He also worked with Senator Henry Jackson, a Democratic hawk and gateway to the intelligence establishment, a subsequent employer of Straussians like Abram Shulsky,[6] not to mention Hans Speier, head of the Rand Corporation and an old friend. Note that these efforts to move American politics to the Right were bipartisan, and not restricted, as it has seemed to some after 2000, to "neoconservative" Republicans.[7]

In contrast to the intellectual "purity" of some of Strauss's correspondence, one finds political themes throughout letters to Walter Berns, Allan Bloom, Joseph Cropsey, Harry Jaffa, and, principally, Robert Goldwin. The political "boys," as he called them, express occasional reverence for Strauss's scholarship. But the correspondence reflects, to a large extent, their personal scholarly and political goals and concerns. They were not concerned with the depth and subtlety of Strauss's argument (Bloom and Cropsey were obviously more interested than Berns and Goldwin, but they all reflect a common political idiom). In a conceptualization drawn from Strauss's 1955 letter to Kojève, Strauss used these rhetors or gentlemen to purse his own reactionary public agenda, including advancing his own students.[8]

2. DEFENDING SEGREGATION AGAINST VALUE-FREE SOCIAL SCIENCE

The debate about *Brown v. Board of Education* involved a number of important issues, including, of course, the role of the Supreme Court in attempting to change what had become "traditional" Southern white subordination of African Americans. But there was also a vigorous debate at the time about the role of social science in public affairs, a topic about which Strauss (and Straussians) had strong views. In *Natural Right and History*, Strauss rightly mocks the empiricist argument for value-free social science or "the fact-value distinction." He seems to defend Socrates and justice against this view. As medicine is concerned with health, he suggests rightly, so social research or "science" should be concerned with justice or a common good.[9] Without self-awareness, social scientists often embrace prevailing values "around here," glossing current prejudices while imagining themselves to do otherwise. Strauss seems to favor Socrates' question: what is justice? Prima facie, this argument is Strauss's strongest, most attractive, and influential claim.[10]

Following what he takes to be the example of philosophers in *Persecution and the Art of Writing*, however, Strauss has two hidden meanings which undercut this argument's force. First, Strauss endorsed Nietzsche and viewed inequality, an aspect of master morality, as what he meant by "justice." For instance, despite the initial lines of *Natural Right and History*, praising the indelible eloquence of asserting each individual's "natural rights" in the Declaration of Independence, Strauss subsequently affirms the "classical view of natural *right*: inequality."[11] Strauss then mocks the argument for equality, suggesting that the mere existence of a division of labor in a city is fatal to that possibility. He oddly ignores Plato's "city in speech" which has no slavery and does not practice the subjection of women. He does not ask whether inequalities harmful to those who experience them are "necessary" in politics, but takes his allusion as sufficient. It is not.[12]

Second, Strauss aimed to defend segregation in the United States against what he called "ss." The "ss" that drew his wrath was that of Gunnar Myrdal as well as Kenneth and Mamie Clark's "doll experiment" cited in *Brown*'s footnote 11. Suffice it to say that this experiment was used to demonstrate that, when given a choice of dolls, both white *and* black children chose the white dolls as "prettier," which for the Clarks (and Chief Justice Warren) was evidence of the assault on the "hearts and minds" of children daily demeaned by state-mandated segregation. Segregation was not conservative. It was authoritarian, anti-liberal, often murderous rule over a large minority (in Mississippi, a majority) of the population which distorted the personalities, as Martin Luther King insisted, of whites as well as African Americans. In the concrete instance, though, we find Strauss and Goldwin promoting "states' rights" and segregation against the Clarks' social science. That difference does not compromise the validity of Strauss's general critique of ostensibly "value neutral" social science. On the contrary, in this instance, the critique indicts Strauss's own political stand. Strauss stood against the justice which he supposedly affirmed, against "ss"; in contrast, the Clarks' social science—and the Warren Court which relied on it—was not "value free" but stood for justice.

When Robert Goldwin became the head of the Public Affairs Conference Center, he took on Strauss as a paid, and more importantly, strategic advisor. On December 17, 1960, Goldwin reported that James Jackson Kilpatrick, the editor of the *Richmond News Leader* and a crusading segregationist, had written one of the four papers for a conference, emphasizing "states' rights" as vital to "the essential strength of the United States in the present situation." As Goldwin put it, "Here is the paper by Mr. Kilpatrick, just received. His assignment was to make the case that a reassertion of States' rights would add to the essential strength of the United States in its present situation. His response in the light of the assignment speaks volumes. Everything proceeds smoothly now, though in a great rush."

On December 24, 1960, Strauss praised Kilpatrick's "contribution," emphasizing that supposed positive impact of "local diversity" on American power to defeat the Soviet Union. (As a matter of fact, briefs submitted by both the Truman and Eisenhower administrations had emphasized the costs to American reputation abroad of segregation at home and in effect pleaded with the Court to do what a Southern-dominated Congress was incapable of doing—ending segregation in the South.[13]) Strauss also emphasizes Morton Grodzins's paper, which focused on federalism, states' rights or "anti-centralism," and also questioned the legitimacy of the Supreme Court's intervention striking down segregation.

As we shall see, Goldwin, like some others among Strauss's students, would extol extreme centralism or authoritarianism: "executive power" or "prerogative." But here, ironically, the affirmation of American imperial purposes seemingly required adopting the

Southern defense of localism or states' rights and opposition to the authority of the Supreme Court.

Upholding the equal rights of each citizen is the core of modern *political* thought or liberalism to which Strauss objected.[14] On no other issue could Strauss's profound aversion to equality manifest itself in such striking terms. Thus he enthusiastically congratulated Goldwin:

> I have read the four articles and can hardly say more than that you ought to be congratulated on the good judgment you have shown in selecting the four writers. *It is not your fault that the States' Rights position is presented in only one paper* but in the future it might be wise to think well in advance of a possible substitute for a senator. The advantage of Kilpatrick's paper is that its main argument (local diversity) is not met in any of the three other papers, and so there is room for discussion. All papers are well and interestingly written. . . . Grodzins' paper is clear, very well written and lucidly argued; *but it does not go into the political reasons of the anti-centralists (especially the desegregation issue and the whole question of whether these kinds of matters can legitimately be settled by the Supreme Court)*. It makes very much sense to me that Grodzins speaks on page 14, line 3 of "the most important services" but this qualification raises a well known "methodological" difficulty which might be brought out on a proper occasion in order to bring in a plug for the anti-SS.[15]

It is, apparently, not enough to criticize the Court's use of social science; one should go beyond and adopt the entire critique of *Brown* and, by the early 1960s, the civil rights movement that was transforming America. On February 13, 1961, speaking of it as "*my* business," Strauss broadened this attack on social science "and its political consequences in the last generation" (desegregation).

It is vital that a new generation be reminded exactly who Kilpatrick was. He was not the equivalent, say, of Herbert Wechsler, a famous professor of constitutional law at Columbia, who with some anguish, misguidedly attacked *Brown* as a violation of "neutral principles" in a lecture at the Harvard Law School. Instead, Kilpatrick praised "the South" and its "traditions" of segregation. To place this within an earlier debate, Kilpatrick was not Stephen A. Douglas, affecting "neutrality" on the goodness or badness of slavery and advocating that the "popular sovereigns" in each state come to their own conclusions about its merits; he was the equivalent instead of John C. Calhoun. Just as slavery had been a "positive good" for Calhoun and partisans of the "slavocracy," so segregation was a positive good for Kilpatrick.

Affecting moderation, Kilpatrick notices that lynching was a problem. (Perhaps this is comparable to a "moderate" Nazi—Schmitt?—agreeing, after defeat and in retrospect, that the Holocaust went too far.) But Kilpatrick was interested in probing the relationship between lynching and the maintenance of the racialized system of power in the South. Kilpatrick does not notice that Democratic politicians by day, particularly sheriffs and other officials, were often Klansmen, or collaborators with Klansmen, by night.[16] Kilpatrick's views were scarcely hidden behind esoteric writings requiring the exegesis of a Straussian seminar to decode. In the late 1950s and early 1960s, Kilpatrick authored three books devoted to the maintenance of white supremacy, including a book forthrightly titled *The Southern Case for School Segregation*. What apparently drew Goldwin's specific attention, and Strauss's plaudits, was the book *The Sovereign States*, setting out his constitutional argument that "sovereign states" comprised the Union. Since the national government, including the Supreme Court, was simply the agent of the principals—that is, the states—a state that disagrees with federal policy—or a judicial decision—on constitutional grounds has the "right to nullify" that policy, or to "interpose" itself to block it. This classic articulation of this argument, of course, was offered by John C. Calhoun, paraphrased by Kilpatrick as follows:

> In this process [of enacting of Tariff of 1828], they [the Congress, meaning "the industrial North"] had gravely encroached upon the rights of the States, but—and here the doctrine of nullification in its most drastic form was asserted for the first time—the States had one remedy remaining to them: They could invoke their inherent right "to interpose to protect their reserved powers" [those not explicitly enumerated in the *Constitution*], and by interposing, *suspend the operation of a law they regarded as unconstitutional pending a decision by all the States in convention assembled.*[17]

Kilpatrick spells out "the transcendent issue" which, ostensibly, will preserve segregation:

> The remedy lies—it must lie—in drastic resistance by the States, *as States*, to Federal encroachment. "If those who voluntarily created the system cannot be trusted to preserve it," asked Calhoun, "who can?" The checking and controlling influence of the people, exerted as of old, though their states, can indeed preserve the constitutional structure. The right to interpose the will of the sovereign people, in order that the evils of encroachment may be arrested, once more can be exerted toward the preservation of a Union and the dignity of States.[18]

Here Kilpatrick emphasizes the "diversity" of state viewpoints, seemingly echoed by Strauss:

> And the necessity for a restraint upon the abuses and excesses to which all governments are inclined, arises largely from the fact that the governed people have dissimilar interests and concerns. Were all the people alike, and all interests of a community identical, no such restraints would be required; a single majority division would justly decide every question submitted to it. But this identity of interest does not exist among the several States who jointly form the American Union. From the very inception of the Republic, the different States zealously have cherished differing institutions: To one, foreign trade may be vital; to another, domestic manufactures; to a third, agriculture; to a fourth, water power and irrigation; to a fifth, the operation of public schools and parts. It is only to a limited extent that these most vital concerns may be subordinated to the "national good." At some point Calhoun argued, compromise must end and oppression begin.[19]

Quite obviously, the specific "oppression" that Kilpatrick is most concerned with is that directed at Southern whites by the American judiciary and their supporters, who were insisting that, in Martin Luther King's terminology, the check written by the Reconstruction Amendments following the Civil War finally be redeemed.

Kilpatrick hastens to point out that the ostensible "right" to nullification cannot be invoked except under circumstances of exigency; otherwise, the central government would collapse. But not to worry, for Kilpatrick and other white Southern racists find just such an "exigency" to be attached to the prospects of desegregation and what was described as "forced intermingling of the races." This is not the occasion for full-scale examination of the merits of "nullification" doctrine. After all, it traces its heritage back to the Virginia and Kentucky resolutions, in which Jefferson and Madison fought the dictatorial implications of the *Alien and Sedition Acts* passed by the Federalist Congress (and signed by John Adams) in 1798, which led to the arrest of immigrant—Scottish and Irish—editors of Republican newspapers and made criticism of the president—though, interestingly, *not* the vice president, one Thomas Jefferson—a serious crime, even, in the draft version of the Sedition Act, a capital offense.[20] If Madison and Jefferson were defending basic freedoms, that most certainly cannot be said of Kilpatrick, and, it should go without saying, it was obtuse of Goldwin and Strauss to offer him the mantle of respectability via participation in the Public Affairs Conference. It appears that he was invited not *in spite* of his political views, but *because of* them. One of the lessons taught by Strauss is the need to read *all* texts very closely, including what might be termed the "social text" of what is suggested by the invitation list to certain conferences and encomia delivered afterward on those who delivered papers.

3. NETWORKING FOR REACTION

Strauss relied on the Public Affairs conferences and on Goldwin, Joseph Cropsey, Herbert Storing (who, it should be emphasized, rejected racism and was a careful student of the Anti-Federalists and Afro-American writers[21]), and Walter Berns to gain public influence.

On February 7, 1961, Goldwin wrote to Strauss:

> I will add only that you would have been very proud of your "boys." Seated in the midst of the famous and the powerful, they conducted themselves admirably and displayed powers of the mind which earned the attention and respect of all. Mr. Grodzins commented especially to me and to others, on the brilliance of some of Mr. Cropsey's formulations in the discussion. Mr. [Martin] Diamond and Mr. [Harry] Jaffa were the other most luminous "stars."[22]

Here is a model of "philosophical" influence, taken from Plato's *Laws*, which would ultimately extend to the role of certain Straussians in the Reagan and Bush administrations. Strauss's "boys" could dazzle, according to Goldwin, "the famous and the power-ful." As a result, Strauss himself and his followers achieved lasting contacts. Strauss set out his wishes in a February 13, 1961 letter to Goldwin:

> I turn immediately to *my* business. I am especially interested in a plan of having a debate on SS and its political consequences in the last generation. But I believe that the subject ought to be broad-ened to prevent the bogging down in methodology—a danger not excluded as you seem to think by the participation of [David] Easton. What I would suggest is a conference devoted to "theory and practice" but not called by that forbidding title. I shall illus-trate what I have in mind by two examples. 1) Economics and its limitations regarding economic policy, i.e. at what typical points "prudence" or "common sense" has to supplement the hand-outs of economic science. Milton Friedman ought to be in on this. You can get ample clarification regarding both subject matter and per-sonnel from Mr. Cropsey. 2) Desegregation and the findings of SS which allegedly demand desegregation. Here I would think we should have a guy from the deep south, say Dean H[W]iggins, a sociologist at Emory.[23] Such a conference could be educative for the non-academicians by making clear to them what they cannot expect from the academicians. . . . I remember a seminar meeting with Rossiter and Grodzins where I put to Grodzins point blank the question: can you tell me a single thing which was discovered by sci-entific political science which was not known to intelligent practitio-ners in advance? He could not remember more than two examples which disproved rather than supported his sanguine position (this English is still better than if I had spoken of his "attitude"). There could be a very easy transition from this conference to the confer-ence on education: what *do* the universities contribute to society?

Among the attendees at the Conference was soon-to-be Senator Charles Percy of Illinois.[24] Strauss stresses Percy's enthusiasm for it, and would attempt to work closely with him.

To be sure, with regard to some issues, Goldwin sought some genuine debate. Thus, regarding a proposed panel on arms con-trol, he hoped to invite a "spokesman for the unilateral disarma-ment position. . . . David Riesman has been recommended by Morton Grodzins . . . James Burnham as the spokesman for the opposite extreme." Attention was also paid to making connections with a broad array of persons from what Goldwin described as "the non-academic side." Thus:

> [W]e have acceptances already from Mr. Percy, Thomas Watson (chairman of the Board of IBM), Emmet Hughes (Eisenhower's former speech writer and now chief advisor and writer for Gov. Rockefeller) and Senator Muskie of Maine. We will invite, in addition, Congressman Ford of Michigan (who attended the first conference and who is a member of the Appropriations Committee and of the subcommittee on defense appropriations [and soon to be president]), Senator Henry Jackson of Washington (a member of the Armed Services Committee), George McGhee (head of the State Department Policy Planning Staff), Eric Sevareid [the newscaster], and Crawford Greenewalt, president of Dupont Co. We also want to invite a Republican member of the Armed Services committee, but I am awaiting Muskie's advice on the best one for our purpose.

Goldwin continues: "I have mentioned all these names as a preface to asking you about Hans Speier." In response, Strauss strongly recommended the participation of his old friend Speier, the head of the Rand Corporation.

To a very unusual and determined extent for a "political theorist," Strauss involved himself with political and military leaders. Steeped in Xenophon's *Hiero* (see his first book in the United States in 1948, *On Tyranny*) and Plato's *Laws*, he sought fiercely to shape policy. The Rand Corporation was central to producing U.S. missile strategy. A connection with Rand also helped to embed Strauss's students like Abram Shulsky or the students of his students such as Gary Schmitt (Herbert Storing), Paul Wolfowitz (Allan Bloom), and Francis Fukuyama (Bloom) in the strategic establishment.

The contact Goldwin had made with Congressman Gerald Ford would prove especially fruitful. After finishing his dissertation on John Locke, Goldwin took a job at Kenyon College where Robert Horwitz, another Strauss student, chaired the political science department and continued a public affairs program. He still worked closely with Ford and then-Congressman Donald Rumsfeld; Goldwin would later describe himself as "a special confidante" of Rumsfeld.[25]

It is worth noting that Strauss himself distinguished between "gentlemen" and "philosophers," and it is quite likely that he viewed at least some of "the boys" as examples more of the former than the latter. Strauss did not intend for all of his students to become dedicated scholars—though that was the aim for his closest ones; it was perhaps of near equal importance, however, for some to influence policy. In Strauss's idiom, they were to be "gentlemen" rather than "philosophers." Not overly concerned with partisan political labels, Strauss was also content to work with Rockefeller Republicans and hawkish Democrats. The aim in policy circles was to create a political voice for specific reactionary ideas, whether offering a defense of segregation and states' rights or an empowered executive capable of acting without significant constraint.

For instance, on June 5, 1969, Joseph Cropsey wrote about Strauss's "old friend" Senator Henry Jackson, the Democratic hawk from the state of Washington. He also notes the increasing influence of Albert Wohlsetter, a University of Chicago nuclear theorist who, though not a Straussian, often helped advise Strauss's students.

4. Conquering Cuba and Nuclear War

Cropsey's letter—written, of course, after the assassinations of John and Robert Kennedy—dismissed Senator Ted Kennedy as "the latest Kennedy" and exemplary of the "huge brood of mediocre aspirants the country will have to suffer, engendered by the unseemly fecundity of that family." Strauss and his students hated President John F. Kennedy and the Kennedy administration. The theme of Strauss's criticism is the weakness of the United States: its failure to exert itself as an empire to intimidate the Soviets. The debacle of the Bay of Pigs aggression and the Cuban missile crisis, which was an American defeat according to Strauss, led to this "unmanly" supineness.

In the 1990s, Robert McNamara, who had served as Kennedy's Secretary of Defense, would go to Cuba for meetings about the Cuban missile crisis with Castro and others. At that point, he discovered that the Soviets, unbeknownst to the U.S. government, had nearly two hundred missiles with nuclear warheads on Cuban soil and, perhaps more importantly (and astoundingly), Soviet field commanders apparently had the authority to order their use.[26] Had the United States, as General Curtis LeMay and Strauss advocated, attacked Cuba, a nuclear war might well have occurred, wiping out at least the East Coast of the United States and, assuming an American response, precipitating a worldwide nuclear holocaust.

But though wary in writing to future Senator Percy about nuclear war, Strauss recognized the danger and wanted to risk it. In fact, in the "Restatement," not easily accessible to Percy, he says optimistically that a return to the Stone Age would be preferable to the supposed decadence of the "last men" (those who fight for freedom, individuality, and peace):

> The end of history would be most exhilarating but for the fact, according to Kojève, that it is the participation in bloody political struggles as well as in real work or, generally expressed, the negating action which raises men above the brutes. The state through which man is said to become reasonably satisfied is, then, the state in which the basis of man's humanity withers away, or in which man loses his humanity. It is the state of Nietzsche's "last man" . . .
>
> There will always be men (*andres*) who will revolt against a state which is destructive of humanity or in which there is no longer the possibility of noble action or of great deeds. They may be forced into a mere negation of the universal and homogeneous state, into a negation not enlightened by any positive goal, into a nihilistic negation. While perhaps doomed to failure, that nihilistic revolution may be the only action on behalf of man's humanity, the only great and noble deed that is possible once the universal and homogeneous state has become inevitable. But no one can know whether it will succeed or fail. We still know too little about the workings of the universal and homogeneous state to say anything about where and when its corruption will start. What we do know is only that it will perish sooner or later (see Friedrich Engels, Ludwig Feuerbach). Someone may object that the successful revolt against the universal and homogeneous state could have no other effect than that the identical historical process that has led from the primitive horde to the final state will be repeated. But would such a repetition of the process—a new lease on life for man's humanity—not be preferable to the indefinite continuation of the inhuman end? Do we not enjoy every spring although we know the cycle of the seasons, although we know that winter will come again? Warriors and workers of all countries, unite, while there is still time to prevent the coming of "the realm of freedom." Defend with might and main, if it needs to be defended, the "realm of necessity."[27]

On February 12, 1963, Strauss suggested an analogy to Percy between the brutal Soviet conquest of rebellious Hungary in 1956 and the United States's "tit for tat" in Cuba. "Strength" means that the United States should respond with the same brutality, using the same methods, as the Soviets. Strauss foolishly suggests that Kennedy shunned such confrontation merely for electoral purposes. He seems not to recognize that Kennedy managed to avoid nuclear war while forcing the Soviets to withdraw nuclear weapons from Cuba, a victory rather than a defeat for American policy, not to mention humankind. Finally, Strauss suggests, brutalizing Cuba would cement American domination in Europe, preventing General de Gaulle in France from suggesting that the United States could not protect "European interests."

Another of Strauss's recommended policies, the Vietnam War, would also damage this alliance, just as a further American invasion of Cuba would have. In Strauss's formulation, one can hear the commanding tone of the would-be philosophical counselor, modeled on the *Laws* or Xenophon's *Hiero*, instructing the political leader:

Dear Mr. Percy

I believe that the following points have not been made, or at least have not been made with sufficient audibility: 1) To speak in the only language which Khrushchev understands, Cuba is our Hungary; just as we did not make the slightest move when he solved the problem in his back yard, Hungary, he cannot, and will not make the slightest move if and when we take care of the problem in our back yard, Cuba. 2) The President has not succeeded in dispelling the impression that what moved him to a moment's action, after which he relapsed into the old inactivity, was not a belated understanding of the true situation but the fear to lose elections. 3) We surely give de Gaulle a wonderful excuse (if it is not more than an excuse but a cause); he can justly say, how can a country be trusted to defend the legitimate European interests if it does not defend its own legitimate interests?

The meetings of the PACC [the Public Affairs Council at Chicago] dealing with foreign affairs convinced me perfectly that the President has surrounded himself with advisors who are completely deluded about the character of the Communist menace. This experience contributed very much toward forming my view about the present administration.

One word about the last meeting of the PACC. I thought it was
without question the best we ever had. We all must be very thankful to
Mr. Goldwin . . .

Strauss also uses the Public Affairs Conference, with attention
to future conferences, to suggest a broad reactionary—anti–
President Kennedy, pro–States' Rights and segregation,[28] pro–
Imperial—policy to Percy. Like the Athenian stranger, he was
using his own arguments and the voices of others to try to shape
policy. Strauss warns repeatedly against making unreciprocated
concessions to the Soviets over Berlin and East Germany. Mirror-
ing his own wishes for the United States, he suggests that the Soviet
Union is limitlessly expansionary. Only with a reversal of Communism in fact—a willingness, as he defines it for Percy, to accept the
existence of "the free world"—would stability be possible. Until
then Strauss recommended, in a memorandum directed to Percy,
the policy of aggression:

To Charles H. Percy
The major premise of American foreign policy must be: no
strengthening of the USSR at the expense of the USA. But concessions
regarding Berlin and East Germany push Germany toward the USSR
and therefore strengthen the USSR. The conclusion: unless concessions in this respect are accompanied by equally great concessions on
the part of the USSR, there must not be the concessions now contemplated. Since it is patent that no acceptable concessions on the part of
the USSR are in sight, there must be no concessions on our part.
    Yet, some people argue, the concessions regarding Berlin and East
Germany correspond to the legitimate demand of Russia. They are
its only demands, its last demands; thereafter there will be genuine
peace. But this argument presupposes that Russia has ceased to be
Communist—which is nonsense. There cannot be genuine peace
with Communism.
    The opponents continue to argue as follows: if we do not seek
genuine peace, then we heighten the danger of thermonuclear war,
which confronts us with the alternative of annihilation or surrender.
Without genuine peace, we must face this alternative. [Emphasis added.]
    There is a profound cleavage of opinion in this country as to which
of the two alternatives is preferable. The issue will be settled not in
journals by the people who call themselves and are called by others
"the intellectuals," but, as is meet in a democracy, ultimately by the
majority vote of the people at large. If this issue is brought before

the American people, I believe the large majority will be opposed to surrender—if for no other reason than for this: because the speakers against surrender will be more trusted by the American people than the speakers for surrender. To make this point quite clear, further considerable setbacks for the United States (super-Cubas) will bring about an anti-"intellectual" reaction compared with which "McCarthyism" will look like child's play. *We must start from the premise that the American people, as a strong, virile, and free people will prefer to perish rather than to surrender.* [Emphasis added.]

As in the end of the "Restatement" in *On Tyranny,* Strauss thought modern Americans were exemplars of the last men. "Virile" here refers to those who seek destruction—and self-destruction. Strauss was hoping for "resistance" even at the risk of nuclear war.

5. A REDUCTION OF LOCKE TO "PREROGATIVE" OR "COMMANDER-IN-CHIEF POWER"

It is hard to overestimate the importance, with regard to understanding central aspects of Leo Strauss's politics, of a May 1933 letter to Karl Loewith:

Just because the German Right will not tolerate us does not mean that there is anything wrong with the principles of the Right. On the contrary only those principles—fascist, authoritarian, *imperial*—and not the laughable and childish imprescriptible rights of man is the only basis on which to oppose the *meskine Unwesen* [on a very rightwing interpretation of Nietzsche, the grubby Jewish reality of the last men].[29]

Even if it were certainly true that Strauss could have had no knowledge of what the "fascist, authoritarian, and imperial" policies of the recently empowered Adolf Hitler would lead to, 1933 is, equally certainly, late enough to wonder about the intellectual judgment of anyone who would find "laughable and childish" those who posited notions of "rights of man" against the grandiose visions of conquest and ethnic cleansing of the Nazis and their advocates like Schmitt or Martin Heidegger (in fact, Strauss was an acolyte of Heidegger all the way through[30]). In *Natural Right and History,* Strauss's dismissiveness toward Locke set the stage for followers, particularly Robert Goldwin, disparaging the rights of each

individual and elevating, in their place, executive—even tyranni-
cal—power. Goldwin's chapter in Strauss and Cropsey's *History
of Political Philosophy* subtly distorts Locke as overemphasizing the
"prerogative" of an authoritarian executive, compared for example to Locke's fierce passages on revolution against a tyrant who
like "any lyon or tiger" in a state of nature may be struck down.
Goldwin's correction reformulates Locke for impact on the American presidency.[31] This *crafting* of their common message coupled
with Goldwin's role as confidant—"philosopher-statesman" or
"one man think-tank"—in Republican politics has had a profound
public impact.

Goldwin had written a thesis on Locke under Strauss's direction. In Goldwin's essay, one can hear Strauss's "Platonic" emphasis
on the best man who rules without laws, but as Simonides in Xenophon's *Hiero* insists, "beneficially." Putatively, action for the public good as opposed to obeying a wooden, "inflexible" rule of law
makes such an executive "godlike." In paragraph 160 of the *Second
Treatise of Government*, Locke defines the idea of "prerogative." As
Goldwin's "John Locke" in Strauss and Cropsey's *History of Political
Philosophy* comments, "The executive may act not only without the
sanction of law, he may also make the laws 'give way' (paragraph
159) to his power where blind adherence to them would be harmful, and he may even go so far as to act contrary to the law for the
public good."[32] He then invokes Locke's formulation: "This power
to act according to discretion for the public good, without the prescription of law and sometimes against it, is that which is called
'*prerogative*' (paragraph 160)."[33] Locke's way of putting it emphasizes the idea of a common good: "*prerogative is nothing but the power
of doing public good without a rule*" (paragraph 165).

Goldwin's interpretation shades toward arbitrary executive
power. The term "prerogative" is a bridge between the word
"authoritarian" in Strauss's 1933 letter to Loewith and the almost
unlimited "Commander-in-Chief Power" that characterized especially the first term of the Bush-Cheney administration, when
torture became near standard operating procedure of what was
labeled the "Global War on Terror." In fact, Goldwin brought this
idiom to the White House, echoed in Saturday afternoon lun-
cheon seminars for President Ford by Harvey Mansfield, Jr., almost

certainly the most exuberant devotee of the supposed necessity of an "untamed prince" as part of the conception of the president.[34]

Goldwin found a receptive audience in President Gerald Ford and his advisors, Secretary of Defense Rumsfeld and Chief of Staff Cheney, for an almost obsessive concern with restoring the powers of the presidency that had been weakened in the aftermath of Richard Nixon's mendacity regarding the Vietnam War and, of course, Watergate. As Ford insisted, "I was absolutely dedicated to doing whatever I could to restore the rightful prerogatives of the Presidency under the constitutional system."[35] As both Goldwin and Mansfield wrote, though, "prerogative" has, at best, an orthogonal relationship to what we usually regard as "the constitutional system," at least if we regard it as establishing genuine constraints that operate upon *all* public officials.

Ford and his aides sought to restore prerogative after Watergate; with "Commander-in-Chief power," "unitary executive," and "lawfare," this idea has now become enmity to law under the Bush administration and is achieving bipartisan consolidation in Obama's odious notion of "state secrets."[36] Following Strauss, Goldwin admired philosopher-kings. He knew that such "wise princes" were above the law, that they were philosopher-tyrants. Goldwin's chapter repeatedly adverts to this idea as a background. He summons this supposed "teaching" of Plato[37] and Strauss as a quasi-esoteric theme. Modeling Socrates' action in the *Apology* and *Crito* as well as the *Republic,* one might of course take the idea of philosopher-kingship as leadership in a democracy to defend philosophy as one small city in the "city of cities" which the Athenian democracy was.[38]

Yet, invoking Locke's account, Goldwin also insists:

> The danger inherent in the executive's prerogative is no less obvious than the necessity for it. The prerogative has always grown most extensively in the reigns of the best princes. The people trust a good and wise prince even while he acts beyond the limits of the law, not fearing for their safety because they see that his purpose is to further their good.

One can imagine Ford Chiefs of Staff Cheney and Rumsfeld perking up their ears at this "philosophical" message from their "special assistant" and "confidante." Goldwin stresses Locke's idiom about a kind of monarch as the best ruler, "as God himself" or sharing in his "wisdom and goodness." Esoterically, it is but a short way from this divine wisdom to a tyrant advised by a wise man (Xenophon's *Simonides* in the *Hiero* and in Strauss's *On Tyranny*). Exaggerating Locke's words, Goldwin's essay draws a metaphorical connection:

> Such godlike princes, indeed, had some title to arbitrary power by the argument that would prove absolute monarchy the best government, as that which God himself governs the universe by, because such kings partake of his wisdom and goodness (paragraph 166).[39]

A few pages later, Goldwin reiterates this theme. He again conjures a prince who like God exercises prerogative.

> There are two places in the *Second Treatise* where Locke speaks of "godlike" princes. In one he speaks of the princes who are allowed the largest prerogative, who have the greatest freedom from the control of the laws. They are like God, who governs the universe as an absolute monarch, because they "partake of his wisdom and goodness" (paragraph 166).

For Goldwin, one might imagine, this is an esoteric emphasis in Locke; like Xenephon and "Mr. Strauss," he is an advocate of philosopher-tyranny.

Yet in a contradiction, Goldwin also invokes Locke's image of a prince who rules "by established laws of liberty" and furthers increased production from the land through labor:

> But in the earlier passage, the prince is said to be wise and godlike who rules "by established laws of liberty." Such a prince is like God as Creator, for established laws of liberty are the means of bringing about "the increase of the lands," which is a kind of creation, as we have seen, although not a creation out of nothing. This increase is not only the cause of domestic prosperity but also the source of the power to protect the society against the hostile attacks of other societies. *The godlike prince whose law-abidingness brings increase "will quickly be too hard for his neighbors"* (paragraph 42).[40]

Locke argues for a lawless executive who still "serves the people" or a "public good."[41] But his defense of a law-adhering leader is part of his core argument on accumulation of property, the lawless executive an error or a rare case, one also limited by the right of revolution. Ironically, Goldwin juxtaposes these opposed arguments as if he notices the contradiction; yet he does not acknowledge, let alone think about, it. He follows the master in a scholarly adherence to the surface (or perhaps pointing to a familiar, for Straussians, *esoteric meaning*) of a text without philosophical analysis.

If Strauss promises cryptography, Goldwin sticks more closely to seeming description. In effect, Goldwin opts for the side of tyranny and downplays Locke's core argument. In his peroration, Goldwin recurs pregnantly to the theme of a philosopher-king: "John Locke has been called America's philosopher, our king in the only way a philosopher has ever been king of a great nation." Esoterically, Goldwin speaks, however, as the student of another "philosopher," Leo Strauss, whose interpretation of Locke would now be brought to bear in the Ford and Reagan administrations through Goldwin directly, through civil service (Shulsky) or political (Wolfowitz) appointments, the colonizing of rightwing foundations (Goldwin's long tenure at the American Enterprise Institute) and matriculation into subsequent reactionary administrations, culminating in the sustained attack on the rule of law of George W. Bush.[42]

Consider in this context an essay by Harvey Mansfield defending extraordinary surveillance by the Bush administration. Mansfield is often regarded as the leading Straussian of his generation, though he was not in fact a direct student of Strauss, having received his doctorate at Harvard. His importance as an "American conservative" comes not only from the quality of his scholarship, but also from his willingness to take part in direct political argument, sometimes in the pages of the *Wall Street Journal* or *Weekly Standard*, both central organs of American conservatism (they are often authoritarian, and not conservative, however). Thus in January 2006, Mansfield published an essay in the *Weekly Standard* under the breezy title "The Law and the President: In a National Emergency, Who You Gonna Call?" The answer, not surprisingly, is the latter, and it is worth quoting Mansfield at some length:

> One can begin from the fact that the American Constitution made the first republic with a strong executive. A strong executive is one that is not confined to executing the laws but has extra-legal powers such as commanding the military, making treaties (and carrying

on foreign policy), and pardoning the convicted, not to mention a veto of legislation. To confirm the extra-legal character of the presidency, the Constitution has him take an oath not to execute the laws but to execute the *office* of president, which is larger.

Mansfield here asserts that legal powers, those of being commander in chief, making treaties, offering pardon, or even the veto, are somehow extralegal. The are not. In any case what is extralegal is not illegal, as with torture. He implicitly links all three, without offering an argument.

> Thus it is wrong to accuse President Bush of acting illegally in the surveillance of possible enemies, as if that were a crime and legality is all that matters. This is simplistic, small-r republican thinking of the kind that our Constitution surpassed when it constructed a strong executive. The Constitution took seriously a difficulty in the rule of law that the republican tradition before 1787 had slighted. The difficulty is obvious enough, but republicans tend to overlook it or minimize it because they believe, as republicans, that power is safer in the hands of many than in those of one or a few. Power is more surely in the hands of many when exercised in the form of law—"standing rules," as opposed to arbitrary decree. Republicans tend to believe in the rule of law and hence to favor legislative power over executive.
>
> Yet the rule of law is not enough to run a government. Any set of standing rules is liable to encounter an emergency requiring an exception from the rule or an improvised response when no rule exists. In Machiavelli's terms, ordinary power needs to be supplemented or corrected by the extraordinary power of a prince, using wise discretion. "Necessity knows no law" is a maxim everyone admits, and takes advantage of, when in need. Small-r republicans especially are reluctant to accept it because they see that wise discretion opens the door to unwise discretion. But there is no way to draw a line between the wise and the unwise without making a law (or something like it) and thus returning to the inflexibility of the rule of law. We need both the rule of law and the power to escape it—and that twofold need is just what the Constitution provides for.

Here is the doctrine of Carl Schmitt—"he is sovereign who makes the decision in the state of the exception" via Strauss—pawned off as: (a) the wisdom of the American constitution (something both Schmitt and Strauss disliked and disparaged); and (b) as a cliché,

"Necessity knows no law," "a maxim everyone admits." Even Mansfield's words, "an emergency requiring an exception from the rule [of law]," are self-consciously redolent of Schmitt. Note that any criminality can be justified in the name of this breezy elision of things sometimes only allegedly "extralegal."

Similarly, Walter Berns, unequivocally one of Strauss's "boys," published a piece in the *Wall Street Journal* on May 23, 2009, with the frank title "Interrogations and Presidential Prerogative: The Founders Created an Executive with Substantial Discretionary Powers." Though this piece appeared in the early days of the Obama administration—and one might wonder if Berns is gratified by the extent to which Obama has proved more than willing to accept the notion of "an executive with substantial discretionary powers"—it was clearly motivated by the discussion of whether those who had been part of the Bush administration's torture apparatus should be subject to punishment. Berns's answer—and, it turned out, Obama's as well—was no. Berns relied, like Goldwin, on Locke:

> But Locke admitted that not everything can be done by law. Or, as he said, there are many things "which the law can by no means provide for." The law cannot "foresee" events, for example, nor can it act with dispatch or with the appropriate subtlety required when dealing with foreign powers. Nor, as we know very well indeed, can a legislative body preserve secrecy.
>
> Such matters, Locke continued in the Second Treatise, should be left to "the discretion of him who has the executive power." It is in this context that he first spoke of the "prerogative": the "power to act according to discretion, for the public good without the prescription of the law, and sometimes even against it." He concluded by saying "prerogative is nothing but the power of doing public good without a rule."
>
> The executive in our case, at least to begin with, is represented by the three Justice Department officials who wrote the memos that Mr. Graham [Senator Bob Graham of Florida] and many members of the Obama administration have found offensive. They have been accused of justifying torture, but they have not yet been given the opportunity in an official setting or forum to defend what they did.
>
> That forum could be a committee of Congress or a "truth commission"—so long as, in addition to the assistance of counsel, they would be judged by "an impartial jury," have the right to call witnesses in their favor, *to call for the release of evidence including the CIA*

memos showing the success of enhanced interrogations, and the right to
"confront the witnesses" against them as the Constitution's Fifth
and Sixth Amendments provide. There is much to be said for a process that, among other things, would require Nancy Pelosi to testify
under oath. [Emphasis added.]

To put it mildly, no widely accepted evidence has emerged that
"enhanced interrogation" was in fact "effective" and, therefore,
even under the crudest form of utilitarianism, "justified." Berns is
also far more concerned with the plight of administration officials
accused of complicity in torture than he is with the fate of those
subjected to medieval brutalities. For him, what might be termed
"patriotic motivation" seems to be the most important thing. His
comments track an earlier 1986 essay, written for a book edited by
Benjamin Netanyahu, and entitled "Constitutional Power and the
Defense of Free Government."[43] Berns begins by quoting James
Madison's comment to Jefferson: "It is a melancholy reflection that
liberty should be equally exposed to danger whether the government have too much or too little power." "But," Berns goes on to ask:

[H]ow much power is too much? . . . [T]he Constitution does not
answer that question. Too much power is beyond what is necessary,
and it is not given to writers of constitutions to foresee what may be
necessary. The ends (or purposes) of government are foreseeable
and capable of being stated explicitly—a more perfect union, justice, domestic tranquillity, the common defense—but the means of
promoting those ends . . . cannot be foreseen. . . .

The body of the Constitution begins by defining the legislative
power, which is to be expected in a document so strongly influenced by the political philosophy of John Locke. . . . The legislative,
Locke says, is the "supreme power." . . . [The Founders] proceeded,
however, to establish an executive whose powers, unlike in a parliamentary system, come not from the legislature but from the people.

By making the executive independent, the Founders acknowledged that, however desirable in principle, in practice not all things
that government may have to do to advance the public good can be
done by law or formulated in law. I hesitate to say this when I lack
the space to say it properly, but under our written Constitution, the
law is not supreme. Above the law, and the lawmaking body, are the
people of the United States, whose will is expressed in the written
Constitution. The supremacy of the people over the law is apparent in the first sentence of Article I: "All legislative powers herein

granted," thereby indicating that certain legislative powers are not granted. But compare this with the first sentence of Article II: "The executive power shall be vested in a President of the United States of America." There is no suggestion here that any part of the executive power is being withheld. And if John Locke was their guide here, as he was elsewhere, the executive power includes the prerogative, "the power to act according to discretion for the public good, without the prescription of law and sometimes even against it." How great those powers are was demonstrated by Lincoln, in my judgment the greatest of American Presidents.

Like Mansfield, Berns elides executive discretion and rampant criminality. The need to justify torture as a common good is alluded to—the CIA's nonexistent evidence he fantasizes must be revealed—but he is expressing a sad preference, not even making an argument, let alone basing one on facts.

Further, Berns does not see in Lincoln the opponent of a war of aggrandizement with Mexico as well as the extension of bondage into the border states. He sees him instead as the employer of emergency powers, violating habeas corpus. Save for a brief mention of the Emancipation Proclamation, Berns's distortion of Lincoln parallels Goldwin's of Locke:

> Lincoln fought a war that was never declared; without congressional authorization, he called for volunteers to fight that war; he established a naval blockade of ports from Texas to Virginia; he suspended the privilege of the writ of habeas corpus; he put enemy sympathizers in army jails without trial and ignored a demand of the Chief Justice to free them; most important, he used his power as commander in chief to free the slaves, something not even Congress was authorized to do. . . .
>
> Beyond the obvious fact that we are not involved in a civil war, or formally in any other kind of war, what distinguishes [the contemporary struggle against terrorism] from Lincoln's? Not a lack of constitutional power: the powers are there when they are needed; the Founders saw to that, and they also authorized the President to decide when they were needed. . . .
>
> Lincoln spoke powerfully of the blessings of liberty and asked his fellow citizens to make sacrifices for it. . . .

There can be no doubt that Berns is fully "American" inasmuch as, like many compatriots, he is obsessed with Madison and then that most complex of all presidents, Abraham Lincoln. The message is that vindication of the Union required doing whatever was thought to be "necessary" to maintain it. And he offers this foolish nostrum for the purpose of making the face of America that of waterboarding. It is hard for people who remember the Vietnam War not to hear overtones of "destroying a village in order to save it."

Strauss's acolytes have therefore done their part to bring into the highest levels of American politics a perspective—anticonstitutional, against individual rights, leader-worshipping, and endlessly war-making—that is similar to his own attraction, in 1933, to the merits of politics that are "fascist, authoritarian, imperial." But, quite obviously, the truly "American conservative" Straussians, like Goldwin and Berns, translated these ideas into an American, quasi-Lockean, pseudo-Constitutional idiom. (What is interesting about Mansfield's essay is that he evokes the authority of Machiavelli instead of the comparatively anodyne Locke.) The political Straussians—the "boys"—were remarkably successful in making Leo Strauss America's philosopher and achieved, in George W. Bush (or Dick Cheney), their wish as to what well-tutored leaders might look like.

Goldwin's final sentence reads: "We, therefore, more than many other peoples in the world, have the duty and experience to judge the rightness of [Locke's] teaching," that is, the teaching about the necessity of claiming prerogative powers. Perhaps paradoxically, the revulsion against Bush and his extreme invocations of executive power was led by, among others, conservative libertarians like Richard Epstein who drew from Locke a distinctly different teaching based on the importance of individual rights and suspicions of overreaching government.

Goldwin was no fool. Like Farabi, he added a Platonic caveat to this account. Although the rule of the best prince and of a mere tyrant are alike in their lawlessness, the latter is only a pathetic imitator of the former. Yet following Locke, Goldwin also notes that even a good ruler smooths the way for an abusive successor:

> But even godlike princes have successors, and there is no assurance that one of them, claiming the precedent, will not make use of the enlarged prerogative to further his own private interests at the peril

of the people's property and safety. "Upon this is founded that saying that the reigns of good princes have been always most dangerous to the liberties of their people" (paragraph 166).

Goldwin played a powerful role in the rise of the modern
Republican Party, as Rumsfeld said in his eulogy. Rumsfeld even
sent Goldwin into the disaster in Iraq as a trusted advisor. There
is, alas, no reason to believe that Goldwin found in Bush, Rumsfeld, Cheney, and others the dangers he himself warned against.
Perhaps he would reply that these men were not using their prerogative powers in order "to further [their] own private interests,"
that they were always motivated by protecting American national
security. Even if one grants, for the sake of argument, the premise,
one might still believe that Goldwin and some of the other "boys"
ended up as apologists for tyranny. "American conservatism"
deserved better.

NOTES

1. Lynne V. Cheney is a senior fellow at AEI. This tribute originally
appeared on AEI's Enterprise Blog on January 13, 2010.
2. Donald Rumsfeld is the former secretary of defense. This tribute
originally appeared on AEI's Enterprise Blog on January 15, 2010. My
emphasis. See also the reflections of Walter Berns, who will also play a role
in the narrative below:

My life changed directions—or took on its purpose—in 1950 when
I began graduate studies at the University of Chicago. It was there—
in fact, the first week there—that I met Bob.

I had come from Reed College, by way of a year at the London
School of Economics, and had intended to study with—better that
I not mention their names—Professors X, Y, and Z. Bob had come
from St. John's College, where he learned about Leo Strauss. He
persuaded me to study with Mr. Strauss, as we called him, and I did,
then and for the next three years; and it was in those seminars that
I met the men—so long as they lived—my life-long friends: Herbert Storing, Allan Bloom, Martin Diamond, Robert Horowitz, and
Ralph Lerner. Bob has a photograph of six of us sitting in a row at
Colgate University in 1976 during a program celebrating the bicen-
tennial of the Declaration of Independence. . . .

[At AEI] he edited and published a series of truly distinguished,
and truly unique, constitutional studies of the sort never before
published. . . .

And what did I do for him? Only this. Herb Storing and I encouraged him to quit his job with an education organization in order to finish his PhD. This required him and his wife and family to live for two—or was it three?—years of dignified poverty, during which Daisy acquired her 100 recipes for serving hamburger. On the other hand, however, with those academic credentials he went on to have his distinguished academic and political careers.

Of his years with Don Rumsfeld at NATO in Brussels and in the Ford White House with Rumsfeld and Dick Cheney, I can say little. I wasn't there. But I can say a good deal about his work at the American Enterprise Institute. There he edited and published a series of truly distinguished, and truly unique, constitutional studies of the sort never before published, studies demonstrating, for example, how the Constitution secures religious liberties, how it separates powers, and, for another example, how it can be said to be democratic. Even before his days at AEI, he had edited a series of constitutional studies published by Rand McNally, and Storing and I and Bloom and Diamond and others contributed to these studies.

Walter Berns is a resident scholar at AEI. Mr. Berns delivered the above remarks at the memorial service for Mr. Goldwin on January 14, 2010.

3. See http://democratic-individuality.blogspot.com/2011/07/distinctions -between-xenophon-plato-and.html. One should neither assume that Xenophon's aphilosophical Socrates is the same as Plato's Socrates nor Socrates himself who founded what we call civil disobedience.

4. Michael Goldfield, who took Strauss's course on Aristotle's *Politics* in 1968, told me about this.

5. After chairing a panel on Strauss's 1933 letter to Loewith at the American Political Science Association in 2008, I engaged in 9 months of negotiations with Nathan Tarcov, Strauss's new literary executor, and was the first non-Straussian admitted to look at the Strauss papers in Regenstein library. Following Strauss's death in 1973, Joseph Cropsey had hidden Strauss's papers for 36 years. He had allowed publication only after 2000 in German by Heinrich Meier, a student of the arcane Schmitt and Strauss. The citations in this chapter are drawn from my research in Regenstein.

6. Senator Daniel P. Moynihan played a comparable role for Gary Schmitt, a student of Storing and to a lesser extent of Strauss, and one of the three principals of the Project for a New American Century.

7. For instance, Bill Kristol, editor of the *Weekly Standard*, columnist praising Strauss at the *New York Times* for a year, and co-leader with Gary Schmitt and Robert Kagan (who studied with Thomas Pangle and shares the politics of aggression and "commander-in-chief power," but is not

interested in political philosophy—a gentleman, in Strauss's idiom) of the Project for a New American Century, or Paul Wolfowitz, who had studied with Bloom and as Assistant Secretary of Defense helped engineer the Iraq disaster.

8. "I do not believe in the possibility of a conversation of Socrates with the people (it is not clear to me what you think about this); the relation of the philosopher to the people is mediated by a certain kind of rhetoricians who arouse fear of punishment after death; the philosopher can guide these rhetoricians but cannot do their work (this is the meaning of the Gorgias)." Leo Strauss, "Strauss-Kojève Correspondence (April 22, 1957)," in Leo Strauss, *On Tyranny*, Rev. ed., ed. Victor Gourevitch and Michael S. Roth (Chicago: University of Chicago Press, 2000), 275.

9. Alan Gilbert, *Democratic Individuality* (Cambridge: Cambridge University Press, 1990), chapter 1.

10. Political science has at times embraced definitions of democracy as two-party competition, which rule out the segregated South but embrace apartheid South Africa. A clear view of justice—that each counts as human—rules out such bizarre results. But Strauss instead favors a transformed anti-urban past, most closely, the vision of Martin Heidegger, "the one great philosopher of our era." See his posthumous "Introduction to [Heideggerian] Existentialism," in *The Rebirth of Classical Political Rationalism: An Introduction to the Thought of Leo Strauss*, ed. Thomas L. Pangle (Chicago: University of Chicago Press, 1989), 27–47. Heidegger was a Nazi, and Strauss, for a long time, pro-Nazi. Here again, Strauss feints at a decent argument to advance a paradigmatic corrupt one.

11. Leo Strauss, *Natural Right and History* (Chicago: University of Chicago Press, 1950), 118.

12. Even more strikingly, the vision of politics in Strauss's 1932 refinement of Carl Schmitt involves a notion of enmity, but makes no mention of a common good. See "Anmerkungen zu Carl Schmitt, Der Begriff des Politischen," *Archiv für Sozialwissenschaft und Sozialpolitik* 67 (August/September 1932): 732–749.

13. See, for example, Mary L. Dudziak, *Cold War Civil Rights: Race and the Image of American Democracy* (Princeton, NJ: Princeton University Press, 2000). All citations from Strauss and Goldwin are drawn from letters whose dates are indicated in the text and are to be found in the Strauss papers/correspondence with Goldwin in Regenstein Library.

14. In *Democratic Individuality*, I take fascist and authoritarian claims about the rule of a Fuehrer to be anti-political.

15. My emphasis. Goldwin would later worry that the conference had been too stridently segregationist, even for him; he includes essays favoring federalism in his subsequent edited collection: Robert A. Goldwin,

ed., *A Nation of States: Essays on the American Federal System*, 2nd ed. (Chicago: Rand McNally, 1974). Thanks to Peter Minowitz for the reference.

16. Those, locally and nationally, who enabled segregation for reasons of achieving power, that is, for other purposes, made themselves responsible for its crimes.

17. James Jackson Kilpatrick, *The Sovereign States: Notes of a Citizen of Virginia* (Chicago: H. Regnery, 1957), 179. Kilpatrick's italics.

18. Kilpatrick, *Sovereign States*, 305.

19. Kilpatrick, *Sovereign States*, 188–189.

20. Madison invoked the rights of states to defend individual rights. Kilpatrick notes the controversy but omits Madison's reasons. Ibid., 180–181.

21. Unlike Strauss and many other Straussians, Storing lived up to Strauss's abstract admonition to pay attention to alternate views (no Straussian has yet paid serious attention to Marx, though Strauss did praise Kojève's—not, until he was older, a Straussian—elaboration of Hegel).

22. My emphasis.

23. James Wiggins.

24. Percy entered politics in the late 1950s. With the encouragement of then U.S. President Dwight D. Eisenhower, Percy helped to write *Decisions for a Better America* (Garden City, NY: Doubleday, 1960), which proposed a long-range program for the Republican Party. He became known as a Rockefeller or liberal Republican. Percy ran for governor of Illinois in 1964, but narrowly lost to Democratic incumbent Otto Kerner. In 1966, Percy ran for senator from Illinois, upsetting the Democratic senator Paul Douglas who had been Percy's teacher at the University of Chicago. Note Percy's broad connection with the university, which prepared a way for his friendship with Leo Strauss. Percy served three terms. He explored the possibility of running for president in 1968 and 1976.

25. Robert A. Goldwin, Special Consultant: Files, 1974–76, Gerald R. Ford Library, Ann Arbor, Michigan.

26. Laurence Chang and Peter Kornbluh, eds., *The Cuban Missile Crisis, 1962: A National Security Archive Documents Reader*, 2nd ed. (New York: New Press, 1998). See Noam Chomsky, "Cuban Missile Crisis: How the US Played Russian Roulette with Nuclear War," *Guardian* (October 15, 2012).

27. Strauss, "Restatement," in *On Tyranny*, 208, 209.

28. Partly because of Goldwater's stand against civil rights, Percy, during his own run for governor in 1964, would endorse Goldwater for president only reluctantly.

29. See Scott Horton's translation of the letter in Leo Strauss, "Letter to Karl Löwith," *Constellations* 16 (March 2009): 82–83. The correction of the last phrase—one which makes clear that Strauss was pro-Nazi at the time—is due to Michael Zank and William Altman.

30. See Heidegger's *Vom Wesen der Wahrheit: zu Platons Hoehlengleich-nis und Theaetet* (On the Essence of Truth: Plato's Cave-Metaphor and the Theatetus) (Frankfurt am Main: V. Klostermann, 1943). Heidegger had lectured on Plato for 20 years. Strauss's interpretation of Plato begins from and is derivative of Heidegger's. See democratic individuality: http://democratic-individuality.blogspot.com/2010/05/mirrors-cave -heideggers-platonic.html; and http://democratic-individuality.blogspot .com/2010/06/mirrors-how-strauss-became-heidegger-in.html.

31. Stanley Rosen was a student of Strauss who spells out ways he differs from the master in "Leo Strauss at Chicago," *Daedalus* 135 (Summer 2006): 104–113. In contrast, Mansfield assures the reader that his views on Machiavelli extend Strauss's *Thoughts on Machiavelli* (Glencoe, IL: Free Press, 1958). The paradigmatic academic Straussian argument is, sadly, closer to the latter than the former.

32. Robert A. Goldwin, "John Locke," in *History of Political Philosophy*, ed. Leo Strauss and Joseph Cropsey (Chicago: Rand McNally, 1963), 502.

33. Locke puts the term prerogative here in quotes, Goldwin does not.

34. Grandiosely and invoking the *idee fixe* of neocons, Cropsey analogized the preemption of Saddam—that is, the U.S. aggression against its almost disarmed former puppet—to an imaginary preemption against Hitler.

35. Kathryn Olmstead, *Challenging the Secret Government: The Post-Watergate Investigations of the CIA and FBI* (Chapel Hill: University of North Carolina Press, 1996), 49. Her footnote is imprecise, however, about when Ford said this. She also notes: "His aides list Ford's renewal of Presidential Power after Watergate as one of the greatest achievements of his administration."

36. This is how Obama attempts to defeat suits for torture or aggression by innocent people. See, for example, the legal brief recently dismissing a suit by an Iraqi woman concerning aggression. But Obama also used this doctrine to repel the suit of Canadian-Syrian engineer Maher Arar, removed from a flight in Laguardia and sent to Syria to be confined in a coffin-size cell and tortured for 10 months, to whom the Canadian government, more honorably, paid damages.

37. In contrast, I argue that Plato's idea of the city in speech and the philosopher-king is largely satiric and represents the dream or vision of Glaucon, a warrior regime for the military leader/potential tyrant. The material on the philosopher king is actually a Platonic satire of Xenophon; the city of philosophers is, on the contrary, a kind of modified Pythagoreanism. See my essays at democratic-individuality.blogspot.com: http://democratic -individuality.blogspot.com/2011/11/socrates-worst-argument-ever.html; http://democratic-individuality.blogspot.com/2011/11/republics-amusing

-answer-to-athenian.html; http://democratic-individuality.blogspot.com/ 2011/11/republics-amusing-answer-to-athenian.html; http://democratic -individuality.blogspot.com/2011/12/if-city-in-speech-is-glaucons-what-city .html; http://democratic-individuality.blogspot.com/2011/12/pythagoras -on-surface-and-in-depths-of.html.

38. See these three essays on "going down" on democratic-individuality: http://democratic-individuality.blogspot.com/2010/08/going-down -on-democratic-interpretation.html; http://democratic-individuality.blog spot.com/2010/08/going-down-on-democratic-interpretation_17.html; http://democratic-individuality.blogspot.com/2010/08/going-down-how -plato-affirms-socrates.html.

39. Goldwin, "John Locke," 503. My emphasis.

40. Ibid., 507–508.

41. Ibid.

42. Strauss said roughly this to Stanley Rosen, as Rosen reported to me in email correspondence. I had written to him to confirm his account to Tracy Strong on January 13, 2007:

> Tracy suggested I talk to you. In addition, he told me a story of yours: that Strauss had said to you that he and his followers would place students in liberal arts colleges where they would be the most knowledgeable and charismatic people on the faculty, and then in rightwing foundations and receptive administrations. Such a pattern is visible.

On January 15, Stanley responded:

> The anecdote via Tracy is substantially accurate. Strauss planned to make an alliance with the Anglophile establishment Conservatives. In other words, WASP power brokers. He never got very close to the Catholic conservatives who correctly sensed that he was an enemy or at least a danger to their tradition. Sometimes it helps politically to know the difference between Aquinas and Aristotle.

43. Benjamin Netanyahu, ed., *Terrorism: How the West Can Win* (New York: Farrar, Straus, Giroux, 1986), 149–154.

INDEX

441